Cram101 Textbook Outlines to accompany:

Biological Psychology

James W. Kalat, 10th Edition

A Cram101 Inc. publication (c) 2010.

PRACTICE EXAMS.

Get all of the self-teaching practice exams for each chapter of this textbook at **www.Cram101.com** and ace the tests. Here is an example:

Chapter 1

Biological Psychology
James W. Kalat, 10th Edition,
All Material Written and Prepared by Cram101

I WANT A BETTER GRADE.

1 _____ as a general concept comprises knowledge of or skill in or observation of some thing or some event gained through involvement in or exposure to that thing or event. The history of the word _____ aligns it closely with the concept of experiment.

○ Experience
○ E Chart
○ E for Ecstasy
○ E.B. v. Order of the Oblates of Mary Immaculate in the Province of British Columbia

2 The _____ is a recurring cycle of physiological changes that occurs in the females of several mammals, including human beings and other apes.

○ Menstrual cycle
○ Margaret Sanger
○ Mental image
○ Mesozoic era

3 In animals, the _____, is the control center of the central nervous system, responsible for behavior. The _____ is located in the head, protected by the skull and close to the primary sensory apparatus of vision, hearing, equilibrioception, sense of acceleration, taste, and olfaction.

○ Brain
○ B cells
○ B.O.M.B.
○ Baader-Meinhof phenomenon

4 The study of _____ draws on both neuroscience and developmental biology to describe the cellular and molecular mechanisms by which complex nervous systems emerge during embryonic development and throughout life.

You get a 50% discount for the online exams. Go to **Cram101.com**, click Sign Up at the top of the screen, and enter DK73DW8588 in the promo code box on the registration screen. Access to Cram101.com is $4.95 per month, cancel at any time.

With Cram101.com online, you also have access to extensive reference material.

You will nail those essays and papers. Here is an example from a Cram101 Biology text:

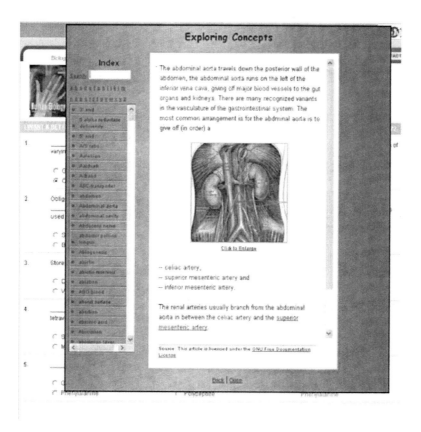

Learning System

Cram101 Textbook Outlines is a learning system. The notes in this book are the highlights of your textbook, you will never have to highlight a book again.

How to use this book. Take this book to class, it is your notebook for the lecture. The notes and highlights on the left hand side of the pages follow the outline and order of the textbook. All you have to do is follow along while your instructor presents the lecture. Circle the items emphasized in class and add other important information on the right side. With Cram101 Textbook Outlines you'll spend less time writing and more time listening. Learning becomes more efficient.

Cram101.com Online

Increase your studying efficiency by using Cram101.com's practice tests and online reference material. It is the perfect complement to Cram101 Textbook Outlines. Use self-teaching matching tests or simulate in-class testing with comprehensive multiple choice tests, or simply use Cram's true and false tests for quick review. Cram101.com even allows you to enter your in-class notes for an integrated studying format combining the textbook notes with your class notes.

Visit **www.Cram101.com**, click Sign Up at the top of the screen, and enter **DK73DW8588** in the promo code box on the registration screen. Access to www.Cram101.com is normally $9.95 per month, but because you have purchased this book, your access fee is only $4.95 per month. Sign up and stop highlighting textbooks forever.

Biological Psychology
James W. Kalat, 10th

CONTENTS

Chapter 1. The Major Issues

Experience	Experience as a general concept comprises knowledge of or skill in or observation of some thing or some event gained through involvement in or exposure to that thing or event. The history of the word experience aligns it closely with the concept of experiment.
Menstrual cycle	The menstrual cycle is a recurring cycle of physiological changes that occurs in the females of several mammals, including human beings and other apes.
Brain	In animals, the brain, is the control center of the central nervous system, responsible for behavior. The brain is located in the head, protected by the skull and close to the primary sensory apparatus of vision, hearing, equilibrioception, sense of acceleration, taste, and olfaction.
Neural development	The study of neural development draws on both neuroscience and developmental biology to describe the cellular and molecular mechanisms by which complex nervous systems emerge during embryonic development and throughout life.
Cycl	CycL in computer science and artificial intelligence is an ontology language used by Doug Lenat"s Cyc artificial intelligence project. Ramanathan V. Guha was instrumental in the design of the language. There is a close variant of CycL known as MELD. The original version of CycL was a frame language, but the modern version is not.
Fertility	Fertility is the natural capability of giving life. As a measure, "Fertility Rate" is the number of children born per couple, person or population.
Hormone	A hormone is a chemical messenger that carries a signal from one cell to another. All multicellular organisms produce hormone s.
Biological psychology	Biological psychology is the application of the principles of biology to the study of mental processes and behavior. The distinguishing characteristic of a biological psychology experiment is that either the independent variable of the experiment is biological, or some dependent variable is biological. In other words, the nervous system of the organism under study is permanently or temporarily altered, or some aspect of the nervous system is measured.
Dorsum	In anatomy, the dorsum is the upper side of animals that typically run, fly or swim in a horizontal position, and the back side of animals that walk upright. In vertebrates the dorsum contains the backbone.
Glial cells	Glial cells are non-neuronal cells that provide support and nutrition, maintain homeostasis, form myelin, and participate in signal transmission in the nervous system.
Nervous system	The nervous system of an animal coordinates the activity of the muscles, monitors the organs, constructs and also stops input from the senses, and initiates actions.
Neuroscience	A field that combines the work of psychologists, biologists, biochemists, medical researchers, and others in the study of the structure and function of the nervous system is neuroscience.

Animal testing	Animal testing refers to the use of animals in experiments. It is estimated that 50 to 100 million vertebrate animals worldwide — from zebrafish to non-human primates — are used annually and either killed during the experiments or subsequently euthanized.
Behavior	Behavior refers to the actions or reactions of an object or organism, usually in relation to the environment. Behavior can be conscious or subconscious, overt or covert, and voluntary or involuntary. Human Behavior (and that of other organisms and mechanisms) can be common, unusual, acceptable, or unacceptable. Humans evaluate the acceptability of Behavior using social norms and regulate Behavior by means of social control
Career	A career is traditionally seen as a course of successive situations that make up a person"s worklife. One can have a sporting career or a musical career without being a professional athlete or musician, but most frequently "career" in the 20th century referenced the series of jobs or positions by which one earned one"s money.
Delusion	A false belief, not generally shared by others, and that cannot be changed despite strong evidence to the contrary is a delusion.
Depression	In everyday language depression refers to any downturn in mood, which may be relatively transitory and perhaps due to something trivial.
Disease	A Disease or medical problem is an abnormal condition of an organism that impairs bodily functions, associated with specific symptoms and signs. It may be caused by external factors, such as invading organisms, or it may be caused by internal dysfunctions, such as autoimmune Disease s. In human beings, Disease is often used more broadly to refer to any condition that causes extreme pain, dysfunction, distress, social problems, and/or death to the person afflicted, or similar problems for those in contact with the person.
Gene	A gene is a locatable region of genomic sequence, corresponding to a unit of inheritance, which is associated with regulatory regions, transcribed regions and/or other functional sequence regions.
Generation	Generation, also known as procreation, is the act of producing offspring. A generation can also be a stage or degree in a succession of natural descent as a grandfather, a father, and the father"s son comprise three generations.
Hallucination	A hallucination is a sensory perception experienced in the absence of an external stimulus, as distinct from an illusion, which is a misperception of an external stimulus. They may occur in any sensory modality - visual, auditory, olfactory, gustatory, tactile, or mixed.

Disability	A disability is a condition or function judged to be significantly impaired relative to the usual standard of an individual or their group. The term is often used to refer to individual functioning, including physical impairments, sensory impairments, cognitive impairments, intellectual impairments or mental health issue.
Impulse	In classical mechanics, an Impulse is defined as the integral of a force with respect to time. When a force is applied to a rigid body it changes the momentum of that body. A small force applied for a long time can produce the same momentum change as a large force applied briefly, because it is the product of the force and the time for which it is applied that is important.
Information	Information as a concept has a diversity of meanings, from everyday usage to technical settings. Generally speaking, the concept of Information is closely related to notions of constraint, communication, control, data, form, instruction, knowledge, meaning, mental stimulus, pattern, perception, and representation. According to the Oxford English Dictionary, the first known historical meaning of the word Information in English was the act of informing, or giving form or shape to the mind, as in education, instruction, or training.
Mechanism	In philosophy, mechanism is a theory that all natural phenomena can be explained by physical causes. It can be contrasted with vitalism, the philosophical theory that vital forces are active in living organisms, so that life cannot be explained solely by mechanism.
Memory	In psychology, memory is an organism"s ability to store, retain, and subsequently retrieve information. In recent decades, it has become one of the principal pillars of a branch of science called cognitive neuroscience, an interdisciplinary link between cognitive psychology and neuroscience.
Cytoplasmic streaming	Cytoplasmic streaming is the flowing of cytoplasm in eukaryotic cells. This occurs in both plant and animal cells.
Not	This catalog is compiled from a source file. Please do not edit this page manually. This is how to edit it.
Other	The Other or constitutive Other is a key concept in continental philosophy, opposed to the Same. It refers, or attempts to refer, to that which is "Other" than the concept being considered. The term often means a person Other than oneself, and is often capitalised.
Physiology	The study of the functions and activities of living cells, tissues, and organs and of the physical and chemical phenomena involved is referred to as physiology.
Experiment	In the scientific method, an experiment is a set of observations performed in the context of solving a particular problem or question, to support or falsify a hypothesis or research concerning phenomena. The experiment is a cornerstone in the empirical approach to acquiring deeper knowledge about the physical world.

Terminology	Terminology is the study of terms and their use. Terms are words and compound words that are used in specific contexts. Not to be confused with "terms" in colloquial usages, the shortened form of technical terms (or terms of art) which are defined within a discipline or speciality field.
Tremor	Tremor is the rhythmic, oscillating shaking movement of the whole body or just a certain part of it, caused by problems of the neurons responsible from muscle action.
Muscle contraction	A muscle contraction occurs when a muscle fiber generates tension through the action of actin and myosin cross-bridge cycling.
Slow-wave sleep	Slow-wave sleep includes stages 3 and 4, during which low-frequency delta waves become prominent in EEG recordings.
Explanation	An explanation is a description which may clarify causes, context, and consequences of a certain object, and a phenomenon such as a process, a state of affairs. This description may establish rules or laws, and may clarify the existing ones in relation to an object, and a phenomenon examined. The components of an explanation can be implicit, and be interwoven with one another.
Sleep stages	Levels of sleep identified by brain-wave patterns and behavioral changes are called sleep stages.
Genetic drift	Genetic drift is a contributing factor in biological evolution, in which traits that do not affect reproductive fitness change in a population over time. Genetic drift is a statistically stochastic process that arises from the role of random sampling in the production of offspring.
Goose	Goose is the English name for a considerable number of birds, belonging to the family Anatidae. This family also includes swans, most of which are larger, and ducks, which are smaller. A goose eats a largely vegetarian diet, and can become pests when flocks feed on arable crops or inhabit ponds or grassy areas in urban environments.
Hair	Hair is a filamentous outgrowth of protein, found only on mammals. It projects from the epidermis, though it grows from hair follicles deep in the dermis.
Ontogenetic	The study of the origin and development of an organism is called ontogenetic.
Poverty	Poverty is the condition of lacking economic access to fundamental human needs such as food, shelter and safe drinking water. While some define poverty primarily in economic terms, others consider social and political arrangements to be intrinsic.
Poverty of the stimulus	The Poverty of the stimulus argument is a variant of the epistemological problem of the indeterminacy of data to theory that claims that grammar is unlearnable given the linguistic data available to children. As such, the argument strikes against empiricist accounts of language acquisition. Inversely, the argument is usually construed as in favor of linguistic nativism because it leads to the conclusion that knowledge of some aspects of grammar must be innate.

Prefrontal cortex	The prefrontal cortex is the anterior part of the frontal lobes of the brain, lying in front of the motor and premotor areas. Cytoarchitectonically, it is defined by the presence of an internal granular layer IV.
Anterior	Anterior is an anatomical term referring to the front part of the body. The anterior is positioned in front of another body part, or towards the head of an animal. It is the opposite of posterior.
Argument	In logic, an Argument is a set of one or more meaningful declarative sentences (or "propositions") known as the premises along with another meaningful declarative sentence (or "proposition") known as the conclusion. A deductive Argument asserts that the truth of the conclusion is a logical consequence of the premises; an inductive Argument asserts that the truth of the conclusion is supported by the premises. Deductive Argument s are valid or invalid, and sound or not sound.
Erection	The erection of the penis, clitoris or a nipple is its enlarged and firm state. It depends on a complex interaction of psychological, neural, vascular and endocrine factors. The ability to maintain the erectile state is key to the reproductive system and many forms of life could not reproduce in a natural way without this ability.
Frontal lobe	The frontal lobe comprises four major folds of cortical tissue: the precentral gyrus, superior gyrus and the middle gyrus of the frontal gyri, the inferior frontal gyrus. It has been found to play a part in impulse control, judgement, language, memory, motor function, problem solving, sexual behavior, socialization and spontaneity.
Need	A Need is something that is necessary for humans to live a healthy life. Need s are distinguished from wants because a deficiency would cause a clear negative outcome, such as dysfunction or death. Need s can be objective and physical, such as food and water, or they can be subjective and psychological, such as the Need for self-esteem.
Signal	In the fields of communications, signal processing, and in electrical engineering more generally, a signal is any time-varying quantity. Signals are often scalar-valued functions of time, but may be vector valued and may be functions of any other relevant independent variable.
Species	Species refers to a reproductively isolated breeding population.
Stimulus	In psychology, a stimulus is part of the stimulus-response relationship of behavioral learning theory.
Structure	Structure is a fundamental and sometimes intangible notion covering the recognition, observation, nature, and stability of patterns and relationships of entities.
Understanding	Understanding is a psychological process related to an abstract or physical object, such as, person, situation, or message whereby one is able to think about it and use concepts to deal adequately with that object.

Dualism	Dualism is the view that two fundamental concepts exist, such as good and evil, light and dark, or male and female. Often, they oppose each other. The word"s origin is the Latin dualis, meaning "two".
Mind	Mind collectively refers to the aspects of intellect and consciousness manifested as combinations of thought, perception, memory, emotion, will and imagination; mind is the stream of consciousness.
Substance abuse	Substance abuse refers to the use of substances when said use is causing detriment to the individual"s physical health or causes the user legal, social, financial or other problems including endangering their lives or the lives of others.
Belief	Belief is the psychological state in which an individual is convinced of the truth or validity of a proposition or premise without the ability to adequately prove their main contention for other people who may disagree.
Mind-body problem	There are three basic views of the mind-body problem: mental and physical events are totally different, and cannot be reduced to each other (dualism); mental events are to be reduced to physical events (materialism); and physical events are to be reduced to mental events (phenomenalism).
Consciousness	The awareness of the sensations, thoughts, and feelings being experienced at a given moment is called consciousness.
Identity	Identity is an umbrella term used throughout the social sciences to describe an individual"s comprehension of him or herself as a discrete, separate entity. This term, though generic, can be further specified by the disciplines of psychology and sociology, including the two forms of social psychology.
Materialism	In philosophy, materialism is a form of physicalism which holds that the only thing that can be truly proven to exist is matter. Fundamentally, all things are composed of material and all phenomena are the result of material interactions; therefore, matter is the only substance.
Mentalism	Mentalism is an ancient performing art in which its practitioners use mental acuity, principles of stage magic, hypnosis and/or suggestion to present the illusion of mind reading, psychokinesis, precognition, clairvoyance or mind control. Some performers add stage hypnotism and/or feats of memory or concentration to the mix.
Monism	Monism is the metaphysical view that there is only one principle, essence, substance or energy.
Gland	A gland is an organ in an animal's body that synthesizes a substance for release such as hormones, often into the bloodstream or into cavities inside the body or its outer surface.
Material	Material refers to physical substances used as inputs to production or manufacturing.

Melatonin	Melatonin is a hormone found in all living creatures from algae to humans, at levels that vary in a daily cycle. It plays a role in the regulation of the circadian rhythm of several biological functions.
Mental processes	The thoughts, feelings, and motives that each of us experiences privately but that cannot be observed directly are called mental processes.
Posterior	In reference to the anatomical terms of location, the posterior end is laterally situated at or toward the hinder part of the body, lying at or extending toward the right or left side. It is the polar opposite to the anterior end, or front end of the body.
Thalamus	An area near the center of the brain involved in the relay of sensory information to the cortex and in the functions of sleep and attention is the thalamus.
View	A View is what can be seen in a range of vision. View may also be used as a synonym of point of View in the first sense. View may also be used figuratively or with special significance--for example, to imply a scenic outlook or significant vantage point: The barrier Rhine hath flashed, through battle-smoke, On men who gaze heart-smitten by the View, As if all Germany had felt the shock! - from The Germans on the Heights of Hochheim by William Wordsworth Laws or regulations in various jurisdictions may protect a View as an easement, preventing property owners from constructing buildings that would block the View from another location.
Archive	An Archive is a collection of historical records, and the location in which the collection is kept. Archive s contain records (primary source documents) which have accumulated over the course of an individual or organization"s lifetime. The Archive s of an individual may include letters, papers, photographs, computer files, scrapbooks, financial records or diaries created or collected by the individual - regardless of media or format.
Audition	An Audition is a sample performance by an actor, singer, musician, dancer or other performer. It involves the performer displaying their talent through a previously-memorized and rehearsed solo piece: for example, a monologue for actors or a song for a singer. Used in the context of performing arts, it is analogous to job interviews in many ways.
Behavioral Neuroscience	Behavioral neuroscience biopsychology in particular neurobiology, to the study of mental processes and behavior. A psychobiologist, for instance, may compare the unfamiliar imprinting behavior in goslings to the early attachment behavior in human infants and construct theory around these two phenomena. Behavioral Neuroscientists may often be interested in measuring some biological variable, e.g. an anatomical, physiological in an attempt to relate it quantitatively or qualitatively to a psychological or behavioral variable, and thus contribute to evidence based practice.

Clinical psychologist	Clinical psychologist usually undergo four to six years of post-Bachelors graduate training in order to demonstrate competence and experience. Central to its practice are psychological assessment and psychotherapy, although clinical psychologists also engage in a range of professional services including research, teaching, consultation, forensic testimony, and program development and administration.
Counseling psychology	Counseling psychology as a psychological specialty is about usually one-on-one engagement between a trained counselor, and a client (McLeod, 2003.) In terms of its formal instantiation, its remit may involve facilitatating personal and interpersonal functioning across the life span with a focus on emotional, social, vocational, educational, health-related, developmental, and organizational concerns. Through the integration of theory, research, and practice, and with a sensitivity to multicultural issues, this specialty encompasses a broad range of practices that help people improve their well-being, alleviate distress and maladjustment, resolve crises, and increase their ability to live more highly functioning lives.
Counseling psychologist	A counseling psychologist is employed in a variety of settings, including universities, hospitals, schools, governmental organizations, businesses, private practice, hospitals, and community mental health centers. It focuses more on normal developmental issues and everyday stress rather than psychopathology, but this distinction has softened over time.
Journal	A journal is a book for writing discrete entries arranged by date reporting on what has happened over the course of a day or other period. Such logs play a role in many aspects of human civilization, including governmental, business ledgers, and military records.
Machine	A Machine is any device that uses energy to perform some activity. In common usage, the meaning is that of a device having parts that perform or assist in performing any type of work. A simple Machine is a device that transforms the direction or magnitude of a force without consuming any energy.
Physical therapists	Physical therapists are health care professionals who evaluate and manage health conditions for people of all ages. Typically individuals consult a PT for the management of medical problems or other health-related conditions that; cause pain, limit their ability to move, and limit the performance of functional activities.
Problem of other minds	The problem of other minds is the philosophical problem of determining how we know that there are minds associated with the bodies we see walking around among us. This is more specifically a problem of epistemology.
Psychiatry	Psychiatry is a branch of medicine dealing with the prevention, assessment, diagnosis, treatment, and rehabilitation of the mind and mental illness. Its primary goal is the relief of mental suffering associated with symptoms of disorder and improvement of mental well-being.

Methylphenidate	Methylphenidate is a prescription stimulant commonly used to treat Attention-deficit hyperactivity disorder, or ADHD. It is also one of the primary drugs used to treat the daytime drowsiness symptoms of narcolepsy and chronic fatigue syndrome.
School psychologist	A school psychologist is educated in child and adolescent development, learning theories, psychological and psychoeducational assessment, personality theories, therapeutic interventions, special education, psychology, consultation, child and adolescent psychopathology, and the ethical, legal and administrative codes of their profession.
Social work	Social work is a discipline involving the application of social theory and research methods to study and improve the lives of people, groups, and societies. It incorporates and uses other social sciences as a means to improve the human condition and positively change society"s response to chronic problems.
Social workers	Social Workers are concerned with social problems, their causes, their solutions and their human impacts.
Solipsism	Solipsism is the epistemological belief that one's self is the only thing that can be known with certainty and verified.
Therapist	A therapist is an individual who specializes in physical therapy or psychotherapy as means of treating psychological disorders. A therapist is often sought when individuals are experiencing extreme levels of stress that can eventually lead to psychological and physical disorders.
Alpha	Alpha is the first letter of the Greek alphabet. In the system of Greek numerals it has a value of 1. It was derived from the Phoenician letter Aleph. Letters that arose from Alpha include the Latin A and the Cyrillic letter A.
Alpha wave	The brain wave associated with deep relaxation is referred to as the alpha wave. Recorded by electroencephalography (EEG), they are synchronous and coherent (regular like sawtooth) and in the frequency range of 8 - 12 Hz. It is also called Berger's wave in memory of the founder of EEG.
Comparative	In grammar, the Comparative is the form of an adjective or adverb which denotes the degree or grade by which a person, thing and is used in this context with a subordinating conjunction, such as than, as...as, etc. The structure of a Comparative in English consists normally of the positive form of the adjective or adverb, plus the suffix -er e.g. "he is taller than his father is", or "the village is less picturesque than the town nearby".
Comparative psychologist	A comparative psychologist is primarily interested in studying and comparing the behavior of different species.
Neuroanatomy	Neuroanatomy is the study of the anatomy of the central nervous system.

Neuropsychologist	A psychologist concerned with the relationships among cognition, affect, behavior, and brain function is a neuropsychologist.
Neuroscientist	A neuroscientist is an individual who studies the scientific field of neuroscience or any of its related sub-fields. Neuroscience as a distinct discipline separate from anatomy, neurology, physiology, psychology, or psychiatry is fairly recent, aided in large part by the advent of newer, faster computing methods and neuroimaging techniques.
Occupational therapists	Occupational therapists work with the disabled, the elderly, newborns, school-aged children, and with anyone who has a permanent or temporary impairment in their physical or mental functioning.
Psychiatrist	A psychiatrist is a physician who specializes in the diagnosis and treatment of psychological disorders.
Field	Field is one of the core concepts used by French social scientist Pierre Bourdieu. A field is a setting in which agents and their social positions are located. The position of each particular agent in the field is a result of interaction between the specific rules of the field, agent"s habitus and agent"s capital social, economic and cultural Bourdieu, 1984. Fields interact with each other, and are hierarchical most are subordinate of the larger field of power and class relations.
Population	In sociology and biology a population is the collection of people or individuals of a particular species. A population shares a particular characteristic of interest most often that of living in a given geographic area.
Chromosome	A chromosome is a single large macromolecule of DNA, and constitutes a physically organized form of DNA in a cell. It is a very long, continuous piece of DNA, which contains many genes, regulatory elements and other intervening nucleotide sequences.
Deoxyribonucleic acid	Deoxyribonucleic acid is a nucleic acid that contains the genetic instructions used in the development and functioning of all known living organisms. The main role of DNA molecules is the long-term storage of information and DNA is often compared to a set of blueprints, since it contains the instructions needed to construct other components of cells, such as proteins and RNA molecules.
Facial expression	A facial expression results from one or more motions or positions of the muscles of the face. These movements convey the emotional state of the individual to observers. It is a form of nonverbal communication.
Genetics	Genetics is the science of heredity and variation in living organisms.Knowledge of the inheritance of characteristics has been implicitly used since prehistoric times for improving crop plants and animals through selective breeding. However, the modern science of genetics, which seeks to understand the mechanisms of inheritance, only began with the work of Gregor Mendel in the mid-1800s.

Hippocampus	The hippocampus is a part of the brain located in the medial temporal lobe. It forms a part of the limbic system and plays a part in memory and spatial navigation.
Learning	Learning is the acquisition and development of memories and behaviors, including skills, knowledge, understanding, values, and wisdom. It is the goal of education, and the product of experience. Learning ranges from simple forms such as habituation to more complex forms such as play, seen only in large vertebrates.
Chemical	A chemical is a material with a definite chemical composition. All samples of a compound have the same composition; that is, all samples have the same proportions, by mass, of the elements present in the compound.
Heredity	Heredity is the transfer of characteristics from parent to offspring through their genes, or the transfer of a title, style or social status through the social convention known as inheritance.
Amino acid	Amino acid is the basic structural building unit of proteins. They form short polymer chains called peptides or polypeptides which in turn form structures called proteins.
Enzyme	An enzyme is a protein that catalyzes, or speeds up, a chemical reaction. Enzymes are essential to sustain life because most chemical reactions in biological cells would occur too slowly, or would lead to different products, without enzymes.
Zygosity	Zygosity refers to the genetic condition of a zygote. In genetics, zygosity describes the similarity or dissimilarity of DNA between homologous chromosomes at a specific allelic position or gene.
Protein	A protein is a complex, high-molecular-weight organic compound that consists of amino acids joined by peptide bonds. It is essential to the structure and function of all living cells and viruses. Many are enzymes or subunits of enzymes.
Recessive gene	Recessive gene refers to an allele that causes a phenotype (visible or detectable characteristic) that is only seen in a homozygous genotype (an organism that has two copies of the same allele). Thus, both parents have to be carriers of a recessive trait in order for a child to express that trait.
Hindbrain	The hindbrain is a developmental categorization of portions of the central nervous system in vertebrates. It can be subdivided in a variable number of transversal swellings called rhombomeres.
Sleep	Sleep is the state of natural rest observed throughout the animal kingdom, in all mammals and birds, and in many reptiles, amphibians, and fish.
X chromosome	The sex chromosomes are one of the 23 pairs of human chromosomes. Each person normally has one pair of sex chromosomes in each cell. Females have two of the X chromosome, while males have one X chromosome and one Y chromosome. The X chromosome carries hundreds of genes but few, if any, of these have anything to do directly with sex determination.

Y chromosome	The Y chromosome is the sex-determining chromosome in humans and most other mammals. In mammals, it contains the gene SRY, which triggers testis development, thus determining sex.
Characteristic	Characteristic has several particular meanings:

· in mathematics
- · Euler characteristic
- · method of characteristic s (partial differential equations)
· in physics and engineering

· any characteristic curve that shows the relationship between certain input- and output parameters, e.g.
· an I-V or current-voltage characteristic is the current in a circuit as a function of the applied voltage
· Receiver-Operator characteristic
· in navigation, the characteristic pattern of a lighted beacon.
· in fiction

· in Dungeons ' Dragons, characteristic is another name for ability score .

Mammal	A mammal is a warm-blooded, vertebrate animal, characterized by the presence of sweat glands, including milk producing sweat glands, and by the presence of: hair, three middle ear bones used in hearing, and a neocortex region in the brain. Most also possess specialized teeth and utilize a placenta in the ontogeny. A mammal encompass approximately 5,400 species, distributed in about 1,200 genera, 153 families, and 29 orders, though this varies by classification scheme.
Sex chromosomes	The sex chromosomes are the 23rd pair of chromosomes. They determine whether the child will be male or female. A pair with two X-shaped chromosomes produces a female. A pair with an X chromosome and a Y chromosome produces a male.
Trait	An enduring personality characteristic that tends to lead to certain behaviors is called a trait. The term trait also means a genetically inherited feature of an organism.
Adoption	Adoption is the legal act of permanently placing a child with a parent or parents other than the birth mother or father. An adoption order has the effect of severing the parental responsibilities and rights of the birth parents and transferring those responsibilities and rights onto the adoptive parent.
Adoption studies	Research studies that assess hereditary influence by examining the resemblance between adopted children and both their biological and their adoptive parents are referred to as adoption studies. The studies have been inconclusive about the relative importance of heredity in intelligence.

Color	Color or colour is the visual perceptual property corresponding in humans to the categories called red, yellow, blue and others. Color derives from the spectrum of light interacting in the eye with the spectral sensitivities of the light receptors. Color categories and physical specifications of Color are also associated with objects, materials, light sources, etc., based on their physical properties such as light absorption, reflection, or emission spectra.
Color blindness	Color blindness in humans is the inability to perceive differences between some or all colors that other people can distinguish. It is most often of genetic nature, but may also occur because of eye, nerve, or brain damage, or due to exposure to certain chemicals.
Color vision	Color vision is the capacity of an organism or machine to distinguish objects based on the wavelengths of the light they reflect or emit. The nervous system derives color by comparing the responses to light from the several types of cone photoreceptors in the eye.
Dizygotic	Fraternal twins (commonly known as "non-identical twins") usually occur when two fertilized eggs are implanted in the uterine wall at the same time. The two eggs form two zygotes, and these twins are therefore also known as dizygotic.
Monozygotic twins	Monozygotic twins derive from a single fertilized egg that divides in two and then goes on to form two separate embryos.
Environmental factor	In epidemiology, environmental factor refers to determinants of disease that are not transmitted genetically.
Heritability	Heritability It is that proportion of the observed variation in a particular phenotype within a particular population, that can be attributed to the contribution of genotype. In other words: it measures the extent to which differences between individuals in a population are due their being different genetically.
Monozygotic	Identical twins occur when a single egg is fertilized to form one zygote, calld monozygotic, but the zygote then divides into two separate embryos. The two embryos develop into foetuses sharing the same womb. Monozygotic twins are genetically identical unless there has been a mutation in development, and they are almost always the same gender.
Prenatal development	Prenatal development is the process in which an embryo or fetus gestates during pregnancy, from fertilization until birth.
Twin	Twin s are a form of multiple birth in which the mother gives birth to two offspring from the same pregnancy, either of the same or opposite sex.
Alcoholism	Alcoholism is a term with multiple and sometimes conflicting definitions. In common and historic usage, alcoholism refers to any condition that results in the continued consumption of alcoholic beverages despite the health problems and negative social consequences it causes.

Androgen	Androgen is the generic term for any natural or synthetic compound, usually a steroid hormone, that stimulates or controls the development and maintenance of masculine characteristics in vertebrates by binding to androgen receptors. This includes the activity of the accessory male sex organs and development of male secondary sex characteristics.
Marxist aesthetics	Marxist aesthetics is a theory of aesthetics based on the theories of Karl Marx. It involves a dialectical approach to the application of Marxism to the cultural sphere, specifically areas related to taste such as art, beauty, etc. Marxists believe that economic and social conditions affect every aspect of an individual"s life, from religious beliefs to legal systems to cultural frameworks.
Estrogen	Estrogen is a group of steroid compounds that function as the primary female sex hormone. They are produced primarily by developing follicles in the ovaries, the corpus luteum and the placenta.
Fraternal twins	Fraternal twins usually occur when two fertilized eggs are implanted in the uterine wall at the same time. The two eggs form two zygotes, and these twins are therefore also known as dizygotic as well as "biovular" twins. When two eggs are independently fertilized by two different sperm cells, fraternal twins result.
Single	In relationships, a single person is one who is not married, or, more broadly, who is not in an exclusive romantic relationship.
Variance	In probability theory and statistics, the variance of a random variable or somewhat more precisely, of a probability distribution is one measure of statistical dispersion, averaging the squared distance of its possible values from the expected value.
Diet	In nutrition, the diet is the sum of food consumed by a person or other organism. Dietary habits are the habitual decisions an individual or culture makes when choosing what foods to eat.
Methyl	Methyl is a hydrophobic alkyl functional group derived from methane. This hydrocarbon unit can be found in many organic compounds. The incorporation of a methyl can have one of three general effects on the rate of metabolism.
PKU	Phenylketonuria (PKU) is an autosomal recessive genetic disorder characterized by a deficiency in the autozome phenylalanine hydroxylase (PAH.) This enzyme is necessary to metabolize the amino acid phenylalanine to the amino acid tyrosine. When PAH is deficient, phenylalanine accumulates and is converted into phenylpyruvate (also known as phenylketone), which is detected in the urine.
Antipsychotic	The term antipsychotic is applied to a group of drugs used to treat psychosis.
Antipsychotics	*Antipsychotics* are a group of psychoactive drugs commonly but not exclusively used to treat psychosis, which is typified by schizophrenia. Over time a wide range of *Antipsychotics* have been developed. A first generation of *Antipsychotics*, known as typical *Antipsychotics*, was discovered in the 1950s.

Chlorpromazine	Chlorpromazine is a phenothiazine antipsychotic. Its principal use is in the treatment of schizophrenia, though it has also been used to treat hiccups and nausea. Its use today has been largely supplanted by the newer atypical antipsychotics such as olanzapine and quetiapine. It works on a variety of receptors in the central nervous system; these include anticholinergic, antidopaminergic and antihistamine effects as well as some antagonism of adrenergic receptors.
Social influence	Social influence occurs when an individual"s thoughts or actions are affected by other people. Social influence takes many forms and can be seen in conformity, socialization, peer pressure, obedience, leadership, persuasion, sales, and marketing. Harvard psychologist, Herbert Kelman identified three broad varieties of Social influence. · Compliance is when people appear to agree with others, but actually keep their dissenting opinions private. · Identification is when people are influenced by someone who is liked and respected, such as a famous celebrity or a favorite uncle. · Internalization is when people accept a belief or behavior and agree both publicly and privately.
Mental retardation	Mental retardation is a term for a pattern of persistently slow learning of basic motor and language skills during childhood, and a significantly below-normal global intellectual capacity as an adult. One common criterion for diagnosis of mental retardation is a tested intelligence quotient of 70 or below and deficits in adaptive functioning. People with mental retardation may be described as having developmental disabilities, global developmental delay, or learning difficulties.
Phenylalanine	Phenylalanine is an essential amino acid. The genetic disorder phenylketonuria is an inability to metabolize phenylalanine.
Artificial selection	In the theory of evolution, artificial selection is the process of intentional or unintentional modification of a species through human actions which encourage the breeding of certain traits over others.
Phylogenetic tree	A phylogenetic tree is a tree showing the evolutionary relationships among various biological species or other entities that are believed to have a common ancestor. In a phylogenetic tree, each node with descendants represents the most recent common ancestor of the descendants, and the edge lengths in some trees correspond to time estimates. Each node is called a taxonomic unit.
Lamarckian evolution	Lamarckian evolution was based on the idea that individuals adapt during their own lifetimes and transmit traits they acquire to their offspring. Offspring then adapt from where the parents left off, enabling evolution to advance. As a mechanism for adaptation, it proposed that individuals increased specific capabilities by exercising them, while losing others through disuse.

31

Mutation	In biology, mutation s are changes to the nucleotide sequence of the genetic material of an organism. mutation s can be caused by copying errors in the genetic material during cell division, by exposure to ultraviolet or ionizing radiation, chemical mutagens, or viruses, or can be induced by the organism itself, by cellular processes such as hyper mutation . In multicellular organisms with dedicated reproductive cells, mutation s can be subdivided into germ line mutation s, which can be passed on to descendants through the reproductive cells, and somatic mutation s, which involve cells outside the dedicated reproductive group and which are not usually transmitted to descendants.
Inheritance	Biological inheritance is the process by which an offspring cell or organism acquires or becomes predisposed to characteristics of its parent cell or organism. Through inheritance, variations exhibited by individuals can accumulate and cause a species to evolve..
Mating	In biology, mating is the pairing of opposite-sex or hermaphroditic internal fertilization animals for reproductive purposes and, in social animals, also to raise their offspring. Mating methods include random mating, disassortative mating, assortative mating, or a mating pool.
Purpose	Purpose in its most general sense is the anticipated aim which guides action. It is used as the synonym of goal and objective.
Altruism	Altruism is selfless concern for the welfare of others. It is a traditional virtue in many cultures, and central to many religious traditions. In English, this idea was often described as the Golden rule of ethics. Some newer philosophies such as egoism have criticized the concept, with writers such as Nietzsche arguing that there is no moral obligation to help others.
Kin selection	Kin selection has been mathematically defined by Hamilton as a mechanism for the evolution of apparently altruistic acts. Under natural selection, a gene that causes itself to increase in frequency should become more common in the population. Since identical copies of genes may be carried in relatives, a gene in one organism that prompts behavior which aids another organism carrying the same gene may become more successful.
Reciprocal altruism	In evolutionary biology and evolutionary psychology, reciprocal altruism is a form of altruism in which one organism provides a benefit to another without expecting any immediate payment or compensation. However, reciprocal altruism is not unconditional.
Ethics	Ethics a major branch of philosophy, is the study of values and customs of a person or group. It covers the analysis and employment of concepts such as right and wrong, good and evil, and responsibility
Sex steroid	Sex steroid refers to steroid hormones that interact with vertebrate androgen or estrogen receptors.
Issue	In computing, the term Issue is a unit of work to accomplish an improvement in a system. An Issue could be a bug, a requested feature, task, missing documentation, and so forth. The word "Issue" is popularly misused in lieu of "problem." This usage is probably related.

Software extension	A Software extension is a computer program designed to be incorporated into another piece of software in order to enhance the functionalities of the latter. On its own, the program is not useful or functional. Examples of software applications that support extensions include the Mozilla Firefox Web browser, Adobe Systems Photoshop and Microsoft Windows Explorer shell extensions.
Muscle	Muscle is contractile tissue of the body and is derived from the mesodermal layer of embryonic germ cells. It is classified as skeletal, cardiac, or smooth muscle, and its function is to produce force and cause motion, either locomotion or movement within internal organs.
Society	A society is a grouping of individuals, which is characterized by common interests and may have distinctive culture and institutions. Society can also refer to an organized group of people associated together for religious, benevolent, cultural, scientific, political, patriotic, or other purposes.
Society for Neuroscience	The Society for Neuroscience is a professional society for basic scientists and physicians around the world whose research is focused on the study of the brain and nervous system.

Chapter 2. Nerve Cells and Nerve Impulses

Nervous system	The nervous system of an animal coordinates the activity of the muscles, monitors the organs, constructs and also stops input from the senses, and initiates actions.
Glial cells	Glial cells are non-neuronal cells that provide support and nutrition, maintain homeostasis, form myelin, and participate in signal transmission in the nervous system.
Sherrington	Sherrington used reflexes in the spinal cord as a way of investigating the general properties of neurons and the nervous system. These experiments led him to postulate "Sherrington's Law," which states that for every neural activation of a muscle, there is a corresponding inhibition of the opposing muscle. He also introduced the concept of the synapse and the concept of the reflex arc.
Impulse	In classical mechanics, an Impulse is defined as the integral of a force with respect to time. When a force is applied to a rigid body it changes the momentum of that body. A small force applied for a long time can produce the same momentum change as a large force applied briefly, because it is the product of the force and the time for which it is applied that is important.
Information	Information as a concept has a diversity of meanings, from everyday usage to technical settings. Generally speaking, the concept of Information is closely related to notions of constraint, communication, control, data, form, instruction, knowledge, meaning, mental stimulus, pattern, perception, and representation. According to the Oxford English Dictionary, the first known historical meaning of the word Information in English was the act of informing, or giving form or shape to the mind, as in education, instruction, or training.
Not	This catalog is compiled from a source file. Please do not edit this page manually. This is how to edit it.
Other	The Other or constitutive Other is a key concept in continental philosophy, opposed to the Same. It refers, or attempts to refer, to that which is "Other" than the concept being considered. The term often means a person Other than oneself, and is often capitalised.
Nucleus	In neuroanatomy, a cluster of cell bodies of neurons within the central nervous system is a nucleus.
Pituitary gland	The pituitary gland is an endocrine gland about the size of a pea that sits in the small, bony cavity at the base of the brain. The pituitary gland secretes hormones regulating a wide variety of bodily activities, including trophic hormones that stimulate other endocrine glands.
Chromosome	A chromosome is a single large macromolecule of DNA, and constitutes a physically organized form of DNA in a cell. It is a very long, continuous piece of DNA, which contains many genes, regulatory elements and other intervening nucleotide sequences.
Endocrine gland	An endocrine gland is one of a set of internal organs involved in the secretion of hormones into the blood. The other major type of gland is the exocrine glands, which secrete substances—usually digestive juices—into the digestive tract or onto the skin.

Hypothalamus	The hypothalamus is a region of the brain located below the thalamus, forming the major portion of the ventral region of the diencephalon and functioning to regulate certain metabolic processes and other autonomic activities.
Structure	Structure is a fundamental and sometimes intangible notion covering the recognition, observation, nature, and stability of patterns and relationships of entities.
Dementia	Dementia is the progressive decline in cognitive function due to damage or disease in the brain beyond what might be expected from normal aging.
Dementia praecox	An older term for schizophrenia, chosen to describe what was believed to be an incurable and progressive deterioration of mental functioning beginning in adolescence is called dementia praecox.
Dendritic spine	A dendritic spine is a small membranous extrusion that protrudes from a dendrite and forms one half of a synapse. Typically spines have a bulbous head which is connected to the parent dendrite through a thin spine neck.
Mitochondrion	In cell biology, a mitochondrion is a membrane-enclosed organelle that is found in most eukaryotic cells. A Mitochondrion is sometimes described as a "cellular power plant," because it generates most of the cell"s supply of adenosine triphosphate, used as a source of chemical energy.
Motor neuron	In vertebrates, the term Motor neuron classically applies to neurons located in the central nervous system that project their axons outside the CNS and directly or indirectly control muscles. Motor neuron is often synonymous with efferent neuron.
Positron emission tomography	Positron emission tomography is a nuclear medicine medical imaging technique which produces a three-dimensional image or map of functional processes in the body. Images of metabolic activity in space are then reconstructed by computer, often in modern scanners aided by results from a CT X-ray scan.
Protein	A protein is a complex, high-molecular-weight organic compound that consists of amino acids joined by peptide bonds. It is essential to the structure and function of all living cells and viruses. Many are enzymes or subunits of enzymes.
Protein channel	A protein channel is a pore-forming protein that help establish the small voltage gradient that exists across the membrane of all living cells, by controlling the flow of ions. They are present in the membranes that surround all biological cells.
Ribosome	A ribosome is an organelle composed of rRNA and ribosomal proteins. It translates mRNA into a polypeptide chain (e.g., a protein). It can be thought of as a factory that builds a protein from a set of genetic instructions.

Disease	A Disease or medical problem is an abnormal condition of an organism that impairs bodily functions, associated with specific symptoms and signs. It may be caused by external factors, such as invading organisms, or it may be caused by internal dysfunctions, such as autoimmune Disease s. In human beings, Disease is often used more broadly to refer to any condition that causes extreme pain, dysfunction, distress, social problems, and/or death to the person afflicted, or similar problems for those in contact with the person.
Energy	The concept of psychic Energy was developed in the field of psychodynamics. In 1874, German scientist Ernst von Brucke proposed that all living organisms are Energy-systems governed by the principle of the conservation of Energy. Brucke was also coincidentally the supervisor at the University of Vienna for first-year medical student Sigmund Freud who adopted this new paradigm.
Muscle	Muscle is contractile tissue of the body and is derived from the mesodermal layer of embryonic germ cells. It is classified as skeletal, cardiac, or smooth muscle, and its function is to produce force and cause motion, either locomotion or movement within internal organs.
Receptor	A sensory receptor is a structure that recognizes a stimulus in the internal or external environment of an organism. In response to stimuli the sensory receptor initiates sensory transduction by creating graded potentials or action potentials in the same cell or in an adjacent one.
Reticulum	The reticulum is the second chamber in the alimentary canal of a ruminant animal. Anatomically it is considered the smaller half of the reticulorumen along with the rumen.
Soma	The soma is the bulbous end of a neuron, containing the cell nucleus.
Spinal cord	The spinal cord is a thin, tubular bundle of nerves that is an extension of the central nervous system from the brain and is enclosed in and protected by the bony vertebral column. The main function of the spinal cord is transmission of neural inputs between the periphery and the brain.
Axon	An axon is a long, slender projection of a nerve cell, or neuron, that conducts electrical impulses away from the neuron"s cell body or soma.
Interneuron	An interneuron (also called relay neuron or association neuron) is a neuron that communicates only to other neurons. They provide connections between sensory and motor neurons, as well as between themselves.
Intrinsic	Intrinsic describes a characteristic or property of some thing or action which is essential and specific to that thing or action, and which is wholly independent of any other object, action or consequence.
Myelin	Myelin is an electrically-insulating phospholipid layer that surrounds the axons of many neurons. It is an outgrowth of glial cells: Schwann cells supply the myelin for peripheral neurons, whereas oligodendrocytes supply it to those of the central nervous system.

Artificial neuron	An artificial neuron is an abstraction of biological neurons and the basic unit in an artificial neural network.
Sensory neurons	*Sensory neurons* are neurons that are activated by sensory input (vision, touch, hearing, etc.), and send projections into the central nervous system that convey sensory information to the brain or spinal cord. Unlike neurons of the central nervous system, whose inputs come from other neurons, *Sensory neurons* are activated by physical modalities such as light, sound, temperature, chemical stimulation, etc. In complex organisms, *Sensory neurons* relay their information to the central nervous system or in less complex organisms, such as the hydra, directly to motor neurons and *Sensory neurons* also transmit information to the brain, where it can be further processed and acted upon.
Chemical	A chemical is a material with a definite chemical composition. All samples of a compound have the same composition; that is, all samples have the same proportions, by mass, of the elements present in the compound.
Constant	A constant is something that does not change, over time or otherwise: a fixed value. In most fields of discourse the term is an antonym of "variable", but in mathematical parlance a mathematical variable may sometimes also be called a constant.
Software extension	A Software extension is a computer program designed to be incorporated into another piece of software in order to enhance the functionalities of the latter. On its own, the program is not useful or functional. Examples of software applications that support extensions include the Mozilla Firefox Web browser, Adobe Systems Photoshop and Microsoft Windows Explorer shell extensions.
Material	Material refers to physical substances used as inputs to production or manufacturing.
Single	In relationships, a single person is one who is not married, or, more broadly, who is not in an exclusive romantic relationship.
Stimulation	Stimulation is the action of various agents on muscles, nerves, or a sensory end organ, by which activity is evoked.
Astrocyte	An astrocyte, also known as astroglia, is a characteristic star-shaped cell in the brain. They are the biggest cells found in brain tissue and outnumber the neurons ten to one. A commonly accepted function is to structure physically the brain. A second function is to provide neurons with nutrients such as glucose. They regulate the flow of nutrients provided by capillaries by forming the blood-brain barrier.
Bipolar cell	A Bipolar cell is a type of neuron which has two extensions. Bipolar cell s are specialized sensory neurons for the transmission of special senses. As such, they are part of the sensory pathways for smell, sight, taste, hearing and vestibular functions.

Brain	In animals, the brain, is the control center of the central nervous system, responsible for behavior. The brain is located in the head, protected by the skull and close to the primary sensory apparatus of vision, hearing, equilibrioception, sense of acceleration, taste, and olfaction.
Cerebellum	The cerebellum is a region of the brain that plays an important role in the integration of sensory perception and motor output. Many neural pathways link the cerebellum with the motor cortex—which sends information to the muscles causing them to move—and the spinocerebellar tract—which provides feedback on the position of the body in space. The cerebellum integrates these pathways, using the constant feedback on body position to fine-tune motor movements.
Purkinje	Purkinje is best known for his 1837 discovery of Purkinje cells, large neurons with many branching fibres found in the cerebellum. He is also known for his discovery, in 1839 of Purkinje fibres, the fibrous tissue that conducts electrical impulses from the atrioventricular node to all parts of the ventricles of the heart.
Purkinje cells	Purkinje cells are a class of GABAergic neuron located in the cerebellar cortex. Purkinje cells send inhibitory projections to the deep cerebellar nuclei, and constitute the sole output of all motor coordination in the cerebellar cortex.
Animal testing	Animal testing refers to the use of animals in experiments. It is estimated that 50 to 100 million vertebrate animals worldwide — from zebrafish to non-human primates — are used annually and either killed during the experiments or subsequently euthanized.
Hindbrain	The hindbrain is a developmental categorization of portions of the central nervous system in vertebrates. It can be subdivided in a variable number of transversal swellings called rhombomeres.
Plan	A Plan is typically any procedure used to achieve an objective. It is a set of intended actions, through which one expects to achieve a goal. Plan s can be formal or informal: · Structured and formal Plan s, used by multiple people, are more likely to occur in projects, diplomacy, careers, economic development, military campaigns, combat, or in the conduct of other business. · Informal or ad-hoc Plan s are created by individuals in all of their pursuits. The most popular ways to describe Plan s are by their breadth, time frame, and specificity; however, these Plan ning classifications are not independent of one another. For instance, there is a close relationship between the short-and long-term categories and the strategic and operational categories.
Retina	The vertebrate Retina is a light sensitive tissue lining the inner surface of the eye. The optics of the eye create an image of the visual world on the Retina which serves much the same function as the film in a camera. Light striking the Retina initiates a cascade of chemical and electrical events that ultimately trigger nerve impulses.

Microglia	Microglia are a type of glial cell that act as the immune cells of the Central nervous system. Microglia, the smallest of the glial cells, can act as phagocytes, cleaning up CNS debris. Most serve as representatives of the immune system in the brain and spinal cord.
Oligodendrocyte	An Oligodendrocyte is a variety of neuroglia. Their main function is the myelination of nerve cells exclusively in the central nervous system of the higher vertebrates. A single oligodendrocyte can extend to about a dozen axons, wrapping around approximately 1mm of each and forming the myelin sheath.
Radial glia	In the developing nervous system, radial glia provide a scaffold for the outward migration of cortical cells.
Schwann cell	A Schwann cell is a variety of neuroglia that wraps around axons in the peripheral nervous system, forming the myelin sheath. The nervous system depends crucially on this sheath for insulation and an increase in impulse speed.
Central nervous system	The central nervous system represents the largest part of the nervous system, including the brain and the spinal cord. Together with the peripheral nervous system, it has a fundamental role in the control of behavior. The CNS is contained within the dorsal cavity, with the brain within the cranial subcavity, and the spinal cord in the spinal cavity. The CNS is covered by the meninges. The brain is also protected by the skull, and the spinal cord is also protected by the vertebrae.
Waste	Waste is unwanted or undesired material.
Active transport	Active transport is the mediated transport of biochemicals, and other atomic/molecular substances, across membranes. Unlike passive transport, this process requires chemical energy. In this form of transport, molecules move against either an electrical or concentration gradient (collectively termed an electrochemical gradient).
Blood-brain barrier	The Blood-brain barrier is a membranic structure that acts primarily to protect the brain from chemicals in the blood, while still allowing essential metabolic function. It is composed of endothelial cells, which are packed very tightly in brain capillaries. This higher density restricts passage of substances from the bloodstream much more than endothelial cells in capillaries elsewhere in the body
Endothelial cell	An endothelial cell forms an interface between circulating blood in the lumen and the rest of the vessel wall. They line the entire circulatory system, from the heart to the smallest capillary. In small blood vessels and capillaries, they are often the only cell-type present.

Behavior	Behavior refers to the actions or reactions of an object or organism, usually in relation to the environment. Behavior can be conscious or subconscious, overt or covert, and voluntary or involuntary.
	Human Behavior (and that of other organisms and mechanisms) can be common, unusual, acceptable, or unacceptable. Humans evaluate the acceptability of Behavior using social norms and regulate Behavior by means of social control
Blood	Blood is a specialized biological fluid consisting of red blood cells.White blood cells also called leukocytes and platelets also called thrombocytes suspended in a complex fluid medium known as blood plasma.
Mechanism	In philosophy, mechanism is a theory that all natural phenomena can be explained by physical causes. It can be contrasted with vitalism, the philosophical theory that vital forces are active in living organisms, so that life cannot be explained solely by mechanism.
Alcoholism	Alcoholism is a term with multiple and sometimes conflicting definitions. In common and historic usage, alcoholism refers to any condition that results in the continued consumption of alcoholic beverages despite the health problems and negative social consequences it causes.
Amino acid	Amino acid is the basic structural building unit of proteins. They form short polymer chains called peptides or polypeptides which in turn form structures called proteins.
Brain damage	Brain damage is the destruction or degeneration of brain cells. It may occur due to a wide range of conditions, illnesses, injuries, and as a result of iatrogenesis. Possible causes of widespread brain damage include prolonged hypoxia, poisoning by teratogens, infection, and neurological illness.
Choline	Choline is an organic compound, classified as an essential nutrient and usually grouped within the Vitamin B complex.
Glucose	Glucose, a simple monosaccharide sugar, is one of the most important carbohydrates and is used as a source of energy in animals and plants. Glucose is one of the main products of photosynthesis and starts respiration.
Ketone	A ketone is either the functional group characterized by a carbonyl group linked to two other carbon atoms or a chemical compound that contains this functional group.
Posttraumatic stress disorder	Posttraumatic stress disorder is the term for a severe and ongoing emotional reaction to an extreme psychological trauma.
Thiamin	Thiamin is one of the B vitamins. It is colorless chemical compound with a chemical formula $C_{12}H_{17}N_4OS$. It is soluble in water, methanol, and glycerol and practically insoluble in acetone, ether, chloroform, and benzene. Thiamin decomposes if heated. Its chemical structure contains a pyrimidine ring and a thiazole ring.

Thiamine	Thiamine, also known as vitamin B1, is a colorless compound with chemical formula $C_{12}H_{17}ClN_4OS$. Systemic thiamine deficiency can lead to myriad problems including neurodegeneration, wasting, and death. Well-known syndromes caused by lack of thiamine due to malnutrition or a diet high in thiaminase-rich foods include Wernicke-Korsakoff syndrome and beriberi, diseases also common in chronic abusers of alcohol.
Wernicke-Korsakoff syndrome	A cluster of symptoms associated with chronic alcohol abuse and characterized by confusion, memory impairment, and filling in gaps in memory with false information is referred to as the Wernicke-Korsakoff syndrome.
Adenosine	Adenosine is a nucleoside composed of adenine attached to a ribose (ribofuranose) moiety via a β-N_9-glycosidic bond. Adenosine plays an important role in biochemical processes, such as energy transfer and Adenosine plays an important role in biochemical processes, such as energy transfer. It is also an inhibitory neurotransmitter, believed to play a role in promoting sleep and suppressing arousal, with levels increasing with each hour an organism is awake.
Amnesia	Amnesia is a condition in which memory is disturbed. The causes of amnesia are organic or functional. Organic causes include damage to the brain, through trauma or disease, or use of certain generally sedative drugs.
Anxiety	Anxiety is a physiological state characterized by cognitive, somatic, emotional, and behavioral components.
Apathy	Apathy is a state of indifference — where an individual has an absence of interest or concern to certain aspects of emotional, social, or physical life. Apathy can be object-specific — toward a person, activity or environment. It is a common reaction to stress where it manifests as "learned helplessness" and is commonly associated with depression. It can also reflect a non-pathological lack of interest in things one does not consider important.
Appetite	The appetite is the desire to eat food, felt as hunger. Appetite exists in all higher lifeforms, and serves to regulate adequate energy intake to maintain metabolic needs. It is regulated by a close interplay between the digestive tract, adipose tissue and the brain. Decreased desire to eat is termed anorexia, while polyphagia or "hyperphagia" is increased eating. Disregulation of appetite contributes to anorexia nervosa, bulimia nervosa, cachexia, overeating, and binge eating disorder.
Arousal	Arousal is a physiological and psychological state involving the activation of the reticular activating system in the brain stem, the autonomic nervous system and the endocrine system, leading to increased heart rate and blood pressure and a condition of alertness and readiness to respond.
Confusion	Severe confusion of a degree considered pathological usually refers to loss of orientation, and often memory. Confusion as such is not synonymous with inability to focus attention, although severe inability to focus attention can cause, or greatly contribute to, confusion.

Delusion	A false belief, not generally shared by others, and that cannot be changed despite strong evidence to the contrary is a delusion.
Dependence	Dependence is compulsively using a substance, despite its negative and sometimes dangerous effects. Other drugs cause addiction without physical dependence.
Depression	In everyday language depression refers to any downturn in mood, which may be relatively transitory and perhaps due to something trivial.
Discovery	Discovery observations form acts of detecting and learning something. Discovery observations are acts in which something is found and given a productive insight. Serendipity is the effect by which one accidentally discovers something fortunate, especially while looking for something else entirely.
Drinking	Drinking is the act of consuming a liquid through the mouth.
Generation	Generation, also known as procreation, is the act of producing offspring. A generation can also be a stage or degree in a succession of natural descent as a grandfather, a father, and the father"s son comprise three generations.
Hallucination	A hallucination is a sensory perception experienced in the absence of an external stimulus, as distinct from an illusion, which is a misperception of an external stimulus. They may occur in any sensory modality - visual, auditory, olfactory, gustatory, tactile, or mixed.
Disability	A disability is a condition or function judged to be significantly impaired relative to the usual standard of an individual or their group. The term is often used to refer to individual functioning, including physical impairments, sensory impairments, cognitive impairments, intellectual impairments or mental health issue.
Intake	An intake is an air intake for an engine.
Intention	Intention is performing an action is their specific purpose in doing so, the end or goal they aim at, or intend to accomplish.
Memory	In psychology, memory is an organism"s ability to store, retain, and subsequently retrieve information. In recent decades, it has become one of the principal pillars of a branch of science called cognitive neuroscience, an interdisciplinary link between cognitive psychology and neuroscience.
Memory loss	Memory loss can have many causes:

· Alzheimer"s disease is an illness which can cause mild to severe memory loss
· Parkinson"s disease is a genetic defect which may result in memory loss
· Huntington"s disease is an inherited disease which can result in memory loss
· It is sometimes a side effect of chemotherapy in which cytotoxic drugs are used to treat cancer.
· Certain forms of mental illness also have memory loss as a key symptom, including fugue states and the much more famous Dissociative Identity Disorder.
· Stress-related activities are another factor which can result in memory loss
· It can also be caused by traumatic brain injury, of which a concussion is a form. .

Metabolism	Metabolism is the biochemical modification of chemical compounds in living organisms and cells.
Noise	In common use the word noise means unwanted sound or noise pollution.
Nutrition	The purposes of nutrition science is to explain metabolic and physiological responses of the body to diet. With advances in molecular biology, biochemistry, and genetics, nutrition science is additionally developing into the study of metabolism, which seeks to disconnect diet and health through the lens of biochemical processes.
Recollection	Recollection is the retrieval of memory. It is not a passive process; people employ metacognitive strategies to make the best use of their memory, and priming and other context can have a large effect on what is retrieved.
Insomnia	Insomnia is a sleep disorder characterized by an inability to sleep and/or inability to remain asleep for a reasonable period.
Spite	In fair division problems, Spite is a phenomenon that occurs when a player"s value of an allocation decreases when one or more other players" valuation increases. Thus, other things being equal, a player exhibiting Spite will prefer an allocation in which other players receive less than more (if the good is desirable.) In this language, Spite is difficult to analyze because one has to assess two sets of preferences.
Attribute-value system	An Attribute-value system is a basic knowledge representation framework comprising a table with columns designating "attributes" and rows designating "objects" Each table cell therefore designates the value of a particular attribute of a particular object. Below is a sample Attribute-value system.
Stimulus	In psychology, a stimulus is part of the stimulus-response relationship of behavioral learning theory.
Stress	Stress is the consequence of the failure to adapt to change. Less simply: it is the condition that results when person-environment transactions lead the individual to perceive a discrepancy, whether real or not, between the demands of a situation and the resources of the person"s biological, psychological or social systems.

Psychological trauma	Psychological trauma involves a singular experience or enduring event or events that completely overwhelm the individual"s ability to cope or integrate the emotion involved with that experience. It usually involves a complete feeling of helplessness in the face of a real or subjective threat to life, bodily integrity, or sanity.
Learning	Learning is the acquisition and development of memories and behaviors, including skills, knowledge, understanding, values, and wisdom. It is the goal of education, and the product of experience. Learning ranges from simple forms such as habituation to more complex forms such as play, seen only in large vertebrates.
Microelectrode	An electrical wire so small that it can be used either to monitor the electrical activity of a single neuron or to stimulate activity within it is a microelectrode.
Polarization	Polarization is the process of preparing a neuron for firing by creating an internal negative charge in relation to the body fluid outside the cell membrane.
Research method	The scope of the research method is to produce some new knowledge. This, in principle, can take three main forms: Exploratory research; Constructive research; and Empirical research.
Resting potential	The resting potential of a cell is the membrane potential that would be maintained if there were no action potentials, synaptic potentials, or other active changes in the membrane potential. In most cells the resting potential has a negative value, which by convention means that there is excess negative charge inside compared to outside.
Vision	Vision is the most important sense for birds, since good eyesight is essential for safe flight, and this group has a number of adaptations which give visual acuity superior to that of other vertebrate groups; a pigeon has been described as "two eyes with wings". The avian eye resembles that of a reptile, but has a better-positioned lens, a feature shared with mammals. Birds have the largest eyes relative to their size within the animal kingdom, and movement is consequently limited within the eye"s bony socket.
Classical conditioning	Classical conditioning is a form of associative learning that was first demonstrated by Ivan Pavlov. The typical procedure for inducing Classical conditioning involves presentations of a neutral stimulus along with a stimulus of some significance. The neutral stimulus could be any event that does not result in an overt behavioral response from the organism under investigation.
Electrical potential	Electrical potential is the potential energy per unit of charge associated with a static electric field, also called the electrostatic potential, typically measured in volts. The electrical potential and the magnetic vector potential together form a four vector, so that the two kinds of potential are mixed under Lorentz transformations.

Control group	A control group augments integrity in experiments by isolating variables as dictated by the scientific method in order to make a conclusion about such variables. In other cases, an experimental control is used to prevent the effects of one variable from being drowned out by the known, greater effects of other variables. this case, the researchers can either use a control group or use statistical techniques to control for the other variables.
Transmission	In medicine, transmission is the passing of a disease from an infected individual or group to a previously uninfected individual or group.
Ion	An Ion is an atom or molecule which has lost or gained one or more electrons, making it positively or negatively charged.
Ion channel	An Ion channel is a pore-forming protein that help establish the small voltage gradient that exists across the membrane of all living cells, by controlling the flow of ions. They are present in the membranes that surround all biological cells.
Potassium	Potassium is the an essential mineral macronutrient and is the main intracellular ion for all types of cells. It is important in maintaining fluid and electrolyte balance in the body.
Sodium-potassium pump	In order to maintain the cell potential, cells must keep a low concentration of sodium ions and high levels of potassium ions within the cell. The sodium-potassium pump is an enzyme located in the plasma membrane. It helps maintain cell potential and regulate cellular volume.
Sodium	Sodium is a chemical element which has the symbol Na, atomic number 11, atomic mass 22.9898 g/mol, common oxidation number +1. Sodium is a soft, silvery white, highly reactive element and is a member of the alkali metals within "group 1". It has only one stable isotope, ^{23}Na.
Concentration gradient	An ion gradient is a concentration gradient of ions, it can be called an electrochemical potential gradient of ions across membranes.
Depolarization	In biology, depolarization is a change in a cell"s membrane potential, making it more positive, or less negative. In neurons and some other cells, a large enough depolarization may result in an action potential. Hyperpolarization is the opposite of depolarization and inhibits the rise of an action potential.
Hypercomplex cells	Hypercomplex cells- Hubel and Wiesel named cells in the visual cortex that exhibit end stopping properties Hypercomplex cells, but later research has found them to be subclasses of the simple and complex cells. End stopping is when a cell"s response increases as a stimulus, for example a bar, expands to fill the receptive field, and then responds less when the stimulus exceeds the size of the receptive field .
Threshold	In general, a threshold is a fixed location or value where an abrupt change is observed. In the sensory modalities, it is the minimum amount of stimulus energy necessary to elicit a sensory response.

Action potential	An action potential is a "spike" of electrical discharge that travels along the membrane of a cell.
Absolute refractory period	The refractory period in a neuron occurs after an action potential. The action potential ends when voltage-gated ion channels allow positively charged potassium ions to leave the cell, between the 2nd and 3rd millisecond after the action potential. During this repolarization period when the potassium ion-channels are open, it is impossible to have another action potential. As a result, this is known as the absolute refractory period.
All-or-none law	The all-or-none law is the principle that the strength by which a nerve or muscle fiber responds to a stimulus is not dependent on the strength of the stimulus. If the stimulus is any strength above threshold, the nerve or muscle fiber will either give a complete response or no response at all.
Local anesthetic	Local anesthetic drugs act mainly by inhibiting sodium influx through sodium-specific ion channels in the neuronal cell membrane, in particular the so-called voltage-gated sodium channels. When the influx of sodium is interrupted, an action potential cannot arise and signal conduction is thus inhibited.
Refractory	The term refractory refers to the quality of a material to retain its strength at high temperatures. Refractory materials are used to make crucibles and linings for furnaces, kilns and incinerators. There is no clearly established boundary between refractory and non-refractory materials, though a practical requirement often cited is the ability of the material to withstand temperatures above 1100 °C without softening.
Refractory period	Refractory period refers to a phase following firing during which a neuron is less sensitive to messages from other neurons and will not fire. In the sexual response cycle, it is a period of time following orgasm during which an individual is not responsive to sexual stimulation.
Relative refractory period	Relative refractory period is a period of time where the stimulus must exceed the usual threshold to produce action potential.
Amplitude	The amplitude is a nonnegative scalar measure of a wave"s magnitude of oscillation, that is, the magnitude of the maximum disturbance in the medium during one wave cycle.
Egodystonic	Egodystonic is a psychological term referring to thoughts and behaviors, (e.g., dreams, impulses, compulsions, desires, etc.), that are in conflict with the needs and goals of the ego in conflict with a person"s ideal self-image. The concept is studied in detail in abnormal psychology, and is the opposite of egosyntonic. Obsessive compulsive disorder is considered to be an ego-dystonic disorder, as the thoughts and compulsions experienced or expressed are often not consistent with the individual"s self-perception, causing extreme distress.
Principle	In user interface design, programming language design, and ergonomics, the principle of least astonishment (or surprise) states that, when two elements of an interface conflict the behaviour should be that which will least surprise the human user or programmer at the time the conflict arises.

For example:

A user interface may have the behaviour that pressing Control-Q causes the program to quit. The same user interface may have a facility for recording macros, a sequence of keystrokes to be played back later, intended to be able to control all aspects of the program.

Tim	TIM is a series of lesser-known psychedelic drugs similar in structure to mescaline. They were first synthesized by Alexander Shulgin. In his book PiHKAL (Phenethylamines i Have Known And Loved), none of their durations are known.
Axon hillock	The axon hillock is the anatomical part of a neuron that connects the cell body to the axon. It is regarded as the place where EPSPs from numerous synaptic inputs on the dendrites or cell body accumulate.
Corpus callosum	The corpus callosum is a structure of the mammalian brain in the longitudal fissure that connects the left and right cerebral hemispheres. Much of the inter-hemispheric communication in the brain is conducted across the corpus callosum.
Consciousness	The awareness of the sensations, thoughts, and feelings being experienced at a given moment is called consciousness.
Saltatory conduction	Saltatory conduction is a means by which action potentials are transmitted along myelinated nerve fibers. In myelinated axons, action potentials do not propagate as waves, but recur at successive nodes.
Fats	Fats consist of a wide group of compounds that are generally soluble in organic solvents and largely insoluble in water. Chemically, fats are generally triesters of glycerol and fatty acids. Fats may be either solid or liquid at normal room temperature, depending on their structure and composition.
Flow	Flow is the mental state of operation in which the person is fully immersed in what he or she is doing by a feeling of energized focus, full involvement, and success in the process of the activity. Proposed by Mihály Csíkszentmihályi, the positive psychology concept has been widely referenced across a variety of fields. Colloquial terms for this or similar mental states include: to be on the ball, in the zone, or in the groove.
Hormone	A hormone is a chemical messenger that carries a signal from one cell to another. All multicellular organisms produce hormone s.

Membrane potential

Membrane potential is the electrical potential difference across a cell"s plasma membrane. The plasma membrane bounds the cell to provide a stable environment for biological processes. Membrane potential arises from the action of ion transporters embedded in the membrane which maintain viable ion concentrations inside the cell. The term "membrane potential" is sometimes used interchangeably with cell potential but is applicable to any lipid bilayer or membrane.

Synapse

A synapse is specialized junction through which cells of the nervous system signal to one another and to non-neuronal cells such as muscles or glands. They allow the neurons of the central nervous system to form interconnected neural circuits.

Chapter 3. Synapses

Synapse	A synapse is specialized junction through which cells of the nervous system signal to one another and to non-neuronal cells such as muscles or glands. They allow the neurons of the central nervous system to form interconnected neural circuits.
Muscle	Muscle is contractile tissue of the body and is derived from the mesodermal layer of embryonic germ cells. It is classified as skeletal, cardiac, or smooth muscle, and its function is to produce force and cause motion, either locomotion or movement within internal organs.
Reflex	A reflex action is an automatic neuromuscular action elicited by a defined stimulus. In most contexts, especially involving humans, a reflex action is mediated via the reflex arc
Reflex arc	A reflex arc is the neural pathway mediating a reflex. It generally does not involve the brain. Instead of the brain it can include a spinal reflex integration center composed of interneurons to connect affector and effector signals.
Sherrington	Sherrington used reflexes in the spinal cord as a way of investigating the general properties of neurons and the nervous system. These experiments led him to postulate "Sherrington's Law," which states that for every neural activation of a muscle, there is a corresponding inhibition of the opposing muscle. He also introduced the concept of the synapse and the concept of the reflex arc.
Sensory neurons	*Sensory neurons* are neurons that are activated by sensory input (vision, touch, hearing, etc.), and send projections into the central nervous system that convey sensory information to the brain or spinal cord. Unlike neurons of the central nervous system, whose inputs come from other neurons, *Sensory neurons* are activated by physical modalities such as light, sound, temperature, chemical stimulation, etc. In complex organisms, *Sensory neurons* relay their information to the central nervous system or in less complex organisms, such as the hydra, directly to motor neurons and *Sensory neurons* also transmit information to the brain, where it can be further processed and acted upon.
Stimulus	In psychology, a stimulus is part of the stimulus-response relationship of behavioral learning theory.
Depolarization	In biology, depolarization is a change in a cell"s membrane potential, making it more positive, or less negative. In neurons and some other cells, a large enough depolarization may result in an action potential. Hyperpolarization is the opposite of depolarization and inhibits the rise of an action potential.
Excitatory postsynaptic potential	In neuroscience, an excitatory postsynaptic potential is a temporary depolarization of postsynaptic membrane potential caused by the flow of positively charged ions into the postsynaptic cell.
Hypercomplex cells	Hypercomplex cells- Hubel and Wiesel named cells in the visual cortex that exhibit end stopping properties Hypercomplex cells, but later research has found them to be subclasses of the simple and complex cells. End stopping is when a cell"s response increases as a stimulus, for example a bar, expands to fill the receptive field, and then responds less when the stimulus exceeds the size of the receptive field .

Sodium	Sodium is a chemical element which has the symbol Na, atomic number 11, atomic mass 22.9898 g/mol, common oxidation number +1. Sodium is a soft, silvery white, highly reactive element and is a member of the alkali metals within "group 1". It has only one stable isotope, ^{23}Na.
Spatial summation	Spatial summation is a way of achieving action potential in a neuron which involves input from multiple cells. Spatial summation is the algebraic summation of potentials from different areas of input, usually on the dendrites. Summation of excitatory postsynaptic potentials allows the potential to reach the threshold to generate an action potential, whereas inhibitory postsynaptic potentials can prevent the cell from achieving action potential.
Temporal summation	Temporal summation is combining the effects of a single or a small number of EPSPs that occur rapidly within a short time at the same synapse until they reach the action potential of the cell.
Membrane potential	Membrane potential is the electrical potential difference across a cell"s plasma membrane. The plasma membrane bounds the cell to provide a stable environment for biological processes. Membrane potential arises from the action of ion transporters embedded in the membrane which maintain viable ion concentrations inside the cell. The term "membrane potential" is sometimes used interchangeably with cell potential but is applicable to any lipid bilayer or membrane.
Not	This catalog is compiled from a source file. Please do not edit this page manually. This is how to edit it.
Single	In relationships, a single person is one who is not married, or, more broadly, who is not in an exclusive romantic relationship.
Stimulation	Stimulation is the action of various agents on muscles, nerves, or a sensory end organ, by which activity is evoked.
Synapses	Chemical synapses are specialized junctions through which neurons signal to each other and to non-neuronal cells such as those in muscles or glands. Chemical synapses allow neurons to form circuits within the central nervous system. They are crucial to the biological computations that underlie perception and thought.
Tim	TIM is a series of lesser-known psychedelic drugs similar in structure to mescaline. They were first synthesized by Alexander Shulgin. In his book PiHKAL (Phenethylamines i Have Known And Loved), none of their durations are known.
Inhibitory postsynaptic potential	Inhibitory postsynaptic potential refers to a local, graded excitatory potential that hyperpolarizes a neuron's membrane--driving the charge farther negative. Driving a cell to negativity will usually lower the firing rate.
Inhibitory synapse	An inhibitory synapse is a synapse in which an action potential in the presynaptic cell decreases the probability of an action potential occurring in the postsynaptic cell.

Interneuron	An interneuron (also called relay neuron or association neuron) is a neuron that communicates only to other neurons. They provide connections between sensory and motor neurons, as well as between themselves.
Intrinsic	Intrinsic describes a characteristic or property of some thing or action which is essential and specific to that thing or action, and which is wholly independent of any other object, action or consequence.
Motor neuron	In vertebrates, the term Motor neuron classically applies to neurons located in the central nervous system that project their axons outside the CNS and directly or indirectly control muscles. Motor neuron is often synonymous with efferent neuron.
Axon	An axon is a long, slender projection of a nerve cell, or neuron, that conducts electrical impulses away from the neuron"s cell body or soma.
Software extension	A Software extension is a computer program designed to be incorporated into another piece of software in order to enhance the functionalities of the latter. On its own, the program is not useful or functional. Examples of software applications that support extensions include the Mozilla Firefox Web browser, Adobe Systems Photoshop and Microsoft Windows Explorer shell extensions.
Hyperpolarization	Hyperpolarization is any change in a cell's membrane potential that makes it more polarized. That is, hyperpolarization is an increase in the absolute value of a cell's membrane potential.
Impulse	In classical mechanics, an Impulse is defined as the integral of a force with respect to time. When a force is applied to a rigid body it changes the momentum of that body. A small force applied for a long time can produce the same momentum change as a large force applied briefly, because it is the product of the force and the time for which it is applied that is important.
Information	Information as a concept has a diversity of meanings, from everyday usage to technical settings. Generally speaking, the concept of Information is closely related to notions of constraint, communication, control, data, form, instruction, knowledge, meaning, mental stimulus, pattern, perception, and representation. According to the Oxford English Dictionary, the first known historical meaning of the word Information in English was the act of informing, or giving form or shape to the mind, as in education, instruction, or training.
Other	The Other or constitutive Other is a key concept in continental philosophy, opposed to the Same. It refers, or attempts to refer, to that which is "Other" than the concept being considered. The term often means a person Other than oneself, and is often capitalised.
Soma	The soma is the bulbous end of a neuron, containing the cell nucleus.

Spinal cord	The spinal cord is a thin, tubular bundle of nerves that is an extension of the central nervous system from the brain and is enclosed in and protected by the bony vertebral column. The main function of the spinal cord is transmission of neural inputs between the periphery and the brain.
Structure	Structure is a fundamental and sometimes intangible notion covering the recognition, observation, nature, and stability of patterns and relationships of entities.
Action potential	An action potential is a "spike" of electrical discharge that travels along the membrane of a cell.
Firing	Firing refers to a decision made by an employer to terminate employment.
Adrenaline	Adrenaline is a hormone when carried in the blood and a neurotransmitter when it is released across a neuronal synapse. It is a catecholamine, a sympathomimetic monoamine derived from the amino acids phenylalanine and tyrosine.
Vagus nerve	The vagus nerve is the tenth of twelve paired cranial nerves, and is the only nerve that starts in the brainstem and extends, through the jugular foramen, down below the head, to the neck, chest and abdomen.
Chemical	A chemical is a material with a definite chemical composition. All samples of a compound have the same composition; that is, all samples have the same proportions, by mass, of the elements present in the compound.
Cranial nerve	A Cranial nerve emerges from the brainstem instead of the spinal cord.
Discovery	Discovery observations form acts of detecting and learning something. Discovery observations are acts in which something is found and given a productive insight. Serendipity is the effect by which one accidentally discovers something fortunate, especially while looking for something else entirely.
Neuropeptide	A neuropeptide is any of the variety of peptides found in neural tissue; e.g. endorphins, enkephalins. Now, about 100 different peptides are known to be released by different populations of neurons in the mammalian brain.
Neurotransmitter	A neurotransmitter is a chemical that is used to relay, amplify and modulate electrical signals between a neurons and another cell.
Synaptic cleft	Synaptic cleft refers to a microscopic gap between the terminal button of a neuron and the cell membrane of another neuron.
Affect	Affect refers to the experience of feeling or emotion. Affect is a key part of the process of an organism's interaction with stimuli. The word also refers sometimes to affect display, which is "a facial, vocal, or gestural behavior that serves as an indicator of affect."

73

Amino acid	Amino acid is the basic structural building unit of proteins. They form short polymer chains called peptides or polypeptides which in turn form structures called proteins.
Axon terminal	A swelling at the end of an axon that is designed to release a chemical substance onto another neuron, muscle cell, or gland cell is called the axon terminal.
Acetic acid	Acetic acid, is an organic chemical compound, giving vinegar its sour taste and pungent smell. Its structural formula is represented as CH_3COOH.
Adenosine	Adenosine is a nucleoside composed of adenine attached to a ribose (ribofuranose) moiety via a β-N_9-glycosidic bond. Adenosine plays an important role in biochemical processes, such as energy transfer and Adenosine plays an important role in biochemical processes, such as energy transfer. It is also an inhibitory neurotransmitter, believed to play a role in promoting sleep and suppressing arousal, with levels increasing with each hour an organism is awake.
Audition	An Audition is a sample performance by an actor, singer, musician, dancer or other performer. It involves the performer displaying their talent through a previously-memorized and rehearsed solo piece: for example, a monologue for actors or a song for a singer. Used in the context of performing arts, it is analogous to job interviews in many ways.
Blood-brain barrier	The Blood-brain barrier is a membranic structure that acts primarily to protect the brain from chemicals in the blood, while still allowing essential metabolic function. It is composed of endothelial cells, which are packed very tightly in brain capillaries. This higher density restricts passage of substances from the bloodstream much more than endothelial cells in capillaries elsewhere in the body
Brain	In animals, the brain, is the control center of the central nervous system, responsible for behavior. The brain is located in the head, protected by the skull and close to the primary sensory apparatus of vision, hearing, equilibrioception, sense of acceleration, taste, and olfaction.
Carbohydrates	Carbohydrates are simple organic compounds that are aldehydes or ketones with many hydroxyl groups added, usually one on each carbon atom that is not part of the aldehyde or ketone functional group.
Choline	Choline is an organic compound, classified as an essential nutrient and usually grouped within the Vitamin B complex.
Diet	In nutrition, the diet is the sum of food consumed by a person or other organism. Dietary habits are the habitual decisions an individual or culture makes when choosing what foods to eat.

Dopamine	Dopamine is a hormone and neurotransmitter occurring in a wide variety of animals, including both vertebrates and invertebrates. In the brain, dopamine functions as a neurotransmitter. Dopamine is also a neurohormone released by the hypothalamus. Its main function as a hormone is to inhibit the release of prolactin from the anterior lobe of the pituitary.
Epinephrine	Epinephrine is a hormone and neurotransmitter. Epinephrine increases the "fight or flight" response of the sympathetic division of the autonomic nervous system. It is a catecholamine, a sympathomimetic monoamine derived from the amino acids phenylalanine and tyrosine.
Insulin	Insulin is an animal hormone whose presence informs the body"s cells that the animal is well fed, causing liver and muscle cells to take in glucose and store it in the form of glycogen, and causing fat cells to take in blood lipids and turn them into triglycerides. In addition it has several other anabolic effects throughout the body.
Nitric oxide	Nitric oxide is a chemical compound with chemical formula NO. This gas is an important signaling molecule in the body of mammals including humans and is an extremely important intermediate in the chemical industry. It is also a toxic air pollutant produced by automobile engines and power plants.
Norepinephrine	Norepinephrine is a catecholamine and a phenethylamine with chemical formula $C_8H_{11}NO_3$.
Serotonin	Serotonin, is a monoamine neurotransmitter synthesized in serotonergic neurons in the central nervous system and enterochromaffin cells in the gastrointestinal tract of animals including humans. Serotonin is also found in many mushrooms and plants, including fruits and vegetables.
Tryptophan	Tryptophan is a sleep-promoting amino acid and a precursor for serotonin (a neurotransmitter) and melatonin (a neurohormone). Tryptophan has been implicated as a possible cause of schizophrenia in people who cannot metabolize it properly.
Tyrosine	Tyrosine is one of the 20 amino acids that are used by cells to synthesize proteins. It plays a key role in signal transduction, since it can be tagged (phosphorylated) with a phosphate group by protein kinases to alter the functionality and activity of certain enzymes.
Vision	Vision is the most important sense for birds, since good eyesight is essential for safe flight, and this group has a number of adaptations which give visual acuity superior to that of other vertebrate groups; a pigeon has been described as "two eyes with wings". The avian eye resembles that of a reptile, but has a better-positioned lens, a feature shared with mammals. Birds have the largest eyes relative to their size within the animal kingdom, and movement is consequently limited within the eye"s bony socket.

Alcoholism	Alcoholism is a term with multiple and sometimes conflicting definitions. In common and historic usage, alcoholism refers to any condition that results in the continued consumption of alcoholic beverages despite the health problems and negative social consequences it causes.
Animal testing	Animal testing refers to the use of animals in experiments. It is estimated that 50 to 100 million vertebrate animals worldwide — from zebrafish to non-human primates — are used annually and either killed during the experiments or subsequently euthanized.
Antipsychotic	The term antipsychotic is applied to a group of drugs used to treat psychosis.
Antipsychotics	*Antipsychotics* are a group of psychoactive drugs commonly but not exclusively used to treat psychosis, which is typified by schizrenia. Over time a wide range of *Antipsychotics* have been developed. A first generation of *Antipsychotics*, known as typical *Antipsychotics*, was discovered in the 1950s.
Behavior	Behavior refers to the actions or reactions of an object or organism, usually in relation to the environment. Behavior can be conscious or subconscious, overt or covert, and voluntary or involuntary. Human Behavior (and that of other organisms and mechanisms) can be common, unusual, acceptable, or unacceptable. Humans evaluate the acceptability of Behavior using social norms and regulate Behavior by means of social control
Blood	Blood is a specialized biological fluid consisting of red blood cells.White blood cells also called leukocytes and platelets also called thrombocytes suspended in a complex fluid medium known as blood plasma.
Body weight	Body weight is a term that is used in biological and medical science contexts to describe the mass of an organism"s body. Body weight is measured in kilograms throughout the world, although in some countries people more often measure and describe body weight in pounds or stones and pounds and thus may not be well acquainted with measurement in kilograms.
Chlorpromazine	Chlorpromazine is a phenothiazine antipsychotic. Its principal use is in the treatment of schizophrenia, though it has also been used to treat hiccups and nausea. Its use today has been largely supplanted by the newer atypical antipsychotics such as olanzapine and quetiapine. It works on a variety of receptors in the central nervous system; these include anticholinergic, antidopaminergic and antihistamine effects as well as some antagonism of adrenergic receptors.
Flow	Flow is the mental state of operation in which the person is fully immersed in what he or she is doing by a feeling of energized focus, full involvement, and success in the process of the activity. Proposed by Mihály Csíkszentmihályi, the positive psychology concept has been widely referenced across a variety of fields. Colloquial terms for this or similar mental states include: to be on the ball, in the zone, or in the groove.

Glucose	Glucose, a simple monosaccharide sugar, is one of the most important carbohydrates and is used as a source of energy in animals and plants. Glucose is one of the main products of photosynthesis and starts respiration.
Hormone	A hormone is a chemical messenger that carries a signal from one cell to another. All multicellular organisms produce hormone s.
Mechanism	In philosophy, mechanism is a theory that all natural phenomena can be explained by physical causes. It can be contrasted with vitalism, the philosophical theory that vital forces are active in living organisms, so that life cannot be explained solely by mechanism.
Pancreas	The pancreas is a retroperitoneal organ that serves two functions: it produces juice containing digestive enzymes; and it produces several important hormones including insulin, glucagon, and several other hormones.
Dementia	Dementia is the progressive decline in cognitive function due to damage or disease in the brain beyond what might be expected from normal aging.
Dementia praecox	An older term for schizophrenia, chosen to describe what was believed to be an incurable and progressive deterioration of mental functioning beginning in adolescence is called dementia praecox.
Constant	A constant is something that does not change, over time or otherwise: a fixed value. In most fields of discourse the term is an antonym of "variable", but in mathematical parlance a mathematical variable may sometimes also be called a constant.
Exocytosis	Exocytosis is the durable process by which a cell directs secretory vesicles out of the cell membrane.
Gamma-aminobutyric acid	Gamma-aminobutyric acid is an inhibitory neurotransmitter found in the nervous systems of widely-divergent species. It is the chief inhibitory neurotransmitter in the central nervous system and also in the retina.
Glutamate	Glutamate is one of the 20 standard amino acids used by all organisms in their proteins. It is critical for proper cell function, but it is not an essential nutrient in humans because it can be manufactured from other compounds.
Glycine	Glycine is the organic compound with the formula $HO_2CCH_2NH_2$. It is one of the 20 amino acids commonly found in proteins, coded by codons GGU, GGC, GGA and GGG. Because of its structural simplicity, this compact amino acid tends to be evolutionarily conserved in, for example, cytochrome c, myoglobin, and hemoglobin. Glycine is the unique amino acid that is not optically active. Most proteins contain only small quantities of glycine. A notable exception is collagen, which contains about 35% glycine.

Manic-depressive disorder	Bipolar affective disorder until recently, the current name is of fairly recent origin and refers to the cycling between high and low episodes; it has replaced the older term Manic-depressive disorder. The new term is designed to be neutral, to avoid the stigma in the non-mental health community.
Nausea	Nausea is the sensation of unease and discomfort in the stomach with an urge to vomit.
Ondansetron	Ondansetron is a serotonin 5-HT$_3$ receptor antagonist used mainly as an antiemetic to treat nausea and vomiting following chemotherapy.
Protein	A protein is a complex, high-molecular-weight organic compound that consists of amino acids joined by peptide bonds. It is essential to the structure and function of all living cells and viruses. Many are enzymes or subunits of enzymes.
Disease	A Disease or medical problem is an abnormal condition of an organism that impairs bodily functions, associated with specific symptoms and signs. It may be caused by external factors, such as invading organisms, or it may be caused by internal dysfunctions, such as autoimmune Disease s. In human beings, Disease is often used more broadly to refer to any condition that causes extreme pain, dysfunction, distress, social problems, and/or death to the person afflicted, or similar problems for those in contact with the person.
Ion channel	An Ion channel is a pore-forming protein that help establish the small voltage gradient that exists across the membrane of all living cells, by controlling the flow of ions. They are present in the membranes that surround all biological cells.
Postsynaptic neurons	Postsynaptic neurons are neurons whose dendritic or somatic receptors bind two neurotransmitters together during a synapse.
Receptor	A sensory receptor is a structure that recognizes a stimulus in the internal or external environment of an organism. In response to stimuli the sensory receptor initiates sensory transduction by creating graded potentials or action potentials in the same cell or in an adjacent one.
Guanosine triphosphate	Guanosine triphosphate is a purine nucleotide. One role is as substrate for the synthesis of RNA during transcription. Its structure is similar to that of the guanine nucleoside, the only difference being that there are three extra phosphate groups added on to the 5" carbon.
Neuromodulator	A neuromodulator is a substance other than a neurotransmitter, released by a neuron at a synapse and conveying information to adjacent or distant neurons, either enhancing or damping their activities.
Message	A message in its most general meaning is an object of communication.
Anterior	Anterior is an anatomical term referring to the front part of the body. The anterior is positioned in front of another body part, or towards the head of an animal. It is the opposite of posterior.

Anterior pituitary	The Anterior pituitary comprises the anterior lobe of the pituitary gland and is part of the endocrine system. Unlike the posterior lobe, the anterior lobe is genuinely glandular, hence the root adeno in its name.
Endocrine gland	An endocrine gland is one of a set of internal organs involved in the secretion of hormones into the blood. The other major type of gland is the exocrine glands, which secrete substances—usually digestive juices—into the digestive tract or onto the skin.
Oxytocin	Oxytocin is a mammalian hormone that also acts as a neurotransmitter in the brain. In females, it is released in large amounts after distension of the cervix and vagina during labor, and after stimulation of the nipples, facilitating birth and breastfeeding, respectively. In humans, oxytocin is released during orgasm in both sexes. In the brain, oxytocin is involved in social recognition and bonding, and might be involved in the formation of trust between people.
Pituitary gland	The pituitary gland is an endocrine gland about the size of a pea that sits in the small, bony cavity at the base of the brain. The pituitary gland secretes hormones regulating a wide variety of bodily activities, including trophic hormones that stimulate other endocrine glands.
Posterior	In reference to the anatomical terms of location, the posterior end is laterally situated at or toward the hinder part of the body, lying at or extending toward the right or left side. It is the polar opposite to the anterior end, or front end of the body.
Posterior pituitary	The posterior pituitary comprises the posterior lobe of the pituitary gland and is part of the endocrine system.
Sex steroid	Sex steroid refers to steroid hormones that interact with vertebrate androgen or estrogen receptors.
Hypothalamus	The hypothalamus is a region of the brain located below the thalamus, forming the major portion of the ventral region of the diencephalon and functioning to regulate certain metabolic processes and other autonomic activities.
Neuropeptides	Brain chemicals, such as enkephalins and endorphins, that regulate the activity of neurons are called neuropeptides.
Cholinesterase	In biochemistry, Cholinesterase is an enzyme that catalyzes the hydrolysis of the neurotransmitter acetylcholine into choline and acetic acid, a reaction necessary to allow a cholinergic neuron to return to its resting state after activation.
Adrenocorticotropic hormone	Adrenocorticotropic hormone is a polypeptide hormone produced and secreted by the pituitary gland. It is an important player in the hypothalamic-pituitary-adrenal axis.

Enzyme	An enzyme is a protein that catalyzes, or speeds up, a chemical reaction. Enzymes are essential to sustain life because most chemical reactions in biological cells would occur too slowly, or would lead to different products, without enzymes.
Experience	Experience as a general concept comprises knowledge of or skill in or observation of some thing or some event gained through involvement in or exposure to that thing or event. The history of the word experience aligns it closely with the concept of experiment.
Follicle-stimulating hormone	Follicle-stimulating hormone is a hormone synthesised and secreted by gonadotropes in the anterior pituitary gland. In the ovary FSH stimulates the growth of immature Graafian follicles to maturation.
Gonadotropins	Gonadotropins are protein hormones secreted by the pituitary gland. The gonads -- testes and ovaries -- are the primary target organs. The gonadotropins stimulates the testes and the ovaries to produce testosterone (and indirectly estradiol).
Growth hormone	Growth hormone is a protein hormone that stimulates growth and cell reproduction in humans and other animals. It has a variety of functions in the body, the most noticeable of which is the increase of height throughout childhood.
Myasthenia gravis	Myasthenia gravis is a neuromuscular disease leading to fluctuating muscle weakness and fatiguability. It is an autoimmune disorder, in which weakness is caused by circulating antibodies that block acetylcholine receptors at the post-synaptic neuromuscular junction, inhibiting the stimulative effect of the neurotransmitter acetylcholine.
Prolactin	Prolactin is a peptide hormone primarily associated with lactation. In breastfeeding, the infant suckling the teat stimulates the production of prolactin, which fills the breast with milk in preparation for the next feed. Oxytocin, a similar hormone, is also released, which triggers milk let-down.
Thyroid-stimulating hormone	Thyroid-stimulating hormone is a hormone synthesized and secreted by thyrotrope cells in the anterior pituitary gland which regulates the endocrine function of the thyroid gland.
Vasopressin	Vasopressin is a peptide hormone. It is derived from a preprohormone precursor that is synthesized in the hypothalamus, from which it is liberated during transport to the posterior pituitary. Most of it is stored in the posterior part of the pituitary gland to be released into the blood stream; some of it is also released directly into the brain.
Acetate	An acetate, is either a salt or ester of acetic acid.
Acetylcholine	The chemical compound acetylcholine, often abbreviated as ACh, was the first neurotransmitter to be identified. It is a chemical transmitter in both the peripheral nervous system and central nervous system in many organisms including humans.

Acetylcholine receptor	An acetylcholine receptor is an integral membrane protein that responds to the binding of the neurotransmitter acetylcholine.
Adrenal cortex	Situated along the perimeter of the adrenal gland, the adrenal cortex mediates the stress response through the production of mineralocorticoids and glucocorticoids, including aldosterone and cortisol respectively. It is also a secondary site of androgen synthesis.
Blood pressure	Blood pressure refers to the force exerted by circulating blood on the walls of blood vessels, and constitutes one of the principal vital signs.
Recess	In education, recess is the daily period, typically ten to thirty minutes, in elementary school where students are allowed to leave the school"s interior to enter its adjacent outdoor playground, where they can play on such recreational equipment or engage in activities.
Corticosterone	Corticosterone is a 21 carbon steroid hormone of the corticosteroid type produced in the cortex of the adrenal glands.
Cortisol	Cortisol is a corticosteroid hormone produced by the adrenal cortex. It is a vital hormone that is often referred to as the "stress hormone" as it is involved in the response to stress. It increases blood pressure, blood sugar levels and has an immunosuppressive action.
Follicle	A follicle is a term to describe a small spherical group of cells containing a cavity, and is often used as a descriptive term in biology, particularly in anatomy.
Prosencephalon	In the anatomy of the brain of vertebrates, the prosencephalon is the rostral-most portion of the brain. The prosencephalon, the mesencephalon, and rhombencephalon are the three primary portions of the brain during early development of the central nervous system.
Immune system	The most important function of the human immune system occurs at the cellular level of the blood and tissues. The lymphatic and blood circulation systems are highways for specialized white blood cells. These cells include B cells, T cells, natural killer cells, and macrophages. All function with the primary objective of recognizing, attacking and destroying bacteria, viruses, cancer cells, and all substances seen as foreign.
Kidney	The kidney is an organ that filters wastes from the blood and excretes them, with water, as urine. In humans, it is located in the posterior part of the abdomen. There is one on each side of the spine. Each kidney receives its blood supply from the renal artery, two of which branch from the abdominal aorta.
Ovary	An ovary is an egg-producing reproductive organ found in female organisms.
Secret	Secrecy or furtiveness is the practice of sharing information among a group of people, which can be as small as one person, while hiding it from all others. That which is kept hidden is known as the Secret.

	Secrecy is often controversial, depending on the content of the Secret, the group or people keeping the Secret, and the motivation for secrecy.
Urine	Urine is an aqueous solution of waste electrolytes and metabolites excreted by mammals, birds, reptiles, fish and amphibians.
Adrenal medulla	Composed mainly of hormone-producing chromaffin cells, the adrenal medulla is the principal site of the conversion of the amino acid tyrosine into the catecholamines epinephrine and norepinephrine (also called adrenaline and noradrenaline, respectively).
Antidepressant	An antidepressant, is a psychiatric medication or other substance (nutrient or herb) used for alleviating depression or dysthymia ("milder" depression). Drug groups known as MAOIs, tricyclics and SSRIs are particularly associated with the term. These medications are now amongst the drugs most commonly prescribed by psychiatrists and general practitioners, and their effectiveness and adverse effects are the subject of many studies and competing claims.
Catechol-o-methyltransferase	Catechol-O-methyltransferase is an enzyme first discovered by biochemist Julius Axelrod. COMT is the name given to the gene that codes for this enzyme. The O in the name stands for oxygen, not for ortho.
Depression	In everyday language depression refers to any downturn in mood, which may be relatively transitory and perhaps due to something trivial.
Fat cells	Fat cells serve as storehouses for liquefied fat in the body and that number from 25 to 35 billion in normal weight individuals; with weight loss, they decrease in size but not in number.
Liver	The liver plays a major role in metabolism and has a number of functions in the body including detoxification, glycogen storage and plasma protein synthesis. It also produces bile, which is important for digestion. The liver converts most carbohydrates, proteing, and fats into glucose.
Parasympathetic nervous system	The parasympathetic nervous system is a division of the autonomic nervous system, along with the sympathetic nervous system and Enteric nervous system. The ANS is a subdivision of the peripheral nervous system.
Physiology	The study of the functions and activities of living cells, tissues, and organs and of the physical and chemical phenomena involved is referred to as physiology.
Prefrontal cortex	The prefrontal cortex is the anterior part of the frontal lobes of the brain, lying in front of the motor and premotor areas. Cytoarchitectonically, it is defined by the presence of an internal granular layer IV.
Reuptake	Reuptake is the reabsorption of a neurotransmitter by the neurotransmitter transporter of a pre-synaptic neuron after it has performed its function of transmitting a neural impulse. This prevents further activity of the neurotransmitter, weakening its effects.

91

Thymus	In human anatomy, the thymus is an organ located in the upper anterior portion of the chest cavity just behind the sternum.
Thyroid	In anatomy, the thyroid is the largest endocrine gland in the body. The primary function of the thyroid is production of hormones.
Thyroid gland	The thyroid gland is one of the largest endocrine glands in the body. This gland is found in the neck just below the laryngeal prominence. The thyroid controls how quickly the body burns energy, makes proteins, and how sensitive the body should be to other hormones.
Membrane transport protein	A membrane transport protein is a protein involved in the movement of ions, small molecules, or macromolecules, such as another protein across a biological membrane. Transport proteins are integral membrane proteins; that is they exist within and span the membrane across which they transport substances. The proteins may assist in the movement of substances by facilitated diffusion or active transport.
Catecholamine	Catecholamine refers to chemical compounds derived from the amino acid tyrosine containing catechol and amine groups.
Explanation	An explanation is a description which may clarify causes, context, and consequences of a certain object, and a phenomenon such as a process, a state of affairs. This description may establish rules or laws, and may clarify the existing ones in relation to an object, and a phenomenon examined. The components of an explanation can be implicit, and be interwoven with one another.
Feminization	In biology and medicine, feminization refers to the development in an organism of physical or behavioral characteristics unique to the female of the species. This may represent a normal developmental process, contributing to sexual differentiation.
Frontal lobe	The frontal lobe comprises four major folds of cortical tissue: the precentral gyrus, superior gyrus and the middle gyrus of the frontal gyri, the inferior frontal gyrus. It has been found to play a part in impulse control, judgement, language, memory, motor function, problem solving, sexual behavior, socialization and spontaneity.
Gonad	The Gonad is the organ that makes gametes. The Gonad s in males are the testes and the Gonad s in females are the ovaries. The product, gametes, are haploid germ cells.
Gonads	The gonad is the organ that makes gametes. The gonads in males are the testes and the gonads in females are the ovaries. The product, gametes, are haploid germ cells.
Melatonin	Melatonin is a hormone found in all living creatures from algae to humans, at levels that vary in a daily cycle. It plays a role in the regulation of the circadian rhythm of several biological functions.

Membrane protein	A membrane protein is a protein molecule that is attached to, or associated with the membrane of a cell or an organelle. It controls sodium entry: as it depolarizes, sodium enters.
Need	A Need is something that is necessary for humans to live a healthy life. Need s are distinguished from wants because a deficiency would cause a clear negative outcome, such as dysfunction or death. Need s can be objective and physical, such as food and water, or they can be subjective and psychological, such as the Need for self-esteem.
Signal	In the fields of communications, signal processing, and in electrical engineering more generally, a signal is any time-varying quantity. Signals are often scalar-valued functions of time, but may be vector valued and may be functions of any other relevant independent variable.
Understanding	Understanding is a psychological process related to an abstract or physical object, such as, person, situation, or message whereby one is able to think about it and use concepts to deal adequately with that object.
Anandamide	Anandamide is a naturally occurring neurotransmitter found in the brain of animals, as well as other organs. Anandamide receptors were originally discovered as being sensitive to tetrahydrocannabinol, which is among the psychoactive cannabinoids found in marijuana.
Autoreceptor	An Autoreceptor is a receptor located on presynaptic nerve cell terminals and serves as a part of a feedback loop in signal transduction. It is sensitive only to those neurotransmitters or hormones, that are released by the neuron in whose membrane the autoreceptor sits.
Cannabinoids	Cannabinoids are a group of terpenophenolic compounds present in Cannabis. The broader definition of cannabinoids refer to a group of substances that are structurally related to tetrahydrocannabinol or that bind to cannabinoid receptors. The chemical definition encompasses a variety of distinct chemical classes: the classical cannabinoids structurally related to THC, the nonclassical cannabinoids, the aminoalkylindoles, the eicosanoids related to the endocannabinoids, 1,5-diarylpyrazoles, quinolines and arylsulphonamides and additional compounds that do not fall into these standard classes but bind to cannabinoid receptors.
Feeding	Feeding is the process by which organisms, typically animals, obtain food. There are many types of feeding that animals exhibit.
Egodystonic	Egodystonic is a psychological term referring to thoughts and behaviors, (e.g., dreams, impulses, compulsions, desires, etc.), that are in conflict with the needs and goals of the ego in conflict with a person"s ideal self-image. The concept is studied in detail in abnormal psychology, and is the opposite of egosyntonic. Obsessive compulsive disorder is considered to be an ego-dystonic disorder, as the thoughts and compulsions experienced or expressed are often not consistent with the individual"s self-perception, causing extreme distress.

Affinity	Affinity in terms of sociology, refers to "kinship of spirit", interest and other interpersonal commonalities. Affinity is characterized by high levels of intimacy and sharing, usually in close groups, also known as Affinity groups. It differs from Affinity in law and canon law which generally refer to the marriage relationship.
Agonist	In pharmacology an agonist is a substance that binds to a specific receptor and triggers a response in the cell. It mimics the action of an endogenous ligand that binds to the same receptor.
Antagonist drugs	Medications that block or counteract the effects of psychoactive or other drugs are called antagonist drugs.
Substance abuse	Substance abuse refers to the use of substances when said use is causing detriment to the individual"s physical health or causes the user legal, social, financial or other problems including endangering their lives or the lives of others.
Addiction	The term Addiction is used in many contexts to describe an obsession, compulsion such as: drug Addiction (e.g. alcoholism), video game Addiction crime, money, work Addiction compulsive overeating, problem gambling, computer Addiction nicotine Addiction pornography Addiction etc. In medical terminology, an Addiction is a chronic neurobiologic disorder that has genetic, psychosocial, and environmental dimensions and is characterized by one of the following: the continued use of a substance despite its detrimental effects, impaired control over the use of a drug (compulsive behavior), and preoccupation with a drug"s use for non-therapeutic purposes (i.e. craving the drug.) Addiction is often accompanied the presence of deviant behaviors (for instance stealing money and forging prescriptions) that are used to obtain a drug.
Mimics	Mimics is an image processing software package for 3-dimensional design and modeling, comercially developed by Materialise NV. Mimics generates and modifies surface 3D models from stacked medical images.
Particular	In philosophy, Particulars are concrete entities existing in space and time as opposed to abstractions. There are, however, theories of abstract Particulars or tropes. For example, Socrates is a Particular (there"s only one Socrates-the-teacher-of-Plato and one cannot make copies of him, e.g., by cloning him, without introducing new, distinct Particulars).
Nucleus	In neuroanatomy, a cluster of cell bodies of neurons within the central nervous system is a nucleus.
Nucleus accumbens	A complex of neurons that is part of the brain's "pleasure pathway" responsible for the experience of reward is referred to as the nucleus accumbens.
Adenosine triphosphate	Adenosine triphosphate is a multifunctional nucleotide that is most important as a "molecular currency" of intracellular energy transfer. It is produced as an energy source during the processes of photosynthesis and cellular respiration and consumed by many enzymes and a multitude of cellular processes including biosynthetic reactions, motility and cell division.

Amphetamine	Amphetamine is a prescription stimulant commonly used to treat Attention-deficit hyperactivity disorder in adults and children. It is also used to treat symptoms of traumatic brain injury and the daytime drowsiness symptoms of narcolepsy and chronic fatigue syndrome
Attention-deficit/hyperactivity disorder	Attention-Deficit/Hyperactivity Disorder is generally considered to be a developmental disorder, largely neurological in nature, affecting about 5% of the world"s population. The disorder typically presents itself during childhood, and is characterized by a persistent pattern of inattention and/or hyperactivity, as well as forgetfulness, poor impulse control or impulsivity, and distractibility.
Consciousness	The awareness of the sensations, thoughts, and feelings being experienced at a given moment is called consciousness.
Dopamine transporter	Dopamine transporter is a membrane spanning protein that binds the neurotransmitter dopamine and moves it from the synapse into a neuron.
Methylphenidate	Methylphenidate is a prescription stimulant commonly used to treat Attention-deficit hyperactivity disorder, or ADHD. It is also one of the primary drugs used to treat the daytime drowsiness symptoms of narcolepsy and chronic fatigue syndrome.
Stimulant	A stimulant is a drug which increases the activity of the sympathetic nervous system and produces a sense of euphoria or awakeness.
Stimulant drugs	*Stimulant drugs* are drugs that temporarily increase alertness and awareness. They usually have increased side-effects with increased effectiveness, and the more powerful variants are therefore often prescription medicines or illegal drugs. Ritalin SR 20mg. Stimulants increase the activity of either the sympathetic nervous system, the central nervous system (CNS) or both.
Alertness	Alertness is the state of paying close and continuous attention being watchful and prompt to meet danger or emergency, or being quick to perceive and act. It is related to psychology as well as to physiology. A lack of Alertness is a symptom of a number of conditions, including narcolepsy, attention deficit disorder, chronic fatigue syndrome, depression, Addison"s disease, or sleep deprivation.
Blocking	If the one of the two members of a compound stimulus fails to produce the CR due to an earlier conditioning of the other member of the compound stimulus, blocking has occurred.
Fatigue	The word fatigue is used in everyday life to describe a range of afflictions, varying from a general state of lethargy to a specific work-induced burning sensation within one"s muscles. It can be both physical and mental. Such a mental fatigue, in turn, can manifest itself both as somnolence just as a general decrease of attention, not necessarily including sleepiness.

99

Mood	A mood is a relatively lasting emotional or affective state. They differ from emotions in that they are less specific, often less intense, less likely to be triggered by a particular stimulus or event, however longer lasting.
Cigarette	A cigarette is a product consumed via smoking and manufactured out of cured and finely cut tobacco leaves and reconstituted tobacco. It contains nicotine, an addictive stimulant which is toxic. It delivers smoke to the lungs immediately and produce a rapid psychoactive effect. The cigarette has been proven to be highly addictive, as well as a cause of multiple types of causes.
Tobacco smoking	Tobacco smoking is the act of burning the dried or cured leaves of the tobacco plant and inhaling the smoke for pleasure, for ritualistic or social purposes, self-medication, or simply to satisfy physical dependence.
Methylenedioxymethamphetamine	Methylenedioxymethamphetamine is a semisynthetic entactogen of the phenethylamine family. It is considered a recreational drug, and has long had a strong association with the rave culture. Some scientists have suggested that it may facilitate self-examination with reduced fear, which may prove useful in some therapeutic settings.
MDMA	MDMA, most commonly known today by the street name ecstasy, is a synthetic entactogen of the phenethylamine family whose primary effect is to stimulate the secretion of large amounts of serotonin as well as dopamine and noradrenaline in the brain, causing a general sense of openness, empathy, energy, euphoria, and well-being.
Nicotinic acetylcholine receptor	Nicotinic acetylcholine receptor are Cholinergic receptors that form ligand-gated ion channels in cells" plasma membranes. Like the other type of acetylcholine receptors, muscarinic acetylcholine receptors, their opening is triggered by the neurotransmitter acetylcholine, but they are also opened by nicotine.
Nicotine	Nicotine is an organic compound, an alkaloid found naturally throughout the tobacco plant, with a high concentration in the leaves. It is a potent nerve poison and is included in many insecticides. In lower concentrations, the substance is a stimulant and is one of the main factors leading to the pleasure and habit-forming qualities of tobacco smoking.
Marinol	Marinol is an FDA-approved cannabinoid and is prescribed as an appetite stimulant, primarily for AIDS, chemotherapy and gastric bypass patients.
Endorphin	An endorphin is an endogenous opioid biochemical compound. They are peptides produced by the pituitary gland and the hypothalamus, and they resemble the opiates in their abilities to produce analgesia and a sense of well-being. In other words, they work as "natural pain killers."
Heroin	Heroin is widely and illegally used as a powerful and addictive drug producing intense euphoria, which often disappears with increasing tolerance. Heroin is a semi-synthetic opioid. It is the 3,6-diacetyl derivative of morphine and is synthesised from it by acetylation.

Marijuana	Marijuana is the dried vegetable matter of the Cannabis sativa plant. It contains large concentrations of compounds that have medicinal and psychoactive effects when consumed, usually by smoking or eating.
Memory	In psychology, memory is an organism"s ability to store, retain, and subsequently retrieve information. In recent decades, it has become one of the principal pillars of a branch of science called cognitive neuroscience, an interdisciplinary link between cognitive psychology and neuroscience.
Methadone	Methadone is a synthetic heroin substitute used for treating heroin addicts that acts as a substitute for heroin by eliminating its effects and the craving for it. Just like heroin, tolerance and dependence frequently develop.
Morphine	Morphine, the principal active agent in opium, is a powerful opioid analgesic drug. According to recent research, it may also be produced naturally by the human brain. Morphine is usually highly addictive, and tolerance and physical and psychological dependence develop quickly.
Opiate	In medicine, the term Opiate describes any of the narcotic alkaloids found in opium.
Retrograde	In males, retrograde ejaculation occurs when the fluid to be ejaculated, which would normally exit via the urethra, is redirected towards the urinary bladder. Normally the sphincter of the bladder contracts and the sperm goes to the urethra towards the area of least pressure. In retrograde ejaculation this sphincter does not function properly.
Marxist aesthetics	Marxist aesthetics is a theory of aesthetics based on the theories of Karl Marx. It involves a dialectical approach to the application of Marxism to the cultural sphere, specifically areas related to taste such as art, beauty, etc. Marxists believe that economic and social conditions affect every aspect of an individual"s life, from religious beliefs to legal systems to cultural frameworks.
Opiates	A group of narcotics derived from the opium poppy that provide a euphoric rush and depress the nervous system are referred to as opiates.
Opium	Opium is a narcotic analgesic drug which is obtained from the unripe seed pods of the opium poppy. Regular use, even for a few days, invariably leads to physical tolerance and dependence. Various degrees of psychological addiction can occur, though this is relatively rare when opioids are properly used..
Genetics	Genetics is the science of heredity and variation in living organisms.Knowledge of the inheritance of characteristics has been implicitly used since prehistoric times for improving crop plants and animals through selective breeding. However, the modern science of genetics, which seeks to understand the mechanisms of inheritance, only began with the work of Gregor Mendel in the mid-1800s.

Lysergic acid diethylamide	Lysergic acid diethylamide, is a semisynthetic psychedelic drug. It is synthesized from lysergic acid derived from ergot, a grain fungus that typically grows on rye. Many clinical trials were conducted on the potential use of it in psychedelic psychotherapy, generally with very positive results.
Lysergic acid	Lysergic acid is a precursor for a wide range of ergoline alkaloids that are produced by the ergot fungus and some plants. Amides of lysergic acid, commonly called lysergamides, are widely used as pharmaceuticals and as hallucinogenic drugs (LSD).
Alcohol abuse	Alcohol abuse, as described in the DSM-IV, is a psychiatric diagnosis describing the use of alcoholic beverages despite negative consequences. It is differentiated from alcohol dependence by the lack of symptoms such as tolerance and withdrawal. Alcohol abuse is sometimes referred to by the less specific term alcoholism. However, many definitions of alcoholism exist, and only some are compatible with alcohol abuse.
Anxiety	Anxiety is a physiological state characterized by cognitive, somatic, emotional, and behavioral components.
Dependence	Dependence is compulsively using a substance, despite its negative and sometimes dangerous effects. Other drugs cause addiction without physical dependence.
Drinking	Drinking is the act of consuming a liquid through the mouth.
Genetic predisposition	A genetic predisposition is a genetic effect which influences the phenotype of an organism but which can be modified by the environmental conditions. Genetic testing is able to identify individuals who have a genetic predisposition to have certain health problems.
Intake	An intake is an air intake for an engine.
Intention	Intention is performing an action is their specific purpose in doing so, the end or goal they aim at, or intend to accomplish.
Perception	In psychology. and the cognitive sciences, perception is the process of acquiring, interpreting, selecting, and organizing sensory information. It is a task far more complex than was imagined in the 1950s and 1960s, when it was proclaimed that building perceiving machines would take about a decade, but, needless to say, that is still very far from reality.
Spite	In fair division problems, Spite is a phenomenon that occurs when a player"s value of an allocation decreases when one or more other players" valuation increases. Thus, other things being equal, a player exhibiting Spite will prefer an allocation in which other players receive less than more (if the good is desirable.) In this language, Spite is difficult to analyze because one has to assess two sets of preferences.

Prenatal development	Prenatal development is the process in which an embryo or fetus gestates during pregnancy, from fertilization until birth.
Amygdala	Amygdala are almond-shaped groups of neurons located deep within the medial temporal lobes of the brain in complex vertebrates, including humans. Shown in research to perform a primary role in the processing and memory of emotional reactions, the amygdala are considered part of the limbic system.
Tolerance	Tolerance is used in social, cultural and religious contexts to describe attitudes and practices that prohibit discrimination against those whose practices or group memberships may be disapproved of by those in the majority. It is used to refer to a wider range of toleramce practices and groups, such as the tolerance of sexual practices and orientations, or of political parties or ideas widely considered objectionable.
Withdrawal	Withdrawal, also known as withdrawal syndrome, refers to the characteristic signs and symptoms that appear when a drug that causes physical dependence is regularly used for a long time and then suddenly discontinued or decreased in dosage.
Withdrawal symptoms	Withdrawal symptoms are physiological changes that occur when the use of a drug is stopped or dosage decreased.
Acamprosate	Acamprosate is a drug used for treating alcohol dependence. Acamprosate is thought to stabilize the chemical balance in the brain that would otherwise be disrupted by alcoholism, possibly by blocking glutaminergic N-methyl-D-aspartate receptors, while gamma-aminobutyric acid type A receptors are activated.
Acetaldehyde	Acetaldehyde is a flammable liquid with a fruity smell. Acetaldehyde occurs naturally in ripe fruit, coffee, and fresh bread, and is produced by plants as part of their normal metabolism. It is popularly known as the chemical that causes hangovers. It is toxic, an irritant, and a probable carcinogen.
Disulfiram	Disulfiram is a drug used to support the treatment of chronic alcoholism by producing an acute sensitivity to alcohol.
Naloxone	Naloxone is a drug used to counter the effects of opioid overdose, for example heroin or morphine overdose. Naloxone is specifically used to counteract life-threatening depression of the central nervous system and respiratory system.
Habit	An habit is an automatic routine of behavior that are repeated regularly, without thinking. They are learned, not instinctive, human behaviors that occur automatically, without the explicit contemporaneous intention of the person. The person may not be paying attention to or be conscious or aware of the behavior.

Choice Set	A Choice Set is one scenario provided for evaluation by respondents in a Choice Experiment. Responses are collected and used to create a Choice Model. Respondents are usually provided with a series of differing Choice Set s for evaluation.
Levomethadyl acetate	Levomethadyl acetate is a synthetic opioid similar in structure to methadone. It has a long duration of action due to its active metabolites. It was approved in 1993 by the U.S. Food and Drug Administration for use in the treatment of opioid dependence.

Chapter 4. Anatomy of the Nervous System

Central nervous system	The central nervous system represents the largest part of the nervous system, including the brain and the spinal cord. Together with the peripheral nervous system, it has a fundamental role in the control of behavior. The CNS is contained within the dorsal cavity, with the brain within the cranial subcavity, and the spinal cord in the spinal cavity. The CNS is covered by the meninges. The brain is also protected by the skull, and the spinal cord is also protected by the vertebrae.
Nervous system	The nervous system of an animal coordinates the activity of the muscles, monitors the organs, constructs and also stops input from the senses, and initiates actions.
Soma	The soma is the bulbous end of a neuron, containing the cell nucleus.
Brain	In animals, the brain, is the control center of the central nervous system, responsible for behavior. The brain is located in the head, protected by the skull and close to the primary sensory apparatus of vision, hearing, equilibrioception, sense of acceleration, taste, and olfaction.
Nerve	A Nerve is an enclosed, cable-like bundle of peripheral axons (the long, slender projections of neurons.) A Nerve provides a common pathway for the electrochemical Nerve impulses that are transmitted along each of the axons. Nerve s are found only in the peripheral nervous system.
Spinal cord	The spinal cord is a thin, tubular bundle of nerves that is an extension of the central nervous system from the brain and is enclosed in and protected by the bony vertebral column. The main function of the spinal cord is transmission of neural inputs between the periphery and the brain.
Terminology	Terminology is the study of terms and their use. Terms are words and compound words that are used in specific contexts. Not to be confused with "terms" in colloquial usages, the shortened form of technical terms (or terms of art) which are defined within a discipline or speciality field.
Anterior	Anterior is an anatomical term referring to the front part of the body. The anterior is positioned in front of another body part, or towards the head of an animal. It is the opposite of posterior.
Autonomic nervous system	The autonomic nervous system is the part of theperipheral nervous system that acts as a control system, maintaining homeostasis in the body. These maintenance activities are primarily performed without conscious control or sensation. . Its most useful definition could be: the sensory and motor neurons that innervate the viscera. These neurons form reflex arcs that pass through the lower brainstem or medulla oblongata.
Contralateral	The term contralateral refers to the opposite side of the body. For example, it can refer to the opposite sides of the right arm and left leg or it can be applied to paired organs such as the kidneys, lungs, breasts, and ovaries.
Coronal plane	A coronal plane is any vertical plane that divides the body into ventral and dorsal sections.
Distal	Students can set both long-term (distal) and short-term (proximal) goals .

Dorsum	In anatomy, the dorsum is the upper side of animals that typically run, fly or swim in a horizontal position, and the back side of animals that walk upright. In vertebrates the dorsum contains the backbone.
Horizontal plane	In astronomy, geography, geometry and related sciences and contexts, a horizontal plane is said to be locally perpendicular to the gradient of the gravity field, i.e., with the direction of the gravitational force at that point.
Ipsilateral	In reference to the anatomical terms of location, ipsilateral is a term that refers to being on the same side of the body as another structure. For example, the right arm would be considered ipsilateral to the right leg.
Nervous system autonomic	Nervous system autonomic is the part of the peripheral nervous system that acts as a control system, maintaining homeostasis in the body.
Posterior	In reference to the anatomical terms of location, the posterior end is laterally situated at or toward the hinder part of the body, lying at or extending toward the right or left side. It is the polar opposite to the anterior end, or front end of the body.
Proximal	Students can set both long-term (distal) and short-term (proximal) goals .
Animal testing	Animal testing refers to the use of animals in experiments. It is estimated that 50 to 100 million vertebrate animals worldwide — from zebrafish to non-human primates — are used annually and either killed during the experiments or subsequently euthanized.
Attachment	In attachment theory psychology, attachment is a product of the activity of a number of behavioral systems that have proximity to a person, e.g. a mother, as a predictable outcome.
Plan	A Plan is typically any procedure used to achieve an objective. It is a set of intended actions, through which one expects to achieve a goal. Plan s can be formal or informal: · Structured and formal Plan s, used by multiple people, are more likely to occur in projects, diplomacy, careers, economic development, military campaigns, combat, or in the conduct of other business. · Informal or ad-hoc Plan s are created by individuals in all of their pursuits. The most popular ways to describe Plan s are by their breadth, time frame, and specificity; however, these Plan ning classifications are not independent of one another. For instance, there is a close relationship between the short-and long-term categories and the strategic and operational categories.
Structure	Structure is a fundamental and sometimes intangible notion covering the recognition, observation, nature, and stability of patterns and relationships of entities.

Axon	An axon is a long, slender projection of a nerve cell, or neuron, that conducts electrical impulses away from the neuron"s cell body or soma.
Bell-Magendie	The Bell-Magendie law states that the anterior branch of spinal nerve roots contain only motor fibers and the posterior roots contain only sensory fibers.
Dorsal root	In anatomy and neurology, the dorsal root is the afferent sensory root of a spinal nerve.
Gray matter	Gray matter is a major component of the central nervous system, consisting of nerve cell bodies, glial cells, capillaries, and short nerve cell extensions/processes.
Motor neuron	In vertebrates, the term Motor neuron classically applies to neurons located in the central nervous system that project their axons outside the CNS and directly or indirectly control muscles. Motor neuron is often synonymous with efferent neuron.
Nucleus	In neuroanatomy, a cluster of cell bodies of neurons within the central nervous system is a nucleus.
Sulcus	A sulcus is a depression or fissure in the surface of an organ, most especially the brain. In the brain it surrounds the gyri, creating the characteristic appearance of the brain.
Blood	Blood is a specialized biological fluid consisting of red blood cells.White blood cells also called leukocytes and platelets also called thrombocytes suspended in a complex fluid medium known as blood plasma.
Chromosome	A chromosome is a single large macromolecule of DNA, and constitutes a physically organized form of DNA in a cell. It is a very long, continuous piece of DNA, which contains many genes, regulatory elements and other intervening nucleotide sequences.
Constant	A constant is something that does not change, over time or otherwise: a fixed value. In most fields of discourse the term is an antonym of "variable", but in mathematical parlance a mathematical variable may sometimes also be called a constant.
Cortex	In anatomy and zoology the cortex is the outermost layer of an organ. Organs with well-defined cortical layers include kidneys, adrenal glands, ovaries, the thymus, and portions of the brain, including the cerebral cortex, the most well-know of all cortices.
Elevation	Elevation is a moral emotion that is pleasant. It involves a desire to act morally and do "good"; as an emotion it has a basis in biology, and can sometimes be characterized by a feeling of expansion in the chest or a tingling feeling on the skin.
Software extension	A Software extension is a computer program designed to be incorporated into another piece of software in order to enhance the functionalities of the latter. On its own, the program is not useful or functional.

Examples of software applications that support extensions include the Mozilla Firefox Web browser, Adobe Systems Photoshop and Microsoft Windows Explorer shell extensions.

Ganglion | In anatomy, a ganglion is a tissue mass.

Gland | A gland is an organ in an animal's body that synthesizes a substance for release such as hormones, often into the bloodstream or into cavities inside the body or its outer surface.

Gyrus | A gyrus is a ridge on the cerebral cortex. It is generally surrounded by one or more sulci.

Scolex | The Scolex of the worm attaches to the intestine of the definitive host. In some groups, the scolex is dominated by bothria, which are sometimes called "sucking grooves," and function like suction cups.

Impulse | In classical mechanics, an Impulse is defined as the integral of a force with respect to time. When a force is applied to a rigid body it changes the momentum of that body. A small force applied for a long time can produce the same momentum change as a large force applied briefly, because it is the product of the force and the time for which it is applied that is important.

Information | Information as a concept has a diversity of meanings, from everyday usage to technical settings. Generally speaking, the concept of Information is closely related to notions of constraint, communication, control, data, form, instruction, knowledge, meaning, mental stimulus, pattern, perception, and representation.
According to the Oxford English Dictionary, the first known historical meaning of the word Information in English was the act of informing, or giving form or shape to the mind, as in education, instruction, or training.

Muscle | Muscle is contractile tissue of the body and is derived from the mesodermal layer of embryonic germ cells. It is classified as skeletal, cardiac, or smooth muscle, and its function is to produce force and cause motion, either locomotion or movement within internal organs.

Observation | Observation is an activity of a sapient or sentient living being, which senses and assimilates the knowledge of a phenomenon in its framework of previous knowledge and ideas.

Other | The Other or constitutive Other is a key concept in continental philosophy, opposed to the Same. It refers, or attempts to refer, to that which is "Other" than the concept being considered. The term often means a person Other than oneself, and is often capitalised.

Root | In vascular plants, the root is the organ of a plant body that typically lies below the surface of the soil. However, this is not always the case, since a root can also be aerial or aerating.

Sense	Sense are the physiological methods of perception. They and their operation, classification, and theory are overlapping topics studied by a variety of fields, most notably neuroscience, cognitive psychology, and philosophy of perception. The nervous system has a sensory system dedicated to each sense.
Sensory neurons	*Sensory neurons* are neurons that are activated by sensory input (vision, touch, hearing, etc.), and send projections into the central nervous system that convey sensory information to the brain or spinal cord. Unlike neurons of the central nervous system, whose inputs come from other neurons, *Sensory neurons* are activated by physical modalities such as light, sound, temperature, chemical stimulation, etc. In complex organisms, *Sensory neurons* relay their information to the central nervous system or in less complex organisms, such as the hydra, directly to motor neurons and *Sensory neurons* also transmit information to the brain, where it can be further processed and acted upon.
Single	In relationships, a single person is one who is not married, or, more broadly, who is not in an exclusive romantic relationship.
Ventral root	In anatomy and neurology, the Ventral root is the efferent motor root of a spinal nerve.
Goose	Goose is the English name for a considerable number of birds, belonging to the family Anatidae. This family also includes swans, most of which are larger, and ducks, which are smaller. A goose eats a largely vegetarian diet, and can become pests when flocks feed on arable crops or inhabit ponds or grassy areas in urban environments.
Hair	Hair is a filamentous outgrowth of protein, found only on mammals. It projects from the epidermis, though it grows from hair follicles deep in the dermis.
Parasympathetic nervous system	The parasympathetic nervous system is a division of the autonomic nervous system, along with the sympathetic nervous system and Enteric nervous system. The ANS is a subdivision of the peripheral nervous system.
Erection	The erection of the penis, clitoris or a nipple is its enlarged and firm state. It depends on a complex interaction of psychological, neural, vascular and endocrine factors. The ability to maintain the erectile state is key to the reproductive system and many forms of life could not reproduce in a natural way without this ability.
Acetic acid	Acetic acid, is an organic chemical compound, giving vinegar its sour taste and pungent smell. Its structural formula is represented as CH_3COOH.
Neurotransmitter	A neurotransmitter is a chemical that is used to relay, amplify and modulate electrical signals between a neurons and another cell.
Norepinephrine	Norepinephrine is a catecholamine and a phenethylamine with chemical formula $C_8H_{11}NO_3$.

Affect	Affect refers to the experience of feeling or emotion. Affect is a key part of the process of an organism's interaction with stimuli. The word also refers sometimes to affect display, which is "a facial, vocal, or gestural behavior that serves as an indicator of affect."
Body weight	Body weight is a term that is used in biological and medical science contexts to describe the mass of an organism"s body. Body weight is measured in kilograms throughout the world, although in some countries people more often measure and describe body weight in pounds or stones and pounds and thus may not be well acquainted with measurement in kilograms.
Chemical	A chemical is a material with a definite chemical composition. All samples of a compound have the same composition; that is, all samples have the same proportions, by mass, of the elements present in the compound.
Discovery	Discovery observations form acts of detecting and learning something. Discovery observations are acts in which something is found and given a productive insight. Serendipity is the effect by which one accidentally discovers something fortunate, especially while looking for something else entirely.
Sympathetic	The sympathetic nervous system activates what is often termed the "fight or flight response". It is an automatic regulation system, that is, one that operates without the intervention of conscious thought.
Brain damage	Brain damage is the destruction or degeneration of brain cells. It may occur due to a wide range of conditions, illnesses, injuries, and as a result of iatrogenesis. Possible causes of widespread brain damage include prolonged hypoxia, poisoning by teratogens, infection, and neurological illness.
Brain stem	The brain stem is the lower part of the brain, adjoining and structurally continuous with the spinal cord. Most sources consider the pons, medulla oblongata, and midbrain all to be part of the brain stem.
Hindbrain	The hindbrain is a developmental categorization of portions of the central nervous system in vertebrates. It can be subdivided in a variable number of transversal swellings called rhombomeres.
Reflex	A reflex action is an automatic neuromuscular action elicited by a defined stimulus. In most contexts, especially involving humans, a reflex action is mediated via the reflex arc
Cerebellum	The cerebellum is a region of the brain that plays an important role in the integration of sensory perception and motor output. Many neural pathways link the cerebellum with the motor cortex—which sends information to the muscles causing them to move—and the spinocerebellar tract—which provides feedback on the position of the body in space. The cerebellum integrates these pathways, using the constant feedback on body position to fine-tune motor movements.
Prosencephalon	In the anatomy of the brain of vertebrates, the prosencephalon is the rostral-most portion of the brain. The prosencephalon, the mesencephalon, and rhombencephalon are the three primary portions of the brain during early development of the central nervous system.

Generation	Generation, also known as procreation, is the act of producing offspring. A generation can also be a stage or degree in a succession of natural descent as a grandfather, a father, and the father"s son comprise three generations.
Medulla	Medulla refers to the middle of something, and derives from the Latin word for "marrow" In medicine it refers to either bone marrow, the spinal cord, or more generally, the middle part of a structure as opposed to the cortex.
Midbrain	The midbrain is the middle of three vesicles that arise from the neural tube that forms the brain of developing animals. In mature human brains, it becomes the least differentiated, from both its developmental form and within its own structure, among the three vesicles. The midbrain is considered part of the brain stem.
Pons	The pons is a structure located on the brain stem. It is rostral to the medulla oblongata, caudal to the midbrain, and ventral to the cerebellum. In humans and other bipeds this means it is above the medulla, below the midbrain, and anterior to the cerebellum.
Stimulus	In psychology, a stimulus is part of the stimulus-response relationship of behavioral learning theory.
Accessory nerve	In anatomy, the Accessory nerve is a nerve that controls specific muscles of the neck. As a part of it was formerly believed to originate in the brain, it is considered a cranial nerve. Based on its location relative to other such nerves, it is designated the eleventh of twelve cranial nerves, and is thus abbreviated CN XI. Although anatomists typically refer to the Accessory nerve in singular, there are in reality two Accessory nerve s, one on each side of the body.
Facial nerve	The facial nerve is the seventh of twelve paired cranial nerves. It emerges from the brainstem between the pons and the medulla, and controls the muscles of facial expression, and taste to the anterior two-thirds of the tongue. It also supplies preganglionic parasympathetic fibers to several head and neck ganglia.
Glossopharyngeal nerve	The glossopharyngeal nerve is the ninth of twelve pairs of cranial nerves. It exits the brainstem out from the sides of the upper medulla, just rostral to the vagus nerve.
Hypocretin	Hypocretin, is the common name given to a pair of highly excitatory neuropeptide hormones that were simultaneously discovered by two groups of researchers in rat brains. . The discovery that hypocretin dysregulation causes the sleep disorder narcolepsy subsequently indicated a major role for this system in sleep regulation.
Oculomotor nerve	The oculomotor nerve is the third of twelve paired cranial nerves. It controls most of the eye movements, constriction of the pupil, and holding the eyelid open.

Olfactory nerve	The olfactory nerve is the first of twelve cranial nerves. The specialized olfactory receptor neurons of the olfactory nerve are located in the olfactory mucosa of the upper parts of the nasal cavity. The olfactory nerve consists of a collection of sensory nerve fibers that extend from the olfactory epithelium to the olfactory bulb, passing through the many openings of the cribriform plate, a sieve-like structure.
Optic nerve	The optic nerve is the nerve that transmits visual information from the retina to the brain. The optic nerve is composed of retinal ganglion cell axons and support cells.
Trigeminal nerve	The Trigeminal nerve is responsible for sensation in the face. It is similar to the spinal nerves C_2–S_5, which are responsible for sensation in the rest of the body. Sensory information from the face and body is processed by parallel pathways in the central nervous system.
Trochlear nerve	The trochlear nerve is a motor nerve that innervates a single muscle: the superior oblique muscle of the eye. An older name is pathetic nerve, which refers to the dejected appearance that is characteristic of patients with fourth nerve palsies.
Vagus nerve	The vagus nerve is the tenth of twelve paired cranial nerves, and is the only nerve that starts in the brainstem and extends, through the jugular foramen, down below the head, to the neck, chest and abdomen.
Cranial nerve	A Cranial nerve emerges from the brainstem instead of the spinal cord.
Ganglion cell	A ganglion cell is a cell found in a ganglion. The term is also sometimes used to refer specifically to a retinal ganglion cell (R ganglion cell) found in the ganglion cell layer of the retina. ganglion cell s reside in the adrenal medulla, where they are involved in the sympathetic nervous system"s release of epinephrine and norepinephrine into the blood stream.
Retina	The vertebrate Retina is a light sensitive tissue lining the inner surface of the eye. The optics of the eye create an image of the visual world on the Retina which serves much the same function as the film in a camera. Light striking the Retina initiates a cascade of chemical and electrical events that ultimately trigger nerve impulses.
Reticular formation	The reticular formation is a part of the brain which is involved in stereotypical actions, such as walking, sleeping, and lying down. It is essential for governing some of the basic functions of higher organisms, and phylogenetically one of the oldest portions of the brain.
Superior colliculus	The superior colliculus is a paired structure that is part of the brain"s tectal area. In humans, the superior colliculus is involved in the generation of saccadic eye movements and eye-head coordination.
Tectum	The tectum is a region of the brain, specifically the dorsal part of the mesencephalon.
Tegmentum	The tegmentum is a general area within the brainstem.

Arousal	Arousal is a physiological and psychological state involving the activation of the reticular activating system in the brain stem, the autonomic nervous system and the endocrine system, leading to increased heart rate and blood pressure and a condition of alertness and readiness to respond.
Attention	Attention is the cognitive process of selectively concentrating on one aspect of the environment while ignoring other things. Examples include listening carefully to what someone is saying while ignoring other conversations in the room or listening to a cell phone conversation while driving a car.
Control group	A control group augments integrity in experiments by isolating variables as dictated by the scientific method in order to make a conclusion about such variables. In other cases, an experimental control is used to prevent the effects of one variable from being drowned out by the known, greater effects of other variables. this case, the researchers can either use a control group or use statistical techniques to control for the other variables.
Eye	Eye s are organs that detect light, and send signals along the optic nerve to the visual and other areas of the brain. Complex optical systems with resolving power have come in ten fundamentally different forms, and 96% of animal species possess a complex optical system. Image-resolving Eye s are present in cnidaria, molluscs, chordates, annelids and arthropods.
Inferior colliculus	The Inferior colliculus is one of the essential auditory centers located in the mesencephalon.
Cytoplasmic streaming	Cytoplasmic streaming is the flowing of cytoplasm in eukaryotic cells. This occurs in both plant and animal cells.
Vision	Vision is the most important sense for birds, since good eyesight is essential for safe flight, and this group has a number of adaptations which give visual acuity superior to that of other vertebrate groups; a pigeon has been described as "two eyes with wings". The avian eye resembles that of a reptile, but has a better-positioned lens, a feature shared with mammals. Birds have the largest eyes relative to their size within the animal kingdom, and movement is consequently limited within the eye"s bony socket.
Amygdala	Amygdala are almond-shaped groups of neurons located deep within the medial temporal lobes of the brain in complex vertebrates, including humans. Shown in research to perform a primary role in the processing and memory of emotional reactions, the amygdala are considered part of the limbic system.
Cingulate gyrus	Cingulate gyrus is a gyrus in the medial part of the brain. It partially wraps around the corpus callosum and is limited above by the cingulate sulcus. It functions as an intergral part of the limbic system, which is involved with emotion formation and processing, learning, and memory.
Diencephalon	The diencephalon is the region of the brain that includes the epithalamus, thalamus, and hypothalamus. It is located above the mesencephalon of the brain stem. Sensory information is relayed between the brain stem and the rest of the brain regions

Hippocampus	The hippocampus is a part of the brain located in the medial temporal lobe. It forms a part of the limbic system and plays a part in memory and spatial navigation.
Hypothalamus	The hypothalamus is a region of the brain located below the thalamus, forming the major portion of the ventral region of the diencephalon and functioning to regulate certain metabolic processes and other autonomic activities.
Lateralization	Lateralization of brain functions is evident in the phenomena of right- or left-handedness, -earedness and -eyedness. Broad generalizations are often made in popular psychology about certain function being lateralised, that is, located in the right or left side of the brain. These ideas need to be treated carefully because the popular lateralization is ften distributed across both sides. However, there is some division of mental processing.
Limbic system	The limbic system includes the putative structures in the human brain involved in emotion, motivation, and emotional association with memory. The limbic system influences the formation of memory by integrating emotional states with stored memories of physical sensations.
Olfactory bulb	The olfactory bulb is a structure of the vertebrate forebrain involved in olfaction, the perception of odors.
Substantia nigra	The substantia nigra is a portion of the midbrain thought to be involved in certain aspects of movement and attention. Degeneration of cells in this region is the principle pathology that underlies Parkinson's disease.
Cerebrum	The cerebrum refers to the cerebral hemispheres and other, smaller structures within the brain. It is the anterior-most embryological division of the brain that develops from the prosencephalon.
Thalamus	An area near the center of the brain involved in the relay of sensory information to the cortex and in the functions of sleep and attention is the thalamus.
Cerebral cortex	The cerebral cortex is a structure within the vertebrate brain with distinct structural and functional properties.
Cerebral hemisphere	A Cerebral hemisphere (hemispherium cerebrale) is defined as one of the two regions of the brain that are delineated by the body"s median plane, (medial longitudinal fissure.) The brain can thus be described as being divided into left and right Cerebral hemisphere s. Each of these hemispheres has an outer layer of grey matter called the cerebral cortex that is supported by an inner layer of white matter.
Depression	In everyday language depression refers to any downturn in mood, which may be relatively transitory and perhaps due to something trivial.

Emotion	Emotion, in its most general definition, is a complex psychophysical process that arises spontaneously, rather than through conscious effort, and evokes either a positive or negative psychological response and physical expressions, often involuntary, related to feelings, perceptions or beliefs about elements, objects or relations between them, in reality or in the imagination. An emotion is often differentiated from a feeling.

View

A View is what can be seen in a range of vision. View may also be used as a synonym of point of View in the first sense. View may also be used figuratively or with special significance--for example, to imply a scenic outlook or significant vantage point:

> The barrier Rhine hath flashed, through battle-smoke,
> On men who gaze heart-smitten by the View,
> As if all Germany had felt the shock!

> - from The Germans on the Heights of Hochheim by William Wordsworth

Laws or regulations in various jurisdictions may protect a View as an easement, preventing property owners from constructing buildings that would block the View from another location.

Hormone

A hormone is a chemical messenger that carries a signal from one cell to another. All multicellular organisms produce hormone s.

Pituitary gland

The pituitary gland is an endocrine gland about the size of a pea that sits in the small, bony cavity at the base of the brain. The pituitary gland secretes hormones regulating a wide variety of bodily activities, including trophic hormones that stimulate other endocrine glands.

Endocrine gland

An endocrine gland is one of a set of internal organs involved in the secretion of hormones into the blood. The other major type of gland is the exocrine glands, which secrete substances—usually digestive juices—into the digestive tract or onto the skin.

Basal ganglia

The basal ganglia are a group of nuclei in the brain associated with motor and learning functions.

Frontal lobe

The frontal lobe comprises four major folds of cortical tissue: the precentral gyrus, superior gyrus and the middle gyrus of the frontal gyri, the inferior frontal gyrus. It has been found to play a part in impulse control, judgement, language, memory, motor function, problem solving, sexual behavior, socialization and spontaneity.

Caudate nucleus

The caudate nucleus is a nucleus located within the basal ganglia of the brains of many animal species. The caudate nuclei are located near the center of the brain, sitting astride the thalamus. There is a caudate nucleus within each hemisphere of the brain.

Central sulcus

The central sulcus is a prominent landmark of the brain, separating the parietal lobe from the frontal lobe. The central sulcus is the site of the primary motor cortex in mammals, a group of cells that controls voluntary movements of the body.

Delusion	A false belief, not generally shared by others, and that cannot be changed despite strong evidence to the contrary is a delusion.
Disease	A Disease or medical problem is an abnormal condition of an organism that impairs bodily functions, associated with specific symptoms and signs. It may be caused by external factors, such as invading organisms, or it may be caused by internal dysfunctions, such as autoimmune Disease s. In human beings, Disease is often used more broadly to refer to any condition that causes extreme pain, dysfunction, distress, social problems, and/or death to the person afflicted, or similar problems for those in contact with the person.
Dopamine	Dopamine is a hormone and neurotransmitter occurring in a wide variety of animals, including both vertebrates and invertebrates. In the brain, dopamine functions as a neurotransmitter. Dopamine is also a neurohormone released by the hypothalamus. Its main function as a hormone is to inhibit the release of prolactin from the anterior lobe of the pituitary.
Globus pallidus	The globus pallidus is a sub-cortical structure of the brain. It is a major element of the basal ganglia system. In this system, it is a major element of the basal ganglia core, consisting of the striatum and its direct targets: globus pallidus and substantia nigra. The last two are made up of the same neuronal elements, have a similar main afferent, have a similar synaptology, and do not receive cortical afferents.
Hallucination	A hallucination is a sensory perception experienced in the absence of an external stimulus, as distinct from an illusion, which is a misperception of an external stimulus. They may occur in any sensory modality - visual, auditory, olfactory, gustatory, tactile, or mixed.
Disability	A disability is a condition or function judged to be significantly impaired relative to the usual standard of an individual or their group. The term is often used to refer to individual functioning, including physical impairments, sensory impairments, cognitive impairments, intellectual impairments or mental health issue.
Memory	In psychology, memory is an organism"s ability to store, retain, and subsequently retrieve information. In recent decades, it has become one of the principal pillars of a branch of science called cognitive neuroscience, an interdisciplinary link between cognitive psychology and neuroscience.
Motor cortex	Motor cortex is a term that describes regions of the cerebral cortex involved in the planning, control, and execution of voluntary motor functions.
Prefrontal cortex	The prefrontal cortex is the anterior part of the frontal lobes of the brain, lying in front of the motor and premotor areas. Cytoarchitectonically, it is defined by the presence of an internal granular layer IV.
Primary	In medicine, the reporting of symptoms by a patient may have significant psychological motivators. Psychologists sometimes categorize these motivators into primary or secondary gain. primary gain is internally good; motivationally.

Primary motor cortex	The primary motor cortex works in association with pre-motor areas to plan and execute movements. It contains large neurons known as Betz cells which send long axons down the spinal cord to synapse onto alpha motor neurons which connect to the muscles.
Putamen	The putamen is a structure in the middle of the brain, which, together with the caudate nucleus forms the dorsal striatum. The putamen is a portion of the basal ganglia that forms the outermost part of the lenticular nucleus.
Rigidity	In psychology, rigidity refers to an obstacle to problem solving which arises from over-dependence on prior experience, which makes it difficult for a person with experience in a specific problem domain to recognize novel solution strategies.
Tremor	Tremor is the rhythmic, oscillating shaking movement of the whole body or just a certain part of it, caused by problems of the neurons responsible from muscle action.
Muscle contraction	A muscle contraction occurs when a muscle fiber generates tension through the action of actin and myosin cross-bridge cycling.
Cerebrospinal fluid	A solution that fills the hollow cavities of the brain and circulates around the brain and spinal cord is called cerebrospinal fluid.
Corpus callosum	The corpus callosum is a structure of the mammalian brain in the longitudal fissure that connects the left and right cerebral hemispheres. Much of the inter-hemispheric communication in the brain is conducted across the corpus callosum.
Hydrocephalus	Hydrocephalus is a condition sometimes known as "water in the brain". People with this condition have abnormal accumulation of cerebrospinal fluid in the ventricles, or cavities, of the brain.
Meninges	The meninges are the system of membranes that envelop the central nervous system. The meninges consist of three layers, the dura mater, the arachnoid mater, and the pia mater.
Meningitis	Meningitis is inflammation of the membranes covering the brain and the spinal cord. Although the most common causes are infection (bacterial, viral, fungal or parasitic), chemical agents and even tumor cells may cause meningitis.
Migraine	Migraine is a form of headache, usually very intense and disabling. It is a neurologic disease.
Parietal lobe	The parietal lobe is a lobe in the brain. It is positioned above the occipital lobe and behind the frontal lobe.
Ventricle	In the heart, a ventricle is a heart chamber which collects blood from an atrium another heart chamber that is smaller than a ventricle and pumps it out of the heart.

Acetylcholine	The chemical compound acetylcholine, often abbreviated as ACh, was the first neurotransmitter to be identified. It is a chemical transmitter in both the peripheral nervous system and central nervous system in many organisms including humans.
Amnesia	Amnesia is a condition in which memory is disturbed. The causes of amnesia are organic or functional. Organic causes include damage to the brain, through trauma or disease, or use of certain generally sedative drugs.
Appetite	The appetite is the desire to eat food, felt as hunger. Appetite exists in all higher lifeforms, and serves to regulate adequate energy intake to maintain metabolic needs. It is regulated by a close interplay between the digestive tract, adipose tissue and the brain. Decreased desire to eat is termed anorexia, while polyphagia or "hyperphagia" is increased eating. Disregulation of appetite contributes to anorexia nervosa, bulimia nervosa, cachexia, overeating, and binge eating disorder.
Basal forebrain	The basal forebrain is a collection of structures located ventrally to the striatum. Cholinergic neurons in the basal forebrain participate in behavioral processes such as attention and memory.
Confusion	Severe confusion of a degree considered pathological usually refers to loss of orientation, and often memory. Confusion as such is not synonymous with inability to focus attention, although severe inability to focus attention can cause, or greatly contribute to, confusion.
Headache	A headache is a condition of pain in the head; sometimes neck or upper back pain may also be interpreted as a headache. It ranks amongst the most common local pain complaints.
Memory loss	Memory loss can have many causes: · Alzheimer"s disease is an illness which can cause mild to severe memory loss · Parkinson"s disease is a genetic defect which may result in memory loss · Huntington"s disease is an inherited disease which can result in memory loss · It is sometimes a side effect of chemotherapy in which cytotoxic drugs are used to treat cancer. · Certain forms of mental illness also have memory loss as a key symptom, including fugue states and the much more famous Dissociative Identity Disorder. · Stress-related activities are another factor which can result in memory loss · It can also be caused by traumatic brain injury, of which a concussion is a form. .
Insomnia	Insomnia is a sleep disorder characterized by an inability to sleep and/or inability to remain asleep for a reasonable period.
Space	The idea of space has been of interest for philosophers and scientists for much of human history. The term is used somewhat differently in different fields of study, hence it is difficult to provide an uncontroversial and clear definition outside of specific defined contexts. Disagreement also exists on whether space itself can be measured or is part of the measuring system.

Brain size	When comparing different species, brain size does present a correlation with intelligence. For example, the ratio of brain weight to body weight for fish is 1:5000; for reptiles it is about 1:1500; for birds, 1:220; for most mammals, 1:180, and for humans, 1:50. However within the human species modern studies using MRI have shown that brain size shows substantial and consistent correlation with IQ among adults of the same sex
Neural development	The study of neural development draws on both neuroscience and developmental biology to describe the cellular and molecular mechanisms by which complex nervous systems emerge during embryonic development and throughout life.
Gorilla	The Gorilla is the largest of the living primates. They are ground-dwelling omnivores that inhabit the forests of Africa.
Mammal	A mammal is a warm-blooded, vertebrate animal, characterized by the presence of sweat glands, including milk producing sweat glands, and by the presence of: hair, three middle ear bones used in hearing, and a neocortex region in the brain. Most also possess specialized teeth and utilize a placenta in the ontogeny. A mammal encompass approximately 5,400 species, distributed in about 1,200 genera, 153 families, and 29 orders, though this varies by classification scheme.
Cortical blindness	Cortical blindness is the total or partial loss of vision in a normal-appearing eye caused by damage to the visual area in the brain"s occipital cortex.
Kluver-Bucy syndrome	Kluver-Bucy syndrome is a behavioral disorder that occurs when both the right and left medial temporal lobes of the brain malfunction. The amygdala has been a particularly implicated brain region in the pathogenesis of this syndrome.
Occipital lobe	The occipital lobe is the visual processing center of the mammalian brain, containing most of the anatomical region of the visual cortex. The primary visual cortex is Brodmann area 17, commonly called V_1.
Postcentral gyrus	The lateral postcentral gyrus is a prominent structure in the parietal lobe of the human brain and an important landmark. It was initially defined from surface stimulation studies of Penfield, and parallel surface potential studies of Bard, Woolsey, and Marshall.
Primary somatosensory cortex	The lateral postcentral gyrus is a prominent structure in the parietal lobe of the human brain and an important landmark. It was initially defined from surface stimulation studies of Penfield, and parallel surface potential studies of Bard, Woolsey, and Marshall. Although initially defined to be roughly the same as Brodmann areas 3, 1 and 2, more recent work by Kaas has suggested that for homogeny with other sensory fields only area 3 should be referred to as "*Primary somatosensory cortex*", as it received the bulk of the thalamocortical projection from the sensory input fields.

Temporal lobe	The temporal lobe is part of the cerebrum. It lies at the side of the brain, beneath the lateral or Sylvian fissure. Adjacent areas in the superior, posterior and lateral parts of the temporal lobe are involved in high-level auditory processing.
Failure	Failure refers to the state or condition of not meeting a desirable or intended objective.
Fear	Fear is an emotional response to tangible and realistic dangers. Fear should be distinguished from anxiety, an emotion that often arises out of proportion to the actual threat or danger involved, and can be subjectively experienced without any specific attention to the threatening object.
Lobes	The four major sections of the cerebral cortex: frontal, parietal, temporal, and occipital are called lobes.
Sensation	Sensation is the first stage in the chain of biochemical and neurologic events that begins with the impinging of a stimulus upon the receptor cells of a sensory organ, which then leads to perception, the mental state that is reflected in statements like "I see a uniformly blue wall."
Somatosensory	Somatosensory system consists of the various sensory receptors that trigger the experiences labelled as touch or pressure, temperature, pain, and the sensations of muscle movement and joint position including posture, movement, and facial expression.
Somatosensory system	The Somatosensory system is made up of the complex of sensations that are experienced by the skin and body. These sensations include the sense of pressure, temperature, pain, body position, and movement.
Visual System	The Visual System is the part of the nervous system which allows organisms to see. It interprets the information from visible light to build a representation of the world surrounding the body.
Somatosensory cortex	The primary somatosensory cortex is across the central sulcus and behind the primary motor cortex configured to generally correspond with the arrangement of nearby motor cells related to specific body parts. It is the main sensory receptive area for the sense of touch.
Message	A message in its most general meaning is an object of communication.
Dementia	Dementia is the progressive decline in cognitive function due to damage or disease in the brain beyond what might be expected from normal aging.
Dementia praecox	An older term for schizophrenia, chosen to describe what was believed to be an incurable and progressive deterioration of mental functioning beginning in adolescence is called dementia praecox.

Need	A Need is something that is necessary for humans to live a healthy life. Need s are distinguished from wants because a deficiency would cause a clear negative outcome, such as dysfunction or death. Need s can be objective and physical, such as food and water, or they can be subjective and psychological, such as the Need for self-esteem.
Signal	In the fields of communications, signal processing, and in electrical engineering more generally, a signal is any time-varying quantity. Signals are often scalar-valued functions of time, but may be vector valued and may be functions of any other relevant independent variable.
Binding	In linguistics, Binding theory is any of a broad class of theories dealing with the distribution of pronominal and anaphoric elements. The idea that there should be a specialised, coherent theory dealing with this particular set of phenomena originated in work in transformational grammar in the 1970s. This work culminated in government and Binding theory (a general theory of innate linguistic structure) whose version of the Binding theory is still considered a reference point, though it is no longer current.
Binding problem	The binding problem is "the problem of how the unity of conscious perception is brought about by the distributed activities of the central nervous system." It arises whenever information from distinct populations of neurons must be combined. The activity of specialised sets of neurons dealing with different aspects of perception are combined to form a unified perceptual experience.
Eating	Eating is the process of consuming nutrition, i.e. food, for the purpose of providing for the nutritional needs of an animal, particularly their energy requirements and to grow.
Lobotomy	A lobotomy is a form of psychosurgery that consists of cutting the connections to and from, or simply destroying, the prefrontal cortex. These procedures often result in major personality changes and possible mental disabilities. This method was used in the past to treat a wide range of severe mental illnesses, including schizophrenia, clinical depression, and various anxiety disorders. After the introduction of the antipsychotic Thorazine, this form of psychosurgery fell out of common use.
Prefrontal lobotomy	A prefrontal lobotomy is a surgical procedure that was pioneered by physician and neurologist Antonio Egas Moniz in 1935 in which the white fibers that connect the thalamus to the prefrontal and frontal lobes of the brain are severed. This procedure was once used as a treatment for excessively violent behavior.
Schizophrenia	Schizophrenia is a psychiatric diagnosis that describes a mental illness characterized by impairments in the perception or expression of reality, most commonly manifesting as auditory hallucinations, paranoid or bizarre delusions or disorganized speech and thinking in the context of significant social or occupational dysfunction.

Sensory system	A sensory system is a part of the nervous system responsible for processing sensory information. A sensory system consists of sensory receptors, neural pathways, and parts of the brain involved in sensory perception The receptive field is the specific part of the world to which a receptor organ and receptor cells respond.
Working memory	Working memory is a theoretical framework within cognitive psychology that refers to the structures and processes used for temporarily storing and manipulating information. There are numerous theories as to both the theoretical structure of working memory as well as to the specific parts of the brain responsible for working memory.
Hearing	Hearing is one of the traditional five senses, and refers to the ability to detect sound. In humans and other vertebrates, hearing is performed primarily by the system: sound is detected by the ear and transduced into nerve impulses that are perceived by the brain.
Disconnection	Disconnection is a practice in Scientology, in which a Scientologist severs all ties between themselves and friends, colleagues, or family members that are deemed to be antagonistic towards Scientology.
Emotional expression	In psychology, emotional expression is observable verbal and nonverbal behavior that communicates emotion.
Personal life	Personal life is the course of an individual human"s life, especially when viewed as the sum of personal choices contributing to one"s personal identity.
Social influence	Social influence occurs when an individual"s thoughts or actions are affected by other people. Social influence takes many forms and can be seen in conformity, socialization, peer pressure, obedience, leadership, persuasion, sales, and marketing. Harvard psychologist, Herbert Kelman identified three broad varieties of Social influence. · Compliance is when people appear to agree with others, but actually keep their dissenting opinions private. · Identification is when people are influenced by someone who is liked and respected, such as a famous celebrity or a favorite uncle. · Internalization is when people accept a belief or behavior and agree both publicly and privately.
Entity	An entity is something that has a distinct, separate existence, though it need not be a material existence. In particular, abstractions and legal fictions are usually regarded as an entity. In general, there is also no presumption that an entity is animate.

Perception	In psychology. and the cognitive sciences, perception is the process of acquiring, interpreting, selecting, and organizing sensory information. It is a task far more complex than was imagined in the 1950s and 1960s, when it was proclaimed that building perceiving machines would take about a decade, but, needless to say, that is still very far from reality.
Homeostasis	Homeostasis is the property of either an open system or a closed system, especially a living organism, which regulates its internal environment so as to maintain a stable, constant condition.
Storage	The human memory has three processes: encoding (input), Storage and retrieval(output.) Storage is the process of retaining information whether in the sensory memory, the short-term memory or the more permanent long-term memory.
Thought disorder	Thought disorder describes a persistent underlying disturbance to conscious thought and is classified largely by its effects on speech and writing. Affected persons may show pressure of speech, derailment or flight of ideas, thought blocking, rhyming, punning, or word salad.
Phrenology	Phrenology is a theory which claims to be able to determine character, personality traits, and criminality on the basis of the shape of the head (reading "bumps"). Developed by Gall around 1800, and very popular in the 19th century, it is now discredited as a pseudoscience.
Research method	The scope of the research method is to produce some new knowledge. This, in principle, can take three main forms: Exploratory research; Constructive research; and Empirical research.
Anatomy	Anatomy is the branch of biology that deals with the structure and organization of living things. It can be divided into animal anatomy zootomy and plant anatomy phytonomy. Major branches of anatomy include comparative anatomy, histology, and human anatomy.
Pseudoscience	Pseudoscience is any body of knowledge, methodology, belief, or practice that claims to be scientific or is made to appear scientific, but does not adhere to the basic requirements of the scientific method.
Skull	The skull is a bony structure found in the head of many animals. The skull supports the structures of the face and protects the head against injury.
Computerized axial tomography	Computerized axial tomography is a medical imaging method employing tomography where digital processing is used to generate a three-dimensional image of the internals of an object from a large series of two-dimensional X-ray images taken around a single axis of rotation.
Intelligence	Intelligence is a property of mind that encompasses many related abilities, such as the capacities to reason, plan, solve problems, think abstractly, comprehend ideas and language, and learn. In some cases intelligence may include traits such as creativity, personality, character, knowledge, or wisdom. However other psychologists prefer not to include these traits in the definition of intelligence.

Magnetic resonance imaging	Magnetic resonance imaging is a non-invasive method used to render images of the inside of an object. It is primarily used in medical imaging to demonstrate pathological or other physiological alterations of living tissues.
Energy	The concept of psychic Energy was developed in the field of psychodynamics. In 1874, German scientist Ernst von Brucke proposed that all living organisms are Energy-systems governed by the principle of the conservation of Energy. Brucke was also coincidentally the supervisor at the University of Vienna for first-year medical student Sigmund Freud who adopted this new paradigm.
Field	Field is one of the core concepts used by French social scientist Pierre Bourdieu. A field is a setting in which agents and their social positions are located. The position of each particular agent in the field is a result of interaction between the specific rules of the field, agent"s habitus and agent"s capital social, economic and cultural Bourdieu, 1984. Fields interact with each other, and are hierarchical most are subordinate of the larger field of power and class relations.
Frequency	In statistics the frequency of an event i is the number ni of times the event occurred in the experiment or the study. These frequencies are often graphically represented in histograms.
X-ray	An X-ray is a form of electromagnetic radiation with a wavelength in the range of 10 to 0.01 nanometers, corresponding to frequencies in the range 30 PHz to 30 EHz.
Electroencephalography	Electroencephalography is the measurement of electrical activity produced by the brain as recorded from electrodes placed on the scalp.
Magnetoencephalograph	Magnetoencephalograph is an imaging technique used to measure the magnetic fields produced by electrical activity in the brain via extremely sensitive devices such as superconducting quantum interference devices. The clinical uses it in detecting and localizing epileptiform spiking activity in patients with epilepsy, and in localizing eloquent cortex for surgical planning in patients with brain tumors or intractable epilepsy.
Positron emission tomography	Positron emission tomography is a nuclear medicine medical imaging technique which produces a three-dimensional image or map of functional processes in the body. Images of metabolic activity in space are then reconstructed by computer, often in modern scanners aided by results from a CT X-ray scan.
Electrode	Any device used to electrically stimulate nerve tissue or to record its activity is an electrode.
Functional magnetic resonance imaging	Functional magnetic resonance imaging is the use of MRI to measure the haemodynamic response related to neural activity in the brain or spinal cord of humans or other animals. It is one of the most recently developed forms of neuroimaging.

MRI	Magnetic resonance imaging (MRI) is primarily a medical imaging technique most commonly used in radiology to visualize the structure and function of the body. It provides detailed images of the body in any plane. MRI provides much greater contrast between the different soft tissues of the body than computed tomography (CT) does, making it especially useful in neurological (brain), musculoskeletal, cardiovascular, and oncological (cancer) imaging.
Hemoglobin	Hemoglobin is the iron-containing oxygen-transport metalloprotein in the red blood cells of the blood in vertebrates and other animals.
Cingulate cortex	The cingulate cortex is a part of the brain situated in the medial aspect of the cortex. It is extended from the corpus callosum below to the cingulate sulcus above, at least anteriorly.
Language	A Language is a system for encoding and decoding information. In its most common use, the term refers to so-called "natural Language s" -- the forms of communication considered peculiar to humankind. In linguistics the term is extended to refer to the human cognitive facility of creating and using Language
Genetics	Genetics is the science of heredity and variation in living organisms.Knowledge of the inheritance of characteristics has been implicitly used since prehistoric times for improving crop plants and animals through selective breeding. However, the modern science of genetics, which seeks to understand the mechanisms of inheritance, only began with the work of Gregor Mendel in the mid-1800s.
Lesion	A lesion is a non-specific term referring to abnormal tissue in the body. It can be caused by any disease process including trauma (physical, chemical, electrical), infection, neoplasm, metabolic and autoimmune.
Transcranial magnetic stimulation	A Transcranial magnetic stimulation is a noninvasive method to excite neurons in the brain.
Experiment	In the scientific method, an experiment is a set of observations performed in the context of solving a particular problem or question, to support or falsify a hypothesis or research concerning phenomena. The experiment is a cornerstone in the empirical approach to acquiring deeper knowledge about the physical world.
Gene	A gene is a locatable region of genomic sequence, corresponding to a unit of inheritance, which is associated with regulatory regions, transcribed regions and/or other functional sequence regions.

Mutation	In biology, mutation s are changes to the nucleotide sequence of the genetic material of an organism. mutation s can be caused by copying errors in the genetic material during cell division, by exposure to ultraviolet or ionizing radiation, chemical mutagens, or viruses, or can be induced by the organism itself, by cellular processes such as hyper mutation . In multicellular organisms with dedicated reproductive cells, mutation s can be subdivided into germ line mutation s, which can be passed on to descendants through the reproductive cells, and somatic mutation s, which involve cells outside the dedicated reproductive group and which are not usually transmitted to descendants.
Not	This catalog is compiled from a source file. Please do not edit this page manually. This is how to edit it.
Particular	In philosophy, Particulars are concrete entities existing in space and time as opposed to abstractions. There are, however, theories of abstract Particulars or tropes. For example, Socrates is a Particular (there"s only one Socrates-the-teacher-of-Plato and one cannot make copies of him, e.g., by cloning him, without introducing new, distinct Particulars).
Receptor	A sensory receptor is a structure that recognizes a stimulus in the internal or external environment of an organism. In response to stimuli the sensory receptor initiates sensory transduction by creating graded potentials or action potentials in the same cell or in an adjacent one.
Albert Einstein	Albert Einstein was a German-born theoretical physicist. He is best known for his theory of relativity and specifically mass-energy equivalence, $E = mc^2$. Einstein received the 1921 Nobel Prize in Physics "for his services to Theoretical Physics, and especially for his discovery of the law of the photoelectric effect."
Ratio	A ratio is a quantity that denotes the proportional amount or magnitude of one quantity relative to another.
Behavior	Behavior refers to the actions or reactions of an object or organism, usually in relation to the environment. Behavior can be conscious or subconscious, overt or covert, and voluntary or involuntary. Human Behavior (and that of other organisms and mechanisms) can be common, unusual, acceptable, or unacceptable. Humans evaluate the acceptability of Behavior using social norms and regulate Behavior by means of social control

Brain	In animals, the brain, is the control center of the central nervous system, responsible for behavior. The brain is located in the head, protected by the skull and close to the primary sensory apparatus of vision, hearing, equilibrioception, sense of acceleration, taste, and olfaction.
Neural development	The study of neural development draws on both neuroscience and developmental biology to describe the cellular and molecular mechanisms by which complex nervous systems emerge during embryonic development and throughout life.
Plasma membrane	A component of every biological cell, the selectively permeable plasma membrane is a thin and structured bilayer of phospholipid and protein molecules that envelopes the cell. It separates a cell's interior from its surroundings and controls what moves in and out.
Central nervous system	The central nervous system represents the largest part of the nervous system, including the brain and the spinal cord. Together with the peripheral nervous system, it has a fundamental role in the control of behavior. The CNS is contained within the dorsal cavity, with the brain within the cranial subcavity, and the spinal cord in the spinal cavity. The CNS is covered by the meninges. The brain is also protected by the skull, and the spinal cord is also protected by the vertebrae.
Gorilla	The Gorilla is the largest of the living primates. They are ground-dwelling omnivores that inhabit the forests of Africa.
Impulse	In classical mechanics, an Impulse is defined as the integral of a force with respect to time. When a force is applied to a rigid body it changes the momentum of that body. A small force applied for a long time can produce the same momentum change as a large force applied briefly, because it is the product of the force and the time for which it is applied that is important.
Information	Information as a concept has a diversity of meanings, from everyday usage to technical settings. Generally speaking, the concept of Information is closely related to notions of constraint, communication, control, data, form, instruction, knowledge, meaning, mental stimulus, pattern, perception, and representation. According to the Oxford English Dictionary, the first known historical meaning of the word Information in English was the act of informing, or giving form or shape to the mind, as in education, instruction, or training.
Mammal	A mammal is a warm-blooded, vertebrate animal, characterized by the presence of sweat glands, including milk producing sweat glands, and by the presence of: hair, three middle ear bones used in hearing, and a neocortex region in the brain. Most also possess specialized teeth and utilize a placenta in the ontogeny. A mammal encompass approximately 5,400 species, distributed in about 1,200 genera, 153 families, and 29 orders, though this varies by classification scheme.
Other	The Other or constitutive Other is a key concept in continental philosophy, opposed to the Same. It refers, or attempts to refer, to that which is "Other" than the concept being considered. The term often means a person Other than oneself, and is often capitalised.

Spinal cord	The spinal cord is a thin, tubular bundle of nerves that is an extension of the central nervous system from the brain and is enclosed in and protected by the bony vertebral column. The main function of the spinal cord is transmission of neural inputs between the periphery and the brain.
Axon	An axon is a long, slender projection of a nerve cell, or neuron, that conducts electrical impulses away from the neuron"s cell body or soma.
Brain damage	Brain damage is the destruction or degeneration of brain cells. It may occur due to a wide range of conditions, illnesses, injuries, and as a result of iatrogenesis. Possible causes of widespread brain damage include prolonged hypoxia, poisoning by teratogens, infection, and neurological illness.
Chemokines	Chemokines are a family of small cytokines, or proteins secreted by cells. Proteins are classified as chemokines according to shared structural characteristics such as small size they are all approximately 8-10 kilodaltons in size, and the presence of four cysteine residues in conserved locations that are key to forming their 3-dimensional shape.
Dementia	Dementia is the progressive decline in cognitive function due to damage or disease in the brain beyond what might be expected from normal aging.
Dementia praecox	An older term for schizophrenia, chosen to describe what was believed to be an incurable and progressive deterioration of mental functioning beginning in adolescence is called dementia praecox.
Inductive reasoning aptitude	The Inductive reasoning aptitude is a measurement which shows how well a person can identify a pattern within a large amount of data. Measurement is generally done in a timed test by showing four pictures or words and asking the test taker to identify which of the pictures or words does not belong in the set.
Eating	Eating is the process of consuming nutrition, i.e. food, for the purpose of providing for the nutritional needs of an animal, particularly their energy requirements and to grow.
Antibodies	Antibodies are proteins that are found in blood or other bodily fluids of vertebrates, and are used by the immune system to identify and neutralize foreign objects, such as bacteria and viruses. They are made of a few basic structural units called chains; each antibody has two large heavy chains and two small light chains.
Myelin	Myelin is an electrically-insulating phospholipid layer that surrounds the axons of many neurons. It is an outgrowth of glial cells: Schwann cells supply the myelin for peripheral neurons, whereas oligodendrocytes supply it to those of the central nervous system.
Schizophrenia	Schizophrenia is a psychiatric diagnosis that describes a mental illness characterized by impairments in the perception or expression of reality, most commonly manifesting as auditory hallucinations, paranoid or bizarre delusions or disorganized speech and thinking in the context of significant social or occupational dysfunction.

Stem cell	A Stem Cell is a primal cell that is found in all multi-cellular organisms.
Synapse	A synapse is specialized junction through which cells of the nervous system signal to one another and to non-neuronal cells such as muscles or glands. They allow the neurons of the central nervous system to form interconnected neural circuits.
Synaptogenesis	Synaptogenesis is the formation of synapses. Although it occurs throughout a healthy person"s lifespan, an explosion of synapse formation occurs during early brain development. Synaptogenesis is particularly important during an individual"s "critical period" of life, during which there is a certain degree of neuronal pruning due to competition for neural growth factors by neurons and synapses.
Constant	A constant is something that does not change, over time or otherwise: a fixed value. In most fields of discourse the term is an antonym of "variable", but in mathematical parlance a mathematical variable may sometimes also be called a constant.
Daughter	A Daughter is a female offspring; a girl, woman, or female animal in relation to her parents. The male equivalent is a son. Analogously the name is used on several areas to show relations between groups or elements.
Delusion	A false belief, not generally shared by others, and that cannot be changed despite strong evidence to the contrary is a delusion.
Emotion	Emotion, in its most general definition, is a complex psychophysical process that arises spontaneously, rather than through conscious effort, and evokes either a positive or negative psychological response and physical expressions, often involuntary, related to feelings, perceptions or beliefs about elements, objects or relations between them, in reality or in the imagination. An emotion is often differentiated from a feeling.
Emotional expression	In psychology, emotional expression is observable verbal and nonverbal behavior that communicates emotion.
Personal life	Personal life is the course of an individual human"s life, especially when viewed as the sum of personal choices contributing to one"s personal identity.
Software extension	A Software extension is a computer program designed to be incorporated into another piece of software in order to enhance the functionalities of the latter. On its own, the program is not useful or functional. Examples of software applications that support extensions include the Mozilla Firefox Web browser, Adobe Systems Photoshop and Microsoft Windows Explorer shell extensions.
Generation	Generation, also known as procreation, is the act of producing offspring. A generation can also be a stage or degree in a succession of natural descent as a grandfather, a father, and the father"s son comprise three generations.

Hallucination	A hallucination is a sensory perception experienced in the absence of an external stimulus, as distinct from an illusion, which is a misperception of an external stimulus. They may occur in any sensory modality - visual, auditory, olfactory, gustatory, tactile, or mixed.
Muscle	Muscle is contractile tissue of the body and is derived from the mesodermal layer of embryonic germ cells. It is classified as skeletal, cardiac, or smooth muscle, and its function is to produce force and cause motion, either locomotion or movement within internal organs.
Homeostasis	Homeostasis is the property of either an open system or a closed system, especially a living organism, which regulates its internal environment so as to maintain a stable, constant condition.
Shape	Shape, refers to the external two-dimensional outline, appearance or configuration of some thing — in contrast to the matter or content or substance of which it is composed.
Single	In relationships, a single person is one who is not married, or, more broadly, who is not in an exclusive romantic relationship.
Synapses	Chemical synapses are specialized junctions through which neurons signal to each other and to non-neuronal cells such as those in muscles or glands. Chemical synapses allow neurons to form circuits within the central nervous system. They are crucial to the biological computations that underlie perception and thought.
Thought disorder	Thought disorder describes a persistent underlying disturbance to conscious thought and is classified largely by its effects on speech and writing. Affected persons may show pressure of speech, derailment or flight of ideas, thought blocking, rhyming, punning, or word salad.
Hippocampus	The hippocampus is a part of the brain located in the medial temporal lobe. It forms a part of the limbic system and plays a part in memory and spatial navigation.
Tectum	The tectum is a region of the brain, specifically the dorsal part of the mesencephalon.
Weight	In the physical sciences, weight is a measurement of the gravitational force acting on an object. Near the surface of the Earth, the acceleration due to gravity is approximately constant; this means that an object"s weight is roughly proportional to its mass.
Cortex	In anatomy and zoology the cortex is the outermost layer of an organ. Organs with well-defined cortical layers include kidneys, adrenal glands, ovaries, the thymus, and portions of the brain, including the cerebral cortex, the most well-know of all cortices.
Prosencephalon	In the anatomy of the brain of vertebrates, the prosencephalon is the rostral-most portion of the brain. The prosencephalon, the mesencephalon, and rhombencephalon are the three primary portions of the brain during early development of the central nervous system.

Memory	In psychology, memory is an organism"s ability to store, retain, and subsequently retrieve information. In recent decades, it has become one of the principal pillars of a branch of science called cognitive neuroscience, an interdisciplinary link between cognitive psychology and neuroscience.
Midbrain	The midbrain is the middle of three vesicles that arise from the neural tube that forms the brain of developing animals. In mature human brains, it becomes the least differentiated, from both its developmental form and within its own structure, among the three vesicles. The midbrain is considered part of the brain stem.
Structure	Structure is a fundamental and sometimes intangible notion covering the recognition, observation, nature, and stability of patterns and relationships of entities.
Thalamus	An area near the center of the brain involved in the relay of sensory information to the cortex and in the functions of sleep and attention is the thalamus.
Language	A Language is a system for encoding and decoding information. In its most common use, the term refers to so-called "natural Language s" -- the forms of communication considered peculiar to humankind. In linguistics the term is extended to refer to the human cognitive facility of creating and using Language
Roger Wolcott Sperry	Roger Wolcott Sperry was a neuropsychologist, neurobiologist and Nobel laureate who, together with David Hunter Hubel and Torsten Nils Wiesel, won the 1981 Nobel Prize in Medicine for his work with split-brain research.
Apoptosis	Apoptosis is one of the main types of programmed cell death. As such, it is a process of deliberate suicide by an unwanted cell in a multicellular organism.
Darwinism	Darwinism is a term for the underlying theory in those ideas of Charles Darwin concerning evolution and natural selection. Discussions of Darwinism usually focus on evolution by natural selection, but sometimes Darwinism is taken to mean evolution more broadly, or other ideas not directly associated with the work of Darwin.
Necrosis	Necrosis is the name given to unprogrammed death of cells/living tissue. There are many causes of necrosis including injury, infection, cancer, infarction, and inflammation.
Nerve	A Nerve is an enclosed, cable-like bundle of peripheral axons (the long, slender projections of neurons.) A Nerve provides a common pathway for the electrochemical Nerve impulses that are transmitted along each of the axons. Nerve s are found only in the peripheral nervous system.
Nerve growth factor	Nerve growth factor, is a small secreted protein which induces the differentiation and survival of particular target neurons. It is perhaps the prototypical growth factor, in that it is one of the first to be described - that work by Rita Levi-Montalcini and Stanley Cohen was rewarded with a Nobel Prize.

Neural Darwinism	Edelman's theory that groups of neurons are in constant competition with one another, each attempting to recruit adjacent neurons to their group and thus perform a particular function is called neural Darwinism.
Gene	A gene is a locatable region of genomic sequence, corresponding to a unit of inheritance, which is associated with regulatory regions, transcribed regions and/or other functional sequence regions.
Population	In sociology and biology a population is the collection of people or individuals of a particular species. A population shares a particular characteristic of interest most often that of living in a given geographic area.
Protein	A protein is a complex, high-molecular-weight organic compound that consists of amino acids joined by peptide bonds. It is essential to the structure and function of all living cells and viruses. Many are enzymes or subunits of enzymes.
Self preservation	Self preservation is part of an animal"s instinct that demands that the organism survives.
Sympathetic	The sympathetic nervous system activates what is often termed the "fight or flight response". It is an automatic regulation system, that is, one that operates without the intervention of conscious thought.
Sympathetic nervous system	The Sympathetic nervous system is a branch of the autonomic nervous system. It is always active at a basal level and becomes more active during times of stress. Its actions during the stress response comprise the fight-or-flight response. The sympathetic nervous system is responsible for up- and down-regulating many homeostatic mechanisms in living organisms.
Brain-derived neurotrophic factor	Brain-derived neurotrophic factor is exactly as it states; a neurotrophic factor found originally in the brain, but also found in the periphery. More specifically, it is a protein which has activity on certain neurons of the central nervous system and the peripheral nervous system; it helps to support the survival of existing neurons, and encourage the growth and differentiation of new neurons and synapses.
Fetal alcohol syndrome	Fetal alcohol syndrome is a disorder of permanent birth defects that occurs in the offspring of women who drink alcohol during pregnancy. Alcohol crosses the placental barrier and can stunt fetal growth or weight, create distinctive facial stigmata, damage neurons and brain structures, and cause other physical, mental, or behavioral problems.
Glucose	Glucose, a simple monosaccharide sugar, is one of the most important carbohydrates and is used as a source of energy in animals and plants. Glucose is one of the main products of photosynthesis and starts respiration.
Neurotransmitter	A neurotransmitter is a chemical that is used to relay, amplify and modulate electrical signals between a neurons and another cell.

Prenatal development	Prenatal development is the process in which an embryo or fetus gestates during pregnancy, from fertilization until birth.
Thyroid	In anatomy, the thyroid is the largest endocrine gland in the body. The primary function of the thyroid is production of hormones.
Active transport	Active transport is the mediated transport of biochemicals, and other atomic/molecular substances, across membranes. Unlike passive transport, this process requires chemical energy. In this form of transport, molecules move against either an electrical or concentration gradient (collectively termed an electrochemical gradient).
Affect	Affect refers to the experience of feeling or emotion. Affect is a key part of the process of an organism's interaction with stimuli. The word also refers sometimes to affect display, which is "a facial, vocal, or gestural behavior that serves as an indicator of affect."
Alcoholism	Alcoholism is a term with multiple and sometimes conflicting definitions. In common and historic usage, alcoholism refers to any condition that results in the continued consumption of alcoholic beverages despite the health problems and negative social consequences it causes.
Alertness	Alertness is the state of paying close and continuous attention being watchful and prompt to meet danger or emergency, or being quick to perceive and act. It is related to psychology as well as to physiology. A lack of Alertness is a symptom of a number of conditions, including narcolepsy, attention deficit disorder, chronic fatigue syndrome, depression, Addison"s disease, or sleep deprivation.
Anxiety	Anxiety is a physiological state characterized by cognitive, somatic, emotional, and behavioral components.
Chemical	A chemical is a material with a definite chemical composition. All samples of a compound have the same composition; that is, all samples have the same proportions, by mass, of the elements present in the compound.
Heart	The heart is a muscular organ responsible for pumping blood through the blood vessels by repeated, rhythmic contractions, or a similar structure in the annelids, mollusks, and arthropods.
Hyperactivity	Hyperactivity can be described as a state in which a individual is abnormally easily excitable and exuberant. Strong emotional reactions and a very short span of attention is also typical for the individual.
Mind	Mind collectively refers to the aspects of intellect and consciousness manifested as combinations of thought, perception, memory, emotion, will and imagination; mind is the stream of consciousness.

Mental retardation	Mental retardation is a term for a pattern of persistently slow learning of basic motor and language skills during childhood, and a significantly below-normal global intellectual capacity as an adult. One common criterion for diagnosis of mental retardation is a tested intelligence quotient of 70 or below and deficits in adaptive functioning. People with mental retardation may be described as having developmental disabilities, global developmental delay, or learning difficulties.
Neurotransmitters	Neurotransmitters are chemicals that are used to relay, amplify and modulate signals between a neuron and another cell. There are many different ways to classify neurotransmitters. Often, dividing them into amino acids, peptides, and monoamines is sufficient for many purposes.
Cigarette	A cigarette is a product consumed via smoking and manufactured out of cured and finely cut tobacco leaves and reconstituted tobacco. It contains nicotine, an addictive stimulant which is toxic. It delivers smoke to the lungs immediately and produce a rapid psychoactive effect. The cigarette has been proven to be highly addictive, as well as a cause of multiple types of causes.
Tobacco smoking	Tobacco smoking is the act of burning the dried or cured leaves of the tobacco plant and inhaling the smoke for pleasure, for ritualistic or social purposes, self-medication, or simply to satisfy physical dependence.
Gamma-aminobutyric acid	Gamma-aminobutyric acid is an inhibitory neurotransmitter found in the nervous systems of widely-divergent species. It is the chief inhibitory neurotransmitter in the central nervous system and also in the retina.
Glutamate	Glutamate is one of the 20 standard amino acids used by all organisms in their proteins. It is critical for proper cell function, but it is not an essential nutrient in humans because it can be manufactured from other compounds.
Stimulant	A stimulant is a drug which increases the activity of the sympathetic nervous system and produces a sense of euphoria or awakeness.
Stimulant drugs	*Stimulant drugs* are drugs that temporarily increase alertness and awareness. They usually have increased side-effects with increased effectiveness, and the more powerful variants are therefore often prescription medicines or illegal drugs. Ritalin SR 20mg. Stimulants increase the activity of either the sympathetic nervous system, the central nervous system (CNS) or both.
Stress	Stress is the consequence of the failure to adapt to change. Less simply: it is the condition that results when person-environment transactions lead the individual to perceive a discrepancy, whether real or not, between the demands of a situation and the resources of the person"s biological, psychological or social systems.

Discovery	Discovery observations form acts of detecting and learning something. Discovery observations are acts in which something is found and given a productive insight. Serendipity is the effect by which one accidentally discovers something fortunate, especially while looking for something else entirely.
Fatigue	The word fatigue is used in everyday life to describe a range of afflictions, varying from a general state of lethargy to a specific work-induced burning sensation within one"s muscles. It can be both physical and mental. Such a mental fatigue, in turn, can manifest itself both as somnolence just as a general decrease of attention, not necessarily including sleepiness.
Mood	A mood is a relatively lasting emotional or affective state. They differ from emotions in that they are less specific, often less intense, less likely to be triggered by a particular stimulus or event, however longer lasting.
Environmental factor	In epidemiology, environmental factor refers to determinants of disease that are not transmitted genetically.
Experience	Experience as a general concept comprises knowledge of or skill in or observation of some thing or some event gained through involvement in or exposure to that thing or event. The history of the word experience aligns it closely with the concept of experiment.
Occipital lobe	The occipital lobe is the visual processing center of the mammalian brain, containing most of the anatomical region of the visual cortex. The primary visual cortex is Brodmann area 17, commonly called V_1.
Practice	Practice or practise is the act of rehearsing a behavior over and over for the purpose of improving or mastering it, as in the phrase "Practice makes perfect". Sports teams Practice to prepare for actual games. Playing a musical instrument well takes a lot of Practice.
Somatosensory	Somatosensory system consists of the various sensory receptors that trigger the experiences labelled as touch or pressure, temperature, pain, and the sensations of muscle movement and joint position including posture, movement, and facial expression.
Somatosensory system	The Somatosensory system is made up of the complex of sensations that are experienced by the skin and body. These sensations include the sense of pressure, temperature, pain, body position, and movement.
Cerebral cortex	The cerebral cortex is a structure within the vertebrate brain with distinct structural and functional properties.
Depression	In everyday language depression refers to any downturn in mood, which may be relatively transitory and perhaps due to something trivial.

Cytoplasmic streaming	Cytoplasmic streaming is the flowing of cytoplasm in eukaryotic cells. This occurs in both plant and animal cells.
Gray matter	Gray matter is a major component of the central nervous system, consisting of nerve cell bodies, glial cells, capillaries, and short nerve cell extensions/processes.
Postcentral gyrus	The lateral postcentral gyrus is a prominent structure in the parietal lobe of the human brain and an important landmark. It was initially defined from surface stimulation studies of Penfield, and parallel surface potential studies of Bard, Woolsey, and Marshall.
Somatosensory cortex	The primary somatosensory cortex is across the central sulcus and behind the primary motor cortex configured to generally correspond with the arrangement of nearby motor cells related to specific body parts. It is the main sensory receptive area for the sense of touch.
Temporal lobe	The temporal lobe is part of the cerebrum. It lies at the side of the brain, beneath the lateral or Sylvian fissure. Adjacent areas in the superior, posterior and lateral parts of the temporal lobe are involved in high-level auditory processing.
Posterior	In reference to the anatomical terms of location, the posterior end is laterally situated at or toward the hinder part of the body, lying at or extending toward the right or left side. It is the polar opposite to the anterior end, or front end of the body.
Primary	In medicine, the reporting of symptoms by a patient may have significant psychological motivators. Psychologists sometimes categorize these motivators into primary or secondary gain. primary gain is internally good; motivationally.
Sensation	Sensation is the first stage in the chain of biochemical and neurologic events that begins with the impinging of a stimulus upon the receptor cells of a sensory organ, which then leads to perception, the mental state that is reflected in statements like "I see a uniformly blue wall."
Functional magnetic resonance imaging	Functional magnetic resonance imaging is the use of MRI to measure the haemodynamic response related to neural activity in the brain or spinal cord of humans or other animals. It is one of the most recently developed forms of neuroimaging.
Closed head injury	A closed head injury is one in which the skull is not broken. A penetrating head injury occurs when an object pierces the skull and breaches the dura mater. Brain injuries may be diffuse, occurring over a wide area, or focal, located in a small, specific area.
Scolex	The Scolex of the worm attaches to the intestine of the definitive host. In some groups, the scolex is dominated by bothria, which are sometimes called "sucking grooves," and function like suction cups.
Optic radiation	The Optic radiation is a collection of axons from relay neurons in the lateral geniculate nucleus of the thalamus carrying visual information to the visual cortex along the calcarine fissure. There is one such tract on each side of the brain.

	A distinctive feature of the Optic radiation s is that they split into two parts on each side: Right superior quadrantanopia.
Assault	Assault is a crime of violence against another person.
Not	This catalog is compiled from a source file. Please do not edit this page manually. This is how to edit it.
Trauma	Trauma (plurals: Trauma ta, Trauma s) can represent: · Physical Trauma an often serious and body-altering physical injury, such as the removal of a limb · Blunt Trauma a type of physical Trauma caused by impact or other force applied from or with a blunt object · Penetrating Trauma a type of physical Trauma in which the skin or tissues are pierced by an object · Psychological Trauma an emotional or psychological injury, usually resulting from an extremely stressful or life-threatening situation · Post-cult Trauma the intense emotional problems that some members of cults and new religious movements experience upon disaffection and disaffiliation ● ● · Also see Troma Entertainment, a film company specializing in independent, horror, and exploitation films ● · "Day Twelve: Trauma , a song by Ayreon on the album The Human Equation · Trauma (song) by Ayumi Hamasaki ● ● · Baltimore Trauma professional paintball team from North Carolina The word Trauma came from Greek τραυμα = "a wound": compare the verb τιτρωσκω " href="/wiki/Root_(linguistics)">root τρω) = "I injure".
Blood-brain barrier	The Blood-brain barrier is a membranic structure that acts primarily to protect the brain from chemicals in the blood, while still allowing essential metabolic function. It is composed of endothelial cells, which are packed very tightly in brain capillaries. This higher density restricts passage of substances from the bloodstream much more than endothelial cells in capillaries elsewhere in the body
Microglia	Microglia are a type of glial cell that act as the immune cells of the Central nervous system. Microglia, the smallest of the glial cells, can act as phagocytes, cleaning up CNS debris. Most serve as representatives of the immune system in the brain and spinal cord.

Sodium-potassium pump	In order to maintain the cell potential, cells must keep a low concentration of sodium ions and high levels of potassium ions within the cell. The sodium-potassium pump is an enzyme located in the plasma membrane. It helps maintain cell potential and regulate cellular volume.
Blood	Blood is a specialized biological fluid consisting of red blood cells.White blood cells also called leukocytes and platelets also called thrombocytes suspended in a complex fluid medium known as blood plasma.
Recess	In education, recess is the daily period, typically ten to thirty minutes, in elementary school where students are allowed to leave the school"s interior to enter its adjacent outdoor playground, where they can play on such recreational equipment or engage in activities.
Material	Material refers to physical substances used as inputs to production or manufacturing.
Mechanism	In philosophy, mechanism is a theory that all natural phenomena can be explained by physical causes. It can be contrasted with vitalism, the philosophical theory that vital forces are active in living organisms, so that life cannot be explained solely by mechanism.
Potassium	Potassium is the an essential mineral macronutrient and is the main intracellular ion for all types of cells. It is important in maintaining fluid and electrolyte balance in the body.
Sodium	Sodium is a chemical element which has the symbol Na, atomic number 11, atomic mass 22.9898 g/mol, common oxidation number +1. Sodium is a soft, silvery white, highly reactive element and is a member of the alkali metals within "group 1". It has only one stable isotope, ^{23}Na.
Stroke	In handwriting research, the concept of stroke is used in various ways. In engineering and computer science, there is a tendency to use the term stroke for a single connected component of ink (in Off-line handwriting recognition) or a complete pen-down trace (in on-line handwriting recognition.) Thus, such stroke may be a complete character or a part of a character.
Waste	Waste is unwanted or undesired material.
Amphetamine	Amphetamine is a prescription stimulant commonly used to treat Attention-deficit hyperactivity disorder in adults and children. It is also used to treat symptoms of traumatic brain injury and the daytime drowsiness symptoms of narcolepsy and chronic fatigue syndrome
Cannabinoids	Cannabinoids are a group of terpenophenolic compounds present in Cannabis. The broader definition of cannabinoids refer to a group of substances that are structurally related to tetrahydrocannabinol or that bind to cannabinoid receptors. The chemical definition encompasses a variety of distinct chemical classes: the classical cannabinoids structurally related to THC, the nonclassical cannabinoids, the aminoalkylindoles, the eicosanoids related to the endocannabinoids, 1,5-diarylpyrazoles, quinolines and arylsulphonamides and additional compounds that do not fall into these standard classes but bind to cannabinoid receptors.

Diaschisis	A process in which a lesion in a specific area of the brain disrupts other intact areas, is referred to as diaschisis.
Oligodendrocyte	An Oligodendrocyte is a variety of neuroglia. Their main function is the myelination of nerve cells exclusively in the central nervous system of the higher vertebrates. A single oligodendrocyte can extend to about a dozen axons, wrapping around approximately 1mm of each and forming the myelin sheath.
Tranquilizer	A sedative, or tranquilizer, is a drug that depresses the central nervous system (CNS), which causes calmness, relaxation, reduction of anxiety, sleepiness, slowed breathing, slurred speech, staggering gait, poor judgment, and slow, uncertain reflexes.
Dopamine	Dopamine is a hormone and neurotransmitter occurring in a wide variety of animals, including both vertebrates and invertebrates. In the brain, dopamine functions as a neurotransmitter. Dopamine is also a neurohormone released by the hypothalamus. Its main function as a hormone is to inhibit the release of prolactin from the anterior lobe of the pituitary.
Fatty acid	In chemistry, especially biochemistry, a Fatty acid is a carboxylic acid often with a long unbranched aliphatic tail (chain), which is either saturated or unsaturated. Carboxylic acids as short as butyric acid (4 carbon atoms) are considered to be Fatty acid s, whereas Fatty acid s derived from natural fats and oils may be assumed to have at least eight carbon atoms, caprylic acid (octanoic acid), for example. The most abundant natural Fatty acid s have an even number of carbon atoms because their biosynthesis involves acetyl-CoA, a coenzyme carrying a two-carbon-atom group
Marijuana	Marijuana is the dried vegetable matter of the Cannabis sativa plant. It contains large concentrations of compounds that have medicinal and psychoactive effects when consumed, usually by smoking or eating.
Stimulation	Stimulation is the action of various agents on muscles, nerves, or a sensory end organ, by which activity is evoked.
Collateral sprouting	Collateral sprouting occurs when disease or injury causes the partial loss of innervation from a muscle, by which the remaining axons "sprout" and form new connections to the denervated muscle fibers.
Fats	Fats consist of a wide group of compounds that are generally soluble in organic solvents and largely insoluble in water. Chemically, fats are generally triesters of glycerol and fatty acids. Fats may be either solid or liquid at normal room temperature, depending on their structure and composition.
Disulfiram	Disulfiram is a drug used to support the treatment of chronic alcoholism by producing an acute sensitivity to alcohol.

Pain	Pain is an unpleasant sensation. It is defined by the International Association for the Study of Pain as "an unpleasant sensory and emotional experience associated with actual or potential tissue damage, or described in terms of such damage".
Animal testing	Animal testing refers to the use of animals in experiments. It is estimated that 50 to 100 million vertebrate animals worldwide — from zebrafish to non-human primates — are used annually and either killed during the experiments or subsequently euthanized.
Sense	Sense are the physiological methods of perception. They and their operation, classification, and theory are overlapping topics studied by a variety of fields, most notably neuroscience, cognitive psychology, and philosophy of perception. The nervous system has a sensory system dedicated to each sense.
Sensitivity	The sensitivity or insensitivity of a human, often considered with regard to a particular kind of stimulus, is the strength of the feeling it results in, in comparison with the strength of the stimulus. The concept applies to physical as well as emotional feeling.
Positron emission tomography	Positron emission tomography is a nuclear medicine medical imaging technique which produces a three-dimensional image or map of functional processes in the body. Images of metabolic activity in space are then reconstructed by computer, often in modern scanners aided by results from a CT X-ray scan.
Phantom limb	Phantom limb is a feeling that a missing limb is still attached to the body and is moving appropriately with other body parts. Phantom pains can also occur in people who are born without limbs and people who are paralyzed.
Behavior	Behavior refers to the actions or reactions of an object or organism, usually in relation to the environment. Behavior can be conscious or subconscious, overt or covert, and voluntary or involuntary. Human Behavior (and that of other organisms and mechanisms) can be common, unusual, acceptable, or unacceptable. Humans evaluate the acceptability of Behavior using social norms and regulate Behavior by means of social control
Neuropsychologist	A psychologist concerned with the relationships among cognition, affect, behavior, and brain function is a neuropsychologist.
Occupational therapists	Occupational therapists work with the disabled, the elderly, newborns, school-aged children, and with anyone who has a permanent or temporary impairment in their physical or mental functioning.
Physical therapists	Physical therapists are health care professionals who evaluate and manage health conditions for people of all ages. Typically individuals consult a PT for the management of medical problems or other health-related conditions that; cause pain, limit their ability to move, and limit the performance of functional activities.

| Therapist | A therapist is an individual who specializes in physical therapy or psychotherapy as means of treating psychological disorders. A therapist is often sought when individuals are experiencing extreme levels of stress that can eventually lead to psychological and physical disorders. |

Vision	Vision is the most important sense for birds, since good eyesight is essential for safe flight, and this group has a number of adaptations which give visual acuity superior to that of other vertebrate groups; a pigeon has been described as "two eyes with wings". The avian eye resembles that of a reptile, but has a better-positioned lens, a feature shared with mammals. Birds have the largest eyes relative to their size within the animal kingdom, and movement is consequently limited within the eye"s bony socket.
Law of specific nerve energies	The Law of Specific Nerve Energies, first proposed by Johannes Peter Muller in 1826, is that the nature of perception is defined by the pathway over which the sensory information is carried. Hence, the origin of the sensation is not important. For example, pressing on the eye elicits sensations of flashes of light because the neurons in the retina send a signal to the occipital lobe. Despite the sensory input"s being mechanical, the experience is visual.
Brain	In animals, the brain, is the control center of the central nervous system, responsible for behavior. The brain is located in the head, protected by the skull and close to the primary sensory apparatus of vision, hearing, equilibrioception, sense of acceleration, taste, and olfaction.
Nerve	A Nerve is an enclosed, cable-like bundle of peripheral axons (the long, slender projections of neurons.) A Nerve provides a common pathway for the electrochemical Nerve impulses that are transmitted along each of the axons. Nerve s are found only in the peripheral nervous system.
Perception	In psychology. and the cognitive sciences, perception is the process of acquiring, interpreting, selecting, and organizing sensory information. It is a task far more complex than was imagined in the 1950s and 1960s, when it was proclaimed that building perceiving machines would take about a decade, but, needless to say, that is still very far from reality.
Principle	In user interface design, programming language design, and ergonomics, the principle of least astonishment (or surprise) states that, when two elements of an interface conflict the behaviour should be that which will least surprise the human user or programmer at the time the conflict arises. For example: A user interface may have the behaviour that pressing Control-Q causes the program to quit. The same user interface may have a facility for recording macros, a sequence of keystrokes to be played back later, intended to be able to control all aspects of the program.
Eye	Eye s are organs that detect light, and send signals along the optic nerve to the visual and other areas of the brain. Complex optical systems with resolving power have come in ten fundamentally different forms, and 96% of animal species possess a complex optical system. Image-resolving Eye s are present in cnidaria, molluscs, chordates, annelids and arthropods.

Eyes	Eyes are organs that detect light. Different kinds of light-sensitive organs are found in a variety of animals. The simplest eyes do nothing but detect whether the surroundings are light or dark, which is sufficient for the entrainment of circadian rhythms but can hardly be called vision. More complex eyes can distinguish shapes and colors. The visual fields of some such complex eyes largely overlap, to allow better depth perception, as in humans; and others are placed so as to minimize the overlap, such as in rabbits and chameleons.
Pupil	The Pupil is a circular opening located in the center of the iris of the eye that controls the amount of light that enters the eye. It appears black because most of the light entering the Pupil is absorbed by the tissues inside the eye. In optical terms, the anatomical Pupil is the eye"s aperture and the iris is the aperture stop.
Retina	The vertebrate Retina is a light sensitive tissue lining the inner surface of the eye. The optics of the eye create an image of the visual world on the Retina which serves much the same function as the film in a camera. Light striking the Retina initiates a cascade of chemical and electrical events that ultimately trigger nerve impulses.
Animal testing	Animal testing refers to the use of animals in experiments. It is estimated that 50 to 100 million vertebrate animals worldwide — from zebrafish to non-human primates — are used annually and either killed during the experiments or subsequently euthanized.
Iris	The iris is the most visible part of the eye. The iris is an annulus (or flattened ring) consisting of pigmented fibrovascular tissue known as a stroma. The stroma connects a sphincter muscle, which contracts the pupil, and a set of dialator muscles which open it.
Receptor	A sensory receptor is a structure that recognizes a stimulus in the internal or external environment of an organism. In response to stimuli the sensory receptor initiates sensory transduction by creating graded potentials or action potentials in the same cell or in an adjacent one.
Amacrine cell	Amacrine cell refers to interneurons in the retina which deliver 70% of the ganglion cells input, and also regulates the output of the cone bipolar cells which deliver the other 30%.
Bipolar cell	A Bipolar cell is a type of neuron which has two extensions. Bipolar cell s are specialized sensory neurons for the transmission of special senses. As such, they are part of the sensory pathways for smell, sight, taste, hearing and vestibular functions.
Blind spot	In anatomy, the blind spot is the region of the retina where the optic nerve and blood vessels pass through to connect to the back of the eye. Since there are no light receptors there, a part of the field of vision is not perceived.
Optic nerve	The optic nerve is the nerve that transmits visual information from the retina to the brain. The optic nerve is composed of retinal ganglion cell axons and support cells.

Axon	An axon is a long, slender projection of a nerve cell, or neuron, that conducts electrical impulses away from the neuron"s cell body or soma.
Ganglion	In anatomy, a ganglion is a tissue mass.
Ganglion cell	A ganglion cell is a cell found in a ganglion. The term is also sometimes used to refer specifically to a retinal ganglion cell (R ganglion cell) found in the ganglion cell layer of the retina. ganglion cell s reside in the adrenal medulla, where they are involved in the sympathetic nervous system"s release of epinephrine and norepinephrine into the blood stream.
Visual acuity	Visual acuity is the eye"s ability to detect fine details and is the quantitative measure of the eye"s ability to see an in-focus image at a certain distance.
Fovea	The fovea, a part of the eye, is a spot located in the center of the macula. The fovea is responsible for sharp central vision, which is necessary in humans for reading, watching television or movies, driving, and any activity where visual detail is of primary importance.
Photopic vision	Photopic vision is the vision of the eye under well-lit conditions. In humans and many animals, photopic vision allows color perception, mediated by cone cells.
Acute	Acute means sudden, sharp, and abrupt. Usually short in duration.
Color	Color or colour is the visual perceptual property corresponding in humans to the categories called red, yellow, blue and others. Color derives from the spectrum of light interacting in the eye with the spectral sensitivities of the light receptors. Color categories and physical specifications of Color are also associated with objects, materials, light sources, etc., based on their physical properties such as light absorption, reflection, or emission spectra.
Color vision	Color vision is the capacity of an organism or machine to distinguish objects based on the wavelengths of the light they reflect or emit. The nervous system derives color by comparing the responses to light from the several types of cone photoreceptors in the eye.
Hearing impairment	A hearing impairment is a full or partial decrease in the ability to detect or understand sounds.[1] Caused by a wide range of biological and environmental factors, loss of hearing can happen to any organism that perceives sound.
Not	This catalog is compiled from a source file. Please do not edit this page manually. This is how to edit it.
Retinal	Retinal is a light-sensitive retinene molecule found in the photoreceptor cells of the retina. Retinal is the fundamental chromophore involved in the transduction of light into visual signals, i.e. nerve impulses, in the visual system of the central nervous system.

Opsin	Opsin s are a group of light-sensitive 35-55 kDa membrane-bound G protein-coupled receptors of the retinylidene protein family found in photoreceptor cells of the retina. Five classical groups of Opsin s are involved in vision, mediating the conversion of a photon of light into an electrochemical signal, the first step in the visual transduction cascade. Another Opsin found in the mammalian retina, melan Opsin , is involved in circadian rhythms and pupillary reflex but not in image-forming.
Opsins	Opsins are a group of light-sensitive 35-55 kDa membrane-bound G protein-coupled receptors of the retinylidene protein family found in photoreceptor cells of the retina. They are involved in vision, mediating the conversion of a photon of light into an electrochemical signal, the first step in the visual transduction cascade.
Photopigment	A Photopigment is an unstable pigment that undergoes a physical or chemical change in the presence of light. The term is generally applied to the non-protein chromophore moiety of photosensitive chromoproteins, such as the pigments involved in photosynthesis and photoreception. In medical terminology, "photopigment" commonly refers to the photoreceptor proteins of the retina.
Chemical	A chemical is a material with a definite chemical composition. All samples of a compound have the same composition; that is, all samples have the same proportions, by mass, of the elements present in the compound.
Energy	The concept of psychic Energy was developed in the field of psychodynamics. In 1874, German scientist Ernst von Brucke proposed that all living organisms are Energy-systems governed by the principle of the conservation of Energy. Brucke was also coincidentally the supervisor at the University of Vienna for first-year medical student Sigmund Freud who adopted this new paradigm.
Trichromatic theory	The trichromatic theory was postulated by Young and later by Helmholtz. They demonstrated that most colors can be matched by superimposing three separate light sources known as primaries; a process known as additive mixing. The Young-Helmholtz theory of color vision was built around the assumption of there being three classes of receptors.
Cone cell	A cone cell is a photoreceptor cell in the retina of the eye which functions best in relatively bright light. The cone cell gradually becomes more sparse towards the periphery of the retina.
Wavelength	In physics, Wavelength is the distance between repeating units of a propagating wave of a given frequency. It is commonly designated by the Greek letter lambda. Examples of wave-like phenonomena are light, water waves, and sound waves.
Opponent-process theory	The opponent-process theory is a color theory that states that the human visual system interprets information about color by processing signals from cones in an antagonistic manner.
Visual field	The visual field is the "spatial array of visual sensations available to observation in introspectionist psychological experiments."

Afterimage	An Afterimage or ghost image is an optical illusion that refers to an image continuing to appear in one"s vision after the exposure to the original image has ceased. One of the most common Afterimage s is the bright glow that seems to float before one"s eyes after staring at a light bulb or a headlight for a few seconds. The phenomenon of Afterimage s may be closely related to persistence of vision, which allows a rapid series of pictures to portray motion, which is the basis of animation and cinema.
Staring	Staring is a prolonged gaze or fixed look. In staring, one object or person is the continual focus of visual interest, for an amount of time. Staring can be interpreted as being either hostile, or the result of intense concentration.
Tim	TIM is a series of lesser-known psychedelic drugs similar in structure to mescaline. They were first synthesized by Alexander Shulgin. In his book PiHKAL (Phenethylamines i Have Known And Loved), none of their durations are known.
Brightness	Brightness is an attribute of visual perception in which a source appears to emit a given amount of light. In other words, brightness is the perception elicited by the luminance of a visual target. This is a subjective attribute/property of an object being observed.
Brightness constancy	The tendency to perceive an object as being just as bright even though lighting conditions change its physical intensity is called brightness constancy.
Color constancy	*Color constancy* is an example of subjective constancy and a feature of the human color perception system which ensures that the perceived color of objects remains relatively constant under varying illumination conditions. A green apple for instance looks green to us at midday, when the main illumination is white sunlight, and also at sunset, when the main illumination is red. This helps us identify objects.
Concept	A Concept is a cognitive unit of meaning-- an abstract idea or a mental symbol sometimes defined as a "unit of knowledge," built from other units which act as a Concept"s characteristics. A Concept is typically associated with a corresponding representation in a language or symbology such as a word. The meaning of "Concept" is explored in mainstream cognitive science and philosophy of mind.
Cortex	In anatomy and zoology the cortex is the outermost layer of an organ. Organs with well-defined cortical layers include kidneys, adrenal glands, ovaries, the thymus, and portions of the brain, including the cerebral cortex, the most well-know of all cortices.
Information	Information as a concept has a diversity of meanings, from everyday usage to technical settings. Generally speaking, the concept of Information is closely related to notions of constraint, communication, control, data, form, instruction, knowledge, meaning, mental stimulus, pattern, perception, and representation.

	According to the Oxford English Dictionary, the first known historical meaning of the word Information in English was the act of informing, or giving form or shape to the mind, as in education, instruction, or training.
Entity	An entity is something that has a distinct, separate existence, though it need not be a material existence. In particular, abstractions and legal fictions are usually regarded as an entity. In general, there is also no presumption that an entity is animate.
Color blindness	Color blindness in humans is the inability to perceive differences between some or all colors that other people can distinguish. It is most often of genetic nature, but may also occur because of eye, nerve, or brain damage, or due to exposure to certain chemicals.
Genetics	Genetics is the science of heredity and variation in living organisms.Knowledge of the inheritance of characteristics has been implicitly used since prehistoric times for improving crop plants and animals through selective breeding. However, the modern science of genetics, which seeks to understand the mechanisms of inheritance, only began with the work of Gregor Mendel in the mid-1800s.
X chromosome	The sex chromosomes are one of the 23 pairs of human chromosomes. Each person normally has one pair of sex chromosomes in each cell. Females have two of the X chromosome, while males have one X chromosome and one Y chromosome. The X chromosome carries hundreds of genes but few, if any, of these have anything to do directly with sex determination.
Brain size	When comparing different species, brain size does present a correlation with intelligence. For example, the ratio of brain weight to body weight for fish is 1:5000; for reptiles it is about 1:1500; for birds, 1:220; for most mammals, 1:180, and for humans, 1:50. However within the human species modern studies using MRI have shown that brain size shows substantial and consistent correlation with IQ among adults of the same sex
Mammal	A mammal is a warm-blooded, vertebrate animal, characterized by the presence of sweat glands, including milk producing sweat glands, and by the presence of: hair, three middle ear bones used in hearing, and a neocortex region in the brain. Most also possess specialized teeth and utilize a placenta in the ontogeny. A mammal encompass approximately 5,400 species, distributed in about 1,200 genera, 153 families, and 29 orders, though this varies by classification scheme.
Other	The Other or constitutive Other is a key concept in continental philosophy, opposed to the Same. It refers, or attempts to refer, to that which is "Other" than the concept being considered. The term often means a person Other than oneself, and is often capitalised.
Hypothalamus	The hypothalamus is a region of the brain located below the thalamus, forming the major portion of the ventral region of the diencephalon and functioning to regulate certain metabolic processes and other autonomic activities.

Lateral geniculate nucleus	The lateral geniculate nucleus of the thalamus is a part of the brain, which is the primary processor of visual information, received from the retina, in the CNS.
Lateral inhibition	Lateral inhibition is a mechanism by which neurons are able to determine more precisely the origin of a stimulus.
Motion perception	Motion perception is the process of inferring the speed and direction of objects and surfaces that move in a visual scene given some visual input. Although this process appears straightforward to most observers, it has proven to be a difficult problem from a computational perspective, and extraordinarily difficult to explain in terms of neural processing.
Optic chiasm	The optic chiasm is the part of the brain where the optic nerves partially cross. Specifically, the nerves connected to the right eye that attend to the left visual field cross with the nerves from the left eye that attend to the right visual field.
Superior colliculus	The superior colliculus is a paired structure that is part of the brain"s tectal area. In humans, the superior colliculus is involved in the generation of saccadic eye movements and eye-head coordination.
Thalamus	An area near the center of the brain involved in the relay of sensory information to the cortex and in the functions of sleep and attention is the thalamus.
Prosencephalon	In the anatomy of the brain of vertebrates, the prosencephalon is the rostral-most portion of the brain. The prosencephalon, the mesencephalon, and rhombencephalon are the three primary portions of the brain during early development of the central nervous system.
Cytoplasmic streaming	Cytoplasmic streaming is the flowing of cytoplasm in eukaryotic cells. This occurs in both plant and animal cells.
Structure	Structure is a fundamental and sometimes intangible notion covering the recognition, observation, nature, and stability of patterns and relationships of entities.
Tectum	The tectum is a region of the brain, specifically the dorsal part of the mesencephalon.
Constant	A constant is something that does not change, over time or otherwise: a fixed value. In most fields of discourse the term is an antonym of "variable", but in mathematical parlance a mathematical variable may sometimes also be called a constant.
Software extension	A Software extension is a computer program designed to be incorporated into another piece of software in order to enhance the functionalities of the latter. On its own, the program is not useful or functional. Examples of software applications that support extensions include the Mozilla Firefox Web browser, Adobe Systems Photoshop and Microsoft Windows Explorer shell extensions.

197

Single	In relationships, a single person is one who is not married, or, more broadly, who is not in an exclusive romantic relationship.
Koniocellular	The lateral geniculate nucleus(LGN) of thalamus in higher mammals(ex.primates) contains three distinct types of cells. Composed of 6 layers in the monkey and human, the LGN is composed primarily of parvocellular cell layers separated by Koniocellular cell layers. A neurochemically distinct population of Koniocellular neurons makes up a third functional channel in primate lateral geniculate nucleus.
Parasympathetic nervous system	The parasympathetic nervous system is a division of the autonomic nervous system, along with the sympathetic nervous system and Enteric nervous system. The ANS is a subdivision of the peripheral nervous system.
Receptive field	The Receptive field of a sensory neuron is a region of space in which the presence of a stimulus will alter the firing of that neuron. Receptive field s have been identified for neurons of the auditory system, the somatosensory system, and the visual system. The concept of Receptive field s can be extended to further up the neural system; if many sensory receptors all form synapses with a single cell further up, they collectively form the Receptive field of that cell.
Depression	In everyday language depression refers to any downturn in mood, which may be relatively transitory and perhaps due to something trivial.
Stimulus	In psychology, a stimulus is part of the stimulus-response relationship of behavioral learning theory.
Visual System	The Visual System is the part of the nervous system which allows organisms to see. It interprets the information from visible light to build a representation of the world surrounding the body.
Blindsight	Blindsight is a phenomenon in which people cannot consciously see a certain portion of their visual field but still behave in some instances as if they can see it. Blindsight may be thought of as a converse of the form of anosognosia known as Anton"s syndrome, in which there is full cortical blindness along with the confabulation of visual experience.
Primary	In medicine, the reporting of symptoms by a patient may have significant psychological motivators. Psychologists sometimes categorize these motivators into primary or secondary gain. primary gain is internally good; motivationally.

Primary somatosensory cortex	The lateral postcentral gyrus is a prominent structure in the parietal lobe of the human brain and an important landmark. It was initially defined from surface stimulation studies of Penfield, and parallel surface potential studies of Bard, Woolsey, and Marshall. Although initially defined to be roughly the same as Brodmann areas 3, 1 and 2, more recent work by Kaas has suggested that for homogeny with other sensory fields only area 3 should be referred to as "*Primary somatosensory cortex*", as it received the bulk of the thalamocortical projection from the sensory input fields.
Somatosensory	Somatosensory system consists of the various sensory receptors that trigger the experiences labelled as touch or pressure, temperature, pain, and the sensations of muscle movement and joint position including posture, movement, and facial expression.
Brain damage	Brain damage is the destruction or degeneration of brain cells. It may occur due to a wide range of conditions, illnesses, injuries, and as a result of iatrogenesis. Possible causes of widespread brain damage include prolonged hypoxia, poisoning by teratogens, infection, and neurological illness.
Dorsum	In anatomy, the dorsum is the upper side of animals that typically run, fly or swim in a horizontal position, and the back side of animals that walk upright. In vertebrates the dorsum contains the backbone.
Dorsal stream	The dorsal stream is a pathway for visual information which flows through the visual cortex, the part of the brain which provides visual processing. It is involved in spatial awareness: recognizing where objects are in space.
Ventral stream	The primate visual system consists of about thirty areas of the cerebral cortex called the visual cortex. The visual cortex is divided into the ventral stream and the dorsal stream. The ventral stream is associated with object recognition and form representation.
Central sulcus	The central sulcus is a prominent landmark of the brain, separating the parietal lobe from the frontal lobe. The central sulcus is the site of the primary motor cortex in mammals, a group of cells that controls voluntary movements of the body.
Cerebral cortex	The cerebral cortex is a structure within the vertebrate brain with distinct structural and functional properties.
Generation	Generation, also known as procreation, is the act of producing offspring. A generation can also be a stage or degree in a succession of natural descent as a grandfather, a father, and the father"s son comprise three generations.
Occipital lobe	The occipital lobe is the visual processing center of the mammalian brain, containing most of the anatomical region of the visual cortex. The primary visual cortex is Brodmann area 17, commonly called V_1.

Visual cortex	The term visual cortex refers to the primary visual cortex and extrastriate visual cortical areas such as V2, V3, V4, and V5. The primary visual cortex is anatomically equivalent to Brodmann area 17, or BA17. Brodmann areas are based on a histological map of the human brain created by Korbinian Brodmann.
Visual processing	Visual processing is the sequence of steps that information takes as it flows from visual sensors to cognitive processing. The sensors may be zoological eyes or they may be cameras or sensor arrays that sense various portions of the electromagnetic spectrum.
Complex	In psychology a Complex is a group of mental factors that are unconsciously associated by the individual with a particular subject or connected by a recognizable theme and influence the individual"s attitude and behavior. Their existence is widely agreed upon in the area of depth psychology at least, being instrumental in the systems of both Freud and Jung. They are generally a way of mapping the psyche, and are crucial theoretical items of common reference to be found in therapy.
Complex cell	Complex cell refers to cells found both in the primary visual cortex and the secondary visual cortex.
David Hunter Hubel	David Hunter Hubel was co-recipient with Torsten Wiesel of the 1981 Nobel Prize in Physiology or Medicine, for their discoveries concerning information processing in the visual system; the prize was shared with Roger W. Sperry for his independent research on the cerebral hemispheres.In 1978, Hubel and Wiesel were awarded the Louisa Gross Horwitz Prize from Columbia University.
Microelectrode	An electrical wire so small that it can be used either to monitor the electrical activity of a single neuron or to stimulate activity within it is a microelectrode.
Research method	The scope of the research method is to produce some new knowledge. This, in principle, can take three main forms: Exploratory research; Constructive research; and Empirical research.
Shape	Shape, refers to the external two-dimensional outline, appearance or configuration of some thing — in contrast to the matter or content or substance of which it is composed.
Simple cell	A neuron in the striate cortex that is maximally sensitive to the position and orientation of edges in the receptive field is called a simple cell.
Torsten Wiesel	Torsten Wiesel was a Swedish co-recipient with David H. Hubel of the 1981 Nobel Prize in Physiology or Medicine, for their discoveries concerning information processing in the visual system; the prize was shared with Roger W. Sperry for his independent research on the cerebral hemispheres.
Particular	In philosophy, Particulars are concrete entities existing in space and time as opposed to abstractions. There are, however, theories of abstract Particulars or tropes. For example, Socrates is a Particular (there"s only one Socrates-the-teacher-of-Plato and one cannot make copies of him, e.g., by cloning him, without introducing new, distinct Particulars).

Anxiety	Anxiety is a physiological state characterized by cognitive, somatic, emotional, and behavioral components.
Escape response	Escape response is a possible reaction in response to stimuli indicative of danger, in particular, it initiates an escape motion of an animal. The term is also used in a more general setting: avoiding of unpleasant situations.
Feature detector	A feature detector is sensory system that is highly attuned to a specific stimulus pattern. They are nerve cells in the brain that respond to specific features of the stimulus, such as shape, angle, or movement.
Feature	A Feature is a concept applied to several fields of linguistics, typically involving the assignment of binary or unary conditions which act as constraints. In phonology, segments are categorized into natural classes on the basis of their distinctive features. Each Feature describes a quality or characteristic of the natural class, such as voice or manner.
Illusion	An Illusion is a distortion of the senses, revealing how the brain normally organizes and interprets sensory stimulation. While Illusion s distort reality, they are generally shared by most people. Illusion s may occur with more of the human senses than vision, but visual Illusion s, optical Illusion s, are the most well known and understood.
Stimulation	Stimulation is the action of various agents on muscles, nerves, or a sensory end organ, by which activity is evoked.
Body weight	Body weight is a term that is used in biological and medical science contexts to describe the mass of an organism"s body. Body weight is measured in kilograms throughout the world, although in some countries people more often measure and describe body weight in pounds or stones and pounds and thus may not be well acquainted with measurement in kilograms.
Fourier analysis	Fourier analysis, named after Joseph Fourier"s introduction of the Fourier series, is the decomposition of a function in terms of a sum of sinusoidal functions of different frequencies that can be recombined to obtain the original function.
Shape constancy	The tendency to perceive an object as being the same shape although the retinal image varies in shape as it rotates, is shape constancy.
Temporal lobe	The temporal lobe is part of the cerebrum. It lies at the side of the brain, beneath the lateral or Sylvian fissure. Adjacent areas in the superior, posterior and lateral parts of the temporal lobe are involved in high-level auditory processing.
Visual agnosia	Visual Agnosia is the inability of the brain to make sense of or make use of some part of otherwise normal visual stimulus, and is typified by the inability to recognize familiar objects or faces.

Recognition	Recognition is a process that occurs in thinking when some event, process, pattern, or object recurs. Thus in order for something to be recognized, it must be familiar. In philosophy recognition became very important in Hegel"s attempt at understanding the emergence of self-consciousness.
Attention	Attention is the cognitive process of selectively concentrating on one aspect of the environment while ignoring other things. Examples include listening carefully to what someone is saying while ignoring other conversations in the room or listening to a cell phone conversation while driving a car.
Face	Face idiomatically meaning "dignity; prestige" is a fundamental concept in the fields of sociology, sociolinguistics, semantics, politeness theory, psychology, political science, and Face Negotiation Theory. Although Lin Yutang (1935:200) claimed "Face cannot be translated or defined", compare these definitions: The term Face may be defined as the positive social value a person effectively claims for himself by the line others assume he has taken during a particular contact. Face is an image of self delineated in terms of approved social attributes.
Face perception	Face perception is the process by which the brain and mind understand and interpret the face, particularly the human face.
Fusiform gyrus	The fusiform gyrus is located on the interior surface of the cortex, extending from the occipital to the temporal lobe.
Bipolar disorder	Bipolar disorder is a psychiatric condition defined as recurrent episodes of significant disturbance in mood. These disturbances can occur on a spectrum that ranges from debilitating depression to unbridled mania. Individuals suffering from bipolar disorder typically experience fluid states of mania, hypomania or what is referred to as a mixed state in conjunction with depressive episodes.
Saccade	A saccade is a fast movement of an eye, head, or other part of an animal's body or of a device. It can also be a fast shift in frequency of an emitted signal, or other such fast change.
Amnesia	Amnesia is a condition in which memory is disturbed. The causes of amnesia are organic or functional. Organic causes include damage to the brain, through trauma or disease, or use of certain generally sedative drugs.
Appetite	The appetite is the desire to eat food, felt as hunger. Appetite exists in all higher lifeforms, and serves to regulate adequate energy intake to maintain metabolic needs. It is regulated by a close interplay between the digestive tract, adipose tissue and the brain. Decreased desire to eat is termed anorexia, while polyphagia or "hyperphagia" is increased eating. Disregulation of appetite contributes to anorexia nervosa, bulimia nervosa, cachexia, overeating, and binge eating disorder.

Confusion	Severe confusion of a degree considered pathological usually refers to loss of orientation, and often memory. Confusion as such is not synonymous with inability to focus attention, although severe inability to focus attention can cause, or greatly contribute to, confusion.
Delusion	A false belief, not generally shared by others, and that cannot be changed despite strong evidence to the contrary is a delusion.
Disease	A Disease or medical problem is an abnormal condition of an organism that impairs bodily functions, associated with specific symptoms and signs. It may be caused by external factors, such as invading organisms, or it may be caused by internal dysfunctions, such as autoimmune Disease s. In human beings, Disease is often used more broadly to refer to any condition that causes extreme pain, dysfunction, distress, social problems, and/or death to the person afflicted, or similar problems for those in contact with the person.
Fixation	Fixation in abnormal psychology is the state where an individual becomes obsessed with an attachment to another human, animal or inanimate object. Fixation in vision refers to maintaining the gaze in a constant direction. .
Hallucination	A hallucination is a sensory perception experienced in the absence of an external stimulus, as distinct from an illusion, which is a misperception of an external stimulus. They may occur in any sensory modality - visual, auditory, olfactory, gustatory, tactile, or mixed.
Memory	In psychology, memory is an organism"s ability to store, retain, and subsequently retrieve information. In recent decades, it has become one of the principal pillars of a branch of science called cognitive neuroscience, an interdisciplinary link between cognitive psychology and neuroscience.
Memory loss	Memory loss can have many causes: · Alzheimer"s disease is an illness which can cause mild to severe memory loss · Parkinson"s disease is a genetic defect which may result in memory loss · Huntington"s disease is an inherited disease which can result in memory loss · It is sometimes a side effect of chemotherapy in which cytotoxic drugs are used to treat cancer. · Certain forms of mental illness also have memory loss as a key symptom, including fugue states and the much more famous Dissociative Identity Disorder. · Stress-related activities are another factor which can result in memory loss · It can also be caused by traumatic brain injury, of which a concussion is a form. .
Insomnia	Insomnia is a sleep disorder characterized by an inability to sleep and/or inability to remain asleep for a reasonable period.
Experience	Experience as a general concept comprises knowledge of or skill in or observation of some thing or some event gained through involvement in or exposure to that thing or event. The history of the word experience aligns it closely with the concept of experiment.

209

Infant	In basic English usage, an Infant is defined as a human child at the youngest stage of life, specifically before they can walk and generally before the age of one.
Neural development	The study of neural development draws on both neuroscience and developmental biology to describe the cellular and molecular mechanisms by which complex nervous systems emerge during embryonic development and throughout life.
Digestive system	The digestive system is the organ system that breaks down and absorbs nutrients that are essential for growth and maintenance. The digestive system includes the mouth, esophagus, stomach, pancreas, liver, gallbladder, duodenum, jejunum, ileum, intestines, rectum, and anus.
Binocular vision	Binocular vision is vision in which both eyes are used together. Having two eyes confers at least four advantages over having one: a spare eye in case one is damaged, a wider field of view, the enhanced ability to detect faint objects and can provide precise depth perception.
Amblyopia	Amblyopia is a disorder of the eye that is characterized by poor or indistinct vision in an eye that is otherwise physically normal, or out of proportion to associated structural abnormalities. It has been estimated to affect 1–5% of the population.
Retinal disparity	A binocular cue for depth based on the difference in the image cast by an object on the retinas of the eyes as the object moves closer or farther away, is called retinal disparity.
Sensitive period	Sensitive periods is a term coined by the Dutch geneticist Hugo de Vries and adopted by the Italian educator Maria Montessori to refer to important periods of childhood development. During a sensitive period it is very easy for children to acquire certain abilities, such as language, discrimination of sensory stimuli, and mental modeling of the environment.
Strabismus	Strabismus is a condition in which the eyes are not properly aligned with each other. It typically involves a lack of coordination between the extraocular muscles that prevents bringing the gaze of each eye to the same point in space and preventing proper binocular vision, which may adversely affect depth perception.
Depth perception	Depth perception is the visual ability to perceive the world in three dimensions. It is a trait common to many higher animals. Depth perception allows the beholder to accurately gauge the distance to an object.
Astigmatism	Astigmatism is a defect of the eye, where vision is blurred by an irregularly shaped cornea. The cornea, instead of being shaped like a sphere, is ellipsoidal and reduces the cornea"s ability to focus light. Astigmatism is a refractive error of the eye in which there is a difference in degree of refraction in different meridians.

211

Gamma-aminobutyric acid	Gamma-aminobutyric acid is an inhibitory neurotransmitter found in the nervous systems of widely-divergent species. It is the chief inhibitory neurotransmitter in the central nervous system and also in the retina.
Cataract	A Cataract is a clouding that develops in the crystalline lens of the eye or in its envelope, varying in degree from slight to complete opacity and obstructing the passage of light. Early in the development of age-related Cataract the power of the lens may be increased, causing near-sightedness (myopia), and the gradual yellowing and opacification of the lens may reduce the perception of blue colours. Cataract s typically progress slowly to cause vision loss and are potentially blinding if untreated.
Cataracts	A cataract is any opacity which develops in the crystalline lens of the eye or in its envelope. Cataracts form for a variety of reasons, including long term ultraviolet exposure, secondary effects of diseases such as diabetes, or simply due to advanced age.
Lateralization	Lateralization of brain functions is evident in the phenomena of right- or left-handedness, -earedness and -eyedness. Broad generalizations are often made in popular psychology about certain function being lateralised, that is, located in the right or left side of the brain. These ideas need to be treated carefully because the popular lateralization is ften distributed across both sides. However, there is some division of mental processing.
Corpus callosum	The corpus callosum is a structure of the mammalian brain in the longitudal fissure that connects the left and right cerebral hemispheres. Much of the inter-hemispheric communication in the brain is conducted across the corpus callosum.

Sensory system	A sensory system is a part of the nervous system responsible for processing sensory information. A sensory system consists of sensory receptors, neural pathways, and parts of the brain involved in sensory perception The receptive field is the specific part of the world to which a receptor organ and receptor cells respond.
Amplitude	The amplitude is a nonnegative scalar measure of a wave"s magnitude of oscillation, that is, the magnitude of the maximum disturbance in the medium during one wave cycle.
Audition	An Audition is a sample performance by an actor, singer, musician, dancer or other performer. It involves the performer displaying their talent through a previously-memorized and rehearsed solo piece: for example, a monologue for actors or a song for a singer. Used in the context of performing arts, it is analogous to job interviews in many ways.
Ear	The ear is the sense organ that detects sounds. The vertebrate ear shows a common biology from fish to humans, with variations in structure according to order and species. It not only acts as a receiver for sound, but plays a major role in the sense of balance and body position. The ear is part of the auditory system.
Frequency	In statistics the frequency of an event i is the number ni of times the event occurred in the experiment or the study. These frequencies are often graphically represented in histograms.
Hertz	The hertz is the International System of Units base unit of frequency. Its base unit is cycle/s or s-1. In English, hertz is used as both singular and plural. As any SI unit, Hz can be prefixed; commonly used multiples are kHz, MHz, GHz and THz.
Loudness	Loudness is the quality of a sound that is the primary psychological correlate of physical intensity. Loudness is often approximated by a power function with an exponent of 0.6 when plotted vs. sound pressure or 0.3 when plotted vs. sound intensity.
Pitch	Pitch is the psychological interpretation of a sound or musical tone corresponding to its physical frequency
Sound	Sound is generally known as vibrational transmission of mechanical energy that propagates through matter as a wave that can be audibly perceived by a living organism through its sense of hearing.
Experience	Experience as a general concept comprises knowledge of or skill in or observation of some thing or some event gained through involvement in or exposure to that thing or event. The history of the word experience aligns it closely with the concept of experiment.
Other	The Other or constitutive Other is a key concept in continental philosophy, opposed to the Same. It refers, or attempts to refer, to that which is "Other" than the concept being considered. The term often means a person Other than oneself, and is often capitalised.

Perception	In psychology. and the cognitive sciences, perception is the process of acquiring, interpreting, selecting, and organizing sensory information. It is a task far more complex than was imagined in the 1950s and 1960s, when it was proclaimed that building perceiving machines would take about a decade, but, needless to say, that is still very far from reality.
Stimulus	In psychology, a stimulus is part of the stimulus-response relationship of behavioral learning theory.
Structure	Structure is a fundamental and sometimes intangible notion covering the recognition, observation, nature, and stability of patterns and relationships of entities.
Oval window	The oval window is a membrane-covered opening which leads from the middle ear to the vestibule of the inner ear.
Pinna	The pinna is the visible outer ear which is comprised of skin and cartilage. The main functions of the pinna are the collection of sound waves into the middle and inner ears, and to assist in heat dissipation.
Cartilage	Cartilage is a type of dense connective tissue.
Eardrum	The tympanum or tympanic membrane, colloquially known as the eardrum, is a thin membrane that separates the outer ear from the middle ear. Its function is to transmit sound from the air to the ossicles inside the middle ear. The malleus bone connects the eardrum to the other ossicles.
Scolex	The Scolex of the worm attaches to the intestine of the definitive host. In some groups, the scolex is dominated by bothria, which are sometimes called "sucking grooves," and function like suction cups.
Inner ear	The inner ear is the anatomical area of the hearing system which triggers nerve impulses that travel towards the brain. The hearing and balance systems can be found within the inner ear.
Stapes	The stapes is the small bone or ossicle in the middle ear which attaches the incus to the fenestra ovalis, the "oval window" which is adjacent to the vestibule of the inner ear. It is the smallest and lightest bone in the human body.
Basilar membrane	The basilar membrane within the cochlea of the inner ear is the part of the auditory system that decomposes incoming auditory signals into their frequency components. This allows higher neural processing of sound information to focus on the frequency spectrum of input, rather than just the time domain waveform.
Cochlea	The Cochlea is the bony tube that contains the basilar membrane and the organ of Corti. The cochlea consists of three fluid-filled chambers - scala tympani and scala vestibuli and scala media.

Frequency theory	Békésy's theory that the pitch of a sound is reflected in the frequency of the neural impulses that are generated in response to the sound is called frequency theory. However, frequences above 1000 Hz nerve impulses cannot follow the wave form.
Place theory	Place theory is a theory of hearing which states that our perception of sound depends on where each component frequency produces vibrations along the basilar membrane. It was first discovered by Helmholtz.
Tectorial membrane	Covering the sulcus spiralis internus and the spiral organ of Corti is the tectorial membrane, which is attached to the limbus laminae spiralis close to the inner edge of the vestibular membrane.
Action potential	An action potential is a "spike" of electrical discharge that travels along the membrane of a cell.
Activity level	Activity level is a way to express your daily physical activity in a number. This number is defined as a multiple of your Basal metabolic rate, which is the amount of energy you consume while inactive.
Hearing	Hearing is one of the traditional five senses, and refers to the ability to detect sound. In humans and other vertebrates, hearing is performed primarily by the system: sound is detected by the ear and transduced into nerve impulses that are perceived by the brain.
Concept	A Concept is a cognitive unit of meaning-- an abstract idea or a mental symbol sometimes defined as a "unit of knowledge," built from other units which act as a Concept"s characteristics. A Concept is typically associated with a corresponding representation in a language or symbology such as a word. The meaning of "Concept" is explored in mainstream cognitive science and philosophy of mind.
Hair	Hair is a filamentous outgrowth of protein, found only on mammals. It projects from the epidermis, though it grows from hair follicles deep in the dermis.
Hair cells	Hair cells are the sensory receptors of both the auditory system and the vestibular system in all vertebrates. In mammals, the auditory hair cells are located within the organ of Corti on a thin basilar membrane in the cochlea of the inner ear.
Receptor	A sensory receptor is a structure that recognizes a stimulus in the internal or external environment of an organism. In response to stimuli the sensory receptor initiates sensory transduction by creating graded potentials or action potentials in the same cell or in an adjacent one.
Sensory receptor	A sensory receptor is a structure that recognizes a stimulus in the environment of an organism. In response to stimuli the sensory receptor initiates sensory transduction by creating graded potentials or action potentials in the same cell or in an adjacent one.
Amusia	Amusia refers to a number of disorders which are indicated by the inability to recognize musical tones or rhythms or to reproduce them. Amusia can be congenital or be acquired sometime later in life.

219

Tone deaf	A person who is Tone deaf lacks relative pitch, the ability to discriminate between musical notes. Being tone deaf is having difficulty or being unable to correctly hear relative differences between notes; however, in common usage, it refers to a person"s inability to reproduce them accurately.
Primary	In medicine, the reporting of symptoms by a patient may have significant psychological motivators. Psychologists sometimes categorize these motivators into primary or secondary gain. primary gain is internally good; motivationally.
Primary auditory cortex	The primary auditory cortex is the region of the brain that is responsible for processing of auditory information.
Cerebral cortex	The cerebral cortex is a structure within the vertebrate brain with distinct structural and functional properties.
Cerebral hemisphere	A Cerebral hemisphere (hemispherium cerebrale) is defined as one of the two regions of the brain that are delineated by the body"s median plane, (medial longitudinal fissure.) The brain can thus be described as being divided into left and right Cerebral hemisphere s. Each of these hemispheres has an outer layer of grey matter called the cerebral cortex that is supported by an inner layer of white matter.
Lobes	The four major sections of the cerebral cortex: frontal, parietal, temporal, and occipital are called lobes.
Particular	In philosophy, Particulars are concrete entities existing in space and time as opposed to abstractions. There are, however, theories of abstract Particulars or tropes. For example, Socrates is a Particular (there"s only one Socrates-the-teacher-of-Plato and one cannot make copies of him, e.g., by cloning him, without introducing new, distinct Particulars).
Temporal lobe	The temporal lobe is part of the cerebrum. It lies at the side of the brain, beneath the lateral or Sylvian fissure. Adjacent areas in the superior, posterior and lateral parts of the temporal lobe are involved in high-level auditory processing.
Conductive deafness	The forms of deafness in which there is loss of conduction of sound through the middle ear is referred to as conductive deafness.
Hearing impairment	A hearing impairment is a full or partial decrease in the ability to detect or understand sounds.[1] Caused by a wide range of biological and environmental factors, loss of hearing can happen to any organism that perceives sound.
Meningitis	Meningitis is inflammation of the membranes covering the brain and the spinal cord. Although the most common causes are infection (bacterial, viral, fungal or parasitic), chemical agents and even tumor cells may cause meningitis.

Nerve deafness	Deafness caused by damage to the hair cells or auditory nerve is nerve deafness.
Prenatal development	Prenatal development is the process in which an embryo or fetus gestates during pregnancy, from fertilization until birth.
Rubella	Rubella is a disease caused by the rubella virus. It is often mild and an attack can pass unnoticed. However, this can make the virus difficult to diagnose.
Sound localization	Sound localization is a listener"s ability to identify the location or origin of a detected sound or the methods in acoustical engineering to simulate the placement of an auditory cue in a virtual 3D space. There are two general methods for sound localization, binaural cues and monaural cues.
Syphilis	Syphilis is a curable sexually transmitted disease caused by the Treponema pallidum spirochete. The route of transmission of syphilis is almost always by sexual contact, although there are examples of congenital syphilis via transmission from mother to child in utero. The signs and symptoms of syphilis are numerous; before the advent of serological testing, precise diagnosis was very difficult.
Thyroid	In anatomy, the thyroid is the largest endocrine gland in the body. The primary function of the thyroid is production of hormones.
Tinnitus	Tinnitus, "ringing ears" or ear noise is a phenomenon of the nervous system connected to the ear, characterized by perception of a ringing, beating or roaring sound (often perceived as sinusoidal) with no external source.
Alcoholism	Alcoholism is a term with multiple and sometimes conflicting definitions. In common and historic usage, alcoholism refers to any condition that results in the continued consumption of alcoholic beverages despite the health problems and negative social consequences it causes.
Auditory nerve	The vestibulocochlear nerve is the eighth of twelve cranial nerves, and also known as the auditory nerve. It is the nerve along which the sensory cells (the hair cells) of the inner ear transmit information to the brain. It consists of the cochlear nerve, carrying information about hearing, and the vestibular nerve, carrying information about balance.
Constant	A constant is something that does not change, over time or otherwise: a fixed value. In most fields of discourse the term is an antonym of "variable", but in mathematical parlance a mathematical variable may sometimes also be called a constant.
Failure	Failure refers to the state or condition of not meeting a desirable or intended objective.
Hormone	A hormone is a chemical messenger that carries a signal from one cell to another. All multicellular organisms produce hormone s.

Middle ear	The middle ear is the portion of the ear internal to the eardrum, and external to the oval window of the cochlea. The mammalian middle ear contains three ossicles, which couple vibration of the eardrum into waves in the fluid and membranes of the inner ear.
Shadow	In Jungian psychology, the Shadow or "Shadow aspect" is a part of the unconscious mind consisting of repressed weaknesses, shortcomings, and instincts. It is one of the three most recognizable archetypes, the others being the anima and animus and the persona. "Everyone carries a Shadow," Jung wrote, "and the less it is embodied in the individual"s conscious life, the blacker and denser it is." It may be (in part) one"s link to more primitive animal instincts, which are superseded during early childhood by the conscious mind.
Positron emission tomography	Positron emission tomography is a nuclear medicine medical imaging technique which produces a three-dimensional image or map of functional processes in the body. Images of metabolic activity in space are then reconstructed by computer, often in modern scanners aided by results from a CT X-ray scan.
Tim	TIM is a series of lesser-known psychedelic drugs similar in structure to mescaline. They were first synthesized by Alexander Shulgin. In his book PiHKAL (Phenethylamines i Have Known And Loved), none of their durations are known.
Otolith	The otolith organs (the utricle and the saccule) are structures in the inner ear that are sensitive to gravity and linear acceleration. Because of their orientation in the head, the utricle is sensitive to a change in horizontal movement, and the saccule gives information about vertical acceleration (such as when in an elevator).
Saccule	Located within the vestibular system of the inner ear, the saccule is one of the otoliths which gathers sensory information to orient the body. The saccule primarily gathers sensory information about linear movement in the vertical plane.
Semicircular canal	The Semicircular canal s are three half-circular, interconnected tubes located inside each ear. The three canals are the horizontal Semicircular canal (also known as the lateral Semicircular canal , superior Semicircular canal (also known as the anterior Semicircular canal , and the posterior Semicircular canal The canals are aligned approximately orthogonally to one another.
Somatosensory	Somatosensory system consists of the various sensory receptors that trigger the experiences labelled as touch or pressure, temperature, pain, and the sensations of muscle movement and joint position including posture, movement, and facial expression.
Somatosensory system	The Somatosensory system is made up of the complex of sensations that are experienced by the skin and body. These sensations include the sense of pressure, temperature, pain, body position, and movement.

Utricle	The utricle, along with the saccule is one of the two otolith organs located in the vertebrate inner ear.
Cytoplasmic streaming	Cytoplasmic streaming is the flowing of cytoplasm in eukaryotic cells. This occurs in both plant and animal cells.
Plan	A Plan is typically any procedure used to achieve an objective. It is a set of intended actions, through which one expects to achieve a goal. Plan s can be formal or informal: · Structured and formal Plan s, used by multiple people, are more likely to occur in projects, diplomacy, careers, economic development, military campaigns, combat, or in the conduct of other business. · Informal or ad-hoc Plan s are created by individuals in all of their pursuits. The most popular ways to describe Plan s are by their breadth, time frame, and specificity; however, these Plan ning classifications are not independent of one another. For instance, there is a close relationship between the short-and long-term categories and the strategic and operational categories.
Sensation	Sensation is the first stage in the chain of biochemical and neurologic events that begins with the impinging of a stimulus upon the receptor cells of a sensory organ, which then leads to perception, the mental state that is reflected in statements like "I see a uniformly blue wall."
Sense	Sense are the physiological methods of perception. They and their operation, classification, and theory are overlapping topics studied by a variety of fields, most notably neuroscience, cognitive psychology, and philosophy of perception. The nervous system has a sensory system dedicated to each sense.
Somatosensation	Somatosensation consists of the various sensory receptors that trigger the experiences labelled as touch or pressure, temperature (warm or cold), pain (including itch and tickle), and the sensations of muscle movement and joint position including posture, movement, and facial expression (collectively also called proprioception).
Capsaicin	Capsaicin is the active component of chilli peppers, which are plants belonging to the genus Capsicum. It is an irritant for mammals, including humans, and produces a sensation of burning in any tissue with which it comes into contact.
Lateralization	Lateralization of brain functions is evident in the phenomena of right- or left-handedness, -earedness and -eyedness. Broad generalizations are often made in popular psychology about certain function being lateralised, that is, located in the right or left side of the brain. These ideas need to be treated carefully because the popular lateralization is ften distributed across both sides. However, there is some division of mental processing.

227

Learning	Learning is the acquisition and development of memories and behaviors, including skills, knowledge, understanding, values, and wisdom. It is the goal of education, and the product of experience. Learning ranges from simple forms such as habituation to more complex forms such as play, seen only in large vertebrates.
Memory	In psychology, memory is an organism"s ability to store, retain, and subsequently retrieve information. In recent decades, it has become one of the principal pillars of a branch of science called cognitive neuroscience, an interdisciplinary link between cognitive psychology and neuroscience.
Ruffini ending	The Ruffini ending is a class of slowly adapting mechanoreceptor thought to exist only in the glabrous dermis and subcutaneous tissue of humans. It is named after Angelo Ruffini.
Skin	In zootomy and dermatology, skin is the largest organ of the integumentary system made up of multiple layers of epithelial tissues that guard underlying muscles and organs.
Brain	In animals, the brain, is the control center of the central nervous system, responsible for behavior. The brain is located in the head, protected by the skull and close to the primary sensory apparatus of vision, hearing, equilibrioception, sense of acceleration, taste, and olfaction.
Neural development	The study of neural development draws on both neuroscience and developmental biology to describe the cellular and molecular mechanisms by which complex nervous systems emerge during embryonic development and throughout life.
Chemical	A chemical is a material with a definite chemical composition. All samples of a compound have the same composition; that is, all samples have the same proportions, by mass, of the elements present in the compound.
Displacement	In psychology, displacement is a subconscious defense mechanism whereby the mind redirects affects from an object felt to be dangerous or unacceptable to an object felt to be safe or acceptable.
Gorilla	The Gorilla is the largest of the living primates. They are ground-dwelling omnivores that inhabit the forests of Africa.
Mammal	A mammal is a warm-blooded, vertebrate animal, characterized by the presence of sweat glands, including milk producing sweat glands, and by the presence of: hair, three middle ear bones used in hearing, and a neocortex region in the brain. Most also possess specialized teeth and utilize a placenta in the ontogeny. A mammal encompass approximately 5,400 species, distributed in about 1,200 genera, 153 families, and 29 orders, though this varies by classification scheme.
Pain	Pain is an unpleasant sensation. It is defined by the International Association for the Study of Pain as "an unpleasant sensory and emotional experience associated with actual or potential tissue damage, or described in terms of such damage".

Substance P	In neuroscience, Substance P is a neuropeptide: a short-chain polypeptide that functions as a neurotransmitter and as a neuromodulator. It belongs to the tachykinin neuropeptide family.
Bipolar disorder	Bipolar disorder is a psychiatric condition defined as recurrent episodes of significant disturbance in mood. These disturbances can occur on a spectrum that ranges from debilitating depression to unbridled mania. Individuals suffering from bipolar disorder typically experience fluid states of mania, hypomania or what is referred to as a mixed state in conjunction with depressive episodes.
Central nervous system	The central nervous system represents the largest part of the nervous system, including the brain and the spinal cord. Together with the peripheral nervous system, it has a fundamental role in the control of behavior. The CNS is contained within the dorsal cavity, with the brain within the cranial subcavity, and the spinal cord in the spinal cavity. The CNS is covered by the meninges. The brain is also protected by the skull, and the spinal cord is also protected by the vertebrae.
Dermatome	A Dermatome is an area of skin that is mainly supplied by a single spinal nerve. There are eight cervical nerves, twelve thoracic nerves, five lumbar nerves and five sacral nerves. Each of these nerves relays sensation (including pain) from a particular region of skin to the brain.
Spinal cord	The spinal cord is a thin, tubular bundle of nerves that is an extension of the central nervous system from the brain and is enclosed in and protected by the bony vertebral column. The main function of the spinal cord is transmission of neural inputs between the periphery and the brain.
Spinal nerve	The term spinal nerve generally refers to the mixed spinal nerve, which is formed from the dorsal and ventral roots that come out of the spinal cord. The spinal nerve passes out of the vertebrae through the intervertebral foramen.
Animal testing	Animal testing refers to the use of animals in experiments. It is estimated that 50 to 100 million vertebrate animals worldwide — from zebrafish to non-human primates — are used annually and either killed during the experiments or subsequently euthanized.
Muscle	Muscle is contractile tissue of the body and is derived from the mesodermal layer of embryonic germ cells. It is classified as skeletal, cardiac, or smooth muscle, and its function is to produce force and cause motion, either locomotion or movement within internal organs.
Postcentral gyrus	The lateral postcentral gyrus is a prominent structure in the parietal lobe of the human brain and an important landmark. It was initially defined from surface stimulation studies of Penfield, and parallel surface potential studies of Bard, Woolsey, and Marshall.
Posterior	In reference to the anatomical terms of location, the posterior end is laterally situated at or toward the hinder part of the body, lying at or extending toward the right or left side. It is the polar opposite to the anterior end, or front end of the body.

Axon	An axon is a long, slender projection of a nerve cell, or neuron, that conducts electrical impulses away from the neuron"s cell body or soma.
Brain damage	Brain damage is the destruction or degeneration of brain cells. It may occur due to a wide range of conditions, illnesses, injuries, and as a result of iatrogenesis. Possible causes of widespread brain damage include prolonged hypoxia, poisoning by teratogens, infection, and neurological illness.
Cutaneous rabbit illusion	The Cutaneous rabbit illusion is a tactile illusion evoked by tapping two separate regions of the skin. Many experiments demonstrating the effect have been carried out on the forearm. A rapid sequence of taps delivered first near the wrist, and then near the elbow creates the sensation of sequential taps hopping up the arm from the wrist towards the elbow, although no physical stimulus was applied between the two actual stimulus locations.
Dopamine hypothesis of schizophrenia	The dopamine hypothesis of schizophrenia is a model attributing symptoms of schizophrenia to a disturbed and hyperactive dopaminergic signal transduction. The model draws evidence from the observation that a large number of antipsychotics have DA-antagonistic effects. The theory, however, does not posit dopamine overabundance as a complete explanation for schizophrenia.
Prefrontal cortex	The prefrontal cortex is the anterior part of the frontal lobes of the brain, lying in front of the motor and premotor areas. Cytoarchitectonically, it is defined by the presence of an internal granular layer IV.
Somatosensory cortex	The primary somatosensory cortex is across the central sulcus and behind the primary motor cortex configured to generally correspond with the arrangement of nearby motor cells related to specific body parts. It is the main sensory receptive area for the sense of touch.
Amnesia	Amnesia is a condition in which memory is disturbed. The causes of amnesia are organic or functional. Organic causes include damage to the brain, through trauma or disease, or use of certain generally sedative drugs.
Anterior	Anterior is an anatomical term referring to the front part of the body. The anterior is positioned in front of another body part, or towards the head of an animal. It is the opposite of posterior.
Appetite	The appetite is the desire to eat food, felt as hunger. Appetite exists in all higher lifeforms, and serves to regulate adequate energy intake to maintain metabolic needs. It is regulated by a close interplay between the digestive tract, adipose tissue and the brain. Decreased desire to eat is termed anorexia, while polyphagia or "hyperphagia" is increased eating. Disregulation of appetite contributes to anorexia nervosa, bulimia nervosa, cachexia, overeating, and binge eating disorder.
Confusion	Severe confusion of a degree considered pathological usually refers to loss of orientation, and often memory. Confusion as such is not synonymous with inability to focus attention, although severe inability to focus attention can cause, or greatly contribute to, confusion.

Delusion	A false belief, not generally shared by others, and that cannot be changed despite strong evidence to the contrary is a delusion.
Depression	In everyday language depression refers to any downturn in mood, which may be relatively transitory and perhaps due to something trivial.
Disease	A Disease or medical problem is an abnormal condition of an organism that impairs bodily functions, associated with specific symptoms and signs. It may be caused by external factors, such as invading organisms, or it may be caused by internal dysfunctions, such as autoimmune Disease s. In human beings, Disease is often used more broadly to refer to any condition that causes extreme pain, dysfunction, distress, social problems, and/or death to the person afflicted, or similar problems for those in contact with the person.
Software extension	A Software extension is a computer program designed to be incorporated into another piece of software in order to enhance the functionalities of the latter. On its own, the program is not useful or functional. Examples of software applications that support extensions include the Mozilla Firefox Web browser, Adobe Systems Photoshop and Microsoft Windows Explorer shell extensions.
Frontal lobe	The frontal lobe comprises four major folds of cortical tissue: the precentral gyrus, superior gyrus and the middle gyrus of the frontal gyri, the inferior frontal gyrus. It has been found to play a part in impulse control, judgement, language, memory, motor function, problem solving, sexual behavior, socialization and spontaneity.
Generation	Generation, also known as procreation, is the act of producing offspring. A generation can also be a stage or degree in a succession of natural descent as a grandfather, a father, and the father"s son comprise three generations.
Glutamate	Glutamate is one of the 20 standard amino acids used by all organisms in their proteins. It is critical for proper cell function, but it is not an essential nutrient in humans because it can be manufactured from other compounds.
Hallucination	A hallucination is a sensory perception experienced in the absence of an external stimulus, as distinct from an illusion, which is a misperception of an external stimulus. They may occur in any sensory modality - visual, auditory, olfactory, gustatory, tactile, or mixed.
Hindbrain	The hindbrain is a developmental categorization of portions of the central nervous system in vertebrates. It can be subdivided in a variable number of transversal swellings called rhombomeres.
Medulla	Medulla refers to the middle of something, and derives from the Latin word for "marrow" In medicine it refers to either bone marrow, the spinal cord, or more generally, the middle part of a structure as opposed to the cortex.
Memory loss	Memory loss can have many causes:

235

· Alzheimer"s disease is an illness which can cause mild to severe memory loss
· Parkinson"s disease is a genetic defect which may result in memory loss
· Huntington"s disease is an inherited disease which can result in memory loss
· It is sometimes a side effect of chemotherapy in which cytotoxic drugs are used to treat cancer.
· Certain forms of mental illness also have memory loss as a key symptom, including fugue states and the much more famous Dissociative Identity Disorder.
· Stress-related activities are another factor which can result in memory loss
· It can also be caused by traumatic brain injury, of which a concussion is a form. .

Need	A Need is something that is necessary for humans to live a healthy life. Need s are distinguished from wants because a deficiency would cause a clear negative outcome, such as dysfunction or death. Need s can be objective and physical, such as food and water, or they can be subjective and psychological, such as the Need for self-esteem.
Neurotransmitter	A neurotransmitter is a chemical that is used to relay, amplify and modulate electrical signals between a neurons and another cell.
Rabbit	The rabbit is a small mammal in he family Leporidae of the order Lagomorpha, found in several parts of the world. It is a ground dweller that lives in environments ranging from desert to tropical forest and wetland. It"s long ears are most likely an adaptation for detecting predators. In addition to their prominent ears, which can measure up to 6 cm long, it has long, powerful hind legs and a short tail.
Schizophrenia	Schizophrenia is a psychiatric diagnosis that describes a mental illness characterized by impairments in the perception or expression of reality, most commonly manifesting as auditory hallucinations, paranoid or bizarre delusions or disorganized speech and thinking in the context of significant social or occupational dysfunction.
Signal	In the fields of communications, signal processing, and in electrical engineering more generally, a signal is any time-varying quantity. Signals are often scalar-valued functions of time, but may be vector valued and may be functions of any other relevant independent variable.
Single	In relationships, a single person is one who is not married, or, more broadly, who is not in an exclusive romantic relationship.
Insomnia	Insomnia is a sleep disorder characterized by an inability to sleep and/or inability to remain asleep for a reasonable period.
Synapse	A synapse is specialized junction through which cells of the nervous system signal to one another and to non-neuronal cells such as muscles or glands. They allow the neurons of the central nervous system to form interconnected neural circuits.

237

Synapses	Chemical synapses are specialized junctions through which neurons signal to each other and to non-neuronal cells such as those in muscles or glands. Chemical synapses allow neurons to form circuits within the central nervous system. They are crucial to the biological computations that underlie perception and thought.
Amygdala	Amygdala are almond-shaped groups of neurons located deep within the medial temporal lobes of the brain in complex vertebrates, including humans. Shown in research to perform a primary role in the processing and memory of emotional reactions, the amygdala are considered part of the limbic system.
Cingulate cortex	The cingulate cortex is a part of the brain situated in the medial aspect of the cortex. It is extended from the corpus callosum below to the cingulate sulcus above, at least anteriorly.
Endorphin	An endorphin is an endogenous opioid biochemical compound. They are peptides produced by the pituitary gland and the hypothalamus, and they resemble the opiates in their abilities to produce analgesia and a sense of well-being. In other words, they work as "natural pain killers."
Hippocampus	The hippocampus is a part of the brain located in the medial temporal lobe. It forms a part of the limbic system and plays a part in memory and spatial navigation.
Opiate	In medicine, the term Opiate describes any of the narcotic alkaloids found in opium.
Opioid	An opioid is any agent that binds to opioid receptors, found principally in the central nervous system and gastrointestinal tract.
Thalamus	An area near the center of the brain involved in the relay of sensory information to the cortex and in the functions of sleep and attention is the thalamus.
Brain stem	The brain stem is the lower part of the brain, adjoining and structurally continuous with the spinal cord. Most sources consider the pons, medulla oblongata, and midbrain all to be part of the brain stem.
Marxist aesthetics	Marxist aesthetics is a theory of aesthetics based on the theories of Karl Marx. It involves a dialectical approach to the application of Marxism to the cultural sphere, specifically areas related to taste such as art, beauty, etc. Marxists believe that economic and social conditions affect every aspect of an individual"s life, from religious beliefs to legal systems to cultural frameworks.
Discovery	Discovery observations form acts of detecting and learning something. Discovery observations are acts in which something is found and given a productive insight. Serendipity is the effect by which one accidentally discovers something fortunate, especially while looking for something else entirely.

Enkephalin	An Enkephalin is a pentapeptide involved in regulating nociception in the body. The Enkephalin s are termed endogenous ligands, or specifically endorphins, as they are internally derived and bind to the body"s opioid receptors. Discovered in 1975, two forms of Enkephalin were revealed, one containing leucine , and the other containing methionine ("met".)
Explanation	An explanation is a description which may clarify causes, context, and consequences of a certain object, and a phenomenon such as a process, a state of affairs. This description may establish rules or laws, and may clarify the existing ones in relation to an object, and a phenomenon examined. The components of an explanation can be implicit, and be interwoven with one another.
Prosencephalon	In the anatomy of the brain of vertebrates, the prosencephalon is the rostral-most portion of the brain. The prosencephalon, the mesencephalon, and rhombencephalon are the three primary portions of the brain during early development of the central nervous system.
Mechanism	In philosophy, mechanism is a theory that all natural phenomena can be explained by physical causes. It can be contrasted with vitalism, the philosophical theory that vital forces are active in living organisms, so that life cannot be explained solely by mechanism.
Opiates	A group of narcotics derived from the opium poppy that provide a euphoric rush and depress the nervous system are referred to as opiates.
Opium	Opium is a narcotic analgesic drug which is obtained from the unripe seed pods of the opium poppy. Regular use, even for a few days, invariably leads to physical tolerance and dependence. Various degrees of psychological addiction can occur, though this is relatively rare when opioids are properly used..
Species	Species refers to a reproductively isolated breeding population.
Understanding	Understanding is a psychological process related to an abstract or physical object, such as, person, situation, or message whereby one is able to think about it and use concepts to deal adequately with that object.
Gate theory	The gate theory of pain, put forward by Ron Melzack and Patrick Wall in 1962, is the idea that pain is not a direct result of activation of pain receptor neurons, but rather its perception is modulated by interaction between different neurons.
Morphine	Morphine, the principal active agent in opium, is a powerful opioid analgesic drug. According to recent research, it may also be produced naturally by the human brain. Morphine is usually highly addictive, and tolerance and physical and psychological dependence develop quickly.

PKU | Phenylketonuria (PKU) is an autosomal recessive genetic disorder characterized by a deficiency in the autozome phenylalanine hydroxylase (PAH.) This enzyme is necessary to metabolize the amino acid phenylalanine to the amino acid tyrosine. When PAH is deficient, phenylalanine accumulates and is converted into phenylpyruvate (also known as phenylketone), which is detected in the urine.

Message | A message in its most general meaning is an object of communication.

Stimulation | Stimulation is the action of various agents on muscles, nerves, or a sensory end organ, by which activity is evoked.

Transmission | In medicine, transmission is the passing of a disease from an infected individual or group to a previously uninfected individual or group.

Cannabinoids | Cannabinoids are a group of terpenophenolic compounds present in Cannabis. The broader definition of cannabinoids refer to a group of substances that are structurally related to tetrahydrocannabinol or that bind to cannabinoid receptors. The chemical definition encompasses a variety of distinct chemical classes: the classical cannabinoids structurally related to THC, the nonclassical cannabinoids, the aminoalkylindoles, the eicosanoids related to the endocannabinoids, 1,5-diarylpyrazoles, quinolines and arylsulphonamides and additional compounds that do not fall into these standard classes but bind to cannabinoid receptors.

Histamine | Histamine is a biogenic amine involved in local immune responses as well as regulating physiological function in the gut and acting as a neurotransmitter. It has been found that about half the patients classified as suffering from schizophrenia have low histamine levels in the blood. This may be because of antipsychotics that have unwanted effect on histamine, such as Quetiapine.

Itch | Itch is an unpleasant sensation that evokes the desire or reflex to scratch. Itch has resisted many attempts to classify it as any one type of sensory experience. Modern science has shown that Itch has many similarities to pain, and while both are unpleasant sensory experiences, their behavioral response patterns are different.

Nerve | A Nerve is an enclosed, cable-like bundle of peripheral axons (the long, slender projections of neurons.) A Nerve provides a common pathway for the electrochemical Nerve impulses that are transmitted along each of the axons. Nerve s are found only in the peripheral nervous system.

Nerve growth factor | Nerve growth factor, is a small secreted protein which induces the differentiation and survival of particular target neurons. It is perhaps the prototypical growth factor, in that it is one of the first to be described - that work by Rita Levi-Montalcini and Stanley Cohen was rewarded with a Nobel Prize.

Marijuana | Marijuana is the dried vegetable matter of the Cannabis sativa plant. It contains large concentrations of compounds that have medicinal and psychoactive effects when consumed, usually by smoking or eating.

Protein	A protein is a complex, high-molecular-weight organic compound that consists of amino acids joined by peptide bonds. It is essential to the structure and function of all living cells and viruses. Many are enzymes or subunits of enzymes.
Self preservation	Self preservation is part of an animal"s instinct that demands that the organism survives.
Sympathetic	The sympathetic nervous system activates what is often termed the "fight or flight response". It is an automatic regulation system, that is, one that operates without the intervention of conscious thought.
Sympathetic nervous system	The Sympathetic nervous system is a branch of the autonomic nervous system. It is always active at a basal level and becomes more active during times of stress. Its actions during the stress response comprise the fight-or-flight response. The sympathetic nervous system is responsible for up- and down-regulating many homeostatic mechanisms in living organisms.
Antihistamine	A histamine antagonist is an agent that serves to inhibit the release or action of histamine. Antihistamine can be used to describe any histamine antagonist, but it is usually reserved for the classical Antihistamine s that act upon the H_1 histamine receptor.
	Antihistamine s are used as treatment for allergies.
Amino acid	Amino acid is the basic structural building unit of proteins. They form short polymer chains called peptides or polypeptides which in turn form structures called proteins.
Cerebrovascular accident	Cerebrovascular accident refers to a sudden stoppage of blood flow to a portion of the brain, leading to a loss of brain function.
Coding	In sensation, Coding is the process by which information about the quality and quantity of a stimulus is preserved in the pattern of action potentials sent through sensory neurons to the central nervous system.
Principle	In user interface design, programming language design, and ergonomics, the principle of least astonishment (or surprise) states that, when two elements of an interface conflict the behaviour should be that which will least surprise the human user or programmer at the time the conflict arises.
	For example:
	A user interface may have the behaviour that pressing Control-Q causes the program to quit. The same user interface may have a facility for recording macros, a sequence of keystrokes to be played back later, intended to be able to control all aspects of the program.
Range	In descriptive statistics, the range is the length of the smallest interval which contains all the data. It is calculated by subtracting the smallest observations from the greatest and provides an indication of statistical dispersion.

Taste bud	The taste bud is a small structure on the upper surface of the tongue that provides information about the taste of food being eaten. It is known that there are five taste sensations: Sweet, Bitter, Umami, Salty and Sour.
Taste buds	Taste buds are small structures on the upper surface of the tongue, soft palate, upper esophagus and epiglottis that provide information about the taste of food being eaten. These structures are involved in detecting the five elements of taste perception: salty, sour, bitter, sweet, and umami (or savory.) Via small openings in the tongue epithelium, called taste pores, parts of the food dissolved in saliva come into contact with the taste receptors.
Tongue	The tongue is the large bundle of skeletal muscles on the floor of the mouth that manipulates food for chewing and swallowing. It is the primary organ of taste. The tongue, with its wide variety of possible movements, assists in forming the sounds of speech. It is sensitive and kept moist by saliva, and is richly supplied with nerves and blood vessels to help it move.
Taste receptor	A Taste receptor is a type of receptor which facilitates the sensation of taste. Examples include TAS2R16 and TAS2R38. They are divided into two families: · Type 1, sweet, first characterized in 2001: TAS1R1 - TAS1R3 · Type 2, bitter, first characterized in 2000: TAS2R1 - TAS2R50, and TAS2R60 .
Adaptation	An adaptation is a positive characteristic of an organism that has been favored by natural selection. The concept is central to biology, particularly in evolutionary biology. The term adaptation is also sometimes used as a synonym for natural selection, but most biologists discourage this usage.
Sodium	Sodium is a chemical element which has the symbol Na, atomic number 11, atomic mass 22.9898 g/mol, common oxidation number +1. Sodium is a soft, silvery white, highly reactive element and is a member of the alkali metals within "group 1". It has only one stable isotope, ^{23}Na.
Facial nerve	The facial nerve is the seventh of twelve paired cranial nerves. It emerges from the brainstem between the pons and the medulla, and controls the muscles of facial expression, and taste to the anterior two-thirds of the tongue. It also supplies preganglionic parasympathetic fibers to several head and neck ganglia.
Hypothalamus	The hypothalamus is a region of the brain located below the thalamus, forming the major portion of the ventral region of the diencephalon and functioning to regulate certain metabolic processes and other autonomic activities.
Insular cortex	The insular cortex is a structure of the human brain. It lies deep to the brain"s lateral surface, within the lateral sulcus which separates the temporal lobe and inferior parietal cortex.

Lateral hypothalamus	The Lateral hypothalamus is a part of the hypothalamus. The Lateral hypothalamus is concerned with hunger. Any damage sustained to the lateral hypothalamus can cause reduced food intake.
Nucleus	In neuroanatomy, a cluster of cell bodies of neurons within the central nervous system is a nucleus.
Pons	The pons is a structure located on the brain stem. It is rostral to the medulla oblongata, caudal to the midbrain, and ventral to the cerebellum. In humans and other bipeds this means it is above the medulla, below the midbrain, and anterior to the cerebellum.
Supertaster	A supertaster is a person who experiences taste with far greater intensity than average.
Antipsychotic	The term antipsychotic is applied to a group of drugs used to treat psychosis.
Antipsychotics	*Antipsychotics* are a group of psychoactive drugs commonly but not exclusively used to treat psychosis, which is typified by schizophrenia. Over time a wide range of *Antipsychotics* have been developed. A first generation of *Antipsychotics*, known as typical *Antipsychotics*, was discovered in the 1950s.
Chlorpromazine	Chlorpromazine is a phenothiazine antipsychotic. Its principal use is in the treatment of schizophrenia, though it has also been used to treat hiccups and nausea. Its use today has been largely supplanted by the newer atypical antipsychotics such as olanzapine and quetiapine. It works on a variety of receptors in the central nervous system; these include anticholinergic, antidopaminergic and antihistamine effects as well as some antagonism of adrenergic receptors.
Drinking	Drinking is the act of consuming a liquid through the mouth.
Eating	Eating is the process of consuming nutrition, i.e. food, for the purpose of providing for the nutritional needs of an animal, particularly their energy requirements and to grow.
Sensitivity	The sensitivity or insensitivity of a human, often considered with regard to a particular kind of stimulus, is the strength of the feeling it results in, in comparison with the strength of the stimulus. The concept applies to physical as well as emotional feeling.
Fungiform papillae	The fungiform papillae are mushroom shaped papillae on the tongue. They are located on the top surface of the tongue, scattered throughout the filiform papilla but mainly at the tip and lateral margins of the tongue. They have taste buds on their superior surface which can distinguish the five tastes: sweet, sour, bitter, salty, and umami. They have a core of connective tissue and the seventh cranial nerve innervates them.
Blood	Blood is a specialized biological fluid consisting of red blood cells.White blood cells also called leukocytes and platelets also called thrombocytes suspended in a complex fluid medium known as blood plasma.

Gland	A gland is an organ in an animal's body that synthesizes a substance for release such as hormones, often into the bloodstream or into cavities inside the body or its outer surface.
Cilium	A cilium is an organelle found in eukaryotic cells. A cilium is a thin, tail-like projection that extends approximately 5–10 micrometers outwards from the cell body.
Epithelium	Epithelium is a tissue composed of a layer of cells. Epithelium can be found lining internal or external free surfaces of the body. Functions of epithelial cells include secretion, absorption and protection.
Olfactory epithelium	The olfactory epithelium is a specialized epithelial tissue inside the nasal cavity that is involved in smell. The tissue is made of three types of cells: the olfactory receptor neurons which transduce the odor to electrical signals, the supporting cells which protect the neurons and secrete mucus, and the basal cells which are a type of stem cell that differentiate into olfactory receptor neurons to replace dead receptor neurons.
Olfactory bulb	The olfactory bulb is a structure of the vertebrate forebrain involved in olfaction, the perception of odors.
Androstenone	Androstenone is a steroid found in both male and female sweat and urine. It is also found in boar"s saliva, and in celery cytoplasm. Androstenone was the first mammalian pheromone to be identified.
Potassium	Potassium is the an essential mineral macronutrient and is the main intracellular ion for all types of cells. It is important in maintaining fluid and electrolyte balance in the body.
Brain size	When comparing different species, brain size does present a correlation with intelligence. For example, the ratio of brain weight to body weight for fish is 1:5000; for reptiles it is about 1:1500; for birds, 1:220; for most mammals, 1:180, and for humans, 1:50. However within the human species modern studies using MRI have shown that brain size shows substantial and consistent correlation with IQ among adults of the same sex
Cortisol	Cortisol is a corticosteroid hormone produced by the adrenal cortex. It is a vital hormone that is often referred to as the "stress hormone" as it is involved in the response to stress. It increases blood pressure, blood sugar levels and has an immunosuppressive action.
Menstrual cycle	The menstrual cycle is a recurring cycle of physiological changes that occurs in the females of several mammals, including human beings and other apes.
Sexual behavior	Human Sexual behavior refers to the manner in which humans experience and express their sexuality. It encompass a wide range of activities such as strategies to find or attract partners (mating and display behaviour), interactions between individuals, physical or emotional intimacy, and sexual contact. Although some cultures hold that sexual activity is acceptable only within marriage, extramarital sexual activities still takes place within such cultures.

Synesthesia	Synesthesia is a neurologically based phenomenon in which stimulation of one sensory or cognitive pathway leads to automatic, involuntary experiences in a second sensory or cognitive pathway. Synesthesia is also sometimes reported by individuals under the influence of psychedelic drugs, after a stroke, or as a consequence of blindness or deafness.
Vomeronasal organ	The vomeronasal organ is an auxiliary olfactory sense organ in some tetrapods. It is the first processing stage of the accessory olfactory system. In adults, it is located in the vomer bone, between the nose and the mouth. It develops from the nasal placode, at the anterior edge of the neural plate.
Adrenal cortex	Situated along the perimeter of the adrenal gland, the adrenal cortex mediates the stress response through the production of mineralocorticoids and glucocorticoids, including aldosterone and cortisol respectively. It is also a secondary site of androgen synthesis.
Affect	Affect refers to the experience of feeling or emotion. Affect is a key part of the process of an organism's interaction with stimuli. The word also refers sometimes to affect display, which is "a facial, vocal, or gestural behavior that serves as an indicator of affect."
CycL	CycL in computer science and artificial intelligence is an ontology language used by Doug Lenat"s Cyc artificial intelligence project. Ramanathan V. Guha was instrumental in the design of the language. There is a close variant of CycL known as MELD. The original version of CycL was a frame language, but the modern version is not.
Fertility	Fertility is the natural capability of giving life. As a measure, "Fertility Rate" is the number of children born per couple, person or population.
Metabolism	Metabolism is the biochemical modification of chemical compounds in living organisms and cells.
Olfactory receptor	Olfactory receptor s expressed in the cell membranes of Olfactory receptor neurons are responsible for the detection of odor molecules. Activated Olfactory receptor s are the initial player in a signal transduction cascade which ultimately produces a nerve impulse which is transmitted to the brain. These receptors are members of the class A rhodopsin-like family of G protein-coupled receptors (GPCRs.)
Olfactory receptors	Olfactory receptors are class A G protein-coupled receptor which play a role in signal transduction to olfactory receptor neurons.
Pheromone	A pheromone is a chemical that triggers a natural behavioral response in another member of the same species.

Acetic acid	Acetic acid, is an organic chemical compound, giving vinegar its sour taste and pungent smell. Its structural formula is represented as CH_3COOH.
Axon	An axon is a long, slender projection of a nerve cell, or neuron, that conducts electrical impulses away from the neuron"s cell body or soma.
Cardiac muscle	Cardiac muscle is a type of involuntary striated muscle found within the heart. Its function is to "pump" blood through the circulatory system through muscular contraction. Cardiac muscle exhibits cross striations formed by alternation segments of thick and thin protein filaments which are anchored by segments called T-lines.
Muscle	Muscle is contractile tissue of the body and is derived from the mesodermal layer of embryonic germ cells. It is classified as skeletal, cardiac, or smooth muscle, and its function is to produce force and cause motion, either locomotion or movement within internal organs.
Myasthenia gravis	Myasthenia gravis is a neuromuscular disease leading to fluctuating muscle weakness and fatiguability. It is an autoimmune disorder, in which weakness is caused by circulating antibodies that block acetylcholine receptors at the post-synaptic neuromuscular junction, inhibiting the stimulative effect of the neurotransmitter acetylcholine.
Neuromuscular junction	A neuromuscular junction is the synapse or junction of the axon terminal of a motoneuron with the motor end plate, the highly-excitable region of muscle fiber plasma membrane responsible for initiation of action potentials across the muscle"s surface, ultimately causing the muscle to contract.
Skeleton	In biology, the skeleton provides a strong, internal framework that supports the body, makes up about 20 percent of its weight, and consists of 206 bones. These bones meet at joints, the majority of which are freely movable, making the skeleton flexible and mobile. The skeleton also contains cartilage.
Skeletal muscle	Skeletal muscle is a type of striated muscle, attached to the skeleton. They are used to facilitate movement, by applying force to bones and joints; via contraction. They generally contract voluntarily (via nerve stimulation), although they can contract involuntarily.
Acetylcholine	The chemical compound acetylcholine, often abbreviated as ACh, was the first neurotransmitter to be identified. It is a chemical transmitter in both the peripheral nervous system and central nervous system in many organisms including humans.
Acetylcholine receptor	An acetylcholine receptor is an integral membrane protein that responds to the binding of the neurotransmitter acetylcholine.
Constant	A constant is something that does not change, over time or otherwise: a fixed value. In most fields of discourse the term is an antonym of "variable", but in mathematical parlance a mathematical variable may sometimes also be called a constant.

Disease	A Disease or medical problem is an abnormal condition of an organism that impairs bodily functions, associated with specific symptoms and signs. It may be caused by external factors, such as invading organisms, or it may be caused by internal dysfunctions, such as autoimmune Disease s. In human beings, Disease is often used more broadly to refer to any condition that causes extreme pain, dysfunction, distress, social problems, and/or death to the person afflicted, or similar problems for those in contact with the person.
Software extension	A Software extension is a computer program designed to be incorporated into another piece of software in order to enhance the functionalities of the latter. On its own, the program is not useful or functional. Examples of software applications that support extensions include the Mozilla Firefox Web browser, Adobe Systems Photoshop and Microsoft Windows Explorer shell extensions.
Heart	The heart is a muscular organ responsible for pumping blood through the blood vessels by repeated, rhythmic contractions, or a similar structure in the annelids, mollusks, and arthropods.
Immune system	The most important function of the human immune system occurs at the cellular level of the blood and tissues. The lymphatic and blood circulation systems are highways for specialized white blood cells. These cells include B cells, T cells, natural killer cells, and macrophages. All function with the primary objective of recognizing, attacking and destroying bacteria, viruses, cancer cells, and all substances seen as foreign.
Muscle fiber	A muscle fiber is a single cell of a muscle. A muscle fiber contains many myofibrils, the contractile unit of muscles. They are very long; a single fiber can reach a length of 30 centimeters.
Single	In relationships, a single person is one who is not married, or, more broadly, who is not in an exclusive romantic relationship.
Synapse	A synapse is specialized junction through which cells of the nervous system signal to one another and to non-neuronal cells such as muscles or glands. They allow the neurons of the central nervous system to form interconnected neural circuits.
Glucose	Glucose, a simple monosaccharide sugar, is one of the most important carbohydrates and is used as a source of energy in animals and plants. Glucose is one of the main products of photosynthesis and starts respiration.
Active transport	Active transport is the mediated transport of biochemicals, and other atomic/molecular substances, across membranes. Unlike passive transport, this process requires chemical energy. In this form of transport, molecules move against either an electrical or concentration gradient (collectively termed an electrochemical gradient).

Go to **Cram101.com** for Interactive Practice Exams for this book or virtually any of your books for $4.95/month.
And, **NEVER** highlight a book again!

Contraction	In medicine, a contraction is a forceful and painful motion of the uterus as part of the process of childbirth. A contraction, and labor in general, is one condition that releases the hormone oxytocin into the body.
Fatigue	The word fatigue is used in everyday life to describe a range of afflictions, varying from a general state of lethargy to a specific work-induced burning sensation within one"s muscles. It can be both physical and mental. Such a mental fatigue, in turn, can manifest itself both as somnolence just as a general decrease of attention, not necessarily including sleepiness.
Not	This catalog is compiled from a source file. Please do not edit this page manually. This is how to edit it.
Tim	TIM is a series of lesser-known psychedelic drugs similar in structure to mescaline. They were first synthesized by Alexander Shulgin. In his book PiHKAL (Phenethylamines i Have Known And Loved), none of their durations are known.
Golgi organ	The Golgi organ, is a proprioceptive sensory receptor organ that is located at the insertion of skeletal muscle fibres into the tendons of skeletal muscle.
Interneuron	An interneuron (also called relay neuron or association neuron) is a neuron that communicates only to other neurons. They provide connections between sensory and motor neurons, as well as between themselves.
Intrinsic	Intrinsic describes a characteristic or property of some thing or action which is essential and specific to that thing or action, and which is wholly independent of any other object, action or consequence.
Muscle spindle	Muscle structure is innervated by both sensory and motor neuron axons. The function of the muscle spindle is to send proprioceptive information about the muscle to the central nervous system, and to respond to muscle stretching.
Reflex	A reflex action is an automatic neuromuscular action elicited by a defined stimulus. In most contexts, especially involving humans, a reflex action is mediated via the reflex arc
Stretch reflex	A stretch reflex is a muscle contraction in response to stretching within the muscle. It is a monosynaptic reflex which provides automatic regulation of skeletal muscle length. Muscle spindles are sensory apparatus sensitive to stretch of the muscle in which they lie.
Stimulus	In psychology, a stimulus is part of the stimulus-response relationship of behavioral learning theory.
Structure	Structure is a fundamental and sometimes intangible notion covering the recognition, observation, nature, and stability of patterns and relationships of entities.

Tendon	A tendon is a tough band of fibrous connective tissue that connects muscle to bone and is built to withstand tension.
Babinski reflex	The Babinski reflex is a reflex that can identify disease of the spinal cord and brain and also exists as a primitive reflex in infants.
Behavior	Behavior refers to the actions or reactions of an object or organism, usually in relation to the environment. Behavior can be conscious or subconscious, overt or covert, and voluntary or involuntary. Human Behavior (and that of other organisms and mechanisms) can be common, unusual, acceptable, or unacceptable. Humans evaluate the acceptability of Behavior using social norms and regulate Behavior by means of social control
Infant	In basic English usage, an Infant is defined as a human child at the youngest stage of life, specifically before they can walk and generally before the age of one.
Primitive reflexes	Primitive reflexes are reflex actions originating in the central nervous system that are exhibited by normal infants but not neurologically in tact adults, in response to particular stimuli. These reflexes disappear or are inhibited by the frontal lobes as a child moves through normal child development.
Vision	Vision is the most important sense for birds, since good eyesight is essential for safe flight, and this group has a number of adaptations which give visual acuity superior to that of other vertebrate groups; a pigeon has been described as "two eyes with wings". The avian eye resembles that of a reptile, but has a better-positioned lens, a feature shared with mammals. Birds have the largest eyes relative to their size within the animal kingdom, and movement is consequently limited within the eye"s bony socket.
Digestive system	The digestive system is the organ system that breaks down and absorbs nutrients that are essential for growth and maintenance. The digestive system includes the mouth, esophagus, stomach, pancreas, liver, gallbladder, duodenum, jejunum, ileum, intestines, rectum, and anus.
Scolex	The Scolex of the worm attaches to the intestine of the definitive host. In some groups, the scolex is dominated by bothria, which are sometimes called "sucking grooves," and function like suction cups.
Cytoplasmic streaming	Cytoplasmic streaming is the flowing of cytoplasm in eukaryotic cells. This occurs in both plant and animal cells.
Entity	An entity is something that has a distinct, separate existence, though it need not be a material existence. In particular, abstractions and legal fictions are usually regarded as an entity. In general, there is also no presumption that an entity is animate.

Somatosensory system	The Somatosensory system is made up of the complex of sensations that are experienced by the skin and body. These sensations include the sense of pressure, temperature, pain, body position, and movement.
Brain	In animals, the brain, is the control center of the central nervous system, responsible for behavior. The brain is located in the head, protected by the skull and close to the primary sensory apparatus of vision, hearing, equilibrioception, sense of acceleration, taste, and olfaction.
Brain damage	Brain damage is the destruction or degeneration of brain cells. It may occur due to a wide range of conditions, illnesses, injuries, and as a result of iatrogenesis. Possible causes of widespread brain damage include prolonged hypoxia, poisoning by teratogens, infection, and neurological illness.
Central pattern generator	A central pattern generator is a system of coupled oscillators often realized as a network of neurons which is able to exhibit rhythmic activity in the absence of sensory input.
Prefrontal cortex	The prefrontal cortex is the anterior part of the frontal lobes of the brain, lying in front of the motor and premotor areas. Cytoarchitectonically, it is defined by the presence of an internal granular layer IV.
Anterior	Anterior is an anatomical term referring to the front part of the body. The anterior is positioned in front of another body part, or towards the head of an animal. It is the opposite of posterior.
Anxiety	Anxiety is a physiological state characterized by cognitive, somatic, emotional, and behavioral components.
Depression	In everyday language depression refers to any downturn in mood, which may be relatively transitory and perhaps due to something trivial.
Frontal lobe	The frontal lobe comprises four major folds of cortical tissue: the precentral gyrus, superior gyrus and the middle gyrus of the frontal gyri, the inferior frontal gyrus. It has been found to play a part in impulse control, judgement, language, memory, motor function, problem solving, sexual behavior, socialization and spontaneity.
Generation	Generation, also known as procreation, is the act of producing offspring. A generation can also be a stage or degree in a succession of natural descent as a grandfather, a father, and the father"s son comprise three generations.
Mechanism	In philosophy, mechanism is a theory that all natural phenomena can be explained by physical causes. It can be contrasted with vitalism, the philosophical theory that vital forces are active in living organisms, so that life cannot be explained solely by mechanism.

Need	A Need is something that is necessary for humans to live a healthy life. Need s are distinguished from wants because a deficiency would cause a clear negative outcome, such as dysfunction or death. Need s can be objective and physical, such as food and water, or they can be subjective and psychological, such as the Need for self-esteem.
Signal	In the fields of communications, signal processing, and in electrical engineering more generally, a signal is any time-varying quantity. Signals are often scalar-valued functions of time, but may be vector valued and may be functions of any other relevant independent variable.
Spinal cord	The spinal cord is a thin, tubular bundle of nerves that is an extension of the central nervous system from the brain and is enclosed in and protected by the bony vertebral column. The main function of the spinal cord is transmission of neural inputs between the periphery and the brain.
Explanation	An explanation is a description which may clarify causes, context, and consequences of a certain object, and a phenomenon such as a process, a state of affairs. This description may establish rules or laws, and may clarify the existing ones in relation to an object, and a phenomenon examined. The components of an explanation can be implicit, and be interwoven with one another.
Species	Species refers to a reproductively isolated breeding population.
Understanding	Understanding is a psychological process related to an abstract or physical object, such as, person, situation, or message whereby one is able to think about it and use concepts to deal adequately with that object.
Cerebral cortex	The cerebral cortex is a structure within the vertebrate brain with distinct structural and functional properties.
Motor cortex	Motor cortex is a term that describes regions of the cerebral cortex involved in the planning, control, and execution of voluntary motor functions.
Primary motor cortex	The primary motor cortex works in association with pre-motor areas to plan and execute movements. It contains large neurons known as Betz cells which send long axons down the spinal cord to synapse onto alpha motor neurons which connect to the muscles.
Central sulcus	The central sulcus is a prominent landmark of the brain, separating the parietal lobe from the frontal lobe. The central sulcus is the site of the primary motor cortex in mammals, a group of cells that controls voluntary movements of the body.
Message	A message in its most general meaning is an object of communication.
Primary	In medicine, the reporting of symptoms by a patient may have significant psychological motivators. Psychologists sometimes categorize these motivators into primary or secondary gain. primary gain is internally good; motivationally.

Postcentral gyrus	The lateral postcentral gyrus is a prominent structure in the parietal lobe of the human brain and an important landmark. It was initially defined from surface stimulation studies of Penfield, and parallel surface potential studies of Bard, Woolsey, and Marshall.
Posterior	In reference to the anatomical terms of location, the posterior end is laterally situated at or toward the hinder part of the body, lying at or extending toward the right or left side. It is the polar opposite to the anterior end, or front end of the body.
Parietal lobe	The parietal lobe is a lobe in the brain. It is positioned above the occipital lobe and behind the frontal lobe.
Monitoring	Monitoring generally means to be aware of the state of a system.
Other	The Other or constitutive Other is a key concept in continental philosophy, opposed to the Same. It refers, or attempts to refer, to that which is "Other" than the concept being considered. The term often means a person Other than oneself, and is often capitalised.
Sensation	Sensation is the first stage in the chain of biochemical and neurologic events that begins with the impinging of a stimulus upon the receptor cells of a sensory organ, which then leads to perception, the mental state that is reflected in statements like "I see a uniformly blue wall."
Somatosensory	Somatosensory system consists of the various sensory receptors that trigger the experiences labelled as touch or pressure, temperature, pain, and the sensations of muscle movement and joint position including posture, movement, and facial expression.
Autism	Autism is a brain development disorder characterized by impairments in social interaction and communication, and restricted and repetitive behavior, all exhibited before a child is three years old. These characteristics distinguish autism from milder autism spectrum disorders.
Dream	A dream is the experience of a sequence of images, like a movie with sounds, ideas, emotions, or other sensations during sleep, especially REM sleep. The dream environment is often much more realistic in a lucid dream, and the senses heightened.
Insular cortex	The insular cortex is a structure of the human brain. It lies deep to the brain"s lateral surface, within the lateral sulcus which separates the temporal lobe and inferior parietal cortex.
Mirror neuron	A Mirror neuron is a neuron that fires both when an animal acts and when the animal observes the same action performed by another animal (especially by another animal of the same species.) Thus, the neuron "mirrors" the behavior of another animal, as though the observer were itself acting. These neurons have been directly observed in primates, and are believed to exist in humans and other species including birds.

Premotor cortex	The premotor cortex is an area of motor cortex in the frontal lobe of the brain. It extends 3mm in front of the Primary motor cortex near the Sylvian fissure before narrowing to approximately 1mm near the Medial longitudinal fissure, where it has the prefrontal cortex. It is responsible for sensory guidance of movement and control of proximal and trunk muscles of the body, and is more or less equivalent with Brodmann area 6.
Sleep	Sleep is the state of natural rest observed throughout the animal kingdom, in all mammals and birds, and in many reptiles, amphibians, and fish.
Arousal	Arousal is a physiological and psychological state involving the activation of the reticular activating system in the brain stem, the autonomic nervous system and the endocrine system, leading to increased heart rate and blood pressure and a condition of alertness and readiness to respond.
Planning	Planning is both the organizational process of creating and maintaining a plan; and the psychological process of thinking about the activities required to create a desired future on some scale.
Consciousness	The awareness of the sensations, thoughts, and feelings being experienced at a given moment is called consciousness.
Amyotrophic lateral sclerosis	Amyotrophic lateral sclerosis is a progressive, fatal, neurodegenerative disease caused by the degeneration of motor neurons, the nerve cells in the central nervous system that control voluntary muscle movement.
Contralateral	The term contralateral refers to the opposite side of the body. For example, it can refer to the opposite sides of the right arm and left leg or it can be applied to paired organs such as the kidneys, lungs, breasts, and ovaries.
Pyramidal tract	The pyramidal tract is a massive collection of axons that travel between the cerebral cortex of the brain and the spinal cord. It mostly contains motor axons.
Hemiplegia	Hemiplegia is a condition where there is paralysis in one vertical half of a patient"s body. This is not hemiparesis wherein one half of the body is weakened, i.e. one arm and its corresponding leg are weak. Hemiplegia is similar to hemiparesis, but hemiparesis is considered less severe.
Ipsilateral	In reference to the anatomical terms of location, ipsilateral is a term that refers to being on the same side of the body as another structure. For example, the right arm would be considered ipsilateral to the right leg.
Paralysis	Paralysis is the complete loss of muscle function for one or more muscle groups. Paralysis can cause loss of feeling or loss of mobility in the affected area.

Paraplegia	*Paraplegia* is an impairment in motor and/or sensory function of the lower extremities. It is usually the result of spinal cord injury or a congenital condition such as spina bifida which affects the neural elements of the spinal canal. The area of the spinal canal which is affected in *Paraplegia* is either the thoracic, lumbar, or sacral regions.
Polio	Polio is an acute viral infectious disease spread from person-to-person, primarily via the fecal-oral route. In less than 1% of polio cases the virus enters the central nervous system, preferentially infecting and destroying motor neurons. The destruction of motor neurons causes muscle weakness and acute flaccid paralysis. It is a highly contagious disease which spreads easily via human-to-human contact.
Red nucleus	The red nucleus is a structure in the rostral midbrain involved in motor coordination. It comprises a caudal magnocellular and a rostral parvocellular part.
Reticular formation	The reticular formation is a part of the brain which is involved in stereotypical actions, such as walking, sleeping, and lying down. It is essential for governing some of the basic functions of higher organisms, and phylogenetically one of the oldest portions of the brain.
Tabes dorsalis	Tabes dorsalis is a slow degeneration of the sensory neurons that carry information. The degenerating nerves are in the dorsal columns (posterior columns) of the spinal cord (the portion closest to the back of the body) and carry information that help maintain a person"s sense of position (proprioception), vibration, and discriminative touch. Tabes dorsalis is caused by demyelination.
Tectum	The tectum is a region of the brain, specifically the dorsal part of the mesencephalon.
Animal testing	Animal testing refers to the use of animals in experiments. It is estimated that 50 to 100 million vertebrate animals worldwide — from zebrafish to non-human primates — are used annually and either killed during the experiments or subsequently euthanized.
Attention	Attention is the cognitive process of selectively concentrating on one aspect of the environment while ignoring other things. Examples include listening carefully to what someone is saying while ignoring other conversations in the room or listening to a cell phone conversation while driving a car.
Brain stem	The brain stem is the lower part of the brain, adjoining and structurally continuous with the spinal cord. Most sources consider the pons, medulla oblongata, and midbrain all to be part of the brain stem.
Control group	A control group augments integrity in experiments by isolating variables as dictated by the scientific method in order to make a conclusion about such variables. In other cases, an experimental control is used to prevent the effects of one variable from being drowned out by the known, greater effects of other variables. this case, the researchers can either use a control group or use statistical techniques to control for the other variables.

Prosencephalon	In the anatomy of the brain of vertebrates, the prosencephalon is the rostral-most portion of the brain. The prosencephalon, the mesencephalon, and rhombencephalon are the three primary portions of the brain during early development of the central nervous system.
Hindbrain	The hindbrain is a developmental categorization of portions of the central nervous system in vertebrates. It can be subdivided in a variable number of transversal swellings called rhombomeres.
Medulla	Medulla refers to the middle of something, and derives from the Latin word for "marrow" In medicine it refers to either bone marrow, the spinal cord, or more generally, the middle part of a structure as opposed to the cortex.
Midbrain	The midbrain is the middle of three vesicles that arise from the neural tube that forms the brain of developing animals. In mature human brains, it becomes the least differentiated, from both its developmental form and within its own structure, among the three vesicles. The midbrain is considered part of the brain stem.
Sense	Sense are the physiological methods of perception. They and their operation, classification, and theory are overlapping topics studied by a variety of fields, most notably neuroscience, cognitive psychology, and philosophy of perception. The nervous system has a sensory system dedicated to each sense.
Tracts	In anatomy, Tracts are a bundle of nerve fibers following a path through the brain, or a collection of related anatomic structures.
Cerebellum	The cerebellum is a region of the brain that plays an important role in the integration of sensory perception and motor output. Many neural pathways link the cerebellum with the motor cortex—which sends information to the muscles causing them to move—and the spinocerebellar tract—which provides feedback on the position of the body in space. The cerebellum integrates these pathways, using the constant feedback on body position to fine-tune motor movements.
Saccade	A saccade is a fast movement of an eye, head, or other part of an animal's body or of a device. It can also be a fast shift in frequency of an emitted signal, or other such fast change.
Eye	Eye s are organs that detect light, and send signals along the optic nerve to the visual and other areas of the brain. Complex optical systems with resolving power have come in ten fundamentally different forms, and 96% of animal species possess a complex optical system. Image-resolving Eye s are present in cnidaria, molluscs, chordates, annelids and arthropods.

Eyes	Eyes are organs that detect light. Different kinds of light-sensitive organs are found in a variety of animals. The simplest eyes do nothing but detect whether the surroundings are light or dark, which is sufficient for the entrainment of circadian rhythms but can hardly be called vision. More complex eyes can distinguish shapes and colors. The visual fields of some such complex eyes largely overlap, to allow better depth perception, as in humans; and others are placed so as to minimize the overlap, such as in rabbits and chameleons.
Fixation	Fixation in abnormal psychology is the state where an individual becomes obsessed with an attachment to another human, animal or inanimate object. Fixation in vision refers to maintaining the gaze in a constant direction. .
Test	A Test or an examination (or "exam") is an assessment, often administered on paper or on the computer, intended to measure the Test-takers" or respondents" (often a student) knowledge, skills, aptitudes beliefs.) Tests are often used in education, professional certification, counseling, psychology (e.g., MMPI), the military, and many other fields. The measurement that is the goal of testing is called a Test score, and is "a summary of the evidence contained in an examinee"s responses to the items of a Test that are related to the construct or constructs being measured." Test scores are interpreted with regards to a norm or criterion, or occasionally both.
Bipolar disorder	Bipolar disorder is a psychiatric condition defined as recurrent episodes of significant disturbance in mood. These disturbances can occur on a spectrum that ranges from debilitating depression to unbridled mania. Individuals suffering from bipolar disorder typically experience fluid states of mania, hypomania or what is referred to as a mixed state in conjunction with depressive episodes.
Impulse	In classical mechanics, an Impulse is defined as the integral of a force with respect to time. When a force is applied to a rigid body it changes the momentum of that body. A small force applied for a long time can produce the same momentum change as a large force applied briefly, because it is the product of the force and the time for which it is applied that is important.
Information	Information as a concept has a diversity of meanings, from everyday usage to technical settings. Generally speaking, the concept of Information is closely related to notions of constraint, communication, control, data, form, instruction, knowledge, meaning, mental stimulus, pattern, perception, and representation. According to the Oxford English Dictionary, the first known historical meaning of the word Information in English was the act of informing, or giving form or shape to the mind, as in education, instruction, or training.
Paradoxical	Paradoxical intention refers to instructing clients to do the opposite of the desired behavior. Telling an impotent man not to have sex or an insomniac not to sleep reduces anxiety to perform.
Rapid eye movement sleep	Rapid eye movement sleep is the normal stage of sleep characterized by rapid movements of the eyes. Criteria for Rapid eye movement sleep include not only rapid eye movements, but also low muscle tone and a rapid, low voltage EEG these features are easily discernible in a polysomnogram, the sleep study typically done for patients with suspected sleep disorders.

Purkinje	Purkinje is best known for his 1837 discovery of Purkinje cells, large neurons with many branching fibres found in the cerebellum. He is also known for his discovery, in 1839 of Purkinje fibres, the fibrous tissue that conducts electrical impulses from the atrioventricular node to all parts of the ventricles of the heart.
Purkinje cells	Purkinje cells are a class of GABAergic neuron located in the cerebellar cortex. Purkinje cells send inhibitory projections to the deep cerebellar nuclei, and constitute the sole output of all motor coordination in the cerebellar cortex.
Plan	A Plan is typically any procedure used to achieve an objective. It is a set of intended actions, through which one expects to achieve a goal. Plan s can be formal or informal: · Structured and formal Plan s, used by multiple people, are more likely to occur in projects, diplomacy, careers, economic development, military campaigns, combat, or in the conduct of other business. · Informal or ad-hoc Plan s are created by individuals in all of their pursuits. The most popular ways to describe Plan s are by their breadth, time frame, and specificity; however, these Plan ning classifications are not independent of one another. For instance, there is a close relationship between the short-and long-term categories and the strategic and operational categories.
Basal ganglia	The basal ganglia are a group of nuclei in the brain associated with motor and learning functions.
Catechol-o-methyltransferase	Catechol-O-methyltransferase is an enzyme first discovered by biochemist Julius Axelrod. COMT is the name given to the gene that codes for this enzyme. The O in the name stands for oxygen, not for ortho.
Gamma-aminobutyric acid	Gamma-aminobutyric acid is an inhibitory neurotransmitter found in the nervous systems of widely-divergent species. It is the chief inhibitory neurotransmitter in the central nervous system and also in the retina.
Globus pallidus	The globus pallidus is a sub-cortical structure of the brain. It is a major element of the basal ganglia system. In this system, it is a major element of the basal ganglia core, consisting of the striatum and its direct targets: globus pallidus and substantia nigra. The last two are made up of the same neuronal elements, have a similar main afferent, have a similar synaptology, and do not receive cortical afferents.
Putamen	The putamen is a structure in the middle of the brain, which, together with the caudate nucleus forms the dorsal striatum. The putamen is a portion of the basal ganglia that forms the outermost part of the lenticular nucleus.
Thalamus	An area near the center of the brain involved in the relay of sensory information to the cortex and in the functions of sleep and attention is the thalamus.

Caudate nucleus	The caudate nucleus is a nucleus located within the basal ganglia of the brains of many animal species. The caudate nuclei are located near the center of the brain, sitting astride the thalamus. There is a caudate nucleus within each hemisphere of the brain.
Delusion	A false belief, not generally shared by others, and that cannot be changed despite strong evidence to the contrary is a delusion.
Hallucination	A hallucination is a sensory perception experienced in the absence of an external stimulus, as distinct from an illusion, which is a misperception of an external stimulus. They may occur in any sensory modality - visual, auditory, olfactory, gustatory, tactile, or mixed.
Hypothalamus	The hypothalamus is a region of the brain located below the thalamus, forming the major portion of the ventral region of the diencephalon and functioning to regulate certain metabolic processes and other autonomic activities.
Disability	A disability is a condition or function judged to be significantly impaired relative to the usual standard of an individual or their group. The term is often used to refer to individual functioning, including physical impairments, sensory impairments, cognitive impairments, intellectual impairments or mental health issue.
Memory	In psychology, memory is an organism"s ability to store, retain, and subsequently retrieve information. In recent decades, it has become one of the principal pillars of a branch of science called cognitive neuroscience, an interdisciplinary link between cognitive psychology and neuroscience.
Tremor	Tremor is the rhythmic, oscillating shaking movement of the whole body or just a certain part of it, caused by problems of the neurons responsible from muscle action.
Muscle contraction	A muscle contraction occurs when a muscle fiber generates tension through the action of actin and myosin cross-bridge cycling.
Learning	Learning is the acquisition and development of memories and behaviors, including skills, knowledge, understanding, values, and wisdom. It is the goal of education, and the product of experience. Learning ranges from simple forms such as habituation to more complex forms such as play, seen only in large vertebrates.
Long-term potentiation	In neuroscience, long-term potentiation is the long-lasting enhancement in communication between two neurons that results from stimulating them simultaneously.
Motor learning	Motor learning is the process of improving the motor skills, the smoothness and accuracy of movements. It is obviously necessary for complicated movements such as speaking, playing the piano, climbing trees and eating bananas but it is also important for calibrating simple movements like reflexes, as parameters of the body and environment change over time. The cerebellum and basal ganglia are critical for Motor learning.

Apoptosis	Apoptosis is one of the main types of programmed cell death. As such, it is a process of deliberate suicide by an unwanted cell in a multicellular organism.
Dopamine	Dopamine is a hormone and neurotransmitter occurring in a wide variety of animals, including both vertebrates and invertebrates. In the brain, dopamine functions as a neurotransmitter. Dopamine is also a neurohormone released by the hypothalamus. Its main function as a hormone is to inhibit the release of prolactin from the anterior lobe of the pituitary.
Mood	A mood is a relatively lasting emotional or affective state. They differ from emotions in that they are less specific, often less intense, less likely to be triggered by a particular stimulus or event, however longer lasting.
Mood disorder	A mood disorder is a condition where the prevailing emotional mood is distorted or inappropriate to the circumstances.
Parasympathetic nervous system	The parasympathetic nervous system is a division of the autonomic nervous system, along with the sympathetic nervous system and Enteric nervous system. The ANS is a subdivision of the peripheral nervous system.
Mental disorder	Mental disorder refes tor a psychological or physiological pattern that occurs in an individual and is usually associated with distress or disability that is not expected as part of normal development or culture.
Substantia nigra	The substantia nigra is a portion of the midbrain thought to be involved in certain aspects of movement and attention. Degeneration of cells in this region is the principle pathology that underlies Parkinson's disease.
Alcoholism	Alcoholism is a term with multiple and sometimes conflicting definitions. In common and historic usage, alcoholism refers to any condition that results in the continued consumption of alcoholic beverages despite the health problems and negative social consequences it causes.
Eating	Eating is the process of consuming nutrition, i.e. food, for the purpose of providing for the nutritional needs of an animal, particularly their energy requirements and to grow.
Eating disorder	An eating disorder is a complex compulsion to eat, or not eat, in a way which disturbs physical and mental health. The eating may be excessive compulsive over-eating, too limited restricting, normal eating punctuated with purging, cycles of binging and purging or ingesting of non-foods.
Nerve	A Nerve is an enclosed, cable-like bundle of peripheral axons (the long, slender projections of neurons.) A Nerve provides a common pathway for the electrochemical Nerve impulses that are transmitted along each of the axons. Nerve s are found only in the peripheral nervous system.

Neurotransmitter	A neurotransmitter is a chemical that is used to relay, amplify and modulate electrical signals between a neurons and another cell.
Rigidity	In psychology, rigidity refers to an obstacle to problem solving which arises from over-dependence on prior experience, which makes it difficult for a person with experience in a specific problem domain to recognize novel solution strategies.
Heritability	Heritability It is that proportion of the observed variation in a particular phenotype within a particular population, that can be attributed to the contribution of genotype. In other words: it measures the extent to which differences between individuals in a population are due their being different genetically.
Characteristic	Characteristic has several particular meanings: · in mathematics ● · Euler characteristic ● · method of characteristic s (partial differential equations) · in physics and engineering · any characteristic curve that shows the relationship between certain input- and output parameters, e.g. · an I-V or current-voltage characteristic is the current in a circuit as a function of the applied voltage · Receiver-Operator characteristic · in navigation, the characteristic pattern of a lighted beacon. · in fiction · in Dungeons ' Dragons, characteristic is another name for ability score .
Heredity	Heredity is the transfer of characteristics from parent to offspring through their genes, or the transfer of a title, style or social status through the social convention known as inheritance.
Population	In sociology and biology a population is the collection of people or individuals of a particular species. A population shares a particular characteristic of interest most often that of living in a given geographic area.
Variance	In probability theory and statistics, the variance of a random variable or somewhat more precisely, of a probability distribution is one measure of statistical dispersion, averaging the squared distance of its possible values from the expected value.

Caffeine	Caffeine is a xanthine alkaloid compound that acts as a psychoactive stimulant in humans. In humans, caffeine is a central nervous system stimulant, having the effect of temporarily warding off drowsiness and restoring alertness. Beverages containing caffeine, such as coffee, tea, soft drinks and energy drinks enjoy great popularity; caffeine is the world"s most widely consumed psychoactive substance, but unlike most other psychoactive substances, it is legal and unregulated in nearly all jurisdictions.
Cigarette	A cigarette is a product consumed via smoking and manufactured out of cured and finely cut tobacco leaves and reconstituted tobacco. It contains nicotine, an addictive stimulant which is toxic. It delivers smoke to the lungs immediately and produce a rapid psychoactive effect. The cigarette has been proven to be highly addictive, as well as a cause of multiple types of causes.
Tobacco smoking	Tobacco smoking is the act of burning the dried or cured leaves of the tobacco plant and inhaling the smoke for pleasure, for ritualistic or social purposes, self-medication, or simply to satisfy physical dependence.
1-methyl 4-phenyl 1,2,3,6-tetrahydropyridine	1-methyl 4-phenyl 1,2,3,6-tetrahydropyridine is a neurotoxin that causes permanent symptoms of Parkinson"s disease by killing certain neurons in the substantia nigra of the brain. It is used to study the disease in monkeys.
Marijuana	Marijuana is the dried vegetable matter of the Cannabis sativa plant. It contains large concentrations of compounds that have medicinal and psychoactive effects when consumed, usually by smoking or eating.
Adenosine	Adenosine is a nucleoside composed of adenine attached to a ribose (ribofuranose) moiety via a β-N_9-glycosidic bond. Adenosine plays an important role in biochemical processes, such as energy transfer and Adenosine plays an important role in biochemical processes, such as energy transfer. It is also an inhibitory neurotransmitter, believed to play a role in promoting sleep and suppressing arousal, with levels increasing with each hour an organism is awake.
Blood	Blood is a specialized biological fluid consisting of red blood cells.White blood cells also called leukocytes and platelets also called thrombocytes suspended in a complex fluid medium known as blood plasma.
Chemical	A chemical is a material with a definite chemical composition. All samples of a compound have the same composition; that is, all samples have the same proportions, by mass, of the elements present in the compound.
Coffee	Coffee is a widely consumed stimulant beverage prepared from roasted seeds. Most studies are contradictory as to whether coffee has any specific health benefits, and results are similarly conflicting regarding negative effects of coffee consumption. Research suggests that drinking caffeinated coffee can cause a temporary increase in the stiffening of arterial walls.

Discovery	Discovery observations form acts of detecting and learning something. Discovery observations are acts in which something is found and given a productive insight. Serendipity is the effect by which one accidentally discovers something fortunate, especially while looking for something else entirely.
Antioxidant	An antioxidant is a molecule capable of slowing or preventing the oxidation of other molecules. Oxidation reactions can produce free radicals, which start chain reactions that damage cells. An antioxidant terminates these chain reactions by removing radical intermediates, and inhibit other oxidation reactions by being oxidized themselves.
Blood-brain barrier	The Blood-brain barrier is a membranic structure that acts primarily to protect the brain from chemicals in the blood, while still allowing essential metabolic function. It is composed of endothelial cells, which are packed very tightly in brain capillaries. This higher density restricts passage of substances from the bloodstream much more than endothelial cells in capillaries elsewhere in the body
Cannabinoids	Cannabinoids are a group of terpenophenolic compounds present in Cannabis. The broader definition of cannabinoids refer to a group of substances that are structurally related to tetrahydrocannabinol or that bind to cannabinoid receptors. The chemical definition encompasses a variety of distinct chemical classes: the classical cannabinoids structurally related to THC, the nonclassical cannabinoids, the aminoalkylindoles, the eicosanoids related to the endocannabinoids, 1,5-diarylpyrazoles, quinolines and arylsulphonamides and additional compounds that do not fall into these standard classes but bind to cannabinoid receptors.
Glutamate	Glutamate is one of the 20 standard amino acids used by all organisms in their proteins. It is critical for proper cell function, but it is not an essential nutrient in humans because it can be manufactured from other compounds.
L-dopa	L-DOPA is used to replace dopamine lost in Parkinson"s disease because dopamine itself cannot cross the blood-brain barrier where its precursor can.
Mitochondrion	In cell biology, a mitochondrion is a membrane-enclosed organelle that is found in most eukaryotic cells. A Mitochondrion is sometimes described as a "cellular power plant," because it generates most of the cell"s supply of adenosine triphosphate, used as a source of chemical energy.
Affect	Affect refers to the experience of feeling or emotion. Affect is a key part of the process of an organism's interaction with stimuli. The word also refers sometimes to affect display, which is "a facial, vocal, or gestural behavior that serves as an indicator of affect."
Catecholamine	Catecholamine refers to chemical compounds derived from the amino acid tyrosine containing catechol and amine groups.

Energy	The concept of psychic Energy was developed in the field of psychodynamics. In 1874, German scientist Ernst von Brucke proposed that all living organisms are Energy-systems governed by the principle of the conservation of Energy. Brucke was also coincidentally the supervisor at the University of Vienna for first-year medical student Sigmund Freud who adopted this new paradigm.
Experience	Experience as a general concept comprises knowledge of or skill in or observation of some thing or some event gained through involvement in or exposure to that thing or event. The history of the word experience aligns it closely with the concept of experiment.
Genetics	Genetics is the science of heredity and variation in living organisms.Knowledge of the inheritance of characteristics has been implicitly used since prehistoric times for improving crop plants and animals through selective breeding. However, the modern science of genetics, which seeks to understand the mechanisms of inheritance, only began with the work of Gregor Mendel in the mid-1800s.
Schizophrenia	Schizophrenia is a psychiatric diagnosis that describes a mental illness characterized by impairments in the perception or expression of reality, most commonly manifesting as auditory hallucinations, paranoid or bizarre delusions or disorganized speech and thinking in the context of significant social or occupational dysfunction.
Stem cell	A Stem Cell is a primal cell that is found in all multi-cellular organisms.
Daughter	A Daughter is a female offspring; a girl, woman, or female animal in relation to her parents. The male equivalent is a son. Analogously the name is used on several areas to show relations between groups or elements.
Emotion	Emotion, in its most general definition, is a complex psychophysical process that arises spontaneously, rather than through conscious effort, and evokes either a positive or negative psychological response and physical expressions, often involuntary, related to feelings, perceptions or beliefs about elements, objects or relations between them, in reality or in the imagination. An emotion is often differentiated from a feeling.
Emotional expression	In psychology, emotional expression is observable verbal and nonverbal behavior that communicates emotion.
Personal life	Personal life is the course of an individual human"s life, especially when viewed as the sum of personal choices contributing to one"s personal identity.
Homeostasis	Homeostasis is the property of either an open system or a closed system, especially a living organism, which regulates its internal environment so as to maintain a stable, constant condition.
Thought disorder	Thought disorder describes a persistent underlying disturbance to conscious thought and is classified largely by its effects on speech and writing. Affected persons may show pressure of speech, derailment or flight of ideas, thought blocking, rhyming, punning, or word salad.

Brain-derived neurotrophic factor	Brain-derived neurotrophic factor is exactly as it states; a neurotrophic factor found originally in the brain, but also found in the periphery. More specifically, it is a protein which has activity on certain neurons of the central nervous system and the peripheral nervous system; it helps to support the survival of existing neurons, and encourage the growth and differentiation of new neurons and synapses.
Hunger	Hunger is a feeling experienced when the glycogen level of the liver falls below a threshold, usually followed by a desire to eat.
Protein	A protein is a complex, high-molecular-weight organic compound that consists of amino acids joined by peptide bonds. It is essential to the structure and function of all living cells and viruses. Many are enzymes or subunits of enzymes.
Sex steroid	Sex steroid refers to steroid hormones that interact with vertebrate androgen or estrogen receptors.

Circadian rhythm	The circadian rhythm is a name given to the "internal body clock" that regulates the roughly 24 hour cycle of biological processes in animals and plants.
Thermoregulation	Thermoregulation is the ability of an organism to keep the temperature of its body within certain boundaries, even when temperature surrounding is very different. This process is one aspect of homeostasis: a dynamic state of stability between an animal"s internal environment and its external environment.
Circannual rhythm	Circannual rhythm is the annual or yearly cycle of light/dark, wakefulness/sleep to which most physiologic processes used by living things are set. During regular intervals every day, the body becomes hungry, tired, active, energized, etc. At the same time, body temperature, heart rate, blood pressure, hormone levels, and urine flow increase and decrease in this rhythmic pattern - a pattern which is initiated and regulated by exposure to sunlight and darkness.
Endogenous	An emotion or behavior is endogenous if it is spontaneously generated from an individual"s internal state.
Cycl	CycL in computer science and artificial intelligence is an ontology language used by Doug Lenat"s Cyc artificial intelligence project. Ramanathan V. Guha was instrumental in the design of the language. There is a close variant of CycL known as MELD. The original version of CycL was a frame language, but the modern version is not.
Day	A Day (symbol d) is a unit of time equivalent to approximately 24 hours. It is not an SI unit but it is accepted for use with SI. The SI unit of time is the second. The word "Day" can also refer to the (roughly) half of the Day that is not night, also known as "Daytime".
Homeostasis	Homeostasis is the property of either an open system or a closed system, especially a living organism, which regulates its internal environment so as to maintain a stable, constant condition.
Year	A Year is the amount of time it takes the Earth to make one revolution around the Sun. By extension, this can be applied to any planet: for example, a "Martian Year" is the time in which Mars completes its own orbit. Although there is no universally accepted symbol for the Year, NIST SP811 and ISO 80000-3:2006 suggest the symbol a in the International System of Units.
Ageing	Ageing is defined as any change in an organism over time. Ageing commences at conception, continues with the changes associated with the gain of function during growth and development and concludes with the loss of function in a system towards the end of life.
Chronobiology	Chronobiology is a field of science that examines periodic phenomena in living organisms.

293

Mechanism	In philosophy, mechanism is a theory that all natural phenomena can be explained by physical causes. It can be contrasted with vitalism, the philosophical theory that vital forces are active in living organisms, so that life cannot be explained solely by mechanism.
Not	This catalog is compiled from a source file. Please do not edit this page manually. This is how to edit it.
Other	The Other or constitutive Other is a key concept in continental philosophy, opposed to the Same. It refers, or attempts to refer, to that which is "Other" than the concept being considered. The term often means a person Other than oneself, and is often capitalised.
Young-Helmholtz theory	The Young-Helmholtz theory is a theory of trichromatic color vision - the manner in which the photoreceptors in the eyes of humans and other primates work to enable color vision.
Cortisol	Cortisol is a corticosteroid hormone produced by the adrenal cortex. It is a vital hormone that is often referred to as the "stress hormone" as it is involved in the response to stress. It increases blood pressure, blood sugar levels and has an immunosuppressive action.
Depression	In everyday language depression refers to any downturn in mood, which may be relatively transitory and perhaps due to something trivial.
Hippocampus	The hippocampus is a part of the brain located in the medial temporal lobe. It forms a part of the limbic system and plays a part in memory and spatial navigation.
Hormone	A hormone is a chemical messenger that carries a signal from one cell to another. All multicellular organisms produce hormone s.
Insomnia	Insomnia is a sleep disorder characterized by an inability to sleep and/or inability to remain asleep for a reasonable period.
Jet lag	Jet lag is a physiological condition which is a consequence of alterations to the circadian rhythm. The condition of jet lag generally lasts many days or more, and medical experts have deemed that a recovery rate of "one day per time zone" is a fair guideline. The condition is generally believed to be the result of disruption of the "light/dark" cycle that entrains the body"s circadian rhythm. It can be exacerbated by environmental factors.
Memory	In psychology, memory is an organism"s ability to store, retain, and subsequently retrieve information. In recent decades, it has become one of the principal pillars of a branch of science called cognitive neuroscience, an interdisciplinary link between cognitive psychology and neuroscience.
Shift work	Shift work is an employment practice designed to make use of the 24 hours of the clock, rather than a standard working day. The term shift work includes both long-term night shifts and work schedules in which employees change or rotate shifts.

295

Sleep	Sleep is the state of natural rest observed throughout the animal kingdom, in all mammals and birds, and in many reptiles, amphibians, and fish.
Stress	Stress is the consequence of the failure to adapt to change. Less simply: it is the condition that results when person-environment transactions lead the individual to perceive a discrepancy, whether real or not, between the demands of a situation and the resources of the person"s biological, psychological or social systems.
Adrenal cortex	Situated along the perimeter of the adrenal gland, the adrenal cortex mediates the stress response through the production of mineralocorticoids and glucocorticoids, including aldosterone and cortisol respectively. It is also a secondary site of androgen synthesis.
Arousal	Arousal is a physiological and psychological state involving the activation of the reticular activating system in the brain stem, the autonomic nervous system and the endocrine system, leading to increased heart rate and blood pressure and a condition of alertness and readiness to respond.
Biological rhythm	A biological rhythm is a hypothetical cyclic pattern of alterations in physiology, emotions, and/or intellect
Blood	Blood is a specialized biological fluid consisting of red blood cells.White blood cells also called leukocytes and platelets also called thrombocytes suspended in a complex fluid medium known as blood plasma.
Chemical	A chemical is a material with a definite chemical composition. All samples of a compound have the same composition; that is, all samples have the same proportions, by mass, of the elements present in the compound.
Feeling	Feeling in psychology is usually reserved for the conscious subjective experience of emotion. As such, it is inherently beyond the reach of scientific method.
Prosencephalon	In the anatomy of the brain of vertebrates, the prosencephalon is the rostral-most portion of the brain. The prosencephalon, the mesencephalon, and rhombencephalon are the three primary portions of the brain during early development of the central nervous system.
Gland	A gland is an organ in an animal's body that synthesizes a substance for release such as hormones, often into the bloodstream or into cavities inside the body or its outer surface.
Lack	Lack , is, in Lacan"s psychoanalytic philosophy, always related to desire. In his seminar Le transfert he states that Lack is what causes desire to arise. However, Lack first designated a Lack of being: what is desired is being itself.
Metabolism	Metabolism is the biochemical modification of chemical compounds in living organisms and cells.

297

Structure	Structure is a fundamental and sometimes intangible notion covering the recognition, observation, nature, and stability of patterns and relationships of entities.
Thalamus	An area near the center of the brain involved in the relay of sensory information to the cortex and in the functions of sleep and attention is the thalamus.
Tim	TIM is a series of lesser-known psychedelic drugs similar in structure to mescaline. They were first synthesized by Alexander Shulgin. In his book PiHKAL (Phenethylamines i Have Known And Loved), none of their durations are known.
Time zone	A time zone is a region of the Earth that has adopted the same standard time.
Hypothalamus	The hypothalamus is a region of the brain located below the thalamus, forming the major portion of the ventral region of the diencephalon and functioning to regulate certain metabolic processes and other autonomic activities.
Melanopsin	Melanopsin is a photopigment found in specialized photosensitive ganglion cells of the retina that are involved in the regulation of circadian rhythms and pupillary reflex. In structure, melanopsin is an opsin, a retinylidene protein variety of G-protein-coupled receptor.
Suprachiasmatic nucleus	The suprachiasmatic nucleus is in the hypothalamus and is so named because it resides immediately above the optic chaism. Its principal function is to create the circadian rhythm, which regulates the body functions over the 24-hour period.
Vision	Vision is the most important sense for birds, since good eyesight is essential for safe flight, and this group has a number of adaptations which give visual acuity superior to that of other vertebrate groups; a pigeon has been described as "two eyes with wings". The avian eye resembles that of a reptile, but has a better-positioned lens, a feature shared with mammals. Birds have the largest eyes relative to their size within the animal kingdom, and movement is consequently limited within the eye"s bony socket.
Optic chiasm	The optic chiasm is the part of the brain where the optic nerves partially cross. Specifically, the nerves connected to the right eye that attend to the left visual field cross with the nerves from the left eye that attend to the right visual field.
Genetics	Genetics is the science of heredity and variation in living organisms.Knowledge of the inheritance of characteristics has been implicitly used since prehistoric times for improving crop plants and animals through selective breeding. However, the modern science of genetics, which seeks to understand the mechanisms of inheritance, only began with the work of Gregor Mendel in the mid-1800s.
Melatonin	Melatonin is a hormone found in all living creatures from algae to humans, at levels that vary in a daily cycle. It plays a role in the regulation of the circadian rhythm of several biological functions.

Physiology	The study of the functions and activities of living cells, tissues, and organs and of the physical and chemical phenomena involved is referred to as physiology.
Protein	A protein is a complex, high-molecular-weight organic compound that consists of amino acids joined by peptide bonds. It is essential to the structure and function of all living cells and viruses. Many are enzymes or subunits of enzymes.
Disease	A Disease or medical problem is an abnormal condition of an organism that impairs bodily functions, associated with specific symptoms and signs. It may be caused by external factors, such as invading organisms, or it may be caused by internal dysfunctions, such as autoimmune Disease s. In human beings, Disease is often used more broadly to refer to any condition that causes extreme pain, dysfunction, distress, social problems, and/or death to the person afflicted, or similar problems for those in contact with the person.
Explanation	An explanation is a description which may clarify causes, context, and consequences of a certain object, and a phenomenon such as a process, a state of affairs. This description may establish rules or laws, and may clarify the existing ones in relation to an object, and a phenomenon examined. The components of an explanation can be implicit, and be interwoven with one another.
Posterior	In reference to the anatomical terms of location, the posterior end is laterally situated at or toward the hinder part of the body, lying at or extending toward the right or left side. It is the polar opposite to the anterior end, or front end of the body.
Understanding	Understanding is a psychological process related to an abstract or physical object, such as, person, situation, or message whereby one is able to think about it and use concepts to deal adequately with that object.
Antioxidant	An antioxidant is a molecule capable of slowing or preventing the oxidation of other molecules. Oxidation reactions can produce free radicals, which start chain reactions that damage cells. An antioxidant terminates these chain reactions by removing radical intermediates, and inhibit other oxidation reactions by being oxidized themselves.
Alpha	Alpha is the first letter of the Greek alphabet. In the system of Greek numerals it has a value of 1. It was derived from the Phoenician letter Aleph. Letters that arose from Alpha include the Latin A and the Cyrillic letter A.
Alpha wave	The brain wave associated with deep relaxation is referred to as the alpha wave. Recorded by electroencephalography (EEG) , they are synchronous and coherent (regular like sawtooth) and in the frequency range of 8 - 12 Hz. It is also called Berger's wave in memory of the founder of EEG.
Brain	In animals, the brain, is the control center of the central nervous system, responsible for behavior. The brain is located in the head, protected by the skull and close to the primary sensory apparatus of vision, hearing, equilibrioception, sense of acceleration, taste, and olfaction.

Brain death	Brain death is a legal definition of death that emerged as a response to the ability to resuscitate individuals and mechanically keep the heart and lungs working. In simple terms, brain death is the irreversible end of all brain activity. It should not be confused with a persistent vegetative state.
Coma	In medicine, a Coma is a profound state of unconsciousness. A Coma tose person cannot be awakened, fails to respond normally to pain or light, does not have sleep-wake cycles, and does not take voluntary actions.
EEG	Electroencephalography (EEG) is the measurement of electrical activity produced by the brain as recorded from electrodes placed on the scalp. Just as the activity in a computer can be understood on multiple levels, from the activity of individual transistors to the function of applications, so can the electrical activity of the brain be described on relatively small to relatively large scales. At one end are action potentials in a single axon or currents within a single dendrite of a single neuron, and at the other end is the activity measured by the EEG which aggregates the electric voltage fields from millions of neurons.
Electroencephalography	Electroencephalography is the measurement of electrical activity produced by the brain as recorded from electrodes placed on the scalp.
Polysomnograph	.Polysomnograph is a multi-parametric test used in the study of sleep; the test is called a polysomnogram . The polysomnogram is usually performed at night, when most people sleep. It monitors many body functions including brain, eye movements, muscle activity or skeletal muscle activation, hearth rhythm, and breathing function or respiratory effort during sleep.
Research method	The scope of the research method is to produce some new knowledge. This, in principle, can take three main forms: Exploratory research; Constructive research; and Empirical research.
Animal testing	Animal testing refers to the use of animals in experiments. It is estimated that 50 to 100 million vertebrate animals worldwide — from zebrafish to non-human primates — are used annually and either killed during the experiments or subsequently euthanized.
Arousal stage	The arousal stage is the phase of sexual activity that include sensations of pleasure with physiological changes, including the erection of the penis in males and the nipples in females. Females also experience vaginal lubrication and blood pooling in the pelvic region.
Data	Data in everyday language is a synonym for information. In the exact sciences there is a clear distinction between data and information, where data is a measurement that can be disorganized and when the data becomes organized it becomes information.
Electrode	Any device used to electrically stimulate nerve tissue or to record its activity is an electrode.

Heart	The heart is a muscular organ responsible for pumping blood through the blood vessels by repeated, rhythmic contractions, or a similar structure in the annelids, mollusks, and arthropods.
Heart rate	Heart rate is a term used to describe the frequency of the cardiac cycle. It is considered one of the four vital signs.
Records	In computer science, a record type is a type whose values are records, i.e. aggregates of several items of possibly different types. The items being aggregated are called fields or members and are usually identified or indexed by field labels, names identifying the fields.
Relaxation	Relaxation is a process or state with the aim of recreation through leisure activities or idling and the opposite of stress or tension
Responsiveness	The responsiveness of an interactive system describes how quickly it responds to user input.
Sign	A Sign is an entity which Sign ifies another entity. A natural Sign is an entity which bears a causal relation to the Sign ified entity, as thunder is a Sign of storm. A conventional Sign Sign ifies by agreement, as a full stop Sign ifies the end of a sentence.
Speech	Speech refers to the processes associated with the production and perception of sounds used in spoken language. A number of academic disciplines study speech and speech sounds, including acoustics, psychology, speech pathology, linguistics, and computer science.
Stages	Stages represent relatively discrete periods of time in which functioning is qualitatively different from functioning at other periods.
Attribute-value system	An Attribute-value system is a basic knowledge representation framework comprising a table with columns designating "attributes" and rows designating "objects" Each table cell therefore designates the value of a particular attribute of a particular object. Below is a sample Attribute-value system.
Stimulus	In psychology, a stimulus is part of the stimulus-response relationship of behavioral learning theory.
Unconsciousness	Unconsciousness, more appropriately referred to as loss of consciousness or lack of consciousness, is a dramatic alteration of mental state that involves complete or near-complete lack of responsiveness to people and other environmental stimuli. Being in a comatose state or coma is an illustration of Unconsciousness. Fainting due to a drop in blood pressure and a decrease of the oxygen supply to the brain is an illustration of a temporary loss of consciousness.

305

Wakefulness	Wakefulness refers to the state of being awake and is the behavioral manifestation of the metabolic state of catabolism. It is the daily recurring period in an organism"s life during which consciousness, awareness and all behaviors necessary for survival, i.e., success in, are conducted. Being awake is the opposite of being asleep a behavioral manifestation of the daily recurring metabolic state of anabolism.
K-complex	A K-complex is an electroencephalography (EEG) waveform that occurs during stage 2 of NREM sleep. It is the "largest event in healthy human EEG". It consists of a brief negative high-voltage peak, usually greater than 100 ÂμV, followed by a slower positive complex around 350 and 550 ms and at 900ms a final negative peak.
Rapid eye movement	Rapid eye movement is the stage of sleep during which the most vivid (though not all) dreams occur. During this stage, the eyes move rapidly, and the activity of the brain's neurons is quite similar to that during waking hours. It is the lightest form of sleep in that people awakened during REM usually feel alert and refreshed.
Rapid eye movement sleep	Rapid eye movement sleep is the normal stage of sleep characterized by rapid movements of the eyes. Criteria for Rapid eye movement sleep include not only rapid eye movements, but also low muscle tone and a rapid, low voltage EEG these features are easily discernible in a polysomnogram, the sleep study typically done for patients with suspected sleep disorders.
Slow-wave sleep	Slow-wave sleep includes stages 3 and 4, during which low-frequency delta waves become prominent in EEG recordings.
Discovery	Discovery observations form acts of detecting and learning something. Discovery observations are acts in which something is found and given a productive insight. Serendipity is the effect by which one accidentally discovers something fortunate, especially while looking for something else entirely.
Eye	Eye s are organs that detect light, and send signals along the optic nerve to the visual and other areas of the brain. Complex optical systems with resolving power have come in ten fundamentally different forms, and 96% of animal species possess a complex optical system. Image-resolving Eye s are present in cnidaria, molluscs, chordates, annelids and arthropods.
Cytoplasmic streaming	Cytoplasmic streaming is the flowing of cytoplasm in eukaryotic cells. This occurs in both plant and animal cells.
Muscle	Muscle is contractile tissue of the body and is derived from the mesodermal layer of embryonic germ cells. It is classified as skeletal, cardiac, or smooth muscle, and its function is to produce force and cause motion, either locomotion or movement within internal organs.
Sleep stages	Levels of sleep identified by brain-wave patterns and behavioral changes are called sleep stages.

Dream	A dream is the experience of a sequence of images, like a movie with sounds, ideas, emotions, or other sensations during sleep, especially REM sleep. The dream environment is often much more realistic in a lucid dream, and the senses heightened.
Non-REM sleep	Sleep stages 1 through 4, which are marked by an absence of rapid eye movements, relatively little dreaming, and varied EEG activity are called non-rem sleep.
Acetic acid	Acetic acid, is an organic chemical compound, giving vinegar its sour taste and pungent smell. Its structural formula is represented as CH_3COOH.
Antihistamine	A histamine antagonist is an agent that serves to inhibit the release or action of histamine. Antihistamine can be used to describe any histamine antagonist, but it is usually reserved for the classical Antihistamine s that act upon the H_1 histamine receptor. Antihistamine s are used as treatment for allergies.
Audition	An Audition is a sample performance by an actor, singer, musician, dancer or other performer. It involves the performer displaying their talent through a previously-memorized and rehearsed solo piece: for example, a monologue for actors or a song for a singer. Used in the context of performing arts, it is analogous to job interviews in many ways.
Axon	An axon is a long, slender projection of a nerve cell, or neuron, that conducts electrical impulses away from the neuron"s cell body or soma.
Consciousness	The awareness of the sensations, thoughts, and feelings being experienced at a given moment is called consciousness.
Glutamate	Glutamate is one of the 20 standard amino acids used by all organisms in their proteins. It is critical for proper cell function, but it is not an essential nutrient in humans because it can be manufactured from other compounds.
Histamine	Histamine is a biogenic amine involved in local immune responses as well as regulating physiological function in the gut and acting as a neurotransmitter. It has been found that about half the patients classified as suffering from schizophrenia have low histamine levels in the blood. This may be because of antipsychotics that have unwanted effect on histamine, such as Quetiapine.
Lateral hypothalamus	The Lateral hypothalamus is a part of the hypothalamus. The Lateral hypothalamus is concerned with hunger. Any damage sustained to the lateral hypothalamus can cause reduced food intake.
Midbrain	The midbrain is the middle of three vesicles that arise from the neural tube that forms the brain of developing animals. In mature human brains, it becomes the least differentiated, from both its developmental form and within its own structure, among the three vesicles. The midbrain is considered part of the brain stem.

Nervous system	The nervous system of an animal coordinates the activity of the muscles, monitors the organs, constructs and also stops input from the senses, and initiates actions.
Orexin	Orexin is the common name given to a pair of highly excititory neuropeptide hormones that were simultaneously discovered by two groups of reseachers in rat brains. The University of Texas, coined the term orexin to reflect the appetite-stimulating activity of these hormones.
Reticular formation	The reticular formation is a part of the brain which is involved in stereotypical actions, such as walking, sleeping, and lying down. It is essential for governing some of the basic functions of higher organisms, and phylogenetically one of the oldest portions of the brain.
Acetylcholine	The chemical compound acetylcholine, often abbreviated as ACh, was the first neurotransmitter to be identified. It is a chemical transmitter in both the peripheral nervous system and central nervous system in many organisms including humans.
Anterior	Anterior is an anatomical term referring to the front part of the body. The anterior is positioned in front of another body part, or towards the head of an animal. It is the opposite of posterior.
Attention	Attention is the cognitive process of selectively concentrating on one aspect of the environment while ignoring other things. Examples include listening carefully to what someone is saying while ignoring other conversations in the room or listening to a cell phone conversation while driving a car.
Basal forebrain	The basal forebrain is a collection of structures located ventrally to the striatum. Cholinergic neurons in the basal forebrain participate in behavioral processes such as attention and memory.
Brain stem	The brain stem is the lower part of the brain, adjoining and structurally continuous with the spinal cord. Most sources consider the pons, medulla oblongata, and midbrain all to be part of the brain stem.
Cerebral cortex	The cerebral cortex is a structure within the vertebrate brain with distinct structural and functional properties.
Constant	A constant is something that does not change, over time or otherwise: a fixed value. In most fields of discourse the term is an antonym of "variable", but in mathematical parlance a mathematical variable may sometimes also be called a constant.
Control group	A control group augments integrity in experiments by isolating variables as dictated by the scientific method in order to make a conclusion about such variables. In other cases, an experimental control is used to prevent the effects of one variable from being drowned out by the known, greater effects of other variables. this case, the researchers can either use a control group or use statistical techniques to control for the other variables.
Drinking	Drinking is the act of consuming a liquid through the mouth.

Eating	Eating is the process of consuming nutrition, i.e. food, for the purpose of providing for the nutritional needs of an animal, particularly their energy requirements and to grow.
Emotion	Emotion, in its most general definition, is a complex psychophysical process that arises spontaneously, rather than through conscious effort, and evokes either a positive or negative psychological response and physical expressions, often involuntary, related to feelings, perceptions or beliefs about elements, objects or relations between them, in reality or in the imagination. An emotion is often differentiated from a feeling.
Software extension	A Software extension is a computer program designed to be incorporated into another piece of software in order to enhance the functionalities of the latter. On its own, the program is not useful or functional. Examples of software applications that support extensions include the Mozilla Firefox Web browser, Adobe Systems Photoshop and Microsoft Windows Explorer shell extensions.
Inferior colliculus	The Inferior colliculus is one of the essential auditory centers located in the mesencephalon.
Medulla	Medulla refers to the middle of something, and derives from the Latin word for "marrow" In medicine it refers to either bone marrow, the spinal cord, or more generally, the middle part of a structure as opposed to the cortex.
Neurotransmitter	A neurotransmitter is a chemical that is used to relay, amplify and modulate electrical signals between a neurons and another cell.
Single	In relationships, a single person is one who is not married, or, more broadly, who is not in an exclusive romantic relationship.
Spinal cord	The spinal cord is a thin, tubular bundle of nerves that is an extension of the central nervous system from the brain and is enclosed in and protected by the bony vertebral column. The main function of the spinal cord is transmission of neural inputs between the periphery and the brain.
Superior colliculus	The superior colliculus is a paired structure that is part of the brain"s tectal area. In humans, the superior colliculus is involved in the generation of saccadic eye movements and eye-head coordination.
Tegmentum	The tegmentum is a general area within the brainstem.
Gamma-aminobutyric acid	Gamma-aminobutyric acid is an inhibitory neurotransmitter found in the nervous systems of widely-divergent species. It is the chief inhibitory neurotransmitter in the central nervous system and also in the retina.

Amnesia	Amnesia is a condition in which memory is disturbed. The causes of amnesia are organic or functional. Organic causes include damage to the brain, through trauma or disease, or use of certain generally sedative drugs.
Appetite	The appetite is the desire to eat food, felt as hunger. Appetite exists in all higher lifeforms, and serves to regulate adequate energy intake to maintain metabolic needs. It is regulated by a close interplay between the digestive tract, adipose tissue and the brain. Decreased desire to eat is termed anorexia, while polyphagia or "hyperphagia" is increased eating. Disregulation of appetite contributes to anorexia nervosa, bulimia nervosa, cachexia, overeating, and binge eating disorder.
Confusion	Severe confusion of a degree considered pathological usually refers to loss of orientation, and often memory. Confusion as such is not synonymous with inability to focus attention, although severe inability to focus attention can cause, or greatly contribute to, confusion.
Delusion	A false belief, not generally shared by others, and that cannot be changed despite strong evidence to the contrary is a delusion.
Hallucination	A hallucination is a sensory perception experienced in the absence of an external stimulus, as distinct from an illusion, which is a misperception of an external stimulus. They may occur in any sensory modality - visual, auditory, olfactory, gustatory, tactile, or mixed.
Memory loss	Memory loss can have many causes: · Alzheimer"s disease is an illness which can cause mild to severe memory loss · Parkinson"s disease is a genetic defect which may result in memory loss · Huntington"s disease is an inherited disease which can result in memory loss · It is sometimes a side effect of chemotherapy in which cytotoxic drugs are used to treat cancer. · Certain forms of mental illness also have memory loss as a key symptom, including fugue states and the much more famous Dissociative Identity Disorder. · Stress-related activities are another factor which can result in memory loss · It can also be caused by traumatic brain injury, of which a concussion is a form. .
Dorsum	In anatomy, the dorsum is the upper side of animals that typically run, fly or swim in a horizontal position, and the back side of animals that walk upright. In vertebrates the dorsum contains the backbone.
Dorsolateral prefrontal cortex	Brodmann area 46, is part of the frontal cortex in the human brain. Brodmann area 46 roughly corresponds with the dorsolateral prefrontal cortex though the borders of area 46 are based on cytoarchitecture rather than function. It is also encompasses part of granular frontal area 9, directly adjacent on the dorsal surface of the cortex.

Limbic system	The limbic system includes the putative structures in the human brain involved in emotion, motivation, and emotional association with memory. The limbic system influences the formation of memory by integrating emotional states with stored memories of physical sensations.
Motor cortex	Motor cortex is a term that describes regions of the cerebral cortex involved in the planning, control, and execution of voluntary motor functions.
Parasympathetic nervous system	The parasympathetic nervous system is a division of the autonomic nervous system, along with the sympathetic nervous system and Enteric nervous system. The ANS is a subdivision of the peripheral nervous system.
Pons	The pons is a structure located on the brain stem. It is rostral to the medulla oblongata, caudal to the midbrain, and ventral to the cerebellum. In humans and other bipeds this means it is above the medulla, below the midbrain, and anterior to the cerebellum.
Positron emission tomography	Positron emission tomography is a nuclear medicine medical imaging technique which produces a three-dimensional image or map of functional processes in the body. Images of metabolic activity in space are then reconstructed by computer, often in modern scanners aided by results from a CT X-ray scan.
Primary	In medicine, the reporting of symptoms by a patient may have significant psychological motivators. Psychologists sometimes categorize these motivators into primary or secondary gain. primary gain is internally good; motivationally.
Primary motor cortex	The primary motor cortex works in association with pre-motor areas to plan and execute movements. It contains large neurons known as Betz cells which send long axons down the spinal cord to synapse onto alpha motor neurons which connect to the muscles.
Primary somatosensory cortex	The lateral postcentral gyrus is a prominent structure in the parietal lobe of the human brain and an important landmark. It was initially defined from surface stimulation studies of Penfield, and parallel surface potential studies of Bard, Woolsey, and Marshall. Although initially defined to be roughly the same as Brodmann areas 3, 1 and 2, more recent work by Kaas has suggested that for homogeny with other sensory fields only area 3 should be referred to as "*Primary somatosensory cortex*", as it received the bulk of the thalamocortical projection from the sensory input fields.
Temporal lobe	The temporal lobe is part of the cerebrum. It lies at the side of the brain, beneath the lateral or Sylvian fissure. Adjacent areas in the superior, posterior and lateral parts of the temporal lobe are involved in high-level auditory processing.
Amygdala	Amygdala are almond-shaped groups of neurons located deep within the medial temporal lobes of the brain in complex vertebrates, including humans. Shown in research to perform a primary role in the processing and memory of emotional reactions, the amygdala are considered part of the limbic system.

Central sulcus	The central sulcus is a prominent landmark of the brain, separating the parietal lobe from the frontal lobe. The central sulcus is the site of the primary motor cortex in mammals, a group of cells that controls voluntary movements of the body.
Cingulate gyrus	Cingulate gyrus is a gyrus in the medial part of the brain. It partially wraps around the corpus callosum and is limited above by the cingulate sulcus. It functions as an intergral part of the limbic system, which is involved with emotion formation and processing, learning, and memory.
Electrical potential	Electrical potential is the potential energy per unit of charge associated with a static electric field, also called the electrostatic potential, typically measured in volts. The electrical potential and the magnetic vector potential together form a four vector, so that the two kinds of potential are mixed under Lorentz transformations.
Hindbrain	The hindbrain is a developmental categorization of portions of the central nervous system in vertebrates. It can be subdivided in a variable number of transversal swellings called rhombomeres.
Message	A message in its most general meaning is an object of communication.
Nerve	A Nerve is an enclosed, cable-like bundle of peripheral axons (the long, slender projections of neurons.) A Nerve provides a common pathway for the electrochemical Nerve impulses that are transmitted along each of the axons. Nerve s are found only in the peripheral nervous system.
Occipital lobe	The occipital lobe is the visual processing center of the mammalian brain, containing most of the anatomical region of the visual cortex. The primary visual cortex is Brodmann area 17, commonly called V_1.
Olfactory bulb	The olfactory bulb is a structure of the vertebrate forebrain involved in olfaction, the perception of odors.
Somatosensory	Somatosensory system consists of the various sensory receptors that trigger the experiences labelled as touch or pressure, temperature, pain, and the sensations of muscle movement and joint position including posture, movement, and facial expression.
Norepinephrine	Norepinephrine is a catecholamine and a phenethylamine with chemical formula $C_8H_{11}NO_3$.
Serotonin	Serotonin, is a monoamine neurotransmitter synthesized in serotonergic neurons in the central nervous system and enterochromaffin cells in the gastrointestinal tract of animals including humans. Serotonin is also found in many mushrooms and plants, including fruits and vegetables.

Behavior	Behavior refers to the actions or reactions of an object or organism, usually in relation to the environment. Behavior can be conscious or subconscious, overt or covert, and voluntary or involuntary. Human Behavior (and that of other organisms and mechanisms) can be common, unusual, acceptable, or unacceptable. Humans evaluate the acceptability of Behavior using social norms and regulate Behavior by means of social control
Body weight	Body weight is a term that is used in biological and medical science contexts to describe the mass of an organism"s body. Body weight is measured in kilograms throughout the world, although in some countries people more often measure and describe body weight in pounds or stones and pounds and thus may not be well acquainted with measurement in kilograms.
Obesity	Obesity is a condition in which excess body fat has accumulated to an extent that health may be negatively affected. It is commonly defined as a body mass index (BMI) of 30 kg/m^2 or higher. This distinguishes it from being pre-obese or overweight as defined by a BMI of 25 kg/m^2 but less than 30 kg/m^2.
Positive Airway Pressure	Positive airway pressure is a method of respiratory ventilation used primarily in the treatment of sleep apnea, for which it was first developed.
Sleep apnea	Sleep apnea refers to a sleep disorder involving periods during sleep when breathing stops and the person must awaken briefly in order to breathe; major symptoms are excessive daytime sleepiness and loud snoring.
Tranquilizer	A sedative, or tranquilizer, is a drug that depresses the central nervous system (CNS), which causes calmness, relaxation, reduction of anxiety, sleepiness, slowed breathing, slurred speech, staggering gait, poor judgment, and slow, uncertain reflexes.
Sleep disorder	A Sleep disorder (somnipathy) is a medical disorder of the sleep patterns of a person or animal. Some Sleep disorder s are serious enough to interfere with normal physical, mental and emotional functioning. A test commonly ordered for some Sleep disorder s is the polysomnogram.
Basal ganglia	The basal ganglia are a group of nuclei in the brain associated with motor and learning functions.
Brain damage	Brain damage is the destruction or degeneration of brain cells. It may occur due to a wide range of conditions, illnesses, injuries, and as a result of iatrogenesis. Possible causes of widespread brain damage include prolonged hypoxia, poisoning by teratogens, infection, and neurological illness.
Cataplexy	Sudden loss of muscle tone that accompanies narcolepsy is called cataplexy.

Dopamine	Dopamine is a hormone and neurotransmitter occurring in a wide variety of animals, including both vertebrates and invertebrates. In the brain, dopamine functions as a neurotransmitter. Dopamine is also a neurohormone released by the hypothalamus. Its main function as a hormone is to inhibit the release of prolactin from the anterior lobe of the pituitary.
Hypnagogic	When in a hypnagogic state a person can have lifelike auditory, visual, or tactile hallucinations, perhaps even accompanied by full body paralysis. The individual is aware that these are hallucinations; the frightening part, in many cases, is the inability to react to them, even being unable to make a sound. In other cases one may enjoy truly vivid imaginations.
Methylphenidate	Methylphenidate is a prescription stimulant commonly used to treat Attention-deficit hyperactivity disorder, or ADHD. It is also one of the primary drugs used to treat the daytime drowsiness symptoms of narcolepsy and chronic fatigue syndrome.
Narcolepsy	A serious sleep disorder characterized by excessive daytime sleepiness and sudden, uncontrollable attacks of REM sleep is called narcolepsy.
Night terror	A night terror is a parasomnia sleep disorder characterized by extreme terror and a temporary inability to regain full consciousness. The subject wakes abruptly from slow-wave sleep, with waking usually accompanied by gasping, moaning, or screaming.
REM behavior disorder	A failure of normal muscle paralysis, leading to violent actions during REM sleep is a rem behavior disorder.
Sleep paralysis	Sleep paralysis is a condition characterized by temporary paralysis of the body shortly after waking up or, less often, shortly before falling asleep.
Sleep talking	Sleep talking is a parasomnia that refers to talking aloud in one"s sleep. It can be quite loud, ranging from simple sounds to long speeches, and can occur many times during sleep. It is harmless and the content should be taken lightly, however it can wake up others and cause them consternation especially when misinterpreted as conscious speech by an observer.
Sleepwalking	Sleepwalking is a sleep disorder where the sufferer engages in activities that are normally associated with wakefulness while he or she is asleep or in a sleeplike state. Sleepwalking is more commonly experienced in people with high levels of stress, anxiety or other psychological factors and in people with genetic factors or sometimes a combination of both.
Stimulant	A stimulant is a drug which increases the activity of the sympathetic nervous system and produces a sense of euphoria or awakeness.
Stimulant drugs	*Stimulant drugs* are drugs that temporarily increase alertness and awareness. They usually have increased side-effects with increased effectiveness, and the more powerful variants are therefore often prescription medicines or illegal drugs. Ritalin SR 20mg.

Stimulants increase the activity of either the sympathetic nervous system, the central nervous system (CNS) or both.

Alcoholism	Alcoholism is a term with multiple and sometimes conflicting definitions. In common and historic usage, alcoholism refers to any condition that results in the continued consumption of alcoholic beverages despite the health problems and negative social consequences it causes.
Alertness	Alertness is the state of paying close and continuous attention being watchful and prompt to meet danger or emergency, or being quick to perceive and act. It is related to psychology as well as to physiology. A lack of Alertness is a symptom of a number of conditions, including narcolepsy, attention deficit disorder, chronic fatigue syndrome, depression, Addison"s disease, or sleep deprivation.
Anxiety	Anxiety is a physiological state characterized by cognitive, somatic, emotional, and behavioral components.
Blocking	If the one of the two members of a compound stimulus fails to produce the CR due to an earlier conditioning of the other member of the compound stimulus, blocking has occurred.
Caudate nucleus	The caudate nucleus is a nucleus located within the basal ganglia of the brains of many animal species. The caudate nuclei are located near the center of the brain, sitting astride the thalamus. There is a caudate nucleus within each hemisphere of the brain.
Experience	Experience as a general concept comprises knowledge of or skill in or observation of some thing or some event gained through involvement in or exposure to that thing or event. The history of the word experience aligns it closely with the concept of experiment.
Fatigue	The word fatigue is used in everyday life to describe a range of afflictions, varying from a general state of lethargy to a specific work-induced burning sensation within one"s muscles. It can be both physical and mental. Such a mental fatigue, in turn, can manifest itself both as somnolence just as a general decrease of attention, not necessarily including sleepiness.
Generation	Generation, also known as procreation, is the act of producing offspring. A generation can also be a stage or degree in a succession of natural descent as a grandfather, a father, and the father"s son comprise three generations.
Globus pallidus	The globus pallidus is a sub-cortical structure of the brain. It is a major element of the basal ganglia system. In this system, it is a major element of the basal ganglia core, consisting of the striatum and its direct targets: globus pallidus and substantia nigra. The last two are made up of the same neuronal elements, have a similar main afferent, have a similar synaptology, and do not receive cortical afferents.

Disability	A disability is a condition or function judged to be significantly impaired relative to the usual standard of an individual or their group. The term is often used to refer to individual functioning, including physical impairments, sensory impairments, cognitive impairments, intellectual impairments or mental health issue.
Mood	A mood is a relatively lasting emotional or affective state. They differ from emotions in that they are less specific, often less intense, less likely to be triggered by a particular stimulus or event, however longer lasting.
Putamen	The putamen is a structure in the middle of the brain, which, together with the caudate nucleus forms the dorsal striatum. The putamen is a portion of the basal ganglia that forms the outermost part of the lenticular nucleus.
Reuptake	Reuptake is the reabsorption of a neurotransmitter by the neurotransmitter transporter of a pre-synaptic neuron after it has performed its function of transmitting a neural impulse. This prevents further activity of the neurotransmitter, weakening its effects.
Rigidity	In psychology, rigidity refers to an obstacle to problem solving which arises from over-dependence on prior experience, which makes it difficult for a person with experience in a specific problem domain to recognize novel solution strategies.
Stimulation	Stimulation is the action of various agents on muscles, nerves, or a sensory end organ, by which activity is evoked.
Synapse	A synapse is specialized junction through which cells of the nervous system signal to one another and to non-neuronal cells such as muscles or glands. They allow the neurons of the central nervous system to form interconnected neural circuits.
Synapses	Chemical synapses are specialized junctions through which neurons signal to each other and to non-neuronal cells such as those in muscles or glands. Chemical synapses allow neurons to form circuits within the central nervous system. They are crucial to the biological computations that underlie perception and thought.
Tremor	Tremor is the rhythmic, oscillating shaking movement of the whole body or just a certain part of it, caused by problems of the neurons responsible from muscle action.
Muscle contraction	A muscle contraction occurs when a muscle fiber generates tension through the action of actin and myosin cross-bridge cycling.
Sexual behavior	Human Sexual behavior refers to the manner in which humans experience and express their sexuality. It encompass a wide range of activities such as strategies to find or attract partners (mating and display behaviour), interactions between individuals, physical or emotional intimacy, and sexual contact.

	Although some cultures hold that sexual activity is acceptable only within marriage, extramarital sexual activities still takes place within such cultures.
Dementia	Dementia is the progressive decline in cognitive function due to damage or disease in the brain beyond what might be expected from normal aging.
Dementia praecox	An older term for schizophrenia, chosen to describe what was believed to be an incurable and progressive deterioration of mental functioning beginning in adolescence is called dementia praecox.
Energy	The concept of psychic Energy was developed in the field of psychodynamics. In 1874, German scientist Ernst von Brucke proposed that all living organisms are Energy-systems governed by the principle of the conservation of Energy. Brucke was also coincidentally the supervisor at the University of Vienna for first-year medical student Sigmund Freud who adopted this new paradigm.
Conservation	Conservation refers to an ability in logical thinking according to the psychologist Jean Piaget who developed four stages in cognitive development. By the third stage, the Concrete operational stage, the child of age 7-11 has mastered this ability, to logically determine that a certain quantity will remain the same despite adjustment of the container, shape, or apparent size.
Hibernation	Hibernation is a state of inactivity and metabolic depression in animals, characterized by lower body temperature, slower breathing, and lower metabolic rate. Hibernation allows animals to conserve energy during the winter when food is short. During hibernation, animals drastically lower their metabolism so as to tap energy reserves stored as body fat at a slower rate.
Species	Species refers to a reproductively isolated breeding population.
Adenosine	Adenosine is a nucleoside composed of adenine attached to a ribose (ribofuranose) moiety via a β-N_9-glycosidic bond. Adenosine plays an important role in biochemical processes, such as energy transfer and Adenosine plays an important role in biochemical processes, such as energy transfer. It is also an inhibitory neurotransmitter, believed to play a role in promoting sleep and suppressing arousal, with levels increasing with each hour an organism is awake.
Caffeine	Caffeine is a xanthine alkaloid compound that acts as a psychoactive stimulant in humans. In humans, caffeine is a central nervous system stimulant, having the effect of temporarily warding off drowsiness and restoring alertness. Beverages containing caffeine, such as coffee, tea, soft drinks and energy drinks enjoy great popularity; caffeine is the world"s most widely consumed psychoactive substance, but unlike most other psychoactive substances, it is legal and unregulated in nearly all jurisdictions.
Sleep deprivation	Sleep deprivation is a general lack of the necessary amount of sleep. This may occur as a result of sleep disorders, active choice or deliberate inducement such as in interrogation or for torture..

Bipolar disorder	Bipolar disorder is a psychiatric condition defined as recurrent episodes of significant disturbance in mood. These disturbances can occur on a spectrum that ranges from debilitating depression to unbridled mania. Individuals suffering from bipolar disorder typically experience fluid states of mania, hypomania or what is referred to as a mixed state in conjunction with depressive episodes.
Coffee	Coffee is a widely consumed stimulant beverage prepared from roasted seeds. Most studies are contradictory as to whether coffee has any specific health benefits, and results are similarly conflicting regarding negative effects of coffee consumption. Research suggests that drinking caffeinated coffee can cause a temporary increase in the stiffening of arterial walls.
Antidepressant	An antidepressant, is a psychiatric medication or other substance (nutrient or herb) used for alleviating depression or dysthymia ("milder" depression). Drug groups known as MAOIs, tricyclics and SSRIs are particularly associated with the term. These medications are now amongst the drugs most commonly prescribed by psychiatrists and general practitioners, and their effectiveness and adverse effects are the subject of many studies and competing claims.
Cornea	The cornea is the transparent front part of the eye that covers the iris, pupil, and anterior chamber and provides most of an eye's optical power. Together with the lens, the cornea refracts light and consequently helps the eye to focus.
Eyes	Eyes are organs that detect light. Different kinds of light-sensitive organs are found in a variety of animals. The simplest eyes do nothing but detect whether the surroundings are light or dark, which is sufficient for the entrainment of circadian rhythms but can hardly be called vision. More complex eyes can distinguish shapes and colors. The visual fields of some such complex eyes largely overlap, to allow better depth perception, as in humans; and others are placed so as to minimize the overlap, such as in rabbits and chameleons.
Intelligence	Intelligence is a property of mind that encompasses many related abilities, such as the capacities to reason, plan, solve problems, think abstractly, comprehend ideas and language, and learn. In some cases intelligence may include traits such as creativity, personality, character, knowledge, or wisdom. However other psychologists prefer not to include these traits in the definition of intelligence.
Long-term potentiation	In neuroscience, long-term potentiation is the long-lasting enhancement in communication between two neurons that results from stimulating them simultaneously.
Activation-synthesis	Activation-Synthesis is a neurobiological theory of dreams, put forward by Allan Hobson and Robert McCarley in 1977, which states that dreams are a random event caused by firing of neurons in the brain.
Hypothesis	A hypothesis consists either of a suggested explanation for a phenomenon or of a reasoned proposal suggesting a possible correlation between multiple phenomena.

| Sensation | Sensation is the first stage in the chain of biochemical and neurologic events that begins with the impinging of a stimulus upon the receptor cells of a sensory organ, which then leads to perception, the mental state that is reflected in statements like "I see a uniformly blue wall." |

| Sense | Sense are the physiological methods of perception. They and their operation, classification, and theory are overlapping topics studied by a variety of fields, most notably neuroscience, cognitive psychology, and philosophy of perception. The nervous system has a sensory system dedicated to each sense. |

View

A View is what can be seen in a range of vision. View may also be used as a synonym of point of View in the first sense. View may also be used figuratively or with special significance--for example, to imply a scenic outlook or significant vantage point:

> The barrier Rhine hath flashed, through battle-smoke,
> On men who gaze heart-smitten by the View,
> As if all Germany had felt the shock!

> - from The Germans on the Heights of Hochheim by William Wordsworth

Laws or regulations in various jurisdictions may protect a View as an easement, preventing property owners from constructing buildings that would block the View from another location.

Prefrontal cortex

The prefrontal cortex is the anterior part of the frontal lobes of the brain, lying in front of the motor and premotor areas. Cytoarchitectonically, it is defined by the presence of an internal granular layer IV.

Working memory

Working memory is a theoretical framework within cognitive psychology that refers to the structures and processes used for temporarily storing and manipulating information. There are numerous theories as to both the theoretical structure of working memory as well as to the specific parts of the brain responsible for working memory.

Frontal lobe

The frontal lobe comprises four major folds of cortical tissue: the precentral gyrus, superior gyrus and the middle gyrus of the frontal gyri, the inferior frontal gyrus. It has been found to play a part in impulse control, judgement, language, memory, motor function, problem solving, sexual behavior, socialization and spontaneity.

Scolex

The Scolex of the worm attaches to the intestine of the definitive host. In some groups, the scolex is dominated by bothria, which are sometimes called "sucking grooves," and function like suction cups.

Need

A Need is something that is necessary for humans to live a healthy life. Need s are distinguished from wants because a deficiency would cause a clear negative outcome, such as dysfunction or death. Need s can be objective and physical, such as food and water, or they can be subjective and psychological, such as the Need for self-esteem.

Signal	In the fields of communications, signal processing, and in electrical engineering more generally, a signal is any time-varying quantity. Signals are often scalar-valued functions of time, but may be vector valued and may be functions of any other relevant independent variable.
Storage	The human memory has three processes: encoding (input), Storage and retrieval(output.) Storage is the process of retaining information whether in the sensory memory, the short-term memory or the more permanent long-term memory.

Behavior	Behavior refers to the actions or reactions of an object or organism, usually in relation to the environment. Behavior can be conscious or subconscious, overt or covert, and voluntary or involuntary. Human Behavior (and that of other organisms and mechanisms) can be common, unusual, acceptable, or unacceptable. Humans evaluate the acceptability of Behavior using social norms and regulate Behavior by means of social control
Thermoregulation	Thermoregulation is the ability of an organism to keep the temperature of its body within certain boundaries, even when temperature surrounding is very different. This process is one aspect of homeostasis: a dynamic state of stability between an animal"s internal environment and its external environment.
Homeostasis	Homeostasis is the property of either an open system or a closed system, especially a living organism, which regulates its internal environment so as to maintain a stable, constant condition.
Allostasis	Allostasis is the process of achieving stability, or homeostasis, through physiological or behavioral change. This can be carried out by means of alteration in HPA axis hormones, the autonomic nervous system, cytokines, or a number of other systems, and is generally adaptive in the short term
Basal metabolic rate	Basal metabolic rate is the amount of energy expended while at rest in a neutrally temperate environment, in the post-absorptive state meaning that the digestive system is inactive, which requires about twelve hours of fasting in humans.
Brain	In animals, the brain, is the control center of the central nervous system, responsible for behavior. The brain is located in the head, protected by the skull and close to the primary sensory apparatus of vision, hearing, equilibrioception, sense of acceleration, taste, and olfaction.
Brain damage	Brain damage is the destruction or degeneration of brain cells. It may occur due to a wide range of conditions, illnesses, injuries, and as a result of iatrogenesis. Possible causes of widespread brain damage include prolonged hypoxia, poisoning by teratogens, infection, and neurological illness.
Caudate nucleus	The caudate nucleus is a nucleus located within the basal ganglia of the brains of many animal species. The caudate nuclei are located near the center of the brain, sitting astride the thalamus. There is a caudate nucleus within each hemisphere of the brain.
Globus pallidus	The globus pallidus is a sub-cortical structure of the brain. It is a major element of the basal ganglia system. In this system, it is a major element of the basal ganglia core, consisting of the striatum and its direct targets: globus pallidus and substantia nigra. The last two are made up of the same neuronal elements, have a similar main afferent, have a similar synaptology, and do not receive cortical afferents.
Hypothalamus	The hypothalamus is a region of the brain located below the thalamus, forming the major portion of the ventral region of the diencephalon and functioning to regulate certain metabolic processes and other autonomic activities.

Negative feedback	Negative feedback occurs when the output of a system acts to partially oppose fluctuations of the input to the system; generally with the result that fluctuations are attenuated. Many real-world systems have one or several points around which the system gravitates. In response to a perturbation, a Negative feedback system with such point(s) will tend to re-establish equilibrium.
Putamen	The putamen is a structure in the middle of the brain, which, together with the caudate nucleus forms the dorsal striatum. The putamen is a portion of the basal ganglia that forms the outermost part of the lenticular nucleus.
Set point	Set point refers to any one of a number of quantities (e.g. body weight, body temperature) which the body tries to keep at a particular value
Perspiration	Perspiration is the production and evaporation of a fluid, consisting primarily of water as well as a smaller amount of sodium chloride, that is excreted by the sweat glands in the skin of mammals.
Constant	A constant is something that does not change, over time or otherwise: a fixed value. In most fields of discourse the term is an antonym of "variable", but in mathematical parlance a mathematical variable may sometimes also be called a constant.
Energy	The concept of psychic Energy was developed in the field of psychodynamics. In 1874, German scientist Ernst von Brucke proposed that all living organisms are Energy-systems governed by the principle of the conservation of Energy. Brucke was also coincidentally the supervisor at the University of Vienna for first-year medical student Sigmund Freud who adopted this new paradigm.
Prosencephalon	In the anatomy of the brain of vertebrates, the prosencephalon is the rostral-most portion of the brain. The prosencephalon, the mesencephalon, and rhombencephalon are the three primary portions of the brain during early development of the central nervous system.
Maxima	In mathematics, maxima and minima, known collectively as extrema (singular: extremum), are the largest value (maximum) or smallest value (minimum), that a function takes in a point either within a given neighbourhood (local extremum) or on the function domain in its entirety (global extremum). Throughout, a point refers to an input (x), while a value refers to an output (y): one distinguishing between the maximum value and the point (or points) at which it occurs. A real-valued function f defined on the real line is said to have a local (or relative) maximum point at the point x^*, if there exists some $\varepsilon > 0$, such that $f(x^*) \geq f(x)$ when $|x - x^*| < \varepsilon$.
Range	In descriptive statistics, the range is the length of the smallest interval which contains all the data. It is calculated by subtracting the smallest observations from the greatest and provides an indication of statistical dispersion.
Structure	Structure is a fundamental and sometimes intangible notion covering the recognition, observation, nature, and stability of patterns and relationships of entities.

Variable	A variable refers to a measurable factor, characteristic, or attribute of an individual or a system.
Goose	Goose is the English name for a considerable number of birds, belonging to the family Anatidae. This family also includes swans, most of which are larger, and ducks, which are smaller. A goose eats a largely vegetarian diet, and can become pests when flocks feed on arable crops or inhabit ponds or grassy areas in urban environments.
Hair	Hair is a filamentous outgrowth of protein, found only on mammals. It projects from the epidermis, though it grows from hair follicles deep in the dermis.
Shivering	Shivering is a bodily function in response to early hypothermia in warm-blooded animals. When the core body temperature drops, the shivering reflex is triggered. Muscle groups around the vital organs begin to shake in small movements in an attempt to create warmth by expending energy. Shivering can also be a response to a fever as a person may feel cold, though their core temperature is already elevated.
Erection	The erection of the penis, clitoris or a nipple is its enlarged and firm state. It depends on a complex interaction of psychological, neural, vascular and endocrine factors. The ability to maintain the erectile state is key to the reproductive system and many forms of life could not reproduce in a natural way without this ability.
Muscle	Muscle is contractile tissue of the body and is derived from the mesodermal layer of embryonic germ cells. It is classified as skeletal, cardiac, or smooth muscle, and its function is to produce force and cause motion, either locomotion or movement within internal organs.
Prenatal development	Prenatal development is the process in which an embryo or fetus gestates during pregnancy, from fertilization until birth.
Protein	A protein is a complex, high-molecular-weight organic compound that consists of amino acids joined by peptide bonds. It is essential to the structure and function of all living cells and viruses. Many are enzymes or subunits of enzymes.
Alcoholism	Alcoholism is a term with multiple and sometimes conflicting definitions. In common and historic usage, alcoholism refers to any condition that results in the continued consumption of alcoholic beverages despite the health problems and negative social consequences it causes.
Animal testing	Animal testing refers to the use of animals in experiments. It is estimated that 50 to 100 million vertebrate animals worldwide — from zebrafish to non-human primates — are used annually and either killed during the experiments or subsequently euthanized.
Disease	A Disease or medical problem is an abnormal condition of an organism that impairs bodily functions, associated with specific symptoms and signs. It may be caused by external factors, such as invading organisms, or it may be caused by internal dysfunctions, such as autoimmune Disease s.

In human beings, Disease is often used more broadly to refer to any condition that causes extreme pain, dysfunction, distress, social problems, and/or death to the person afflicted, or similar problems for those in contact with the person.

Cytokines	Cytokines are a group of proteins and peptides that are used in organisms as signaling compounds. These chemical signals are similar to hormones and neurotransmitters and are used to allow one cell to communicate with another. The cytokine family consists mainly of smaller water-soluble proteins and glycoproteins with a mass of between 8 and 30 kDa.
Fever	Fever is a frequent medical symptom that describes an increase in internal body temperature to levels that are above normal.
Immune system	The most important function of the human immune system occurs at the cellular level of the blood and tissues. The lymphatic and blood circulation systems are highways for specialized white blood cells. These cells include B cells, T cells, natural killer cells, and macrophages. All function with the primary objective of recognizing, attacking and destroying bacteria, viruses, cancer cells, and all substances seen as foreign.
Prostaglandin	A prostaglandin is any member of a group of lipid compounds that are derived from fatty acids and have important functions. They act on a variety of cells such as vascular smooth muscle cells causing constriction or dilation, on platelets causing aggregation or disaggregation and on spinal neurons causing pain.
Vagus nerve	The vagus nerve is the tenth of twelve paired cranial nerves, and is the only nerve that starts in the brainstem and extends, through the jugular foramen, down below the head, to the neck, chest and abdomen.
Antipsychotic	The term antipsychotic is applied to a group of drugs used to treat psychosis.
Antipsychotics	*Antipsychotics* are a group of psychoactive drugs commonly but not exclusively used to treat psychosis, which is typified by schizophrenia. Over time a wide range of *Antipsychotics* have been developed. A first generation of *Antipsychotics*, known as typical *Antipsychotics*, was discovered in the 1950s.
Blood	Blood is a specialized biological fluid consisting of red blood cells.White blood cells also called leukocytes and platelets also called thrombocytes suspended in a complex fluid medium known as blood plasma.
Chemical	A chemical is a material with a definite chemical composition. All samples of a compound have the same composition; that is, all samples have the same proportions, by mass, of the elements present in the compound.
Cranial nerve	A Cranial nerve emerges from the brainstem instead of the spinal cord.

Infection	An infection is the detrimental colonization of a host organism by a foreign species.
Information	Information as a concept has a diversity of meanings, from everyday usage to technical settings. Generally speaking, the concept of Information is closely related to notions of constraint, communication, control, data, form, instruction, knowledge, meaning, mental stimulus, pattern, perception, and representation. According to the Oxford English Dictionary, the first known historical meaning of the word Information in English was the act of informing, or giving form or shape to the mind, as in education, instruction, or training.
Other	The Other or constitutive Other is a key concept in continental philosophy, opposed to the Same. It refers, or attempts to refer, to that which is "Other" than the concept being considered. The term often means a person Other than oneself, and is often capitalised.
Extracellular	In cell biology, molecular biology and related fields, the word extracellular means "outside the cell". This space is usually taken to be outside the plasma membranes, and occupied by fluid. The term is used in contrast to intracellular.
Extracellular fluid	Extracellular fluid usually denotes all body fluid outside of cells. The remainder is called intracellular fluid.
Hypovolemic thirst	Hypovolemic thirst is a type of thirst that is attributed to the low volume of bodily fluids. It is triggered by the release of the hormones vasopressin and angiotensin II, which constrict blood vessels to make up for a drop in blood pressure.
Intracellular	The intracellular means "inside the cell". The cell membrane is the barrier between the two, and chemical composition of intracellular and extracellular milieu can be radically different.
Cytosol	The priya cytosol is the internal fluid of the cell, and a portion of cell metabolism occurs here. Proteins within the cytosol play an important role in signal transduction pathways and glycolysis. They also act as intracellular receptors and form part of the ribosomes, enabling protein synthesis.
Osmotic pressure	Osmotic pressure is the hydrostatic pressure produced by a solution in a space divided by a semipermeable membrane due to a differential in the concentrations of solute.
Osmotic thirst	Osmotic thirst is a kind of thirst that is the result of eating salty foods. It occurs for the reason that the human body maintains a combined concentration of solutes at a fixed level of .15 molar. The internal and external soutes of a cell produce osmotic pressure, which is defined as the tendency of water to flow across a semi-permeable membrane from an area of low solute concentration to one of high concentration.

Pituitary gland	The pituitary gland is an endocrine gland about the size of a pea that sits in the small, bony cavity at the base of the brain. The pituitary gland secretes hormones regulating a wide variety of bodily activities, including trophic hormones that stimulate other endocrine glands.
Posterior	In reference to the anatomical terms of location, the posterior end is laterally situated at or toward the hinder part of the body, lying at or extending toward the right or left side. It is the polar opposite to the anterior end, or front end of the body.
Posterior pituitary	The posterior pituitary comprises the posterior lobe of the pituitary gland and is part of the endocrine system.
Sodium	Sodium is a chemical element which has the symbol Na, atomic number 11, atomic mass 22.9898 g/mol, common oxidation number +1. Sodium is a soft, silvery white, highly reactive element and is a member of the alkali metals within "group 1". It has only one stable isotope, ^{23}Na.
Thirst	Thirst is the basic instinct of humans or animals to drink. It arises from a lack of fluids and/or an increase in the concentration of certain osmolites such as salt. If the water volume of the body falls below a certain threshold, or the osmolite concentration becomes too high, the brain signals thirst.
Vasopressin	Vasopressin is a peptide hormone. It is derived from a preprohormone precursor that is synthesized in the hypothalamus, from which it is liberated during transport to the posterior pituitary. Most of it is stored in the posterior part of the pituitary gland to be released into the blood stream; some of it is also released directly into the brain.
Anxiety	Anxiety is a physiological state characterized by cognitive, somatic, emotional, and behavioral components.
Blood pressure	Blood pressure refers to the force exerted by circulating blood on the walls of blood vessels, and constitutes one of the principal vital signs.
Dependence	Dependence is compulsively using a substance, despite its negative and sometimes dangerous effects. Other drugs cause addiction without physical dependence.
Drinking	Drinking is the act of consuming a liquid through the mouth.
Endocrine gland	An endocrine gland is one of a set of internal organs involved in the secretion of hormones into the blood. The other major type of gland is the exocrine glands, which secrete substances—usually digestive juices—into the digestive tract or onto the skin.
Flow	Flow is the mental state of operation in which the person is fully immersed in what he or she is doing by a feeling of energized focus, full involvement, and success in the process of the activity. Proposed by Mihály Csíkszentmihályi, the positive psychology concept has been widely referenced across a variety of fields.

347

	Colloquial terms for this or similar mental states include: to be on the ball, in the zone, or in the groove.
Hormone	A hormone is a chemical messenger that carries a signal from one cell to another. All multicellular organisms produce hormone s.
Intake	An intake is an air intake for an engine.
Intention	Intention is performing an action is their specific purpose in doing so, the end or goal they aim at, or intend to accomplish.
Kidney	The kidney is an organ that filters wastes from the blood and excretes them, with water, as urine. In humans, it is located in the posterior part of the abdomen. There is one on each side of the spine. Each kidney receives its blood supply from the renal artery, two of which branch from the abdominal aorta.
Secret	Secrecy or furtiveness is the practice of sharing information among a group of people, which can be as small as one person, while hiding it from all others. That which is kept hidden is known as the Secret. Secrecy is often controversial, depending on the content of the Secret, the group or people keeping the Secret, and the motivation for secrecy.
Spite	In fair division problems, Spite is a phenomenon that occurs when a player"s value of an allocation decreases when one or more other players" valuation increases. Thus, other things being equal, a player exhibiting Spite will prefer an allocation in which other players receive less than more (if the good is desirable.) In this language, Spite is difficult to analyze because one has to assess two sets of preferences.
Urine	Urine is an aqueous solution of waste electrolytes and metabolites excreted by mammals, birds, reptiles, fish and amphibians.
Blood-brain barrier	The Blood-brain barrier is a membranic structure that acts primarily to protect the brain from chemicals in the blood, while still allowing essential metabolic function. It is composed of endothelial cells, which are packed very tightly in brain capillaries. This higher density restricts passage of substances from the bloodstream much more than endothelial cells in capillaries elsewhere in the body
Intestine	In anatomy, the intestine is the segment of the alimentary canal extending from the stomach to the anus and, in humans and other mammals, consists of two segments, the small intestine and the large intestine.

Parasympathetic nervous system	The parasympathetic nervous system is a division of the autonomic nervous system, along with the sympathetic nervous system and Enteric nervous system. The ANS is a subdivision of the peripheral nervous system.
Subfornical organ	The subfornical organ, situated on the ventral surface of the fornix, at the foramen of Monro, is one of the circumventricular organs of the brain.
Axon	An axon is a long, slender projection of a nerve cell, or neuron, that conducts electrical impulses away from the neuron"s cell body or soma.
Lead	Lead is a poisonous metal that can damage nervous connections and cause blood and brain disorders. Long term exposure to lead or its salts can cause nephropathy, and colic-like abdominal pains. The concern about lead"s role in cognitive deficits in children has brought about widespread reduction in its use. The majority of cases of adult elevate blood lead levels are workplace-related.
Mechanism	In philosophy, mechanism is a theory that all natural phenomena can be explained by physical causes. It can be contrasted with vitalism, the philosophical theory that vital forces are active in living organisms, so that life cannot be explained solely by mechanism.
Preoptic area	The preoptic area is a region of the hypothalamus. According to the MeSH classification, it is considered part of the anterior hypothalamus.
Third ventricle	The third ventricle is one of four connected fluid-filled cavities comprising the ventricular system within the human brain. It is a median cleft between the two thalami, and is filled with cerebrospinal fluid.
Adrenocorticotropic hormone	Adrenocorticotropic hormone is a polypeptide hormone produced and secreted by the pituitary gland. It is an important player in the hypothalamic-pituitary-adrenal axis.
Aldosterone	Aldosterone is a steroid hormone produced by the outer-section of the adrenal cortex in the adrenal gland to regulate sodium and potassium balance in the blood. It was first isolated by Simpson and Tait in 1953.
Angel dust	Angel dust is a dissociative drug formerly used as an anesthetic agent, exhibiting hallucinogenic and neurotoxic effects. It is consumed in a recreational manner mainly in the United States, where the demand is met by illegal production. It comes in both powder and liquid forms, but typically it is sprayed onto leafy material such as marijuana, mint, oregano, parsley or Ginger Leaves, and smoked.
Cerebrovascular accident	Cerebrovascular accident refers to a sudden stoppage of blood flow to a portion of the brain, leading to a loss of brain function.
Neurotransmitter	A neurotransmitter is a chemical that is used to relay, amplify and modulate electrical signals between a neurons and another cell.

Nucleus	In neuroanatomy, a cluster of cell bodies of neurons within the central nervous system is a nucleus.
Rapid eye movement sleep	Rapid eye movement sleep is the normal stage of sleep characterized by rapid movements of the eyes. Criteria for Rapid eye movement sleep include not only rapid eye movements, but also low muscle tone and a rapid, low voltage EEG these features are easily discernible in a polysomnogram, the sleep study typically done for patients with suspected sleep disorders.
Adrenal cortex	Situated along the perimeter of the adrenal gland, the adrenal cortex mediates the stress response through the production of mineralocorticoids and glucocorticoids, including aldosterone and cortisol respectively. It is also a secondary site of androgen synthesis.
Affect	Affect refers to the experience of feeling or emotion. Affect is a key part of the process of an organism's interaction with stimuli. The word also refers sometimes to affect display, which is "a facial, vocal, or gestural behavior that serves as an indicator of affect."
Corticosterone	Corticosterone is a 21 carbon steroid hormone of the corticosteroid type produced in the cortex of the adrenal glands.
Cortisol	Cortisol is a corticosteroid hormone produced by the adrenal cortex. It is a vital hormone that is often referred to as the "stress hormone" as it is involved in the response to stress. It increases blood pressure, blood sugar levels and has an immunosuppressive action.
Hunger	Hunger is a feeling experienced when the glycogen level of the liver falls below a threshold, usually followed by a desire to eat.
Medulla	Medulla refers to the middle of something, and derives from the Latin word for "marrow" In medicine it refers to either bone marrow, the spinal cord, or more generally, the middle part of a structure as opposed to the cortex.
Receptor	A sensory receptor is a structure that recognizes a stimulus in the internal or external environment of an organism. In response to stimuli the sensory receptor initiates sensory transduction by creating graded potentials or action potentials in the same cell or in an adjacent one.
Taste receptor	A Taste receptor is a type of receptor which facilitates the sensation of taste. Examples include TAS2R16 and TAS2R38. They are divided into two families: · Type 1, sweet, first characterized in 2001: TAS1R1 - TAS1R3 · Type 2, bitter, first characterized in 2000: TAS2R1 - TAS2R50, and TAS2R60 .
Digestive system	The digestive system is the organ system that breaks down and absorbs nutrients that are essential for growth and maintenance. The digestive system includes the mouth, esophagus, stomach, pancreas, liver, gallbladder, duodenum, jejunum, ileum, intestines, rectum, and anus.

Eating	Eating is the process of consuming nutrition, i.e. food, for the purpose of providing for the nutritional needs of an animal, particularly their energy requirements and to grow.
Enzyme	An enzyme is a protein that catalyzes, or speeds up, a chemical reaction. Enzymes are essential to sustain life because most chemical reactions in biological cells would occur too slowly, or would lead to different products, without enzymes.
Experience	Experience as a general concept comprises knowledge of or skill in or observation of some thing or some event gained through involvement in or exposure to that thing or event. The history of the word experience aligns it closely with the concept of experiment.
Hydrochloric acid	Hydrochloric acid is the aqueous solution of hydrogen chloride gas. It is also widely used in industry. Hydrochloric acid must be handled with appropriate safety precautions because it is a highly corrosive liquid. Hydrochloric acid in high concentrations forms acidic mists. Both the mist and the solution have a corrosive effect on human tissue, with the potential to damage respiratory organs, eyes, skin, and intestines.
Saliva	Saliva (also referred to as spit , spittle or slobber) is the watery and usually frothy substance produced in the mouths of humans and most other animals. Saliva is produced in and secreted from the Saliva ry glands. Human Saliva is composed mostly of water, but also includes electrolytes, mucus, antibacterial compounds, and various enzymes.
Carnivore	A carnivore is an animal with a diet consisting mainly of meat, whether it comes from animals living or dead. An obligate or true carnivore is an animal that subsists on a diet consisting only of meat. Characteristics commonly "associated" with it include organs for capturing and disarticulating prey and status as a predator.
Genetics	Genetics is the science of heredity and variation in living organisms.Knowledge of the inheritance of characteristics has been implicitly used since prehistoric times for improving crop plants and animals through selective breeding. However, the modern science of genetics, which seeks to understand the mechanisms of inheritance, only began with the work of Gregor Mendel in the mid-1800s.
Herbivore	A herbivore is an animal that is adapted to eat primarily plant matter. Although such animals are sometimes referred to as being vegetarian, this term is more properly reserved for humans who choose not to eat meat as opposed to animals that are unable to make such choices. A herbivore adaption to plant defense has been likened to "offensive traits" and consist of those traits that allow for increased feeding and use of a host.
Infant	In basic English usage, an Infant is defined as a human child at the youngest stage of life, specifically before they can walk and generally before the age of one.

Lactose intolerance	Lactose intolerance is the term for the normal decline in the level of lactase, an enzyme needed for proper metabolization of lactose, in human beings after weaning. Lactose intolerance is an autosomal recessive trait, while lactase persistence is the dominant allele. The gene is expressed and the enzyme synthesized if at least one of the two genes are able to express properly.
Omnivore	An omnivore is a species of animal that eats both plants and animals as its primary food source. They are opportunistic, general feeders not specifically adapted to eat and digest either meat or plant material exclusively.
Explanation	An explanation is a description which may clarify causes, context, and consequences of a certain object, and a phenomenon such as a process, a state of affairs. This description may establish rules or laws, and may clarify the existing ones in relation to an object, and a phenomenon examined. The components of an explanation can be implicit, and be interwoven with one another.
Selection	Under selection, individuals with advantageous or "adaptive" traits tend to be more successful than their peers reproductively--meaning they contribute more offspring to the succeeding generation than others do.
Species	Species refers to a reproductively isolated breeding population.
Understanding	Understanding is a psychological process related to an abstract or physical object, such as, person, situation, or message whereby one is able to think about it and use concepts to deal adequately with that object.
Conditioned taste aversion	Conditioned taste aversion occurs when a subject associates the taste of a certain food with symptoms caused by a toxic, spoiled, or poisonous substance. It is an example of classical conditioning. However, conditioned taste aversion sometimes occurs in subjects when sickness was merely coincidental and not related to the food.
Taste aversion	Taste aversion occurs when a subject associates the taste of a certain food with symptoms caused by a toxic, spoiled, or poisonous substance. The ability to develop a taste aversion is considered an adaptive trait or survival mechanism that trains the body to avoid poisonous substances before they can cause harm.
Illness	Illness can be defined as a state of poor health. The mode of being healthy includes "a state of complete physical, mental and social well-being and not merely the absence of disease or infirmity". When these conditions are not fulfilled, then one can be considered to have an illness or be ill.
Learning	Learning is the acquisition and development of memories and behaviors, including skills, knowledge, understanding, values, and wisdom. It is the goal of education, and the product of experience. Learning ranges from simple forms such as habituation to more complex forms such as play, seen only in large vertebrates.

Chlorpromazine	Chlorpromazine is a phenothiazine antipsychotic. Its principal use is in the treatment of schizophrenia, though it has also been used to treat hiccups and nausea. Its use today has been largely supplanted by the newer atypical antipsychotics such as olanzapine and quetiapine. It works on a variety of receptors in the central nervous system; these include anticholinergic, antidopaminergic and antihistamine effects as well as some antagonism of adrenergic receptors.
Glucagon	Glucagon is an important hormone involved in carbohydrate metabolism. Produced by the pancreas, it is released when the glucose level in the blood is low, causing the liver to convert stored glycogen into glucose and release it into the bloodstream. The action of glucagon is thus opposite to that of insulin, which instructs the body"s cells to take in glucose from the blood in times of satiation.
Glucose	Glucose, a simple monosaccharide sugar, is one of the most important carbohydrates and is used as a source of energy in animals and plants. Glucose is one of the main products of photosynthesis and starts respiration.
Insulin	Insulin is an animal hormone whose presence informs the body"s cells that the animal is well fed, causing liver and muscle cells to take in glucose and store it in the form of glycogen, and causing fat cells to take in blood lipids and turn them into triglycerides. In addition it has several other anabolic effects throughout the body.
Pancreas	The pancreas is a retroperitoneal organ that serves two functions: it produces juice containing digestive enzymes; and it produces several important hormones including insulin, glucagon, and several other hormones.
Satiety	Satiety refers to the state of being satisfied; fullness.
Sex steroid	Sex steroid refers to steroid hormones that interact with vertebrate androgen or estrogen receptors.
Sexual behavior	Human Sexual behavior refers to the manner in which humans experience and express their sexuality. It encompass a wide range of activities such as strategies to find or attract partners (mating and display behaviour), interactions between individuals, physical or emotional intimacy, and sexual contact. Although some cultures hold that sexual activity is acceptable only within marriage, extramarital sexual activities still takes place within such cultures.
Active transport	Active transport is the mediated transport of biochemicals, and other atomic/molecular substances, across membranes. Unlike passive transport, this process requires chemical energy. In this form of transport, molecules move against either an electrical or concentration gradient (collectively termed an electrochemical gradient).

Glycogen	Glycogen is a polysaccharide of glucose which functions as the primary short term energy storage in animal cells. It is made primarily by the liver and the muscles, but can also be made by the brain, uterus, and the vagina. Glycogen is the analogue of starch, a less branched glucose polymer in plants, and is commonly referred to as animal starch, having a similar structure to amylopectin.
Impulse	In classical mechanics, an Impulse is defined as the integral of a force with respect to time. When a force is applied to a rigid body it changes the momentum of that body. A small force applied for a long time can produce the same momentum change as a large force applied briefly, because it is the product of the force and the time for which it is applied that is important.
Liver	The liver plays a major role in metabolism and has a number of functions in the body including detoxification, glycogen storage and plasma protein synthesis. It also produces bile, which is important for digestion. The liver converts most carbohydrates, proteing, and fats into glucose.
Lumbar	In anatomy, lumbar is an adjective that means of or pertaining to the abdominal segment of the torso, between the diaphragm and the sacrum.
Nutrient	A Nutrient is a chemical that an organism needs to live and grow or a substance used in an organism"s metabolism which must be taken in from its environment. Nutrient s are the substances that enrich the body. They build and repair tissues, give heat and energy, and regulate body processes.
Negative symptoms	Negative symptoms are indications of deficiency in specific mental functions and of an absence of typical behavior; these can include reduced or inappropriate emotions, lack of eill, loss of verbal expression, and the lack of logic. Negative symptoms are often displayed in the residual phase of schizophrenia.
Small intestine	In biology the small intestine is the part of the gastrointestinal tract between the stomach and the large intestine and comprises the duodenum, jejunum, and ileum.
Spinal cord	The spinal cord is a thin, tubular bundle of nerves that is an extension of the central nervous system from the brain and is enclosed in and protected by the bony vertebral column. The main function of the spinal cord is transmission of neural inputs between the periphery and the brain.
Thorax	The thorax is a division of an animal"s body that lies between the head and the abdomen. It extends from the neck to the diaphragm, not including the upper limbs. The inner organs are protected by the rib cage and the sternum.
Diabetes	Diabetes is a medical disorder characterized by varying or persistent elevated blood sugar levels, especially after eating. All types of diabetes share similar symptoms and complications at advanced stages: dehydration and ketoacidosis, cardiovascular disease, chronic renal failure, retinal damage which can lead to blindness, nerve damage which can lead to erectile dysfunction, gangrene with risk of amputation of toes, feet, and even legs.

Body weight	Body weight is a term that is used in biological and medical science contexts to describe the mass of an organism"s body. Body weight is measured in kilograms throughout the world, although in some countries people more often measure and describe body weight in pounds or stones and pounds and thus may not be well acquainted with measurement in kilograms.
Fat cells	Fat cells serve as storehouses for liquefied fat in the body and that number from 25 to 35 billion in normal weight individuals; with weight loss, they decrease in size but not in number.
Leptin	Leptin is a 16 kDa protein hormone that plays a key role in regulating energy intake and energy expenditure, including the regulation decrease of appetite and increase of metabolism.
Memory	In psychology, memory is an organism"s ability to store, retain, and subsequently retrieve information. In recent decades, it has become one of the principal pillars of a branch of science called cognitive neuroscience, an interdisciplinary link between cognitive psychology and neuroscience.
Nutrition	The purposes of nutrition science is to explain metabolic and physiological responses of the body to diet. With advances in molecular biology, biochemistry, and genetics, nutrition science is additionally developing into the study of metabolism, which seeks to disconnect diet and health through the lens of biochemical processes.
Discovery	Discovery observations form acts of detecting and learning something. Discovery observations are acts in which something is found and given a productive insight. Serendipity is the effect by which one accidentally discovers something fortunate, especially while looking for something else entirely.
Neuropeptide	A neuropeptide is any of the variety of peptides found in neural tissue; e.g. endorphins, enkephalins. Now, about 100 different peptides are known to be released by different populations of neurons in the mammalian brain.
Weight loss	Weight loss is a reduction of the total body weight, due to a mean loss of fluid, body fat or adipose tissue and/or lean mass, namely bone mineral deposits, muscle, tendon and other connective tissue. Infections such as HIV may alter metabolism, leading to weight loss.
Weight-loss	Weight-loss is a reduction of the total body weight, due to a mean loss of fluid, body fat or adipose tissue and/or lean mass. It occurs when an individual is in a state of negative energy balance. When the human body is spending more energy in work and heat than it is gaining from food or other nutritional supplements, it will catabolise stored reserves of fat or muscle.
Arcuate nucleus	The arcuate nucleus is an aggregation of neurons in the mediobasal hypothalamus, adjacent to the third ventricle and the median eminence.
Gamma-aminobutyric acid	Gamma-aminobutyric acid is an inhibitory neurotransmitter found in the nervous systems of widely-divergent species. It is the chief inhibitory neurotransmitter in the central nervous system and also in the retina.

Ghrelin	Ghrelin is a hormone that is produced by cells lining the stomach and stimulates the appetite. Ghrelin levels are increased prior to a meal and decreased after a meal. It is considered the counterpart of the hormone leptin, produced by adipose tissue, which induces satiation when present at higher levels.
Deprivation	Deprivation, is the loss or withholding of normal stimulation, nutrition, comfort, love, and so forth; a condition of lacking. The level of stimulation is less than what is required.
Signal	In the fields of communications, signal processing, and in electrical engineering more generally, a signal is any time-varying quantity. Signals are often scalar-valued functions of time, but may be vector valued and may be functions of any other relevant independent variable.
Agouti-related protein	Agouti-related protein is a neuropeptide produced in the brain by the AgRP/NPY neuron that increases appetite and decreases metabolism and energy expenditure. It is one of the most potent and long-lasting of appetite stimulators.
Lateral hypothalamus	The Lateral hypothalamus is a part of the hypothalamus. The Lateral hypothalamus is concerned with hunger. Any damage sustained to the lateral hypothalamus can cause reduced food intake.
Neuropeptide Y	Neuropeptide Y is a 36 amino acid peptide neurotransmitter found in the brain and autonomic nervous system.
Orexin	Orexin is the common name given to a pair of highly excititory neuropeptide hormones that were simultaneously discovered by two groups of reseachers in rat brains. The University of Texas, coined the term orexin to reflect the appetite-stimulating activity of these hormones.
Amino acid	Amino acid is the basic structural building unit of proteins. They form short polymer chains called peptides or polypeptides which in turn form structures called proteins.
Arousal	Arousal is a physiological and psychological state involving the activation of the reticular activating system in the brain stem, the autonomic nervous system and the endocrine system, leading to increased heart rate and blood pressure and a condition of alertness and readiness to respond.
Feeding	Feeding is the process by which organisms, typically animals, obtain food. There are many types of feeding that animals exhibit.
Paraventricular nucleus	The paraventricular nucleus is an aggregation of neurons in the hypothalamus, which produces many hormones.
Wakefulness	Wakefulness refers to the state of being awake and is the behavioral manifestation of the metabolic state of catabolism. It is the daily recurring period in an organism"s life during which consciousness, awareness and all behaviors necessary for survival, i.e., success in, are conducted. Being awake is the opposite of being asleep a behavioral manifestation of the daily recurring metabolic state of anabolism.

Dopamine	Dopamine is a hormone and neurotransmitter occurring in a wide variety of animals, including both vertebrates and invertebrates. In the brain, dopamine functions as a neurotransmitter. Dopamine is also a neurohormone released by the hypothalamus. Its main function as a hormone is to inhibit the release of prolactin from the anterior lobe of the pituitary.
Depression	In everyday language depression refers to any downturn in mood, which may be relatively transitory and perhaps due to something trivial.
Scolex	The Scolex of the worm attaches to the intestine of the definitive host. In some groups, the scolex is dominated by bothria, which are sometimes called "sucking grooves," and function like suction cups.
Sense	Sense are the physiological methods of perception. They and their operation, classification, and theory are overlapping topics studied by a variety of fields, most notably neuroscience, cognitive psychology, and philosophy of perception. The nervous system has a sensory system dedicated to each sense.
Ventromedial hypothalamus	Ventromedial hypothalamus acts as a satiety center and, when activated, signals an animal to stop eating; when destroyed, the animal overeats, becoming obese.
Software extension	A Software extension is a computer program designed to be incorporated into another piece of software in order to enhance the functionalities of the latter. On its own, the program is not useful or functional. Examples of software applications that support extensions include the Mozilla Firefox Web browser, Adobe Systems Photoshop and Microsoft Windows Explorer shell extensions.
Single	In relationships, a single person is one who is not married, or, more broadly, who is not in an exclusive romantic relationship.
Eating disorder	An eating disorder is a complex compulsion to eat, or not eat, in a way which disturbs physical and mental health. The eating may be excessive compulsive over-eating, too limited restricting, normal eating punctuated with purging, cycles of binging and purging or ingesting of non-foods.
Norepinephrine	Norepinephrine is a catecholamine and a phenethylamine with chemical formula $C_8H_{11}NO_3$.
Obesity	Obesity is a condition in which excess body fat has accumulated to an extent that health may be negatively affected. It is commonly defined as a body mass index (BMI) of 30 kg/m^2 or higher. This distinguishes it from being pre-obese or overweight as defined by a BMI of 25 kg/m^2 but less than 30 kg/m^2.
Mental disorder	Mental disorder refes tor a psychological or physiological pattern that occurs in an individual and is usually associated with distress or disability that is not expected as part of normal development or culture.

Audition	An Audition is a sample performance by an actor, singer, musician, dancer or other performer. It involves the performer displaying their talent through a previously-memorized and rehearsed solo piece: for example, a monologue for actors or a song for a singer. Used in the context of performing arts, it is analogous to job interviews in many ways.
Dieting	Dieting is the practice of ingesting food in a regulated fashion to achieve a particular objective.
Environmental factor	In epidemiology, environmental factor refers to determinants of disease that are not transmitted genetically.
Exercise	Exercise is manual activity that develops or maintains physical fitness and overall health. It is often practiced to strengthen muscles and the cardiovascular system, and to hone athletic skills.
Frontal lobe	The frontal lobe comprises four major folds of cortical tissue: the precentral gyrus, superior gyrus and the middle gyrus of the frontal gyri, the inferior frontal gyrus. It has been found to play a part in impulse control, judgement, language, memory, motor function, problem solving, sexual behavior, socialization and spontaneity.
Prader-Willi syndrome	Prader-Willi syndrome is a genetic disorder, in which seven genes on chromosome 15 are missing or unexpressed on the paternal chromosome. It is characterized by hyperphagia and food preoccupations, as well as small stature and learning difficulties.
Prefrontal cortex	The prefrontal cortex is the anterior part of the frontal lobes of the brain, lying in front of the motor and premotor areas. Cytoarchitectonically, it is defined by the presence of an internal granular layer IV.
Primary	In medicine, the reporting of symptoms by a patient may have significant psychological motivators. Psychologists sometimes categorize these motivators into primary or secondary gain. primary gain is internally good; motivationally.
Primary motor cortex	The primary motor cortex works in association with pre-motor areas to plan and execute movements. It contains large neurons known as Betz cells which send long axons down the spinal cord to synapse onto alpha motor neurons which connect to the muscles.
Serotonin	Serotonin, is a monoamine neurotransmitter synthesized in serotonergic neurons in the central nervous system and enterochromaffin cells in the gastrointestinal tract of animals including humans. Serotonin is also found in many mushrooms and plants, including fruits and vegetables.
Sibutramine	Sibutramine, usually as Sibutramine hydrochloride monohydrate, is an orally administered agent for the treatment of obesity, as an appetite suppressant. It is a centrally-acting serotonin-norepinephrine reuptake inhibitor structurally related to amphetamines, although its mechanism of action is distinct. Sibutramine is manufactured by Abbott Laboratories.

Temporal lobe	The temporal lobe is part of the cerebrum. It lies at the side of the brain, beneath the lateral or Sylvian fissure. Adjacent areas in the superior, posterior and lateral parts of the temporal lobe are involved in high-level auditory processing.
Vision	Vision is the most important sense for birds, since good eyesight is essential for safe flight, and this group has a number of adaptations which give visual acuity superior to that of other vertebrate groups; a pigeon has been described as "two eyes with wings". The avian eye resembles that of a reptile, but has a better-positioned lens, a feature shared with mammals. Birds have the largest eyes relative to their size within the animal kingdom, and movement is consequently limited within the eye"s bony socket.
Anterior	Anterior is an anatomical term referring to the front part of the body. The anterior is positioned in front of another body part, or towards the head of an animal. It is the opposite of posterior.
Central sulcus	The central sulcus is a prominent landmark of the brain, separating the parietal lobe from the frontal lobe. The central sulcus is the site of the primary motor cortex in mammals, a group of cells that controls voluntary movements of the body.
Cerebral cortex	The cerebral cortex is a structure within the vertebrate brain with distinct structural and functional properties.
Addiction	The term Addiction is used in many contexts to describe an obsession, compulsion such as: drug Addiction (e.g. alcoholism), video game Addiction crime, money, work Addiction compulsive overeating, problem gambling, computer Addiction nicotine Addiction pornography Addiction etc. In medical terminology, an Addiction is a chronic neurobiologic disorder that has genetic, psychosocial, and environmental dimensions and is characterized by one of the following: the continued use of a substance despite its detrimental effects, impaired control over the use of a drug (compulsive behavior), and preoccupation with a drug"s use for non-therapeutic purposes (i.e. craving the drug.) Addiction is often accompanied the presence of deviant behaviors (for instance stealing money and forging prescriptions) that are used to obtain a drug.
Anorexia	Anorexia is the decreased sensation of appetite. While the term in non-scientific publications is often used interchangeably with one of its causes, anorexia nervosa, there are many possible causes for a decreased appetite, some of which may be harmless while others pose significant risk for the person.
Anorexia nervosa	Anorexia nervosa is a psychiatric diagnosis that describes an eating disorder characterized by low body weight and body image distortion with an obsessive fear of gaining weight. Anorexia Nervosa is a disease condition that can put a serious strain on many of the body"s organs and physiological resources.

Bulimia	Bulimia refers to a disorder in which a person binges on incredibly large quantities of food, then purges by vomiting or by using laxatives. Bulimia is often less about food, and more to do with deep psychological issues and profound feelings of lack of control.
Bulimia nervosa	Bulimia nervosa is an eating disorder. It is a psychological condition in which the subject engages in recurrent binge eating followed by intentional purging. This purging is done in order to compensate for the excessive intake of food, usually to prevent weight gain. It is often less about food, more to do with deep psychological issues and profound feelings of lack of control.
Gastric bypass	Gastric bypass procedures (Gastric bypass P) are any of a group of similar operations used to treat morbid obesity--the severe accumulation of excess weight as fatty tissue--and the health problems (comorbidities) it causes. Bariatric surgery is the term encompassing all of the surgical treatments for morbid obesity, not just Gastric bypass es, which make up only one class of such operations. A Gastric bypass first divides the stomach into a small upper pouch and a much larger, lower "remnant" pouch and then re-arranges the small intestine to allow both pouches to stay connected to it.
Opioid	An opioid is any agent that binds to opioid receptors, found principally in the central nervous system and gastrointestinal tract.
Orlistat	Orlistat is a drug designed to treat obesity. Its primary function is preventing the absorption of fats from the human diet, thereby reducing caloric intake. It is intended for use in conjunction with a physician-supervised reduced-calorie diet.
Brain size	When comparing different species, brain size does present a correlation with intelligence. For example, the ratio of brain weight to body weight for fish is 1:5000; for reptiles it is about 1:1500; for birds, 1:220; for most mammals, 1:180, and for humans, 1:50. However within the human species modern studies using MRI have shown that brain size shows substantial and consistent correlation with IQ among adults of the same sex
Neurotransmitters	Neurotransmitters are chemicals that are used to relay, amplify and modulate signals between a neuron and another cell. There are many different ways to classify neurotransmitters. Often, dividing them into amino acids, peptides, and monoamines is sufficient for many purposes.
Nitric oxide	Nitric oxide is a chemical compound with chemical formula NO. This gas is an important signaling molecule in the body of mammals including humans and is an extremely important intermediate in the chemical industry. It is also a toxic air pollutant produced by automobile engines and power plants.
Opiate	In medicine, the term Opiate describes any of the narcotic alkaloids found in opium.

Sexual reproduction	Sexual reproduction is a biological process by which organisms create descendants through the combination of genetic material taken randomly and independently from two different members of the species.
Explanation	An explanation is a description which may clarify causes, context, and consequences of a certain object, and a phenomenon such as a process, a state of affairs. This description may establish rules or laws, and may clarify the existing ones in relation to an object, and a phenomenon examined. The components of an explanation can be implicit, and be interwoven with one another.
Species	Species refers to a reproductively isolated breeding population.
Understanding	Understanding is a psychological process related to an abstract or physical object, such as, person, situation, or message whereby one is able to think about it and use concepts to deal adequately with that object.
Androgen	Androgen is the generic term for any natural or synthetic compound, usually a steroid hormone, that stimulates or controls the development and maintenance of masculine characteristics in vertebrates by binding to androgen receptors. This includes the activity of the accessory male sex organs and development of male secondary sex characteristics.
Brain	In animals, the brain, is the control center of the central nervous system, responsible for behavior. The brain is located in the head, protected by the skull and close to the primary sensory apparatus of vision, hearing, equilibrioception, sense of acceleration, taste, and olfaction.
Cholesterol	Cholesterol is a steroid, a lipid, and an alcohol, found in the cell membranes of all body tissues, and transported in the blood plasma of all animals. Cholesterol is an important component of the membranes of cells, providing stability; it makes the membrane"s fluidity stable over a bigger temperature interval.
Estradiol	Estradiol is a sex hormone. Labelled the "female" hormone but also present in males, it represents the major estrogen in humans. Estradiol has not only a critical impact on reproductive and sexual functioning, but also affects other organs including bone structure.
Estrogen	Estrogen is a group of steroid compounds that function as the primary female sex hormone. They are produced primarily by developing follicles in the ovaries, the corpus luteum and the placenta.
Progesterone	Progesterone is a C-21 steroid hormone involved in the female menstrual cycle, pregnancy and embryogenesis of humans and other species. Progesterone belongs to a class of hormones called progestogens, and is the major naturally occurring human progestogen.
Sex steroid	Sex steroid refers to steroid hormones that interact with vertebrate androgen or estrogen receptors.

Steroid	A steroid is a terpenoid lipid characterized by its sterane or steroid nucleus: a carbon skeleton with four fused rings, generally arranged in a 6-6-6-5 fashion. steroid s vary by the functional groups attached to these rings and the oxidation state of the rings. Hundreds of distinct steroid s are found in plants, animals, and fungi.
Animal testing	Animal testing refers to the use of animals in experiments. It is estimated that 50 to 100 million vertebrate animals worldwide — from zebrafish to non-human primates — are used annually and either killed during the experiments or subsequently euthanized.
Brain size	When comparing different species, brain size does present a correlation with intelligence. For example, the ratio of brain weight to body weight for fish is 1:5000; for reptiles it is about 1:1500; for birds, 1:220; for most mammals, 1:180, and for humans, 1:50. However within the human species modern studies using MRI have shown that brain size shows substantial and consistent correlation with IQ among adults of the same sex
Gene	A gene is a locatable region of genomic sequence, corresponding to a unit of inheritance, which is associated with regulatory regions, transcribed regions and/or other functional sequence regions.
Other	The Other or constitutive Other is a key concept in continental philosophy, opposed to the Same. It refers, or attempts to refer, to that which is "Other" than the concept being considered. The term often means a person Other than oneself, and is often capitalised.
Ovum	Ovum is a female sex cell or gamete.
Uterus	The uterus or womb is the major female reproductive organ. The main function of the uterus is to accept a fertilized ovum which becomes implanted into the endometrium, and derives nourishment from blood vessels which develop exclusively for this purpose.
Activating effect	The arousal-producing effects of sex hormones that increase the likelihood of sexual behavior is called the activating effect.
Genitals	Genitals refers to the internal and external reproductive organs.
Gonad	The Gonad is the organ that makes gametes. The Gonad s in males are the testes and the Gonad s in females are the ovaries. The product, gametes, are haploid germ cells.
Gonads	The gonad is the organ that makes gametes. The gonads in males are the testes and the gonads in females are the ovaries. The product, gametes, are haploid germ cells.
Heritability	Heritability It is that proportion of the observed variation in a particular phenotype within a particular population, that can be attributed to the contribution of genotype. In other words: it measures the extent to which differences between individuals in a population are due their being different genetically.

Organizing effect	The organizing effect is the directional predisposition of sex hormones to move development along stereotypically masculine or feminine lines.
Ovary	An ovary is an egg-producing reproductive organ found in female organisms.
Prenatal development	Prenatal development is the process in which an embryo or fetus gestates during pregnancy, from fertilization until birth.
Seminal vesicles	The seminal vesicles are a pair of glands on the posterior surface of the urinary bladder of males. They secrete a significant proportion of the fluid that ultimately becomes semen.
Testosterone	Testosterone is a steroid hormone from the androgen group. It is the principal male sex hormone and the "original" anabolic steroid.
Vas deferens	The vas deferens are two muscular tubes that carry sperm from the testes to the urethra.
Wolffian duct	The Wolffian duct is a paired organ found in mammals including humans during embryogenesis. It connects the primitive kidney Wolffian body to the cloaca and serves as the anlage for certain male reproductive organs.
Alcoholism	Alcoholism is a term with multiple and sometimes conflicting definitions. In common and historic usage, alcoholism refers to any condition that results in the continued consumption of alcoholic beverages despite the health problems and negative social consequences it causes.
Anatomy	Anatomy is the branch of biology that deals with the structure and organization of living things. It can be divided into animal anatomy zootomy and plant anatomy phytonomy. Major branches of anatomy include comparative anatomy, histology, and human anatomy.
Behavior	Behavior refers to the actions or reactions of an object or organism, usually in relation to the environment. Behavior can be conscious or subconscious, overt or covert, and voluntary or involuntary. Human Behavior (and that of other organisms and mechanisms) can be common, unusual, acceptable, or unacceptable. Humans evaluate the acceptability of Behavior using social norms and regulate Behavior by means of social control
Inductive reasoning aptitude	The Inductive reasoning aptitude is a measurement which shows how well a person can identify a pattern within a large amount of data. Measurement is generally done in a timed test by showing four pictures or words and asking the test taker to identify which of the pictures or words does not belong in the set.
Feminization	In biology and medicine, feminization refers to the development in an organism of physical or behavioral characteristics unique to the female of the species. This may represent a normal developmental process, contributing to sexual differentiation.

Sensitive period	Sensitive periods is a term coined by the Dutch geneticist Hugo de Vries and adopted by the Italian educator Maria Montessori to refer to important periods of childhood development. During a sensitive period it is very easy for children to acquire certain abilities, such as language, discrimination of sensory stimuli, and mental modeling of the environment.
Sexual differentiation	Sexual differentiation is the process of development of the differences between males and females from an undifferentiated zygote. Current theories of mechanisms of sexual differentiation of brain and behaviors in humans are based primarily on three sources of evidence: animal research involving manipulation of hormones in early life, observation of outcomes of small numbers of individuals with disorders of sexual development .
Structure	Structure is a fundamental and sometimes intangible notion covering the recognition, observation, nature, and stability of patterns and relationships of entities.
Test	A Test or an examination (or "exam") is an assessment, often administered on paper or on the computer, intended to measure the Test-takers" or respondents" (often a student) knowledge, skills, aptitudes beliefs.) Tests are often used in education, professional certification, counseling, psychology (e.g., MMPI), the military, and many other fields. The measurement that is the goal of testing is called a Test score, and is "a summary of the evidence contained in an examinee"s responses to the items of a Test that are related to the construct or constructs being measured." Test scores are interpreted with regards to a norm or criterion, or occasionally both.
Testes	The testes is the male generative gland in animals.
Aspirin	Aspirin is a salicylate drug often used as an analgesic, antipyretic, and as an anti-inflammatory. It also has an antiplatelet effect and is used in long-term, low doses to prevent heart attacks and blood clot formation in people at high risk for developing blood clots.
Haloperidol	Haloperidol is a conventional butyrophenone antipsychotic drug. It posesses a strong activity against delusions and hallucinations, most likely due to an effective dopaminergic receptor blockage in the mesocortex and the limbic system of the brain.
Marijuana	Marijuana is the dried vegetable matter of the Cannabis sativa plant. It contains large concentrations of compounds that have medicinal and psychoactive effects when consumed, usually by smoking or eating.
Sexual behavior	Human Sexual behavior refers to the manner in which humans experience and express their sexuality. It encompass a wide range of activities such as strategies to find or attract partners (mating and display behaviour), interactions between individuals, physical or emotional intimacy, and sexual contact. Although some cultures hold that sexual activity is acceptable only within marriage, extramarital sexual activities still takes place within such cultures.

Stimulant	A stimulant is a drug which increases the activity of the sympathetic nervous system and produces a sense of euphoria or awakeness.
Stimulant drugs	*Stimulant drugs* are drugs that temporarily increase alertness and awareness. They usually have increased side-effects with increased effectiveness, and the more powerful variants are therefore often prescription medicines or illegal drugs. Ritalin SR 20mg. Stimulants increase the activity of either the sympathetic nervous system, the central nervous system (CNS) or both.
Alertness	Alertness is the state of paying close and continuous attention being watchful and prompt to meet danger or emergency, or being quick to perceive and act. It is related to psychology as well as to physiology. A lack of Alertness is a symptom of a number of conditions, including narcolepsy, attention deficit disorder, chronic fatigue syndrome, depression, Addison"s disease, or sleep deprivation.
Anxiety	Anxiety is a physiological state characterized by cognitive, somatic, emotional, and behavioral components.
Discovery	Discovery observations form acts of detecting and learning something. Discovery observations are acts in which something is found and given a productive insight. Serendipity is the effect by which one accidentally discovers something fortunate, especially while looking for something else entirely.
Fatigue	The word fatigue is used in everyday life to describe a range of afflictions, varying from a general state of lethargy to a specific work-induced burning sensation within one"s muscles. It can be both physical and mental. Such a mental fatigue, in turn, can manifest itself both as somnolence just as a general decrease of attention, not necessarily including sleepiness.
Mood	A mood is a relatively lasting emotional or affective state. They differ from emotions in that they are less specific, often less intense, less likely to be triggered by a particular stimulus or event, however longer lasting.
Tim	TIM is a series of lesser-known psychedelic drugs similar in structure to mescaline. They were first synthesized by Alexander Shulgin. In his book PiHKAL (Phenethylamines i Have Known And Loved), none of their durations are known.
Alpha-fetoprotein	Alpha-fetoprotein is a molecule produced in the developing embryo and fetus. In humans, AFP levels decrease gradually after birth, reaching adult levels by 8 to 12 months. Normal adult AFP levels are low, but detectable; however, AFP has no known function in normal adults.
Aromaticity	Aromaticity is a chemical property in which a conjugated ring of unsaturated bonds, lone pairs, or empty orbitals exhibit a stabilization stronger than would be expected by the stabilization of conjugation alone. It can also be considered a manifestation of cyclic delocalization and of resonance.

383

Hypothalamus	The hypothalamus is a region of the brain located below the thalamus, forming the major portion of the ventral region of the diencephalon and functioning to regulate certain metabolic processes and other autonomic activities.
Prosencephalon	In the anatomy of the brain of vertebrates, the prosencephalon is the rostral-most portion of the brain. The prosencephalon, the mesencephalon, and rhombencephalon are the three primary portions of the brain during early development of the central nervous system.
Mammal	A mammal is a warm-blooded, vertebrate animal, characterized by the presence of sweat glands, including milk producing sweat glands, and by the presence of: hair, three middle ear bones used in hearing, and a neocortex region in the brain. Most also possess specialized teeth and utilize a placenta in the ontogeny. A mammal encompass approximately 5,400 species, distributed in about 1,200 genera, 153 families, and 29 orders, though this varies by classification scheme.
Nucleus	In neuroanatomy, a cluster of cell bodies of neurons within the central nervous system is a nucleus.
Audition	An Audition is a sample performance by an actor, singer, musician, dancer or other performer. It involves the performer displaying their talent through a previously-memorized and rehearsed solo piece: for example, a monologue for actors or a song for a singer. Used in the context of performing arts, it is analogous to job interviews in many ways.
Cerebrovascular accident	Cerebrovascular accident refers to a sudden stoppage of blood flow to a portion of the brain, leading to a loss of brain function.
Dihydrotestosterone	Dihydrotestosterone is a biologically active metabolite of the hormone testosterone, formed primarily in the prostate gland, testes, hair follicles, and adrenal glands by the enzyme 5α-reductase by means of reducing the 4,5 double-bond. Dihydrotestosterone belongs to the class of compounds called androgens, also commonly called androgenic hormones or testoids.
Dopamine	Dopamine is a hormone and neurotransmitter occurring in a wide variety of animals, including both vertebrates and invertebrates. In the brain, dopamine functions as a neurotransmitter. Dopamine is also a neurohormone released by the hypothalamus. Its main function as a hormone is to inhibit the release of prolactin from the anterior lobe of the pituitary.
Hippocampus	The hippocampus is a part of the brain located in the medial temporal lobe. It forms a part of the limbic system and plays a part in memory and spatial navigation.
Preoptic area	The preoptic area is a region of the hypothalamus. According to the MeSH classification, it is considered part of the anterior hypothalamus.
Memory	In psychology, memory is an organism"s ability to store, retain, and subsequently retrieve information. In recent decades, it has become one of the principal pillars of a branch of science called cognitive neuroscience, an interdisciplinary link between cognitive psychology and neuroscience.

Nitric oxide	Nitric oxide is a chemical compound with chemical formula NO. This gas is an important signaling molecule in the body of mammals including humans and is an extremely important intermediate in the chemical industry. It is also a toxic air pollutant produced by automobile engines and power plants.
Nucleus accumbens	A complex of neurons that is part of the brain's "pleasure pathway" responsible for the experience of reward is referred to as the nucleus accumbens.
Posttraumatic stress disorder	Posttraumatic stress disorder is the term for a severe and ongoing emotional reaction to an extreme psychological trauma.
Prefrontal cortex	The prefrontal cortex is the anterior part of the frontal lobes of the brain, lying in front of the motor and premotor areas. Cytoarchitectonically, it is defined by the presence of an internal granular layer IV.
Serotonin	Serotonin, is a monoamine neurotransmitter synthesized in serotonergic neurons in the central nervous system and enterochromaffin cells in the gastrointestinal tract of animals including humans. Serotonin is also found in many mushrooms and plants, including fruits and vegetables.
Sildenafil	Sildenafil is a drug used to treat male erectile dysfunction, developed by the pharmaceutical company Pfizer.
Ventromedial hypothalamus	Ventromedial hypothalamus acts as a satiety center and, when activated, signals an animal to stop eating; when destroyed, the animal overeats, becoming obese.
Viagra	Sildenafil citrate, sold as Viagra Revatio and under various other trade names, is a drug used to treat erectile dysfunction and pulmonary arterial hypertension (PAH.) It was developed and is being marketed by the pharmaceutical company Pfizer. It acts by inhibiting cGMP specific phosphodiesterase type 5, an enzyme that regulates blood flow in the penis.
Vision	Vision is the most important sense for birds, since good eyesight is essential for safe flight, and this group has a number of adaptations which give visual acuity superior to that of other vertebrate groups; a pigeon has been described as "two eyes with wings". The avian eye resembles that of a reptile, but has a better-positioned lens, a feature shared with mammals. Birds have the largest eyes relative to their size within the animal kingdom, and movement is consequently limited within the eye"s bony socket.
Anterior	Anterior is an anatomical term referring to the front part of the body. The anterior is positioned in front of another body part, or towards the head of an animal. It is the opposite of posterior.
Blood	Blood is a specialized biological fluid consisting of red blood cells.White blood cells also called leukocytes and platelets also called thrombocytes suspended in a complex fluid medium known as blood plasma.

Erection	The erection of the penis, clitoris or a nipple is its enlarged and firm state. It depends on a complex interaction of psychological, neural, vascular and endocrine factors. The ability to maintain the erectile state is key to the reproductive system and many forms of life could not reproduce in a natural way without this ability.
Flow	Flow is the mental state of operation in which the person is fully immersed in what he or she is doing by a feeling of energized focus, full involvement, and success in the process of the activity. Proposed by Mihály Csíkszentmihályi, the positive psychology concept has been widely referenced across a variety of fields. Colloquial terms for this or similar mental states include: to be on the ball, in the zone, or in the groove.
Frontal lobe	The frontal lobe comprises four major folds of cortical tissue: the precentral gyrus, superior gyrus and the middle gyrus of the frontal gyri, the inferior frontal gyrus. It has been found to play a part in impulse control, judgement, language, memory, motor function, problem solving, sexual behavior, socialization and spontaneity.
Insulin	Insulin is an animal hormone whose presence informs the body"s cells that the animal is well fed, causing liver and muscle cells to take in glucose and store it in the form of glycogen, and causing fat cells to take in blood lipids and turn them into triglycerides. In addition it has several other anabolic effects throughout the body.
Lead	Lead is a poisonous metal that can damage nervous connections and cause blood and brain disorders. Long term exposure to lead or its salts can cause nephropathy, and colic-like abdominal pains. The concern about lead"s role in cognitive deficits in children has brought about widespread reduction in its use. The majority of cases of adult elevate blood lead levels are workplace-related.
Need	A Need is something that is necessary for humans to live a healthy life. Need s are distinguished from wants because a deficiency would cause a clear negative outcome, such as dysfunction or death. Need s can be objective and physical, such as food and water, or they can be subjective and psychological, such as the Need for self-esteem.
Neurotransmitter	A neurotransmitter is a chemical that is used to relay, amplify and modulate electrical signals between a neurons and another cell.
Receptor	A sensory receptor is a structure that recognizes a stimulus in the internal or external environment of an organism. In response to stimuli the sensory receptor initiates sensory transduction by creating graded potentials or action potentials in the same cell or in an adjacent one.
Sense	Sense are the physiological methods of perception. They and their operation, classification, and theory are overlapping topics studied by a variety of fields, most notably neuroscience, cognitive psychology, and philosophy of perception. The nervous system has a sensory system dedicated to each sense.

389

Signal	In the fields of communications, signal processing, and in electrical engineering more generally, a signal is any time-varying quantity. Signals are often scalar-valued functions of time, but may be vector valued and may be functions of any other relevant independent variable.
Stimulus	In psychology, a stimulus is part of the stimulus-response relationship of behavioral learning theory.
Anterior pituitary	The Anterior pituitary comprises the anterior lobe of the pituitary gland and is part of the endocrine system. Unlike the posterior lobe, the anterior lobe is genuinely glandular, hence the root adeno in its name.
Corpus luteum	The corpus luteum is a temporary endocrine structure in mammals, involved in the production of the progestogens which are needed for the maintenance of a pregnancy.
Follicle-stimulating hormone	Follicle-stimulating hormone is a hormone synthesised and secreted by gonadotropes in the anterior pituitary gland. In the ovary FSH stimulates the growth of immature Graafian follicles to maturation.
Menstrual cycle	The menstrual cycle is a recurring cycle of physiological changes that occurs in the females of several mammals, including human beings and other apes.
Pituitary gland	The pituitary gland is an endocrine gland about the size of a pea that sits in the small, bony cavity at the base of the brain. The pituitary gland secretes hormones regulating a wide variety of bodily activities, including trophic hormones that stimulate other endocrine glands.
Sexual offender	A sexual offender is a person who has been criminally charged and convicted of, or has pled guilty to, or pled Nolo contendere to a sex crime. Behavior modification programs have been shown to reduce recidivism in a sexual offender. Often such programs use principles of applied behavior analysis two such approaches from this line of research have promise the first uses operant conditioning approaches which use reward and punishment to train new behavior.
CycL	CycL in computer science and artificial intelligence is an ontology language used by Doug Lenat"s Cyc artificial intelligence project. Ramanathan V. Guha was instrumental in the design of the language. There is a close variant of CycL known as MELD. The original version of CycL was a frame language, but the modern version is not.
Endocrine gland	An endocrine gland is one of a set of internal organs involved in the secretion of hormones into the blood. The other major type of gland is the exocrine glands, which secrete substances—usually digestive juices—into the digestive tract or onto the skin.
Fertility	Fertility is the natural capability of giving life. As a measure, "Fertility Rate" is the number of children born per couple, person or population.
Follicle	A follicle is a term to describe a small spherical group of cells containing a cavity, and is often used as a descriptive term in biology, particularly in anatomy.

Oxytocin	Oxytocin is a mammalian hormone that also acts as a neurotransmitter in the brain. In females, it is released in large amounts after distension of the cervix and vagina during labor, and after stimulation of the nipples, facilitating birth and breastfeeding, respectively. In humans, oxytocin is released during orgasm in both sexes. In the brain, oxytocin is involved in social recognition and bonding, and might be involved in the formation of trust between people.
Parasympathetic nervous system	The parasympathetic nervous system is a division of the autonomic nervous system, along with the sympathetic nervous system and Enteric nervous system. The ANS is a subdivision of the peripheral nervous system.
Prolactin	Prolactin is a peptide hormone primarily associated with lactation. In breastfeeding, the infant suckling the teat stimulates the production of prolactin, which fills the breast with milk in preparation for the next feed. Oxytocin, a similar hormone, is also released, which triggers milk let-down.
Nerve	A Nerve is an enclosed, cable-like bundle of peripheral axons (the long, slender projections of neurons.) A Nerve provides a common pathway for the electrochemical Nerve impulses that are transmitted along each of the axons. Nerve s are found only in the peripheral nervous system.
Posterior	In reference to the anatomical terms of location, the posterior end is laterally situated at or toward the hinder part of the body, lying at or extending toward the right or left side. It is the polar opposite to the anterior end, or front end of the body.
Posterior pituitary	The posterior pituitary comprises the posterior lobe of the pituitary gland and is part of the endocrine system.
Vasopressin	Vasopressin is a peptide hormone. It is derived from a preprohormone precursor that is synthesized in the hypothalamus, from which it is liberated during transport to the posterior pituitary. Most of it is stored in the posterior part of the pituitary gland to be released into the blood stream; some of it is also released directly into the brain.
Blood pressure	Blood pressure refers to the force exerted by circulating blood on the walls of blood vessels, and constitutes one of the principal vital signs.
Kidney	The kidney is an organ that filters wastes from the blood and excretes them, with water, as urine. In humans, it is located in the posterior part of the abdomen. There is one on each side of the spine. Each kidney receives its blood supply from the renal artery, two of which branch from the abdominal aorta.
Secret	Secrecy or furtiveness is the practice of sharing information among a group of people, which can be as small as one person, while hiding it from all others. That which is kept hidden is known as the Secret. Secrecy is often controversial, depending on the content of the Secret, the group or people keeping the Secret, and the motivation for secrecy.

393

Urine	Urine is an aqueous solution of waste electrolytes and metabolites excreted by mammals, birds, reptiles, fish and amphibians.
Experience	Experience as a general concept comprises knowledge of or skill in or observation of some thing or some event gained through involvement in or exposure to that thing or event. The history of the word experience aligns it closely with the concept of experiment.
Vomeronasal organ	The vomeronasal organ is an auxiliary olfactory sense organ in some tetrapods. It is the first processing stage of the accessory olfactory system. In adults, it is located in the vomer bone, between the nose and the mouth. It develops from the nasal placode, at the anterior edge of the neural plate.
Affect	Affect refers to the experience of feeling or emotion. Affect is a key part of the process of an organism's interaction with stimuli. The word also refers sometimes to affect display, which is "a facial, vocal, or gestural behavior that serves as an indicator of affect."
Antipsychotic	The term antipsychotic is applied to a group of drugs used to treat psychosis.
Antipsychotics	*Antipsychotics* are a group of psychoactive drugs commonly but not exclusively used to treat psychosis, which is typified by schizophrenia. Over time a wide range of *Antipsychotics* have been developed. A first generation of *Antipsychotics*, known as typical *Antipsychotics*, was discovered in the 1950s.
Neural development	The study of neural development draws on both neuroscience and developmental biology to describe the cellular and molecular mechanisms by which complex nervous systems emerge during embryonic development and throughout life.
Chemical	A chemical is a material with a definite chemical composition. All samples of a compound have the same composition; that is, all samples have the same proportions, by mass, of the elements present in the compound.
Chlorpromazine	Chlorpromazine is a phenothiazine antipsychotic. Its principal use is in the treatment of schizophrenia, though it has also been used to treat hiccups and nausea. Its use today has been largely supplanted by the newer atypical antipsychotics such as olanzapine and quetiapine. It works on a variety of receptors in the central nervous system; these include anticholinergic, antidopaminergic and antihistamine effects as well as some antagonism of adrenergic receptors.
Olfactory receptor	Olfactory receptor s expressed in the cell membranes of Olfactory receptor neurons are responsible for the detection of odor molecules. Activated Olfactory receptor s are the initial player in a signal transduction cascade which ultimately produces a nerve impulse which is transmitted to the brain. These receptors are members of the class A rhodopsin-like family of G protein-coupled receptors (GPCRs.)

Olfactory receptors	Olfactory receptors are class A G protein-coupled receptor which play a role in signal transduction to olfactory receptor neurons.
Ageing	Ageing is defined as any change in an organism over time. Ageing commences at conception, continues with the changes associated with the gain of function during growth and development and concludes with the loss of function in a system towards the end of life.
Jealousy	Jealousy typically refers to the thoughts, feelings, and behaviors that occur when a person believes a valued relationship is being threatened by a rival.
Major histocompatibility complex	The major histocompatibility complex is a large genomic region or gene family found in most vertebrates. It is the most gene-dense region of the mammalian genome and plays an important role in the immune system, autoimmunity, and reproductive success.
Circadian rhythm	The circadian rhythm is a name given to the "internal body clock" that regulates the roughly 24 hour cycle of biological processes in animals and plants.
Assortative mating	Assortative mating takes place when sexually reproducing organisms tend to mate with individuals that are like themselves in some respect or dissimilar. In evolution, these two types of assortative mating have the effect, respectively, of increasing and reducing the range of variation, or trait variance, when the assorting is cued on heritable traits.
Adrenocorticotropic hormone	Adrenocorticotropic hormone is a polypeptide hormone produced and secreted by the pituitary gland. It is an important player in the hypothalamic-pituitary-adrenal axis.
Congenital	A condition existing at birth is referred to as congenital.
Congenital adrenal hyperplasia	Congenital adrenal hyperplasia refers to any of several autosomal recessive conditions resulting from biochemical paths of the steroidogenesis of cortisol from cholesterol by the adrenal glands
Cortisol	Cortisol is a corticosteroid hormone produced by the adrenal cortex. It is a vital hormone that is often referred to as the "stress hormone" as it is involved in the response to stress. It increases blood pressure, blood sugar levels and has an immunosuppressive action.
Gender	Gender in common usage, refers to the differences between men and women. An individual"s self-conception as being male or female, as distinguished from actual biological sex." Although "gender" is commonly used interchangeably with "sex," within the academic fields of cultural studies, gender studies and the social sciences in general, the term "gender" often refers to purely social rather than biological differences. Some view gender as a social construction rather than a biological phenomenon.

397

Gender identity	Gender identity describes the gender with which a person identifies, but can also be used to refer to the gender that other people attribute to the individual on the basis of what they know from gender role indications.
Genetics	Genetics is the science of heredity and variation in living organisms.Knowledge of the inheritance of characteristics has been implicitly used since prehistoric times for improving crop plants and animals through selective breeding. However, the modern science of genetics, which seeks to understand the mechanisms of inheritance, only began with the work of Gregor Mendel in the mid-1800s.
Hormone	A hormone is a chemical messenger that carries a signal from one cell to another. All multicellular organisms produce hormone s.
Adrenal cortex	Situated along the perimeter of the adrenal gland, the adrenal cortex mediates the stress response through the production of mineralocorticoids and glucocorticoids, including aldosterone and cortisol respectively. It is also a secondary site of androgen synthesis.
Adrenal glands	The adrenal glands sit atop the kidneys. They are chiefly responsible for regulating the stress response through the synthesis of corticosteroids and catecholamines, including cortisol and adrenalin.
Ambiguity	In sociology and social psychology, the term ambiguity is used to indicate situations that involve uncertainty. Much of this focuses on ambiguity tolerance. A number of correlations have been found between an individual's reaction and tolerance to ambiguity and a range of factors.
Corticosterone	Corticosterone is a 21 carbon steroid hormone of the corticosteroid type produced in the cortex of the adrenal glands.
Metabolism	Metabolism is the biochemical modification of chemical compounds in living organisms and cells.
Sexual development	Sexual development is the process by which an immature and sterile organism develops the capacity to reproduce. In humans, this process is called puberty.
Hermaphrodite	Hermaphrodite refers to a person with parts of both male and female genitalia.
Not	This catalog is compiled from a source file. Please do not edit this page manually. This is how to edit it.
Androgen insensitivity	Androgen insensitivity syndrome is a set of disorders of sexual differentiation that results from mutations of the gene encoding the androgen receptor. If androgen insensitivity is total, XY males develop as females in the sense that their bodies look completely female and they develop a female gender identity.

Clitoris	The clitoris is a sexual organ that is present in biologically female mammals. In humans, the visible knob-like portion is located near the anterior junction of the labia minora, above the opening of the urethra and vagina.
Cloacal exstrophy	Cloacal exstrophy is a severe birth defect wherein much of the abdominal organs are exposed. It often causes the splitting of both male and female genitalia, and the anus is occasionally sealed.
Sexual orientation	Sexual orientation refers to the direction of an individual"s sexuality, usually conceived of as classifiable according to the sex or gender of the persons whom the individual finds sexually attractive. Most definitions of sexual orientation include a psychological component and/or a behavioral component.
Vagina	The vagina is a fibromuscular tubular tract leading from the uterus to the exterior of the body in female placental mammals and marsupials, or to the cloaca in female birds, monotremes, and some reptiles. Female insects and other invertebrates also have a vagina, which is the terminal part of the oviduct.
Lack	Lack , is, in Lacan"s psychoanalytic philosophy, always related to desire. In his seminar Le transfert he states that Lack is what causes desire to arise. However, Lack first designated a Lack of being: what is desired is being itself.
Mechanism	In philosophy, mechanism is a theory that all natural phenomena can be explained by physical causes. It can be contrasted with vitalism, the philosophical theory that vital forces are active in living organisms, so that life cannot be explained solely by mechanism.
Generation	Generation, also known as procreation, is the act of producing offspring. A generation can also be a stage or degree in a succession of natural descent as a grandfather, a father, and the father"s son comprise three generations.
Amygdala	Amygdala are almond-shaped groups of neurons located deep within the medial temporal lobes of the brain in complex vertebrates, including humans. Shown in research to perform a primary role in the processing and memory of emotional reactions, the amygdala are considered part of the limbic system.
Prepulse inhibition	Prepulse inhibition is a neurological phenomenon in which a weaker prestimulus (prepulse) inhibits the reaction of an organism to a subsequent strong startling stimulus (pulse.) The stimuli are usually acoustic, but tactile, light, airpuff stimuli are also used. The reduction of the amplitude of startle reflects the ability of the nervous system to temporarily adapt to a strong sensory stimulus when a preceding weaker signal is given to warn the organism.
Reflex	A reflex action is an automatic neuromuscular action elicited by a defined stimulus. In most contexts, especially involving humans, a reflex action is mediated via the reflex arc

Selective serotonin reuptake inhibitor	Selective serotonin reuptake inhibitor is a class of antidepressants used in the treatment of depression, anxiety disorders, and some personality disorders. They are also typically effective and used in treating premature ejaculation problems.
Depression	In everyday language depression refers to any downturn in mood, which may be relatively transitory and perhaps due to something trivial.
Startle Reflex	Startle reflex is the response of mind and body to a sudden unexpected stimulus, such as a flash of light, a loud noise, or a quick movement near the face. In human beings, the reaction includes physical movement away from the stimulus, a contraction of the muscles of the arms and legs, and often blinking.
Kin selection	Kin selection has been mathematically defined by Hamilton as a mechanism for the evolution of apparently altruistic acts. Under natural selection, a gene that causes itself to increase in frequency should become more common in the population. Since identical copies of genes may be carried in relatives, a gene in one organism that prompts behavior which aids another organism carrying the same gene may become more successful.
Immune system	The most important function of the human immune system occurs at the cellular level of the blood and tissues. The lymphatic and blood circulation systems are highways for specialized white blood cells. These cells include B cells, T cells, natural killer cells, and macrophages. All function with the primary objective of recognizing, attacking and destroying bacteria, viruses, cancer cells, and all substances seen as foreign.
Methyl	Methyl is a hydrophobic alkyl functional group derived from methane. This hydrocarbon unit can be found in many organic compounds. The incorporation of a methyl can have one of three general effects on the rate of metabolism.
Stress	Stress is the consequence of the failure to adapt to change. Less simply: it is the condition that results when person-environment transactions lead the individual to perceive a discrepancy, whether real or not, between the demands of a situation and the resources of the person"s biological, psychological or social systems.
Suprachiasmatic nucleus	The suprachiasmatic nucleus is in the hypothalamus and is so named because it resides immediately above the optic chaism. Its principal function is to create the circadian rhythm, which regulates the body functions over the 24-hour period.
Axon	An axon is a long, slender projection of a nerve cell, or neuron, that conducts electrical impulses away from the neuron"s cell body or soma.
Chronobiology	Chronobiology is a field of science that examines periodic phenomena in living organisms.

403

Cerebral hemisphere	A Cerebral hemisphere (hemispherium cerebrale) is defined as one of the two regions of the brain that are delineated by the body"s median plane, (medial longitudinal fissure.) The brain can thus be described as being divided into left and right Cerebral hemisphere s. Each of these hemispheres has an outer layer of grey matter called the cerebral cortex that is supported by an inner layer of white matter.
Corpus callosum	The corpus callosum is a structure of the mammalian brain in the longitudal fissure that connects the left and right cerebral hemispheres. Much of the inter-hemispheric communication in the brain is conducted across the corpus callosum.
Optic chiasm	The optic chiasm is the part of the brain where the optic nerves partially cross. Specifically, the nerves connected to the right eye that attend to the left visual field cross with the nerves from the left eye that attend to the right visual field.

Emotion	Emotion, in its most general definition, is a complex psychophysical process that arises spontaneously, rather than through conscious effort, and evokes either a positive or negative psychological response and physical expressions, often involuntary, related to feelings, perceptions or beliefs about elements, objects or relations between them, in reality or in the imagination. An emotion is often differentiated from a feeling.
Methylphenidate	Methylphenidate is a prescription stimulant commonly used to treat Attention-deficit hyperactivity disorder, or ADHD. It is also one of the primary drugs used to treat the daytime drowsiness symptoms of narcolepsy and chronic fatigue syndrome.
Arousal	Arousal is a physiological and psychological state involving the activation of the reticular activating system in the brain stem, the autonomic nervous system and the endocrine system, leading to increased heart rate and blood pressure and a condition of alertness and readiness to respond.
Autonomic nervous system	The autonomic nervous system is the part of theperipheral nervous system that acts as a control system, maintaining homeostasis in the body. These maintenance activities are primarily performed without conscious control or sensation. . Its most useful definition could be: the sensory and motor neurons that innervate the viscera. These neurons form reflex arcs that pass through the lower brainstem or medulla oblongata.
Walter Bradford Cannon	Walter Bradford Cannon was an American physiologist. He was President of the American Physiological Society from 1914 to 1916.
Cognition	In psychology, cognition refers to an information processing view of an individual"s psychological functions. Other interpretations of the meaning of cognition link it to the development of concepts; individual minds, groups, organizations, and even larger coalitions of entities, can be modelled as societies which cooperate to form concepts.
James-Lange	The James-Lange theory concerns the origin and nature of emotions as developed independently by two 19th-century scholars. As a response to experiences in the world, the autonomic nervous system creates physiological events. Emotions are feelings which come about as a result of these physiological changes, rather than being their cause.
James-Lange theory	The James-Lange theory refers to a hypothesis on the origin and nature of emotions developed independently, William James and Carl Lange. It states that within human beings, as a response to experiences in the world, the autonomic nervous system creates physiological events such as muscular tension, a rise in heart rate, perspiration, and dryness of the mouth. Emotions, then, are feelings which come about as a result of these physiological changes, rather than being their cause.
Nervous system	The nervous system of an animal coordinates the activity of the muscles, monitors the organs, constructs and also stops input from the senses, and initiates actions.
Nervous system autonomic	Nervous system autonomic is the part of the peripheral nervous system that acts as a control system, maintaining homeostasis in the body.

407

Parasympathetic nervous system	The parasympathetic nervous system is a division of the autonomic nervous system, along with the sympathetic nervous system and Enteric nervous system. The ANS is a subdivision of the peripheral nervous system.
Nerve	A Nerve is an enclosed, cable-like bundle of peripheral axons (the long, slender projections of neurons.) A Nerve provides a common pathway for the electrochemical Nerve impulses that are transmitted along each of the axons. Nerve s are found only in the peripheral nervous system.
Perception	In psychology. and the cognitive sciences, perception is the process of acquiring, interpreting, selecting, and organizing sensory information. It is a task far more complex than was imagined in the 1950s and 1960s, when it was proclaimed that building perceiving machines would take about a decade, but, needless to say, that is still very far from reality.
Skeleton	In biology, the skeleton provides a strong, internal framework that supports the body, makes up about 20 percent of its weight, and consists of 206 bones. These bones meet at joints, the majority of which are freely movable, making the skeleton flexible and mobile. The skeleton also contains cartilage.
Muscle	Muscle is contractile tissue of the body and is derived from the mesodermal layer of embryonic germ cells. It is classified as skeletal, cardiac, or smooth muscle, and its function is to produce force and cause motion, either locomotion or movement within internal organs.
Failure	Failure refers to the state or condition of not meeting a desirable or intended objective.
Brain	In animals, the brain, is the control center of the central nervous system, responsible for behavior. The brain is located in the head, protected by the skull and close to the primary sensory apparatus of vision, hearing, equilibrioception, sense of acceleration, taste, and olfaction.
Functional magnetic resonance imaging	Functional magnetic resonance imaging is the use of MRI to measure the haemodynamic response related to neural activity in the brain or spinal cord of humans or other animals. It is one of the most recently developed forms of neuroimaging.
Limbic system	The limbic system includes the putative structures in the human brain involved in emotion, motivation, and emotional association with memory. The limbic system influences the formation of memory by integrating emotional states with stored memories of physical sensations.
MRI	Magnetic resonance imaging (MRI) is primarily a medical imaging technique most commonly used in radiology to visualize the structure and function of the body. It provides detailed images of the body in any plane. MRI provides much greater contrast between the different soft tissues of the body than computed tomography (CT) does, making it especially useful in neurological (brain), musculoskeletal, cardiovascular, and oncological (cancer) imaging.

Magnetic resonance imaging	Magnetic resonance imaging is a non-invasive method used to render images of the inside of an object. It is primarily used in medical imaging to demonstrate pathological or other physiological alterations of living tissues.
Panic	Panic is a sudden fear which dominates or replaces thinking and often affects groups of people or animals. Panic s typically occur in disaster situations, or violent situations (such as robbery, home invasion, a shooting rampage, etc.) which may endanger the overall health of the affected group.
Panic attack	An attack of overwhelming anxiety, fear, or terror is called panic attack.
Panic disorder	Panic Disorder is a psychiatric condition characterized by reccurring panic attacks in combination with significant behavioral change or at least a month of ongoing worry about the implications or concern about having other attacks. Panic Disorder is real and potentially disabling, but it can be controlled and successfully treated. Because of the disturbing symptoms that accompany panic disorder, it may be mistaken for a life-threatening physical illness.
Positron emission tomography	Positron emission tomography is a nuclear medicine medical imaging technique which produces a three-dimensional image or map of functional processes in the body. Images of metabolic activity in space are then reconstructed by computer, often in modern scanners aided by results from a CT X-ray scan.
Research method	The scope of the research method is to produce some new knowledge. This, in principle, can take three main forms: Exploratory research; Constructive research; and Empirical research.
Amygdala	Amygdala are almond-shaped groups of neurons located deep within the medial temporal lobes of the brain in complex vertebrates, including humans. Shown in research to perform a primary role in the processing and memory of emotional reactions, the amygdala are considered part of the limbic system.
Animal testing	Animal testing refers to the use of animals in experiments. It is estimated that 50 to 100 million vertebrate animals worldwide — from zebrafish to non-human primates — are used annually and either killed during the experiments or subsequently euthanized.
Blood	Blood is a specialized biological fluid consisting of red blood cells.White blood cells also called leukocytes and platelets also called thrombocytes suspended in a complex fluid medium known as blood plasma.
Brain stem	The brain stem is the lower part of the brain, adjoining and structurally continuous with the spinal cord. Most sources consider the pons, medulla oblongata, and midbrain all to be part of the brain stem.

Chemical	A chemical is a material with a definite chemical composition. All samples of a compound have the same composition; that is, all samples have the same proportions, by mass, of the elements present in the compound.
Cingulate gyrus	Cingulate gyrus is a gyrus in the medial part of the brain. It partially wraps around the corpus callosum and is limited above by the cingulate sulcus. It functions as an intergral part of the limbic system, which is involved with emotion formation and processing, learning, and memory.
Depression	In everyday language depression refers to any downturn in mood, which may be relatively transitory and perhaps due to something trivial.
Prosencephalon	In the anatomy of the brain of vertebrates, the prosencephalon is the rostral-most portion of the brain. The prosencephalon, the mesencephalon, and rhombencephalon are the three primary portions of the brain during early development of the central nervous system.
Hemoglobin	Hemoglobin is the iron-containing oxygen-transport metalloprotein in the red blood cells of the blood in vertebrates and other animals.
Hypothalamus	The hypothalamus is a region of the brain located below the thalamus, forming the major portion of the ventral region of the diencephalon and functioning to regulate certain metabolic processes and other autonomic activities.
Olfactory bulb	The olfactory bulb is a structure of the vertebrate forebrain involved in olfaction, the perception of odors.
Other	The Other or constitutive Other is a key concept in continental philosophy, opposed to the Same. It refers, or attempts to refer, to that which is "Other" than the concept being considered. The term often means a person Other than oneself, and is often capitalised.
Structure	Structure is a fundamental and sometimes intangible notion covering the recognition, observation, nature, and stability of patterns and relationships of entities.
Sympathetic	The sympathetic nervous system activates what is often termed the "fight or flight response". It is an automatic regulation system, that is, one that operates without the intervention of conscious thought.
Syndrome	The term syndrome is the association of several clinically recognizable features, signs, symptoms, phenomena or characteristics which often occur together, so that the presence of one feature indicates the presence of the others.

413

Behavioral Activation	Behavioral activation is a third generation behavior therapy for treating depression. It is one of many functional analytic psychotherapies which are based on a Skinnerian psychological model of behavior change, generally referred to as Applied Behavior Analysis. This area is also a part of what is called Clinical Behavior Analysis (C behavioral activation) and makes up one of the most effective practices in the professional practice of behavior analysis.
Behavioral Inhibition	Physiological probes of children with behavioral inhibition show significantly higher measures of activity in the sympathetic nervous system and hypothalamic-pituitary axis than in non-inhibited children. Kagan postulates that anxiety-prone children are born with a lower firing threshold in amygdala and hypothalamic neurons. His work provides a robust model for predicting temperamental forerunners of anxiety disorders.
Behavioral Inhibition System	The behavioral inhibition system is a circuit in the limbic system that responds to threat signals by inhibiting activity and causing anxiety.
Cerebrovascular accident	Cerebrovascular accident refers to a sudden stoppage of blood flow to a portion of the brain, leading to a loss of brain function.
Disgust	Disgust is an emotion that is typically associated with things that are perceived as unclean, inedible, or infectious. Disgust is one of the basic emotions of Robert Plutchik"s theory of emotions. Disgust invokes a characteristic facial expression, one of Paul Ekman"s six universal facial expressions of emotion.
Escape response	Escape response is a possible reaction in response to stimuli indicative of danger, in particular, it initiates an escape motion of an animal. The term is also used in a more general setting: avoiding of unpleasant situations.
Insular cortex	The insular cortex is a structure of the human brain. It lies deep to the brain"s lateral surface, within the lateral sulcus which separates the temporal lobe and inferior parietal cortex.
Lateralization	Lateralization of brain functions is evident in the phenomena of right- or left-handedness, -earedness and -eyedness. Broad generalizations are often made in popular psychology about certain function being lateralised, that is, located in the right or left side of the brain. These ideas need to be treated carefully because the popular lateralization is ften distributed across both sides. However, there is some division of mental processing.
Temporal lobe	The temporal lobe is part of the cerebrum. It lies at the side of the brain, beneath the lateral or Sylvian fissure. Adjacent areas in the superior, posterior and lateral parts of the temporal lobe are involved in high-level auditory processing.
Attention	Attention is the cognitive process of selectively concentrating on one aspect of the environment while ignoring other things. Examples include listening carefully to what someone is saying while ignoring other conversations in the room or listening to a cell phone conversation while driving a car.

Brain damage	Brain damage is the destruction or degeneration of brain cells. It may occur due to a wide range of conditions, illnesses, injuries, and as a result of iatrogenesis. Possible causes of widespread brain damage include prolonged hypoxia, poisoning by teratogens, infection, and neurological illness.
Decision making	Decision making is the cognitive process leading to the selection of a course of action among variations. Every decision making process produces a final choice. It can be an action or an opinion. It begins when we need to do something but know not what. Therefore, decision making is a reasoning process which can be rational or irrational, and can be based on explicit assumptions or tacit assumptions.
Ethics	Ethics a major branch of philosophy, is the study of values and customs of a person or group. It covers the analysis and employment of concepts such as right and wrong, good and evil, and responsibility
Prefrontal cortex	The prefrontal cortex is the anterior part of the frontal lobes of the brain, lying in front of the motor and premotor areas. Cytoarchitectonically, it is defined by the presence of an internal granular layer IV.
Sex steroid	Sex steroid refers to steroid hormones that interact with vertebrate androgen or estrogen receptors.
Anterior	Anterior is an anatomical term referring to the front part of the body. The anterior is positioned in front of another body part, or towards the head of an animal. It is the opposite of posterior.
Explanation	An explanation is a description which may clarify causes, context, and consequences of a certain object, and a phenomenon such as a process, a state of affairs. This description may establish rules or laws, and may clarify the existing ones in relation to an object, and a phenomenon examined. The components of an explanation can be implicit, and be interwoven with one another.
Frontal lobe	The frontal lobe comprises four major folds of cortical tissue: the precentral gyrus, superior gyrus and the middle gyrus of the frontal gyri, the inferior frontal gyrus. It has been found to play a part in impulse control, judgement, language, memory, motor function, problem solving, sexual behavior, socialization and spontaneity.
Generation	Generation, also known as procreation, is the act of producing offspring. A generation can also be a stage or degree in a succession of natural descent as a grandfather, a father, and the father"s son comprise three generations.
Issue	In computing, the term Issue is a unit of work to accomplish an improvement in a system. An Issue could be a bug, a requested feature, task, missing documentation, and so forth. The word "Issue" is popularly misused in lieu of "problem." This usage is probably related.

Need	A Need is something that is necessary for humans to live a healthy life. Need s are distinguished from wants because a deficiency would cause a clear negative outcome, such as dysfunction or death. Need s can be objective and physical, such as food and water, or they can be subjective and psychological, such as the Need for self-esteem.
Signal	In the fields of communications, signal processing, and in electrical engineering more generally, a signal is any time-varying quantity. Signals are often scalar-valued functions of time, but may be vector valued and may be functions of any other relevant independent variable.
Species	Species refers to a reproductively isolated breeding population.
Stimulus	In psychology, a stimulus is part of the stimulus-response relationship of behavioral learning theory.
Understanding	Understanding is a psychological process related to an abstract or physical object, such as, person, situation, or message whereby one is able to think about it and use concepts to deal adequately with that object.
Phineas Gage	Phineas Gage was a railroad construction foreman who suffered a traumatic brain injury when a tamping iron accidentally passed through his skull, damaging the frontal lobes of his brain. This injury is supposed to have negatively affected his emotional, social and personal traits—leaving him in a temperamental and unsociable state, so much so that his friends said he was "no longer Gage".
Behavior	Behavior refers to the actions or reactions of an object or organism, usually in relation to the environment. Behavior can be conscious or subconscious, overt or covert, and voluntary or involuntary. Human Behavior (and that of other organisms and mechanisms) can be common, unusual, acceptable, or unacceptable. Humans evaluate the acceptability of Behavior using social norms and regulate Behavior by means of social control
Cigarette	A cigarette is a product consumed via smoking and manufactured out of cured and finely cut tobacco leaves and reconstituted tobacco. It contains nicotine, an addictive stimulant which is toxic. It delivers smoke to the lungs immediately and produce a rapid psychoactive effect. The cigarette has been proven to be highly addictive, as well as a cause of multiple types of causes.
Tobacco smoking	Tobacco smoking is the act of burning the dried or cured leaves of the tobacco plant and inhaling the smoke for pleasure, for ritualistic or social purposes, self-medication, or simply to satisfy physical dependence.
Environmental factor	In epidemiology, environmental factor refers to determinants of disease that are not transmitted genetically.

Genetics	Genetics is the science of heredity and variation in living organisms.Knowledge of the inheritance of characteristics has been implicitly used since prehistoric times for improving crop plants and animals through selective breeding. However, the modern science of genetics, which seeks to understand the mechanisms of inheritance, only began with the work of Gregor Mendel in the mid-1800s.
Heritability	Heritability It is that proportion of the observed variation in a particular phenotype within a particular population, that can be attributed to the contribution of genotype. In other words: it measures the extent to which differences between individuals in a population are due their being different genetically.
Lead	Lead is a poisonous metal that can damage nervous connections and cause blood and brain disorders. Long term exposure to lead or its salts can cause nephropathy, and colic-like abdominal pains. The concern about lead"s role in cognitive deficits in children has brought about widespread reduction in its use. The majority of cases of adult elevate blood lead levels are workplace-related.
Manic-depressive disorder	Bipolar affective disorder until recently, the current name is of fairly recent origin and refers to the cycling between high and low episodes; it has replaced the older term Manic-depressive disorder. The new term is designed to be neutral, to avoid the stigma in the non-mental health community.
Prenatal development	Prenatal development is the process in which an embryo or fetus gestates during pregnancy, from fertilization until birth.
Alcoholism	Alcoholism is a term with multiple and sometimes conflicting definitions. In common and historic usage, alcoholism refers to any condition that results in the continued consumption of alcoholic beverages despite the health problems and negative social consequences it causes.
Characteristic	Characteristic has several particular meanings: · in mathematics • · Euler characteristic • · method of characteristic s (partial differential equations) · in physics and engineering · any characteristic curve that shows the relationship between certain input- and output parameters, e.g. · an I-V or current-voltage characteristic is the current in a circuit as a function of the applied voltage · Receiver-Operator characteristic · in navigation, the characteristic pattern of a lighted beacon. · in fiction · in Dungeons ' Dragons, characteristic is another name for ability score .
Heredity	Heredity is the transfer of characteristics from parent to offspring through their genes, or the transfer of a title, style or social status through the social convention known as inheritance.

Population	In sociology and biology a population is the collection of people or individuals of a particular species. A population shares a particular characteristic of interest most often that of living in a given geographic area.
Variance	In probability theory and statistics, the variance of a random variable or somewhat more precisely, of a probability distribution is one measure of statistical dispersion, averaging the squared distance of its possible values from the expected value.
Hormone	A hormone is a chemical messenger that carries a signal from one cell to another. All multicellular organisms produce hormone s.
Testosterone	Testosterone is a steroid hormone from the androgen group. It is the principal male sex hormone and the "original" anabolic steroid.
Activating effect	The arousal-producing effects of sex hormones that increase the likelihood of sexual behavior is called the activating effect.
Androgen	Androgen is the generic term for any natural or synthetic compound, usually a steroid hormone, that stimulates or controls the development and maintenance of masculine characteristics in vertebrates by binding to androgen receptors. This includes the activity of the accessory male sex organs and development of male secondary sex characteristics.
Gland	A gland is an organ in an animal's body that synthesizes a substance for release such as hormones, often into the bloodstream or into cavities inside the body or its outer surface.
5-Hydroxyindoleacetic acid	*5-hydroxyindoleacetic acid* (5-HIAA) is the main metabolite of serotonin in the human body. In chemical analysis of urine samples, 5-HIAA is used to determine the body"s levels of serotonin. 5-HIAA, Quantitative, 24-Hour Urine; Serotonin Metabolite, 24-Hour Urine 24-hour urine volume is measured and recorded on the request form.
Audition	An Audition is a sample performance by an actor, singer, musician, dancer or other performer. It involves the performer displaying their talent through a previously-memorized and rehearsed solo piece: for example, a monologue for actors or a song for a singer. Used in the context of performing arts, it is analogous to job interviews in many ways.
Cerebrospinal fluid	A solution that fills the hollow cavities of the brain and circulates around the brain and spinal cord is called cerebrospinal fluid.
Corpus callosum	The corpus callosum is a structure of the mammalian brain in the longitudal fissure that connects the left and right cerebral hemispheres. Much of the inter-hemispheric communication in the brain is conducted across the corpus callosum.

Parietal lobe	The parietal lobe is a lobe in the brain. It is positioned above the occipital lobe and behind the frontal lobe.
Serotonin	Serotonin, is a monoamine neurotransmitter synthesized in serotonergic neurons in the central nervous system and enterochromaffin cells in the gastrointestinal tract of animals including humans. Serotonin is also found in many mushrooms and plants, including fruits and vegetables.
Turnover	Turnover, in a human resources context refers to the characteristic of a given company or industry, relative to rate at which an employer gains and loses staff. The ease of replacing these employees provides little incentive to employers to offer generous employment contracts: conversely, contracts may strongly favour the employer and lead to increased turnover as employees seek, and eventually find, more favourable employment.
Vision	Vision is the most important sense for birds, since good eyesight is essential for safe flight, and this group has a number of adaptations which give visual acuity superior to that of other vertebrate groups; a pigeon has been described as "two eyes with wings". The avian eye resembles that of a reptile, but has a better-positioned lens, a feature shared with mammals. Birds have the largest eyes relative to their size within the animal kingdom, and movement is consequently limited within the eye"s bony socket.
Metabolite	Metabolite is the intermediate and product of metabolism. The term metabolite is usually restricted to small molecules. A primary metabolite is directly involved in the normal growth, development, and reproduction.
Neurotransmitter	A neurotransmitter is a chemical that is used to relay, amplify and modulate electrical signals between a neurons and another cell.
Spinal cord	The spinal cord is a thin, tubular bundle of nerves that is an extension of the central nervous system from the brain and is enclosed in and protected by the bony vertebral column. The main function of the spinal cord is transmission of neural inputs between the periphery and the brain.
Ventricle	In the heart, a ventricle is a heart chamber which collects blood from an atrium another heart chamber that is smaller than a ventricle and pumps it out of the heart.
Amino acid	Amino acid is the basic structural building unit of proteins. They form short polymer chains called peptides or polypeptides which in turn form structures called proteins.
Anxiety	Anxiety is a physiological state characterized by cognitive, somatic, emotional, and behavioral components.

425

Blood-brain barrier	The Blood-brain barrier is a membranic structure that acts primarily to protect the brain from chemicals in the blood, while still allowing essential metabolic function. It is composed of endothelial cells, which are packed very tightly in brain capillaries. This higher density restricts passage of substances from the bloodstream much more than endothelial cells in capillaries elsewhere in the body
Diet	In nutrition, the diet is the sum of food consumed by a person or other organism. Dietary habits are the habitual decisions an individual or culture makes when choosing what foods to eat.
Fear	Fear is an emotional response to tangible and realistic dangers. Fear should be distinguished from anxiety, an emotion that often arises out of proportion to the actual threat or danger involved, and can be subjectively experienced without any specific attention to the threatening object.
Nucleus	In neuroanatomy, a cluster of cell bodies of neurons within the central nervous system is a nucleus.
Nucleus accumbens	A complex of neurons that is part of the brain's "pleasure pathway" responsible for the experience of reward is referred to as the nucleus accumbens.
Reflex	A reflex action is an automatic neuromuscular action elicited by a defined stimulus. In most contexts, especially involving humans, a reflex action is mediated via the reflex arc
Selective serotonin reuptake inhibitor	Selective serotonin reuptake inhibitor is a class of antidepressants used in the treatment of depression, anxiety disorders, and some personality disorders. They are also typically effective and used in treating premature ejaculation problems.
Tryptophan	Tryptophan is a sleep-promoting amino acid and a precursor for serotonin (a neurotransmitter) and melatonin (a neurohormone). Tryptophan has been implicated as a possible cause of schizophrenia in people who cannot metabolize it properly.
Tryptophan hydroxylase	Tryptophan hydroxylase is an enzyme involved in the synthesis of the neurotransmitter serotonin.
Antipsychotic	The term antipsychotic is applied to a group of drugs used to treat psychosis.
Antipsychotics	*Antipsychotics* are a group of psychoactive drugs commonly but not exclusively used to treat psychosis, which is typified by schizophrenia. Over time a wide range of *Antipsychotics* have been developed. A first generation of *Antipsychotics*, known as typical *Antipsychotics*, was discovered in the 1950s.

Chlorpromazine	Chlorpromazine is a phenothiazine antipsychotic. Its principal use is in the treatment of schizophrenia, though it has also been used to treat hiccups and nausea. Its use today has been largely supplanted by the newer atypical antipsychotics such as olanzapine and quetiapine. It works on a variety of receptors in the central nervous system; these include anticholinergic, antidopaminergic and antihistamine effects as well as some antagonism of adrenergic receptors.
Dopamine	Dopamine is a hormone and neurotransmitter occurring in a wide variety of animals, including both vertebrates and invertebrates. In the brain, dopamine functions as a neurotransmitter. Dopamine is also a neurohormone released by the hypothalamus. Its main function as a hormone is to inhibit the release of prolactin from the anterior lobe of the pituitary.
Mechanism	In philosophy, mechanism is a theory that all natural phenomena can be explained by physical causes. It can be contrasted with vitalism, the philosophical theory that vital forces are active in living organisms, so that life cannot be explained solely by mechanism.
Receptor	A sensory receptor is a structure that recognizes a stimulus in the internal or external environment of an organism. In response to stimuli the sensory receptor initiates sensory transduction by creating graded potentials or action potentials in the same cell or in an adjacent one.
Startle Reflex	Startle reflex is the response of mind and body to a sudden unexpected stimulus, such as a flash of light, a loud noise, or a quick movement near the face. In human beings, the reaction includes physical movement away from the stimulus, a contraction of the muscles of the arms and legs, and often blinking.
Axon	An axon is a long, slender projection of a nerve cell, or neuron, that conducts electrical impulses away from the neuron"s cell body or soma.
Midbrain	The midbrain is the middle of three vesicles that arise from the neural tube that forms the brain of developing animals. In mature human brains, it becomes the least differentiated, from both its developmental form and within its own structure, among the three vesicles. The midbrain is considered part of the brain stem.
Pain	Pain is an unpleasant sensation. It is defined by the International Association for the Study of Pain as "an unpleasant sensory and emotional experience associated with actual or potential tissue damage, or described in terms of such damage".
Pons	The pons is a structure located on the brain stem. It is rostral to the medulla oblongata, caudal to the midbrain, and ventral to the cerebellum. In humans and other bipeds this means it is above the medulla, below the midbrain, and anterior to the cerebellum.

Toxoplasma	Toxoplasma gondii is a species of parasitic protozoa in the genus Toxoplasma. Acute stage toxoplasma infections can be asymptomatic, but often gives flu-like symptoms in the early acute stages, and like flu can become, in very rare cases, fatal. Several independent pieces of evidence point towards a possible role of Toxoplasma infection in some cases of schizophrenia and paranoia, but this theory does not seem to account for many cases.
Toxoplasma gondii	Toxoplasma gondii is a species of parasitic protozoa in the genus Toxoplasma. The definitive host of Toxoplasma gondii is the cat, but the parasite can be carried by the vast majority of warm-blooded animals, including humans. Toxoplasma gondii infections have the ability to change the behavior of rats and mice, making them drawn to rather than fearful of the scent of cats. This effect is advantageous to the parasite, which will be able to sexually reproduce if its host is eaten by a cat.
Constant	A constant is something that does not change, over time or otherwise: a fixed value. In most fields of discourse the term is an antonym of "variable", but in mathematical parlance a mathematical variable may sometimes also be called a constant.
Software extension	A Software extension is a computer program designed to be incorporated into another piece of software in order to enhance the functionalities of the latter. On its own, the program is not useful or functional. Examples of software applications that support extensions include the Mozilla Firefox Web browser, Adobe Systems Photoshop and Microsoft Windows Explorer shell extensions.
Hindbrain	The hindbrain is a developmental categorization of portions of the central nervous system in vertebrates. It can be subdivided in a variable number of transversal swellings called rhombomeres.
Inferior colliculus	The Inferior colliculus is one of the essential auditory centers located in the mesencephalon.
Medulla	Medulla refers to the middle of something, and derives from the Latin word for "marrow" In medicine it refers to either bone marrow, the spinal cord, or more generally, the middle part of a structure as opposed to the cortex.
Sense	Sense are the physiological methods of perception. They and their operation, classification, and theory are overlapping topics studied by a variety of fields, most notably neuroscience, cognitive psychology, and philosophy of perception. The nervous system has a sensory system dedicated to each sense.
Single	In relationships, a single person is one who is not married, or, more broadly, who is not in an exclusive romantic relationship.
Superior colliculus	The superior colliculus is a paired structure that is part of the brain"s tectal area. In humans, the superior colliculus is involved in the generation of saccadic eye movements and eye-head coordination.

Tegmentum	The tegmentum is a general area within the brainstem.
Kluver-Bucy syndrome	Kluver-Bucy syndrome is a behavioral disorder that occurs when both the right and left medial temporal lobes of the brain malfunction. The amygdala has been a particularly implicated brain region in the pathogenesis of this syndrome.
Lobes	The four major sections of the cerebral cortex: frontal, parietal, temporal, and occipital are called lobes.
Cortical blindness	Cortical blindness is the total or partial loss of vision in a normal-appearing eye caused by damage to the visual area in the brain"s occipital cortex.
Disease	A Disease or medical problem is an abnormal condition of an organism that impairs bodily functions, associated with specific symptoms and signs. It may be caused by external factors, such as invading organisms, or it may be caused by internal dysfunctions, such as autoimmune Disease s. In human beings, Disease is often used more broadly to refer to any condition that causes extreme pain, dysfunction, distress, social problems, and/or death to the person afflicted, or similar problems for those in contact with the person.
Gamma-aminobutyric acid	Gamma-aminobutyric acid is an inhibitory neurotransmitter found in the nervous systems of widely-divergent species. It is the chief inhibitory neurotransmitter in the central nervous system and also in the retina.
Negative symptoms	Negative symptoms are indications of deficiency in specific mental functions and of an absence of typical behavior; these can include reduced or inappropriate emotions, lack of eill, loss of verbal expression, and the lack of logic. Negative symptoms are often displayed in the residual phase of schizophrenia.
Benzodiazepine	A benzodiazepine is a psychoactive drug whose core chemical structure is the fusion of a benzene ring and a diazepine ring. benzodiazepine s have varying sedative, hypnotic , anxiolytic (anti-anxiety), anticonvulsant, muscle relaxant and amnesic properties. These properties make benzodiazepine s useful in treating anxiety, insomnia, agitation, seizures, muscle spasms, alcohol withdrawal and as a premedication for medical or dental procedures.
Benzodiazepines	The Benzodiazepines are a commonly prescribed class of sedative hypnotic psychoactive drugs with varying sedative, hypnotic, anxiolytic , anticonvulsant, muscle relaxant and amnesic properties. Benzodiazepines are useful in treating anxiety, insomnia, agitation, seizures, muscle spasms and alcohol withdrawal. They can also be used before certain medical procedures such as endoscopies or dental work where tension and anxiety are present to induce sedation and amnesia.
Microdialysis	Microdialysis is a technique used to determine the chemical components of the fluid in the extracellular space of tissues.

433

Antianxiety drugs	Drugs that can reduce a person's level of excitability while increasing feelings of well-being are called antianxiety drugs.
Discovery	Discovery observations form acts of detecting and learning something. Discovery observations are acts in which something is found and given a productive insight. Serendipity is the effect by which one accidentally discovers something fortunate, especially while looking for something else entirely.
GABA receptor	A GABA receptor is a receptor that responds to the neurotransmitter γ-aminobutyric acid, the chief inhibitory neurotransmitter in the vertebrate central nervous system. There are three distinct classes: $GABA_A$, $GABA_B$, and $GABA_C$.
Glial cells	Glial cells are non-neuronal cells that provide support and nutrition, maintain homeostasis, form myelin, and participate in signal transmission in the nervous system.
Memory	In psychology, memory is an organism"s ability to store, retain, and subsequently retrieve information. In recent decades, it has become one of the principal pillars of a branch of science called cognitive neuroscience, an interdisciplinary link between cognitive psychology and neuroscience.
Protein	A protein is a complex, high-molecular-weight organic compound that consists of amino acids joined by peptide bonds. It is essential to the structure and function of all living cells and viruses. Many are enzymes or subunits of enzymes.
Protein channel	A protein channel is a pore-forming protein that help establish the small voltage gradient that exists across the membrane of all living cells, by controlling the flow of ions. They are present in the membranes that surround all biological cells.
Thalamus	An area near the center of the brain involved in the relay of sensory information to the cortex and in the functions of sleep and attention is the thalamus.
Cerebral hemisphere	A Cerebral hemisphere (hemispherium cerebrale) is defined as one of the two regions of the brain that are delineated by the body"s median plane, (medial longitudinal fissure.) The brain can thus be described as being divided into left and right Cerebral hemisphere s. Each of these hemispheres has an outer layer of grey matter called the cerebral cortex that is supported by an inner layer of white matter.
Complex	In psychology a Complex is a group of mental factors that are unconsciously associated by the individual with a particular subject or connected by a recognizable theme and influence the individual"s attitude and behavior. Their existence is widely agreed upon in the area of depth psychology at least, being instrumental in the systems of both Freud and Jung. They are generally a way of mapping the psyche, and are crucial theoretical items of common reference to be found in therapy.

Diazepam	Diazepam, brand names: Valium, Seduxen, in Europe Apozepam, Diapam, is a 1,4-benzodiazepine derivative, which possesses anxiolytic, anticonvulsant, sedative and skeletal muscle relaxant properties. Diazepam is used to treat anxiety and tension, and is the most effective benzodiazepine for treating muscle spasms.
Impulse	In classical mechanics, an Impulse is defined as the integral of a force with respect to time. When a force is applied to a rigid body it changes the momentum of that body. A small force applied for a long time can produce the same momentum change as a large force applied briefly, because it is the product of the force and the time for which it is applied that is important.
Not	This catalog is compiled from a source file. Please do not edit this page manually. This is how to edit it.
Adrenal cortex	Situated along the perimeter of the adrenal gland, the adrenal cortex mediates the stress response through the production of mineralocorticoids and glucocorticoids, including aldosterone and cortisol respectively. It is also a secondary site of androgen synthesis.
Adrenocorticotropic hormone	Adrenocorticotropic hormone is a polypeptide hormone produced and secreted by the pituitary gland. It is an important player in the hypothalamic-pituitary-adrenal axis.
Behavioral medicine	Behavioral Medicine is an interdisciplinary field of medicine concerned with the development and integration of psychosocial, behavioral and biomedical knowledge relevant to health and illness. The term is often used interchangeably with health psychology, however, behavioral medicine development teams include psychiatrists, nurses, and other medical support staff.
Cortisol	Cortisol is a corticosteroid hormone produced by the adrenal cortex. It is a vital hormone that is often referred to as the "stress hormone" as it is involved in the response to stress. It increases blood pressure, blood sugar levels and has an immunosuppressive action.
Exhaustion stage	The third stage of the general adaptation syndrome, characterized by weakened resistance and possible deterioration is referred to as the exhaustion stage.
General adaptation syndrome	General Adaptation Syndrome is the sequence of physiological reactions in relation to pronlonged and intense stress.
Hypothalamic-pituitary-adrenal axis	The hypothalamic-pituitary-adrenal axis is a complex set of direct influences and feedback interactions between: the hypothalamus, a hollow, funnel-shaped part of the brain; the pituitary gland, a pea-shaped structure located below the hypothalamus; and the adrenal or suprarenal gland, a small, paired, pyramidal organ located at the top of each kidney.
Pituitary gland	The pituitary gland is an endocrine gland about the size of a pea that sits in the small, bony cavity at the base of the brain. The pituitary gland secretes hormones regulating a wide variety of bodily activities, including trophic hormones that stimulate other endocrine glands.

Resistance	An idea originally established by Sigmund Freud following his work with patient Elizabeth, who had been suffering from hysterical symptoms with no organic basis. As was the norm for Freud at the time, he attempted hypnotizing her, but found she was prone to awaking from the trance with no memory of what had happened, consequentely causing there to be no therapeutic benefit to the hypnotic sessions. This phenomenon was coined resistance, and was regarded as a general obstinacy toward discussing, remembering, or thinking about troubling or threatening past events.
Resistance stage	The resistance stage is the second stage of the general adaptation syndrome. It is characterized by prolonged sympathetic activity in an effort to restore lost energy and repair damage.
Stress	Stress is the consequence of the failure to adapt to change. Less simply: it is the condition that results when person-environment transactions lead the individual to perceive a discrepancy, whether real or not, between the demands of a situation and the resources of the person"s biological, psychological or social systems.
Adaptation	An adaptation is a positive characteristic of an organism that has been favored by natural selection. The concept is central to biology, particularly in evolutionary biology. The term adaptation is also sometimes used as a synonym for natural selection, but most biologists discourage this usage.
Concept	A Concept is a cognitive unit of meaning-- an abstract idea or a mental symbol sometimes defined as a "unit of knowledge," built from other units which act as a Concept"s characteristics. A Concept is typically associated with a corresponding representation in a language or symbology such as a word. The meaning of "Concept" is explored in mainstream cognitive science and philosophy of mind.
Concepts	There are two prevailing theories in contemporary philosophy which attempt to explain the nature of Concepts The representational theory of mind proposes that Concepts are mental representations, while the semantic theory of Concepts (originating with Frege"s distinction between concept and object) holds that they are abstract objects. Ideas are taken to be Concepts, although abstract Concepts do not necessarily appear to the mind as images as some ideas do.
Corticosterone	Corticosterone is a 21 carbon steroid hormone of the corticosteroid type produced in the cortex of the adrenal glands.
Drinking	Drinking is the act of consuming a liquid through the mouth.
Eating	Eating is the process of consuming nutrition, i.e. food, for the purpose of providing for the nutritional needs of an animal, particularly their energy requirements and to grow.
Endocrine gland	An endocrine gland is one of a set of internal organs involved in the secretion of hormones into the blood. The other major type of gland is the exocrine glands, which secrete substances—usually digestive juices—into the digestive tract or onto the skin.

Exercise	Exercise is manual activity that develops or maintains physical fitness and overall health. It is often practiced to strengthen muscles and the cardiovascular system, and to hone athletic skills.
Field	Field is one of the core concepts used by French social scientist Pierre Bourdieu. A field is a setting in which agents and their social positions are located. The position of each particular agent in the field is a result of interaction between the specific rules of the field, agent"s habitus and agent"s capital social, economic and cultural Bourdieu, 1984. Fields interact with each other, and are hierarchical most are subordinate of the larger field of power and class relations.
Habit	An habit is an automatic routine of behavior that are repeated regularly, without thinking. They are learned, not instinctive, human behaviors that occur automatically, without the explicit contemporaneous intention of the person. The person may not be paying attention to or be conscious or aware of the behavior.
Social influence	Social influence occurs when an individual"s thoughts or actions are affected by other people. Social influence takes many forms and can be seen in conformity, socialization, peer pressure, obedience, leadership, persuasion, sales, and marketing. Harvard psychologist, Herbert Kelman identified three broad varieties of Social influence. · Compliance is when people appear to agree with others, but actually keep their dissenting opinions private. · Identification is when people are influenced by someone who is liked and respected, such as a famous celebrity or a favorite uncle. · Internalization is when people accept a belief or behavior and agree both publicly and privately.
Metabolism	Metabolism is the biochemical modification of chemical compounds in living organisms and cells.
Stress Hormones	Group of hormones including cortico steroids, that are involved in the body's physiological stress response are referred to as stress hormones.
Variable	A variable refers to a measurable factor, characteristic, or attribute of an individual or a system.
Antibody	An antibody is a protein used by the immune system to identify and neutralize foreign objects like bacteria and viruses. Each antibody recognizes a specific antigen unique to its target.
Antidiuretic hormone	Antidiuretic hormone is a peptide hormone produced by the hypothalamus, and stored in the posterior part of the pituitary gland. It acts on the kidneys, concentrating the urine by promoting the reabsorption of water from the cortical collecting duct.

B cells	B cells are lymphocytes that play a large role in the humoral immune response as opposed to the cell-mediated immune response that is governed by T cells. B cells are produced in the bone marrow of most mammals and are therefore called B cells. The principal function of B cells is to make antibodies against soluble antigens. B cells are an essential component of the adaptive immune system.
Cytokines	Cytokines are a group of proteins and peptides that are used in organisms as signaling compounds. These chemical signals are similar to hormones and neurotransmitters and are used to allow one cell to communicate with another. The cytokine family consists mainly of smaller water-soluble proteins and glycoproteins with a mass of between 8 and 30 kDa.
Immune system	The most important function of the human immune system occurs at the cellular level of the blood and tissues. The lymphatic and blood circulation systems are highways for specialized white blood cells. These cells include B cells, T cells, natural killer cells, and macrophages. All function with the primary objective of recognizing, attacking and destroying bacteria, viruses, cancer cells, and all substances seen as foreign.
Mood	A mood is a relatively lasting emotional or affective state. They differ from emotions in that they are less specific, often less intense, less likely to be triggered by a particular stimulus or event, however longer lasting.
Mood disorder	A mood disorder is a condition where the prevailing emotional mood is distorted or inappropriate to the circumstances.
Myasthenia gravis	Myasthenia gravis is a neuromuscular disease leading to fluctuating muscle weakness and fatiguability. It is an autoimmune disorder, in which weakness is caused by circulating antibodies that block acetylcholine receptors at the post-synaptic neuromuscular junction, inhibiting the stimulative effect of the neurotransmitter acetylcholine.
Prostaglandin	A prostaglandin is any member of a group of lipid compounds that are derived from fatty acids and have important functions. They act on a variety of cells such as vascular smooth muscle cells causing constriction or dilation, on platelets causing aggregation or disaggregation and on spinal neurons causing pain.
Psychoneuroimmunology	Psychoneuroimmunology is the study of the interaction between psychological processes and the nervous and immune systems of the human body. PNI has an interdisciplinary approach, interlacing disciplines as psychology, neuroscience, immunology, physiology, pharmacology, psychiatry, behavioral medicine, infectious diseases, endocrinology, rheumatology and others.
Rheumatoid arthritis	Rheumatoid arthritis is a chronic, inflammatory autoimmune disorder that causes the immune system to attack the joints. It is a disabling and painful inflammatory condition, which can lead to substantial loss of mobility due to pain and joint destruction.

Schizophrenia	Schizophrenia is a psychiatric diagnosis that describes a mental illness characterized by impairments in the perception or expression of reality, most commonly manifesting as auditory hallucinations, paranoid or bizarre delusions or disorganized speech and thinking in the context of significant social or occupational dysfunction.
Substance abuse	Substance abuse refers to the use of substances when said use is causing detriment to the individual"s physical health or causes the user legal, social, financial or other problems including endangering their lives or the lives of others.
Thymus	In human anatomy, the thymus is an organ located in the upper anterior portion of the chest cavity just behind the sternum.
Acetylcholine	The chemical compound acetylcholine, often abbreviated as ACh, was the first neurotransmitter to be identified. It is a chemical transmitter in both the peripheral nervous system and central nervous system in many organisms including humans.
Acetylcholine receptor	An acetylcholine receptor is an integral membrane protein that responds to the binding of the neurotransmitter acetylcholine.
Antigen	An antigen is a molecule that stimulates the production of antibodies. Usually, it is a protein or a polysaccharide, but can be any type of molecule, including small molecules (haptens) coupled to a protein (carrier).
Central nervous system	The central nervous system represents the largest part of the nervous system, including the brain and the spinal cord. Together with the peripheral nervous system, it has a fundamental role in the control of behavior. The CNS is contained within the dorsal cavity, with the brain within the cranial subcavity, and the spinal cord in the spinal cavity. The CNS is covered by the meninges. The brain is also protected by the skull, and the spinal cord is also protected by the vertebrae.
Experience	Experience as a general concept comprises knowledge of or skill in or observation of some thing or some event gained through involvement in or exposure to that thing or event. The history of the word experience aligns it closely with the concept of experiment.
Infection	An infection is the detrimental colonization of a host organism by a foreign species.
Experiment	In the scientific method, an experiment is a set of observations performed in the context of solving a particular problem or question, to support or falsify a hypothesis or research concerning phenomena. The experiment is a cornerstone in the empirical approach to acquiring deeper knowledge about the physical world.
Hippocampus	The hippocampus is a part of the brain located in the medial temporal lobe. It forms a part of the limbic system and plays a part in memory and spatial navigation.

Ageing	Ageing is defined as any change in an organism over time. Ageing commences at conception, continues with the changes associated with the gain of function during growth and development and concludes with the loss of function in a system towards the end of life.
Posttraumatic stress disorder	Posttraumatic stress disorder is the term for a severe and ongoing emotional reaction to an extreme psychological trauma.
Circadian rhythm	The circadian rhythm is a name given to the "internal body clock" that regulates the roughly 24 hour cycle of biological processes in animals and plants.
Noise	In common use the word noise means unwanted sound or noise pollution.
Recollection	Recollection is the retrieval of memory. It is not a passive process; people employ metacognitive strategies to make the best use of their memory, and priming and other context can have a large effect on what is retrieved.
Attribute-value system	An Attribute-value system is a basic knowledge representation framework comprising a table with columns designating "attributes" and rows designating "objects" Each table cell therefore designates the value of a particular attribute of a particular object. Below is a sample Attribute-value system.
Psychological trauma	Psychological trauma involves a singular experience or enduring event or events that completely overwhelm the individual"s ability to cope or integrate the emotion involved with that experience. It usually involves a complete feeling of helplessness in the face of a real or subjective threat to life, bodily integrity, or sanity.

446

Learning	Learning is the acquisition and development of memories and behaviors, including skills, knowledge, understanding, values, and wisdom. It is the goal of education, and the product of experience. Learning ranges from simple forms such as habituation to more complex forms such as play, seen only in large vertebrates.
Memory	In psychology, memory is an organism"s ability to store, retain, and subsequently retrieve information. In recent decades, it has become one of the principal pillars of a branch of science called cognitive neuroscience, an interdisciplinary link between cognitive psychology and neuroscience.
Brain	In animals, the brain, is the control center of the central nervous system, responsible for behavior. The brain is located in the head, protected by the skull and close to the primary sensory apparatus of vision, hearing, equilibrioception, sense of acceleration, taste, and olfaction.
Classical conditioning	Classical conditioning is a form of associative learning that was first demonstrated by Ivan Pavlov. The typical procedure for inducing Classical conditioning involves presentations of a neutral stimulus along with a stimulus of some significance. The neutral stimulus could be any event that does not result in an overt behavioral response from the organism under investigation.
Conditioned stimulus	A previously neutral stimulus that elicits the conditioned response because of being repeatedly paired with a stimulus that naturally elicited that response, is called a conditioned stimulus.
Operant conditioning	Operant conditioning is the use of consequences to modify the occurrence and form of behavior. Operant conditioning is distinguished from classical conditioning (also called respondent conditioning, or Pavlovian conditioning) in that Operant conditioning deals with the modification of "voluntary behavior" or operant behavior. Operant behavior "operates" on the environment and is maintained by its consequences, while classical conditioning deals with the conditioning of respondent behaviors which are elicited by antecedent conditions.
Punishment	Punishment is the practice of imposing something unpleasant or aversive on a person or animal in response to an unwanted, disobedient or morally wrong behavior.
Reinforcer	In operant conditioning, a reinforcer is any stimulus that increases the probability that a preceding behavior will occur again. In Classical Conditioning, the unconditioned stimulus (US) is the reinforcer.
Unconditioned response	An Unconditioned Response is the response elicited to an unconditioned stimulus. It is a natural, automatic response.
Unconditioned stimulus	In classical conditioning, an unconditioned stimulus elicits a response from an organism prior to conditioning. It is a naturally occurring stimulus and a naturally occurring response..
Animal testing	Animal testing refers to the use of animals in experiments. It is estimated that 50 to 100 million vertebrate animals worldwide — from zebrafish to non-human primates — are used annually and either killed during the experiments or subsequently euthanized.

Behavior	Behavior refers to the actions or reactions of an object or organism, usually in relation to the environment. Behavior can be conscious or subconscious, overt or covert, and voluntary or involuntary.
	Human Behavior (and that of other organisms and mechanisms) can be common, unusual, acceptable, or unacceptable. Humans evaluate the acceptability of Behavior using social norms and regulate Behavior by means of social control
Frequency	In statistics the frequency of an event i is the number ni of times the event occurred in the experiment or the study. These frequencies are often graphically represented in histograms.
Future	In a linear conception of time, the future is the portion of the time line that has yet to occur.
Particular	In philosophy, Particulars are concrete entities existing in space and time as opposed to abstractions. There are, however, theories of abstract Particulars or tropes. For example, Socrates is a Particular (there"s only one Socrates-the-teacher-of-Plato and one cannot make copies of him, e.g., by cloning him, without introducing new, distinct Particulars).
Reinforcement	In operant conditioning, reinforcement is an increase in the strength of a response following the change in environment immediately following that response. Response strength can be assessed by measures such as the frequency with which the response is made, or the speed with which it is made.
Stimulus	In psychology, a stimulus is part of the stimulus-response relationship of behavioral learning theory.
Engram	An engram is a hypothetical means by which memories are stored as physical or biochemical change in the brain in response to external stimuli.
Depression	In everyday language depression refers to any downturn in mood, which may be relatively transitory and perhaps due to something trivial.
Representation	Representation is a term used in cognitive psychology, neuroscience, and cognitive science to refer to a hypothetical internal cognitive symbol that represents external reality. David Marr defines Representation as "a formal system for making explicit certain entities or types of information, together with a specification of how the system does this." Representationalism (also known as indirect realism) is the view that representations are the main way we access external reality.
Action theory	A motivation theory that links a person's goals to his or her behavior is action theory.
Cortex	In anatomy and zoology the cortex is the outermost layer of an organ. Organs with well-defined cortical layers include kidneys, adrenal glands, ovaries, the thymus, and portions of the brain, including the cerebral cortex, the most well-know of all cortices.

Cerebellum	The cerebellum is a region of the brain that plays an important role in the integration of sensory perception and motor output. Many neural pathways link the cerebellum with the motor cortex—which sends information to the muscles causing them to move—and the spinocerebellar tract—which provides feedback on the position of the body in space. The cerebellum integrates these pathways, using the constant feedback on body position to fine-tune motor movements.
Long-term memory	Long-term memory is memory, stored as meaning, that can last as little as 30 seconds or as long as decades. It differs structurally and functionally from working memory or short-term memory, which ostensibly stores items for only around 30 seconds.
Red nucleus	The red nucleus is a structure in the rostral midbrain involved in motor coordination. It comprises a caudal magnocellular and a rostral parvocellular part.
Short-term memory	Short-term memory is that part of memory which is said to be able to hold a small amount of information for about 20 seconds. The information held in short-term memory may be: recently processed sensory input; items recently retrieved from long-term memory; or the result of recent mental processing, although that is more generally related to the concept of working memory.
Attention	Attention is the cognitive process of selectively concentrating on one aspect of the environment while ignoring other things. Examples include listening carefully to what someone is saying while ignoring other conversations in the room or listening to a cell phone conversation while driving a car.
Axon	An axon is a long, slender projection of a nerve cell, or neuron, that conducts electrical impulses away from the neuron"s cell body or soma.
Pyramidal tract	The pyramidal tract is a massive collection of axons that travel between the cerebral cortex of the brain and the spinal cord. It mostly contains motor axons.
Hindbrain	The hindbrain is a developmental categorization of portions of the central nervous system in vertebrates. It can be subdivided in a variable number of transversal swellings called rhombomeres.
Midbrain	The midbrain is the middle of three vesicles that arise from the neural tube that forms the brain of developing animals. In mature human brains, it becomes the least differentiated, from both its developmental form and within its own structure, among the three vesicles. The midbrain is considered part of the brain stem.
Muscle	Muscle is contractile tissue of the body and is derived from the mesodermal layer of embryonic germ cells. It is classified as skeletal, cardiac, or smooth muscle, and its function is to produce force and cause motion, either locomotion or movement within internal organs.
Not	This catalog is compiled from a source file. Please do not edit this page manually. This is how to edit it.

Structure	Structure is a fundamental and sometimes intangible notion covering the recognition, observation, nature, and stability of patterns and relationships of entities.
Working memory	Working memory is a theoretical framework within cognitive psychology that refers to the structures and processes used for temporarily storing and manipulating information. There are numerous theories as to both the theoretical structure of working memory as well as to the specific parts of the brain responsible for working memory.
Storage	The human memory has three processes: encoding (input), Storage and retrieval(output.) Storage is the process of retaining information whether in the sensory memory, the short-term memory or the more permanent long-term memory.
Ageing	Ageing is defined as any change in an organism over time. Ageing commences at conception, continues with the changes associated with the gain of function during growth and development and concludes with the loss of function in a system towards the end of life.
Amnesia	Amnesia is a condition in which memory is disturbed. The causes of amnesia are organic or functional. Organic causes include damage to the brain, through trauma or disease, or use of certain generally sedative drugs.
Anterograde amnesia	Anterograde amnesia is a form of amnesia, or memory loss; in which new events are not transferred from short-termed memory to long-term memory. This may be a permanent deficit, or it may be temporary, such as is sometimes seen for a period of hours or days after head trauma or for a period of intoxication with an amnestic drug.
Brain damage	Brain damage is the destruction or degeneration of brain cells. It may occur due to a wide range of conditions, illnesses, injuries, and as a result of iatrogenesis. Possible causes of widespread brain damage include prolonged hypoxia, poisoning by teratogens, infection, and neurological illness.
Epilepsy	Epilepsy is a chronic neurological condition characterized by recurrent unprovoked neural discharges. It is commonly controlled with medication, although surgical methods are used as well.
Gamma-aminobutyric acid	Gamma-aminobutyric acid is an inhibitory neurotransmitter found in the nervous systems of widely-divergent species. It is the chief inhibitory neurotransmitter in the central nervous system and also in the retina.
Hippocampus	The hippocampus is a part of the brain located in the medial temporal lobe. It forms a part of the limbic system and plays a part in memory and spatial navigation.
Prefrontal cortex	The prefrontal cortex is the anterior part of the frontal lobes of the brain, lying in front of the motor and premotor areas. Cytoarchitectonically, it is defined by the presence of an internal granular layer IV.

Retrograde	In males, retrograde ejaculation occurs when the fluid to be ejaculated, which would normally exit via the urethra, is redirected towards the urinary bladder. Normally the sphincter of the bladder contracts and the sperm goes to the urethra towards the area of least pressure. In retrograde ejaculation this sphincter does not function properly.
Retrograde amnesia	Retrograde amnesia is a form of amnesia where someone will be unable to recall events that occurred before the onset of amnesia. The term is used to categorise patterns of symptoms, rather than to indicate a particular cause or etiology.
Stimulant	A stimulant is a drug which increases the activity of the sympathetic nervous system and produces a sense of euphoria or awakeness.
Stimulant drugs	*Stimulant drugs* are drugs that temporarily increase alertness and awareness. They usually have increased side-effects with increased effectiveness, and the more powerful variants are therefore often prescription medicines or illegal drugs. Ritalin SR 20mg. Stimulants increase the activity of either the sympathetic nervous system, the central nervous system (CNS) or both.
Alertness	Alertness is the state of paying close and continuous attention being watchful and prompt to meet danger or emergency, or being quick to perceive and act. It is related to psychology as well as to physiology. A lack of Alertness is a symptom of a number of conditions, including narcolepsy, attention deficit disorder, chronic fatigue syndrome, depression, Addison"s disease, or sleep deprivation.
Anterior	Anterior is an anatomical term referring to the front part of the body. The anterior is positioned in front of another body part, or towards the head of an animal. It is the opposite of posterior.
Circadian rhythm	The circadian rhythm is a name given to the "internal body clock" that regulates the roughly 24 hour cycle of biological processes in animals and plants.
Discovery	Discovery observations form acts of detecting and learning something. Discovery observations are acts in which something is found and given a productive insight. Serendipity is the effect by which one accidentally discovers something fortunate, especially while looking for something else entirely.
Disease	A Disease or medical problem is an abnormal condition of an organism that impairs bodily functions, associated with specific symptoms and signs. It may be caused by external factors, such as invading organisms, or it may be caused by internal dysfunctions, such as autoimmune Disease s. In human beings, Disease is often used more broadly to refer to any condition that causes extreme pain, dysfunction, distress, social problems, and/or death to the person afflicted, or similar problems for those in contact with the person.

Fatigue	The word fatigue is used in everyday life to describe a range of afflictions, varying from a general state of lethargy to a specific work-induced burning sensation within one"s muscles. It can be both physical and mental. Such a mental fatigue, in turn, can manifest itself both as somnolence just as a general decrease of attention, not necessarily including sleepiness.
Frontal lobe	The frontal lobe comprises four major folds of cortical tissue: the precentral gyrus, superior gyrus and the middle gyrus of the frontal gyri, the inferior frontal gyrus. It has been found to play a part in impulse control, judgement, language, memory, motor function, problem solving, sexual behavior, socialization and spontaneity.
Generation	Generation, also known as procreation, is the act of producing offspring. A generation can also be a stage or degree in a succession of natural descent as a grandfather, a father, and the father"s son comprise three generations.
Memory loss	Memory loss can have many causes: · Alzheimer"s disease is an illness which can cause mild to severe memory loss · Parkinson"s disease is a genetic defect which may result in memory loss · Huntington"s disease is an inherited disease which can result in memory loss · It is sometimes a side effect of chemotherapy in which cytotoxic drugs are used to treat cancer. · Certain forms of mental illness also have memory loss as a key symptom, including fugue states and the much more famous Dissociative Identity Disorder. · Stress-related activities are another factor which can result in memory loss · It can also be caused by traumatic brain injury, of which a concussion is a form. .
Mood	A mood is a relatively lasting emotional or affective state. They differ from emotions in that they are less specific, often less intense, less likely to be triggered by a particular stimulus or event, however longer lasting.
Need	A Need is something that is necessary for humans to live a healthy life. Need s are distinguished from wants because a deficiency would cause a clear negative outcome, such as dysfunction or death. Need s can be objective and physical, such as food and water, or they can be subjective and psychological, such as the Need for self-esteem.
Signal	In the fields of communications, signal processing, and in electrical engineering more generally, a signal is any time-varying quantity. Signals are often scalar-valued functions of time, but may be vector valued and may be functions of any other relevant independent variable.
Single	In relationships, a single person is one who is not married, or, more broadly, who is not in an exclusive romantic relationship.

Declarative memory	Declarative memory is the aspect of human memory that stores facts. It is so called because it refers to memories that can be consciously discussed, or declared. It applies to standard textbook learning and knowledge, as well memories that can be "travelled back to" in one"s "mind"s eye".
Environmental factor	In epidemiology, environmental factor refers to determinants of disease that are not transmitted genetically.
Explicit memory	Explicit memory is the conscious, intentional recollection of previous experiences and information.
Implicit memory	Implicit memory is a type of memory in which previous experiences aid in the performance of a task without conscious awareness of these previous experiences. Evidence for implicit memory arises in priming, a process whereby subjects show improved performance on tasks for which they have been subconsciously prepared.
Procedural memory	Procedural memory is the long-term memory of skills and procedures, or "how to" knowledge.
Experience	Experience as a general concept comprises knowledge of or skill in or observation of some thing or some event gained through involvement in or exposure to that thing or event. The history of the word experience aligns it closely with the concept of experiment.
Social influence	Social influence occurs when an individual"s thoughts or actions are affected by other people. Social influence takes many forms and can be seen in conformity, socialization, peer pressure, obedience, leadership, persuasion, sales, and marketing. Harvard psychologist, Herbert Kelman identified three broad varieties of Social influence. · Compliance is when people appear to agree with others, but actually keep their dissenting opinions private. · Identification is when people are influenced by someone who is liked and respected, such as a famous celebrity or a favorite uncle. · Internalization is when people accept a belief or behavior and agree both publicly and privately.
Information	Information as a concept has a diversity of meanings, from everyday usage to technical settings. Generally speaking, the concept of Information is closely related to notions of constraint, communication, control, data, form, instruction, knowledge, meaning, mental stimulus, pattern, perception, and representation. According to the Oxford English Dictionary, the first known historical meaning of the word Information in English was the act of informing, or giving form or shape to the mind, as in education, instruction, or training.
Motor skill	A Motor skill is a learned series of movements that combine to produce a smooth, efficient action.

· Gross Motor skill s include lifting one"s head, rolling over, sitting up, balancing, crawling, and walking. Gross motor development usually follows a pattern. Generally large muscles develop before smaller ones, thus, gross motor development is the foundation for developing skills in other areas (such as fine Motor skill s.) Development also generally moves from top to bottom. The first thing a baby usually learns to control is its eyes.

· Fine Motor skill s include the ability to manipulate small objects, transfer objects from hand to hand, and various hand-eye coordination tasks. Fine Motor skill s may involve the use of very precise motor movement in order to achieve an especially delicate task. Some examples of fine Motor skill s are using the pincer grasp (thumb and forefinger) to pick up small objects, cutting, coloring, writing, or threading beads. Fine motor development refers to the development of skills involving the smaller muscle groups.

· Ambidexterity is a specialized skill in which there is no dominance between body symmetries, so tasks requiring fine Motor skill s can be performed with the left or right extremities. The most common example of ambidexterity is the ability to write with the left or right hand, rather than one dominant side.

Recollection	Recollection is the retrieval of memory. It is not a passive process; people employ metacognitive strategies to make the best use of their memory, and priming and other context can have a large effect on what is retrieved.
Attribute-value system	An Attribute-value system is a basic knowledge representation framework comprising a table with columns designating "attributes" and rows designating "objects" Each table cell therefore designates the value of a particular attribute of a particular object. Below is a sample Attribute-value system.
Word	A word is the smallest free form (an item that may be uttered in isolation with semantic or pragmatic content) in a language, in contrast to a morpheme, which is the smallest unit of meaning. A word may consist of only one morpheme (e.g. cat), but a single morpheme may not be able to exist as a free form . Typically, a word will consist of a root or stem, and zero or more affixes.
Basal ganglia	The basal ganglia are a group of nuclei in the brain associated with motor and learning functions.
Caudate nucleus	The caudate nucleus is a nucleus located within the basal ganglia of the brains of many animal species. The caudate nuclei are located near the center of the brain, sitting astride the thalamus. There is a caudate nucleus within each hemisphere of the brain.
Prosencephalon	In the anatomy of the brain of vertebrates, the prosencephalon is the rostral-most portion of the brain. The prosencephalon, the mesencephalon, and rhombencephalon are the three primary portions of the brain during early development of the central nervous system.

Globus pallidus	The globus pallidus is a sub-cortical structure of the brain. It is a major element of the basal ganglia system. In this system, it is a major element of the basal ganglia core, consisting of the striatum and its direct targets: globus pallidus and substantia nigra. The last two are made up of the same neuronal elements, have a similar main afferent, have a similar synaptology, and do not receive cortical afferents.
Hypothalamus	The hypothalamus is a region of the brain located below the thalamus, forming the major portion of the ventral region of the diencephalon and functioning to regulate certain metabolic processes and other autonomic activities.
Musth	Musth is a periodic condition in bull elephants, characterized by a thick, tar-like secretion called temporin from the temporal ducts and, far more notably, by highly aggressive behavior. It is accompanied by a significant rise in reproductive hormones - testosterone levels in an elephant in musth can be as much as 60 times greater than in the same elephant at other times.
Entity	An entity is something that has a distinct, separate existence, though it need not be a material existence. In particular, abstractions and legal fictions are usually regarded as an entity. In general, there is also no presumption that an entity is animate.
Putamen	The putamen is a structure in the middle of the brain, which, together with the caudate nucleus forms the dorsal striatum. The putamen is a portion of the basal ganglia that forms the outermost part of the lenticular nucleus.
Sample	In statistics, a sample is a subset of a population. Typically, the population is very large, making a census or a complete enumeration of all the values in the population impractical or impossible. The sample represents a subset of manageable size. Samples are collected and statistics are calculated from the samples so that one can make inferences or extrapolations from the sample to the population.
Morris water maze	In neuroscience, the Morris water maze is a behavioral procedure designed to test spatial memory. It was developed by neuroscientist Richard G. Morris in 1984, and is commonly used today to explore the role of the hippocampus in the formation of said spatial memories.
Spatial memory	In cognitive psychology and neuroscience, spatial memory is the part of memory responsible for recording information about one"s environment and its spatial orientation.
Thalamus	An area near the center of the brain involved in the relay of sensory information to the cortex and in the functions of sleep and attention is the thalamus.
Subject	In biostatistics or psychological statistics, a research subject is any object or phenomenon that is observed for purposes of research.

Context	In Psychology, context refers to the background stimuli that accompany some kind of foreground event.
Emotion	Emotion, in its most general definition, is a complex psychophysical process that arises spontaneously, rather than through conscious effort, and evokes either a positive or negative psychological response and physical expressions, often involuntary, related to feelings, perceptions or beliefs about elements, objects or relations between them, in reality or in the imagination. An emotion is often differentiated from a feeling.
Memory consolidation	The broad definition of memory consolidation is the process by which recent memories are crystallised into long-term memory.
Adrenaline	Adrenaline is a hormone when carried in the blood and a neurotransmitter when it is released across a neuronal synapse. It is a catecholamine, a sympathomimetic monoamine derived from the amino acids phenylalanine and tyrosine.
Alcoholism	Alcoholism is a term with multiple and sometimes conflicting definitions. In common and historic usage, alcoholism refers to any condition that results in the continued consumption of alcoholic beverages despite the health problems and negative social consequences it causes.
Amygdala	Amygdala are almond-shaped groups of neurons located deep within the medial temporal lobes of the brain in complex vertebrates, including humans. Shown in research to perform a primary role in the processing and memory of emotional reactions, the amygdala are considered part of the limbic system.
Confabulation	Confabulation is the confusion of imagination with memory, and/or the confusion of true memories with false recollections. Confabulation can result from both organic and psychological causes.
Cortisol	Cortisol is a corticosteroid hormone produced by the adrenal cortex. It is a vital hormone that is often referred to as the "stress hormone" as it is involved in the response to stress. It increases blood pressure, blood sugar levels and has an immunosuppressive action.
Epinephrine	Epinephrine is a hormone and neurotransmitter. Epinephrine increases the "fight or flight" response of the sympathetic division of the autonomic nervous system. It is a catecholamine, a sympathomimetic monoamine derived from the amino acids phenylalanine and tyrosine.
Stress	Stress is the consequence of the failure to adapt to change. Less simply: it is the condition that results when person-environment transactions lead the individual to perceive a discrepancy, whether real or not, between the demands of a situation and the resources of the person"s biological, psychological or social systems.

Thiamin	Thiamin is one of the B vitamins. It is colorless chemical compound with a chemical formula $C_{12}H_{17}N_4OS$. It is soluble in water, methanol, and glycerol and practically insoluble in acetone, ether, chloroform, and benzene. Thiamin decomposes if heated. Its chemical structure contains a pyrimidine ring and a thiazole ring.
Thiamine	Thiamine, also known as vitamin B1, is a colorless compound with chemical formula $C_{12}H_{17}CIN_4OS$. Systemic thiamine deficiency can lead to myriad problems including neurodegeneration, wasting, and death. Well-known syndromes caused by lack of thiamine due to malnutrition or a diet high in thiaminase-rich foods include Wernicke-Korsakoff syndrome and beriberi, diseases also common in chronic abusers of alcohol.
Wernicke-Korsakoff syndrome	A cluster of symptoms associated with chronic alcohol abuse and characterized by confusion, memory impairment, and filling in gaps in memory with false information is referred to as the Wernicke-Korsakoff syndrome.
Adrenal cortex	Situated along the perimeter of the adrenal gland, the adrenal cortex mediates the stress response through the production of mineralocorticoids and glucocorticoids, including aldosterone and cortisol respectively. It is also a secondary site of androgen synthesis.
Anxiety	Anxiety is a physiological state characterized by cognitive, somatic, emotional, and behavioral components.
Apathy	Apathy is a state of indifference — where an individual has an absence of interest or concern to certain aspects of emotional, social, or physical life. Apathy can be object-specific — toward a person, activity or environment. It is a common reaction to stress where it manifests as "learned helplessness" and is commonly associated with depression. It can also reflect a non-pathological lack of interest in things one does not consider important.
Blood	Blood is a specialized biological fluid consisting of red blood cells.White blood cells also called leukocytes and platelets also called thrombocytes suspended in a complex fluid medium known as blood plasma.
Chemical	A chemical is a material with a definite chemical composition. All samples of a compound have the same composition; that is, all samples have the same proportions, by mass, of the elements present in the compound.
Confusion	Severe confusion of a degree considered pathological usually refers to loss of orientation, and often memory. Confusion as such is not synonymous with inability to focus attention, although severe inability to focus attention can cause, or greatly contribute to, confusion.
Dependence	Dependence is compulsively using a substance, despite its negative and sometimes dangerous effects. Other drugs cause addiction without physical dependence.

Drinking	Drinking is the act of consuming a liquid through the mouth.
Glucose	Glucose, a simple monosaccharide sugar, is one of the most important carbohydrates and is used as a source of energy in animals and plants. Glucose is one of the main products of photosynthesis and starts respiration.
Hormone	A hormone is a chemical messenger that carries a signal from one cell to another. All multicellular organisms produce hormone s.
Disability	A disability is a condition or function judged to be significantly impaired relative to the usual standard of an individual or their group. The term is often used to refer to individual functioning, including physical impairments, sensory impairments, cognitive impairments, intellectual impairments or mental health issue.
Intake	An intake is an air intake for an engine.
Intention	Intention is performing an action is their specific purpose in doing so, the end or goal they aim at, or intend to accomplish.
Inventive spelling	Inventive spelling is the non-conventional spelling of a word created by a novice reader or writer. It contrasts with conventional spelling, the correct or standard spelling. Inventive spelling is not an instructional technique but rather something that is encouraged or discouraged by a child"s teachers and parents.
Metabolism	Metabolism is the biochemical modification of chemical compounds in living organisms and cells.
Spite	In fair division problems, Spite is a phenomenon that occurs when a player"s value of an allocation decreases when one or more other players" valuation increases. Thus, other things being equal, a player exhibiting Spite will prefer an allocation in which other players receive less than more (if the good is desirable.) In this language, Spite is difficult to analyze because one has to assess two sets of preferences.
Down syndrome	Down syndrome or is a genetic disorder caused by the presence of all or part of an extra 21st chromosome. Often Down syndrome is associated with some impairment of cognitive ability and physical growth as well as facial appearance. Down syndrome can be identified during pregnancy or at birth.
Genetics	Genetics is the science of heredity and variation in living organisms.Knowledge of the inheritance of characteristics has been implicitly used since prehistoric times for improving crop plants and animals through selective breeding. However, the modern science of genetics, which seeks to understand the mechanisms of inheritance, only began with the work of Gregor Mendel in the mid-1800s.

Plaques	Plaques refer to small, round areas composed of remnants of lost neurons and beta-amyloid, a waxy protein deposit; present in the brains of patients with Alzheimer's disease.
Protein	A protein is a complex, high-molecular-weight organic compound that consists of amino acids joined by peptide bonds. It is essential to the structure and function of all living cells and viruses. Many are enzymes or subunits of enzymes.
Tau protein	The tau protein is a microtubule-associated protein that is abundant in neurons in the central nervous system and is less common elsewhere. It was discovered in 1975 in Marc Kirschner"s laboratory at Princeton University.
Appetite	The appetite is the desire to eat food, felt as hunger. Appetite exists in all higher lifeforms, and serves to regulate adequate energy intake to maintain metabolic needs. It is regulated by a close interplay between the digestive tract, adipose tissue and the brain. Decreased desire to eat is termed anorexia, while polyphagia or "hyperphagia" is increased eating. Disregulation of appetite contributes to anorexia nervosa, bulimia nervosa, cachexia, overeating, and binge eating disorder.
Cerebral hemisphere	A Cerebral hemisphere (hemispherium cerebrale) is defined as one of the two regions of the brain that are delineated by the body"s median plane, (medial longitudinal fissure.) The brain can thus be described as being divided into left and right Cerebral hemisphere s. Each of these hemispheres has an outer layer of grey matter called the cerebral cortex that is supported by an inner layer of white matter.
Delusion	A false belief, not generally shared by others, and that cannot be changed despite strong evidence to the contrary is a delusion.
Hallucination	A hallucination is a sensory perception experienced in the absence of an external stimulus, as distinct from an illusion, which is a misperception of an external stimulus. They may occur in any sensory modality - visual, auditory, olfactory, gustatory, tactile, or mixed.
Intracellular	The intracellular means "inside the cell". The cell membrane is the barrier between the two, and chemical composition of intracellular and extracellular milieu can be radically different.
Insomnia	Insomnia is a sleep disorder characterized by an inability to sleep and/or inability to remain asleep for a reasonable period.
Acetic acid	Acetic acid, is an organic chemical compound, giving vinegar its sour taste and pungent smell. Its structural formula is represented as CH_3COOH.
Fear	Fear is an emotional response to tangible and realistic dangers. Fear should be distinguished from anxiety, an emotion that often arises out of proportion to the actual threat or danger involved, and can be subjectively experienced without any specific attention to the threatening object.

Parasympathetic nervous system	The parasympathetic nervous system is a division of the autonomic nervous system, along with the sympathetic nervous system and Enteric nervous system. The ANS is a subdivision of the peripheral nervous system.
Selective serotonin reuptake inhibitor	Selective serotonin reuptake inhibitor is a class of antidepressants used in the treatment of depression, anxiety disorders, and some personality disorders. They are also typically effective and used in treating premature ejaculation problems.
Tangles	Tangles are twisted fibers that build up inside nerve cells.
Temporal lobe	The temporal lobe is part of the cerebrum. It lies at the side of the brain, beneath the lateral or Sylvian fissure. Adjacent areas in the superior, posterior and lateral parts of the temporal lobe are involved in high-level auditory processing.
Central sulcus	The central sulcus is a prominent landmark of the brain, separating the parietal lobe from the frontal lobe. The central sulcus is the site of the primary motor cortex in mammals, a group of cells that controls voluntary movements of the body.
Cerebral cortex	The cerebral cortex is a structure within the vertebrate brain with distinct structural and functional properties.
Nerve	A Nerve is an enclosed, cable-like bundle of peripheral axons (the long, slender projections of neurons.) A Nerve provides a common pathway for the electrochemical Nerve impulses that are transmitted along each of the axons. Nerve s are found only in the peripheral nervous system.
Neurotransmitter	A neurotransmitter is a chemical that is used to relay, amplify and modulate electrical signals between a neurons and another cell.
Occipital lobe	The occipital lobe is the visual processing center of the mammalian brain, containing most of the anatomical region of the visual cortex. The primary visual cortex is Brodmann area 17, commonly called V_1.
Other	The Other or constitutive Other is a key concept in continental philosophy, opposed to the Same. It refers, or attempts to refer, to that which is "Other" than the concept being considered. The term often means a person Other than oneself, and is often capitalised.
Reuptake	Reuptake is the reabsorption of a neurotransmitter by the neurotransmitter transporter of a pre-synaptic neuron after it has performed its function of transmitting a neural impulse. This prevents further activity of the neurotransmitter, weakening its effects.
Serotonin	Serotonin, is a monoamine neurotransmitter synthesized in serotonergic neurons in the central nervous system and enterochromaffin cells in the gastrointestinal tract of animals including humans. Serotonin is also found in many mushrooms and plants, including fruits and vegetables.

Cingulate cortex	The cingulate cortex is a part of the brain situated in the medial aspect of the cortex. It is extended from the corpus callosum below to the cingulate sulcus above, at least anteriorly.
EffeCtiveness	Effectiveness means the capability of producing an effect. In mathematics, effective is sometimes used as a synonym of algorithmically computable. In physics, an effective theory is, similar to a phenomenological theory, a framework intended to explain certain (observed) effects without the claim that the theory correctly models the underlying (unobserved) processes.
Simultaneity	Simultaneity is the property of two events happening at the same time in at least one reference frame.
Synapse	A synapse is specialized junction through which cells of the nervous system signal to one another and to non-neuronal cells such as muscles or glands. They allow the neurons of the central nervous system to form interconnected neural circuits.
Aplysia	The genus Aplysia belongs to the family Aplysiidae and is a genus of sea hares, which are a type of large sea slug. The general description of these sea hares can be found under the entry about the superfamily Aplysioidea.
Habituation	In psychology, habituation is an example of non-associative learning in which there is a progressive diminution of behavioral response probability with repetition of a stimulus.
Hebbian theory	Hebbian theory describes a basic mechanism for synaptic plasticity wherein an increase in synaptic efficacy arises from the presynaptic cell"s repeated and persistent stimulation of the postsynaptic cell.
Eric Kandel	Eric Kandel is a psychiatrist, a neuroscientist and professor of biochemistry and biophysics at the Columbia University College of Physicians and Surgeons. He was a recipient of the 2000 Nobel Prize in Physiology or Medicine for his research on the physiological basis of memory storage in neurons. He shared the prize with fellow recipients Arvid Carlsson and Paul Greengard.
Invertebrate	Invertebrate is an English word that describes any animal without a spinal column. The group includes 97% of all animal species — all animals except those in the Chordate subphylum Vertebrata.
Experiment	In the scientific method, an experiment is a set of observations performed in the context of solving a particular problem or question, to support or falsify a hypothesis or research concerning phenomena. The experiment is a cornerstone in the empirical approach to acquiring deeper knowledge about the physical world.
Audition	An Audition is a sample performance by an actor, singer, musician, dancer or other performer. It involves the performer displaying their talent through a previously-memorized and rehearsed solo piece: for example, a monologue for actors or a song for a singer. Used in the context of performing arts, it is analogous to job interviews in many ways.

Dementia	Dementia is the progressive decline in cognitive function due to damage or disease in the brain beyond what might be expected from normal aging.
Dementia praecox	An older term for schizophrenia, chosen to describe what was believed to be an incurable and progressive deterioration of mental functioning beginning in adolescence is called dementia praecox.
Interneuron	An interneuron (also called relay neuron or association neuron) is a neuron that communicates only to other neurons. They provide connections between sensory and motor neurons, as well as between themselves.
Intrinsic	Intrinsic describes a characteristic or property of some thing or action which is essential and specific to that thing or action, and which is wholly independent of any other object, action or consequence.
Long-term potentiation	In neuroscience, long-term potentiation is the long-lasting enhancement in communication between two neurons that results from stimulating them simultaneously.
Motor neuron	In vertebrates, the term Motor neuron classically applies to neurons located in the central nervous system that project their axons outside the CNS and directly or indirectly control muscles. Motor neuron is often synonymous with efferent neuron.
Potassium	Potassium is the an essential mineral macronutrient and is the main intracellular ion for all types of cells. It is important in maintaining fluid and electrolyte balance in the body.
Sensitization	Sensitization is an example of non-associative learning in which the progressive amplification of a response follows repeated administrations of a stimulus (Bell et al., 1995). An everyday example of this mechanism is the repeated tonic stimulation of peripheral nerves that will occur if a person rubs his arm continuously.
Sensory neurons	*Sensory neurons* are neurons that are activated by sensory input (vision, touch, hearing, etc.), and send projections into the central nervous system that convey sensory information to the brain or spinal cord. Unlike neurons of the central nervous system, whose inputs come from other neurons, *Sensory neurons* are activated by physical modalities such as light, sound, temperature, chemical stimulation, etc. In complex organisms, *Sensory neurons* relay their information to the central nervous system or in less complex organisms, such as the hydra, directly to motor neurons and *Sensory neurons* also transmit information to the brain, where it can be further processed and acted upon.
Vision	Vision is the most important sense for birds, since good eyesight is essential for safe flight, and this group has a number of adaptations which give visual acuity superior to that of other vertebrate groups; a pigeon has been described as "two eyes with wings". The avian eye resembles that of a reptile, but has a better-positioned lens, a feature shared with mammals. Birds have the largest eyes relative to their size within the animal kingdom, and movement is consequently limited within the eye"s bony socket.

Day	A Day (symbol d) is a unit of time equivalent to approximately 24 hours. It is not an SI unit but it is accepted for use with SI. The SI unit of time is the second. The word "Day" can also refer to the (roughly) half of the Day that is not night, also known as "Daytime".
Impulse	In classical mechanics, an Impulse is defined as the integral of a force with respect to time. When a force is applied to a rigid body it changes the momentum of that body. A small force applied for a long time can produce the same momentum change as a large force applied briefly, because it is the product of the force and the time for which it is applied that is important.
Property	In modern philosophy, mathematics, and logic, a Property is an attribute of an object; thus a red object is said to have the Property of redness. The Property may be considered a form of object in its own right, able to possess other properties. Properties are therefore subject to the Russell"s paradox/Grelling-Nelson paradox.
Soma	The soma is the bulbous end of a neuron, containing the cell nucleus.
Spinal cord	The spinal cord is a thin, tubular bundle of nerves that is an extension of the central nervous system from the brain and is enclosed in and protected by the bony vertebral column. The main function of the spinal cord is transmission of neural inputs between the periphery and the brain.
Stimulation	Stimulation is the action of various agents on muscles, nerves, or a sensory end organ, by which activity is evoked.
AMPA receptor	The Ampa receptor is a non-NMDA-type ionotropic transmembrane receptor for glutamate that mediates fast synaptic transmission in the central nervous system. Its name is derived from its ability to be activated by the artificial glutamate analog, AMPA. AMPARs are found in many parts of the brain and are the most commonly found receptor in the nervous system.
Depolarization	In biology, depolarization is a change in a cell"s membrane potential, making it more positive, or less negative. In neurons and some other cells, a large enough depolarization may result in an action potential. Hyperpolarization is the opposite of depolarization and inhibits the rise of an action potential.
Glutamate	Glutamate is one of the 20 standard amino acids used by all organisms in their proteins. It is critical for proper cell function, but it is not an essential nutrient in humans because it can be manufactured from other compounds.
Locus coeruleus	The Locus coeruleus is a nucleus in the brain stem responsible for physiological responses to stress and panic. It is the primary area of noradrenergic neurons in the brain, which modulate brain function to be able to regulate and initiate the activation and mood of the organism.

N-methyl d-aspartate receptor	The N-methyl d-aspartate receptor is an ionotropic receptor for glutamate is a name of its selective specific agonist). Activation of NMDA receptors results in the opening of an ion channel that is nonselective to cations. This allows flow of Na^+ and small amounts of Ca^{2+} ions into the cell and K^+ out of the cell.
Polarization	Polarization is the process of preparing a neuron for firing by creating an internal negative charge in relation to the body fluid outside the cell membrane.
Caffeine	Caffeine is a xanthine alkaloid compound that acts as a psychoactive stimulant in humans. In humans, caffeine is a central nervous system stimulant, having the effect of temporarily warding off drowsiness and restoring alertness. Beverages containing caffeine, such as coffee, tea, soft drinks and energy drinks enjoy great popularity; caffeine is the world"s most widely consumed psychoactive substance, but unlike most other psychoactive substances, it is legal and unregulated in nearly all jurisdictions.
Dopamine	Dopamine is a hormone and neurotransmitter occurring in a wide variety of animals, including both vertebrates and invertebrates. In the brain, dopamine functions as a neurotransmitter. Dopamine is also a neurohormone released by the hypothalamus. Its main function as a hormone is to inhibit the release of prolactin from the anterior lobe of the pituitary.
Ginkgo	Ginkgo is a genus of highly unusual non-flowering plants with one extant species, G. biloba, which is regarded as a living fossil. Fossils recognisably related to modern Ginkgo date back to the Permian, some 270 million years ago. The genus diversified and spread throughout Laurasia during the middle Jurassic and Cretaceous, but became much rarer thereafter.
Posttraumatic stress disorder	Posttraumatic stress disorder is the term for a severe and ongoing emotional reaction to an extreme psychological trauma.
Acetylcholine	The chemical compound acetylcholine, often abbreviated as ACh, was the first neurotransmitter to be identified. It is a chemical transmitter in both the peripheral nervous system and central nervous system in many organisms including humans.
Adenosine	Adenosine is a nucleoside composed of adenine attached to a ribose (ribofuranose) moiety via a β-N_9-glycosidic bond. Adenosine plays an important role in biochemical processes, such as energy transfer and Adenosine plays an important role in biochemical processes, such as energy transfer. It is also an inhibitory neurotransmitter, believed to play a role in promoting sleep and suppressing arousal, with levels increasing with each hour an organism is awake.
Arousal	Arousal is a physiological and psychological state involving the activation of the reticular activating system in the brain stem, the autonomic nervous system and the endocrine system, leading to increased heart rate and blood pressure and a condition of alertness and readiness to respond.

Coffee	Coffee is a widely consumed stimulant beverage prepared from roasted seeds. Most studies are contradictory as to whether coffee has any specific health benefits, and results are similarly conflicting regarding negative effects of coffee consumption. Research suggests that drinking caffeinated coffee can cause a temporary increase in the stiffening of arterial walls.
Noise	In common use the word noise means unwanted sound or noise pollution.
Psychological trauma	Psychological trauma involves a singular experience or enduring event or events that completely overwhelm the individual"s ability to cope or integrate the emotion involved with that experience. It usually involves a complete feeling of helplessness in the face of a real or subjective threat to life, bodily integrity, or sanity.

Lateralization	Lateralization of brain functions is evident in the phenomena of right- or left-handedness, -earedness and -eyedness. Broad generalizations are often made in popular psychology about certain function being lateralised, that is, located in the right or left side of the brain. These ideas need to be treated carefully because the popular lateralization is ften distributed across both sides. However, there is some division of mental processing.
Brain	In animals, the brain, is the control center of the central nervous system, responsible for behavior. The brain is located in the head, protected by the skull and close to the primary sensory apparatus of vision, hearing, equilibrioception, sense of acceleration, taste, and olfaction.
Asymmetry	Asymmetry is the absence of a symmetry. Due to how cells divide in organisms, Asymmetry in organisms is fairly usual in at least one dimension, with biological symmetry also being common in at least one dimension. Louis Pasteur proposed that biological molecules are asymmetric because the cosmic [i.e. physical] forces that preside over their formation are themselves asymmetric.
Corpus callosum	The corpus callosum is a structure of the mammalian brain in the longitudal fissure that connects the left and right cerebral hemispheres. Much of the inter-hemispheric communication in the brain is conducted across the corpus callosum.
Vision	Vision is the most important sense for birds, since good eyesight is essential for safe flight, and this group has a number of adaptations which give visual acuity superior to that of other vertebrate groups; a pigeon has been described as "two eyes with wings". The avian eye resembles that of a reptile, but has a better-positioned lens, a feature shared with mammals. Birds have the largest eyes relative to their size within the animal kingdom, and movement is consequently limited within the eye"s bony socket.
Visual field	The visual field is the "spatial array of visual sensations available to observation in introspectionist psychological experiments."
Axon	An axon is a long, slender projection of a nerve cell, or neuron, that conducts electrical impulses away from the neuron"s cell body or soma.
Cerebral cortex	The cerebral cortex is a structure within the vertebrate brain with distinct structural and functional properties.
Cerebral hemisphere	A Cerebral hemisphere (hemispherium cerebrale) is defined as one of the two regions of the brain that are delineated by the body"s median plane, (medial longitudinal fissure.) The brain can thus be described as being divided into left and right Cerebral hemisphere s. Each of these hemispheres has an outer layer of grey matter called the cerebral cortex that is supported by an inner layer of white matter.

Sensory system	A sensory system is a part of the nervous system responsible for processing sensory information. A sensory system consists of sensory receptors, neural pathways, and parts of the brain involved in sensory perception The receptive field is the specific part of the world to which a receptor organ and receptor cells respond.
Tim	TIM is a series of lesser-known psychedelic drugs similar in structure to mescaline. They were first synthesized by Alexander Shulgin. In his book PiHKAL (Phenethylamines i Have Known And Loved), none of their durations are known.
Audition	An Audition is a sample performance by an actor, singer, musician, dancer or other performer. It involves the performer displaying their talent through a previously-memorized and rehearsed solo piece: for example, a monologue for actors or a song for a singer. Used in the context of performing arts, it is analogous to job interviews in many ways.
Brain damage	Brain damage is the destruction or degeneration of brain cells. It may occur due to a wide range of conditions, illnesses, injuries, and as a result of iatrogenesis. Possible causes of widespread brain damage include prolonged hypoxia, poisoning by teratogens, infection, and neurological illness.
Epilepsy	Epilepsy is a chronic neurological condition characterized by recurrent unprovoked neural discharges. It is commonly controlled with medication, although surgical methods are used as well.
Gamma-aminobutyric acid	Gamma-aminobutyric acid is an inhibitory neurotransmitter found in the nervous systems of widely-divergent species. It is the chief inhibitory neurotransmitter in the central nervous system and also in the retina.
Optic chiasm	The optic chiasm is the part of the brain where the optic nerves partially cross. Specifically, the nerves connected to the right eye that attend to the left visual field cross with the nerves from the left eye that attend to the right visual field.
Split-brain	Split-brain is a lay term to describe the result when the corpus callosum connecting the two halves of the brain is severed to some degree. The surgical operation to produce this condition is called corpus callosotomy. It is rarely performed, usually to treat epilepsy; people with generalized seizures who injure themselves during falls may have less violent seizures, and hence less injury during those seizures, after the procedure.
Discovery	Discovery observations form acts of detecting and learning something. Discovery observations are acts in which something is found and given a productive insight. Serendipity is the effect by which one accidentally discovers something fortunate, especially while looking for something else entirely.
Generation	Generation, also known as procreation, is the act of producing offspring. A generation can also be a stage or degree in a succession of natural descent as a grandfather, a father, and the father"s son comprise three generations.

489

Nerve	A Nerve is an enclosed, cable-like bundle of peripheral axons (the long, slender projections of neurons.) A Nerve provides a common pathway for the electrochemical Nerve impulses that are transmitted along each of the axons. Nerve s are found only in the peripheral nervous system.
Optic nerve	The optic nerve is the nerve that transmits visual information from the retina to the brain. The optic nerve is composed of retinal ganglion cell axons and support cells.
Other	The Other or constitutive Other is a key concept in continental philosophy, opposed to the Same. It refers, or attempts to refer, to that which is "Other" than the concept being considered. The term often means a person Other than oneself, and is often capitalised.
Seizure	A seizure is a temporary alteration in brain function expressed as a changed mental state, tonic or clonic movements and various other symptoms. They are due to temporary abnormal electrical activity of a group of brain cells.
Language	A Language is a system for encoding and decoding information. In its most common use, the term refers to so-called "natural Language s" -- the forms of communication considered peculiar to humankind. In linguistics the term is extended to refer to the human cognitive facility of creating and using Language
Speech	Speech refers to the processes associated with the production and perception of sounds used in spoken language. A number of academic disciplines study speech and speech sounds, including acoustics, psychology, speech pathology, linguistics, and computer science.
Roger Wolcott Sperry	Roger Wolcott Sperry was a neuropsychologist, neurobiologist and Nobel laureate who, together with David Hunter Hubel and Torsten Nils Wiesel, won the 1981 Nobel Prize in Medicine for his work with split-brain research.
Stuttering	Stuttering is a speech disorder in which the flow of speech is disrupted by involuntary repetitions and prolongations of sounds, syllables, words or phrases; and involuntary silent pauses or blocks in which the stutterer is unable to produce sounds. Stuttering is generally not a problem with the physical production of speech sounds or putting thoughts into words. Despite popular perceptions to the contrary, stuttering does not affect and has no bearing on intelligence . Apart from their speech impediment, people who stutter may well be "normal" in the clinical sense of the term.
Emotion	Emotion, in its most general definition, is a complex psychophysical process that arises spontaneously, rather than through conscious effort, and evokes either a positive or negative psychological response and physical expressions, often involuntary, related to feelings, perceptions or beliefs about elements, objects or relations between them, in reality or in the imagination. An emotion is often differentiated from a feeling.
Jerre Levy	*Jerre Levy*, a student of Roger Sperry, has studied the relationship between the cerebral hemispheres and visual-oriented versus language-oriented tasks in split-brain surgery patients.

She has also found evidence that the left hemisphere specializes in analytical processing, while the right brain is more holistic.

She claims that the two hemispheres of the brain work together for every human function rather than act as two separate brains, as Sperry believed.

Brain hemisphere	Brain hemisphere is defined as one of the two regions of the brain that are delineated by the body"s median plane. Each has an outer layer of grey matter that is supported by an inner layer of white matter.
Neural development	The study of neural development draws on both neuroscience and developmental biology to describe the cellular and molecular mechanisms by which complex nervous systems emerge during embryonic development and throughout life.
Planum temporale	The planum temporale is the posterior superior surface of the superior temporal gyrus in the cerebrum. It is a highly lateralized brain structure involved with language.
Right hemisphere	The brain is divided into left and right cerebral hemispheres. The right hemisphere of the cortex controls the left side of the body.
Handedness	Handedness is an attribute of human beings defined by their unequal distribution of fine motor skill between the left and right hands. An individual who is more dextrous with the right hand is called right-handed, and one who is more skilled with the left is said to be left-handed.
Gorilla	The Gorilla is the largest of the living primates. They are ground-dwelling omnivores that inhabit the forests of Africa.
Idea	In the most narrow sense, an Idea is just whatever is before the mind when one thinks. Very often, Idea s are construed as representational images; i.e. images of some object. In other contexts, Idea s are taken to be concepts, although abstract concepts do not necessarily appear as images.
Mammal	A mammal is a warm-blooded, vertebrate animal, characterized by the presence of sweat glands, including milk producing sweat glands, and by the presence of: hair, three middle ear bones used in hearing, and a neocortex region in the brain. Most also possess specialized teeth and utilize a placenta in the ontogeny. A mammal encompass approximately 5,400 species, distributed in about 1,200 genera, 153 families, and 29 orders, though this varies by classification scheme.
Signal	In the fields of communications, signal processing, and in electrical engineering more generally, a signal is any time-varying quantity. Signals are often scalar-valued functions of time, but may be vector valued and may be functions of any other relevant independent variable.

Bonobo	The Bonobo is one of the two species making up the chimpanzee genus, Pan. The other species in genus Pan is Pan troglodytes, or the Common Chimpanzee. Although the name "chimpanzee" is sometimes used to refer to both species together, it is usually understood as referring to the Common Chimpanzee.
Sexual behavior	Human Sexual behavior refers to the manner in which humans experience and express their sexuality. It encompass a wide range of activities such as strategies to find or attract partners (mating and display behaviour), interactions between individuals, physical or emotional intimacy, and sexual contact. Although some cultures hold that sexual activity is acceptable only within marriage, extramarital sexual activities still takes place within such cultures.
Explanation	An explanation is a description which may clarify causes, context, and consequences of a certain object, and a phenomenon such as a process, a state of affairs. This description may establish rules or laws, and may clarify the existing ones in relation to an object, and a phenomenon examined. The components of an explanation can be implicit, and be interwoven with one another.
Primates	A primate is any member of the biological order Primates, the group that contains all the species commonly related to the lemurs, monkeys, and apes, with the last category including humans. Non-human primates occur mostly in Central and South America, Africa, and South Asia. The Primates order is divided informally into three main groupings: prosimians, monkeys of the New World, and monkeys and apes of the Old World.
Parasympathetic nervous system	The parasympathetic nervous system is a division of the autonomic nervous system, along with the sympathetic nervous system and Enteric nervous system. The ANS is a subdivision of the peripheral nervous system.
Parrot	Parrot is a bird of the roughly 350 species in the order Psittaciformes, found in most warm and tropical regions. It"s characteristics include a strong curved bill, an upright stance, strong legs, and clawed zygodactyl feet. Most predominantly green, with other bright colors, and some species are multi-colored. Many species can imitate human speech or other sounds.
Frontal lobe	The frontal lobe comprises four major folds of cortical tissue: the precentral gyrus, superior gyrus and the middle gyrus of the frontal gyri, the inferior frontal gyrus. It has been found to play a part in impulse control, judgement, language, memory, motor function, problem solving, sexual behavior, socialization and spontaneity.
Genetics	Genetics is the science of heredity and variation in living organisms.Knowledge of the inheritance of characteristics has been implicitly used since prehistoric times for improving crop plants and animals through selective breeding. However, the modern science of genetics, which seeks to understand the mechanisms of inheritance, only began with the work of Gregor Mendel in the mid-1800s.

Intelligence	Intelligence is a property of mind that encompasses many related abilities, such as the capacities to reason, plan, solve problems, think abstractly, comprehend ideas and language, and learn. In some cases intelligence may include traits such as creativity, personality, character, knowledge, or wisdom. However other psychologists prefer not to include these traits in the definition of intelligence.
Animal testing	Animal testing refers to the use of animals in experiments. It is estimated that 50 to 100 million vertebrate animals worldwide — from zebrafish to non-human primates — are used annually and either killed during the experiments or subsequently euthanized.
Anterior	Anterior is an anatomical term referring to the front part of the body. The anterior is positioned in front of another body part, or towards the head of an animal. It is the opposite of posterior.
Central sulcus	The central sulcus is a prominent landmark of the brain, separating the parietal lobe from the frontal lobe. The central sulcus is the site of the primary motor cortex in mammals, a group of cells that controls voluntary movements of the body.
Motor cortex	Motor cortex is a term that describes regions of the cerebral cortex involved in the planning, control, and execution of voluntary motor functions.
Prefrontal cortex	The prefrontal cortex is the anterior part of the frontal lobes of the brain, lying in front of the motor and premotor areas. Cytoarchitectonically, it is defined by the presence of an internal granular layer IV.
Primary	In medicine, the reporting of symptoms by a patient may have significant psychological motivators. Psychologists sometimes categorize these motivators into primary or secondary gain. primary gain is internally good; motivationally.
Primary motor cortex	The primary motor cortex works in association with pre-motor areas to plan and execute movements. It contains large neurons known as Betz cells which send long axons down the spinal cord to synapse onto alpha motor neurons which connect to the muscles.
Species	Species refers to a reproductively isolated breeding population.
Understanding	Understanding is a psychological process related to an abstract or physical object, such as, person, situation, or message whereby one is able to think about it and use concepts to deal adequately with that object.
Hearing impairment	A hearing impairment is a full or partial decrease in the ability to detect or understand sounds.[1] Caused by a wide range of biological and environmental factors, loss of hearing can happen to any organism that perceives sound.

Language acquisition	Language acquisition is the process by which the language capability develops in a human. First language acquisition concerns the development of language in children, while second language acquisition focuses on language development in adults as well. Historically, theorists are often divided between emphasising either nature or nurture as the most important explanatory factor for acquisition.
Language acquisition device	The Language Acquisition Device is a postulated "organ" of the brain that is supposed to function as a congenital device for learning symbolic language. Its concept is a component of the nativist theory of language which dominates contemporary formal linguistics, which asserts that humans are born with the instinct or "innate facility" for acquiring language.
Sign	A Sign is an entity which Sign ifies another entity. A natural Sign is an entity which bears a causal relation to the Sign ified entity, as thunder is a Sign of storm. A conventional Sign Sign ifies by agreement, as a full stop Sign ifies the end of a sentence.
Sign language	A Sign Language (also signed language) is a language which, instead of acoustically conveyed sound patterns, uses visually transmitted sign patterns (manual communication, body language and lip patterns) to convey meaning--simultaneously combining hand shapes, orientation and movement of the hands, arms or body, and facial expressions to fluidly express a speaker"s thoughts. Sign Language s commonly develop in deaf communities, which can include interpreters and friends and families of deaf people as well as people who are deaf or hard of hearing themselves. Wherever communities of deaf people exist, Sign Language s develop.
Williams syndrome	Williams syndrome is a rare genetic disorder, occurring in fewer than 1 in 7,500 live births. It is characterized by a distinctive, "elfin" facial appearance, along with a low nasal bridge; an unusually cheerful demeanor and ease with strangers, coupled with unpredictably occurring negative outbursts; mental retardation coupled with unusual language skills; a love for music; and cardiovascular problems, such as supravalvular aortic stenosis and transient hypercalcaemia. The syndrome was first identified in 1961 by Dr. J. C. P. Williams of New Zealand.
Mechanism	In philosophy, mechanism is a theory that all natural phenomena can be explained by physical causes. It can be contrasted with vitalism, the philosophical theory that vital forces are active in living organisms, so that life cannot be explained solely by mechanism.
Mind	Mind collectively refers to the aspects of intellect and consciousness manifested as combinations of thought, perception, memory, emotion, will and imagination; mind is the stream of consciousness.
Mental retardation	Mental retardation is a term for a pattern of persistently slow learning of basic motor and language skills during childhood, and a significantly below-normal global intellectual capacity as an adult. One common criterion for diagnosis of mental retardation is a tested intelligence quotient of 70 or below and deficits in adaptive functioning. People with mental retardation may be described as having developmental disabilities, global developmental delay, or learning difficulties.

Skill	A Skill is the learned capacity to carry out pre-determined results often with the minimum outlay of time, energy, or both. Skill s can often be divided into domain-general and domain-specific Skill s. For example, in the domain of work, some general Skill s would include time management, teamwork and leadership, self motivation and others, whereas domain-specific Skill s would be useful only for a certain job.
Spite	In fair division problems, Spite is a phenomenon that occurs when a player"s value of an allocation decreases when one or more other players" valuation increases. Thus, other things being equal, a player exhibiting Spite will prefer an allocation in which other players receive less than more (if the good is desirable.) In this language, Spite is difficult to analyze because one has to assess two sets of preferences.
Aphasia	Aphasia is a loss or impairment of the ability to produce or comprehend language, due to brain damage. It is usually a result of damage to the language centers of the brain.
Broca's aphasia	Broca"s aphasia is an aphasia caused by damage to anterior regions of the brain, including the left inferior frontal region Broca"s area. It is also a classification of non-fluent aphasia, as opposed to fluent aphasia. Diagnosis is done on a case by case basis, as lesions often affect surrounding cortex and deficits are not well conserved between patients.
Sensitive period	Sensitive periods is a term coined by the Dutch geneticist Hugo de Vries and adopted by the Italian educator Maria Montessori to refer to important periods of childhood development. During a sensitive period it is very easy for children to acquire certain abilities, such as language, discrimination of sensory stimuli, and mental modeling of the environment.
Temporal lobe	The temporal lobe is part of the cerebrum. It lies at the side of the brain, beneath the lateral or Sylvian fissure. Adjacent areas in the superior, posterior and lateral parts of the temporal lobe are involved in high-level auditory processing.
Disability	A disability is a condition or function judged to be significantly impaired relative to the usual standard of an individual or their group. The term is often used to refer to individual functioning, including physical impairments, sensory impairments, cognitive impairments, intellectual impairments or mental health issue.
Word	A word is the smallest free form (an item that may be uttered in isolation with semantic or pragmatic content) in a language, in contrast to a morpheme, which is the smallest unit of meaning. A word may consist of only one morpheme (e.g. cat), but a single morpheme may not be able to exist as a free form . Typically, a word will consist of a root or stem, and zero or more affixes.
Consciousness	The awareness of the sensations, thoughts, and feelings being experienced at a given moment is called consciousness.

Optic radiation	The Optic radiation is a collection of axons from relay neurons in the lateral geniculate nucleus of the thalamus carrying visual information to the visual cortex along the calcarine fissure. There is one such tract on each side of the brain. A distinctive feature of the Optic radiation s is that they split into two parts on each side: Right superior quadrantanopia.
Depression	In everyday language depression refers to any downturn in mood, which may be relatively transitory and perhaps due to something trivial.
Comprehension	The comprehension of an object is the totality of intensions, that is, attributes, characters, marks, properties, or qualities, that the object possesses, or else the totality of intensions that are pertinent to the context of a given discussion. This is the correct technical term for the whole collection of intensions of an object.
Language comprehension	Language comprehension takes place whenever a reader or listener processes a language utterance, either in isolation or in the context of a conversation or a text. Many studies of the language comprehension process have focused on reading of single utterances without context. Extensive research has shown, however, that language comprehension is affected also by context preceding a given utterance, as well as many other factors.
Entity	An entity is something that has a distinct, separate existence, though it need not be a material existence. In particular, abstractions and legal fictions are usually regarded as an entity. In general, there is also no presumption that an entity is animate.
Remembering	Remembering is the retrieval of memory. It is not a passive process; people employ metacognitive strategies to make the best use of their memory, and priming and other context can have a large effect on what is retrieved.
Nominal aphasia	Nominal aphasia is a form of aphasia in which the subject has difficulty remembering or recognizing names which the subject should know well. The subject speaks fluently and grammatically, and has normal comprehension; the only deficit is trouble with "word finding," that is, finding appropriate words for what they mean to say.
Basal ganglia	The basal ganglia are a group of nuclei in the brain associated with motor and learning functions.
Multilingualism	The term multilingualism can refer to phenomena regarding an individual speaker who uses two or more languages, a community of speakers where two or more languages are used, or between speakers of different languages.
Dyslexia	Dyslexia is a specific learning disability that manifests primarily as a difficulty with written language, particularly with reading and spelling. Dyslexia is the result of a neurological difference but is not an intellectual disability. Most people with dyslexia have average or above-average intelligence.

Central tendency	In mathematics, the central tendency of a data set refers to a measure of the "middle" or "expected" value of the data set. There are many different descriptive statistics that can be chosen as a measurement of the central tendency of the data items. The most common method is the arithmetic mean, but there are many other types of averages.
Brain size	When comparing different species, brain size does present a correlation with intelligence. For example, the ratio of brain weight to body weight for fish is 1:5000; for reptiles it is about 1:1500; for birds, 1:220; for most mammals, 1:180, and for humans, 1:50. However within the human species modern studies using MRI have shown that brain size shows substantial and consistent correlation with IQ among adults of the same sex
Caudate nucleus	The caudate nucleus is a nucleus located within the basal ganglia of the brains of many animal species. The caudate nuclei are located near the center of the brain, sitting astride the thalamus. There is a caudate nucleus within each hemisphere of the brain.
Prosencephalon	In the anatomy of the brain of vertebrates, the prosencephalon is the rostral-most portion of the brain. The prosencephalon, the mesencephalon, and rhombencephalon are the three primary portions of the brain during early development of the central nervous system.
Globus pallidus	The globus pallidus is a sub-cortical structure of the brain. It is a major element of the basal ganglia system. In this system, it is a major element of the basal ganglia core, consisting of the striatum and its direct targets: globus pallidus and substantia nigra. The last two are made up of the same neuronal elements, have a similar main afferent, have a similar synaptology, and do not receive cortical afferents.
Hypothalamus	The hypothalamus is a region of the brain located below the thalamus, forming the major portion of the ventral region of the diencephalon and functioning to regulate certain metabolic processes and other autonomic activities.
Putamen	The putamen is a structure in the middle of the brain, which, together with the caudate nucleus forms the dorsal striatum. The putamen is a portion of the basal ganglia that forms the outermost part of the lenticular nucleus.
Structure	Structure is a fundamental and sometimes intangible notion covering the recognition, observation, nature, and stability of patterns and relationships of entities.
Amygdala	Amygdala are almond-shaped groups of neurons located deep within the medial temporal lobes of the brain in complex vertebrates, including humans. Shown in research to perform a primary role in the processing and memory of emotional reactions, the amygdala are considered part of the limbic system.

505

Attention	Attention is the cognitive process of selectively concentrating on one aspect of the environment while ignoring other things. Examples include listening carefully to what someone is saying while ignoring other conversations in the room or listening to a cell phone conversation while driving a car.
Spoonerism	A Spoonerism is an error in speech or deliberate play on words in which corresponding consonants, vowels, or morphemes are switched . It is named after the Reverend William Archibald Spooner (1844-1930), Warden of New College, Oxford, who was notoriously prone to this tendency. It is also known as a marrowsky, after a Polish count who suffered from the same impediment.
Bipolar disorder	Bipolar disorder is a psychiatric condition defined as recurrent episodes of significant disturbance in mood. These disturbances can occur on a spectrum that ranges from debilitating depression to unbridled mania. Individuals suffering from bipolar disorder typically experience fluid states of mania, hypomania or what is referred to as a mixed state in conjunction with depressive episodes.
Inattentional blindness	Inattentional blindness is the phenomenon of not being able to see things that are actually there. This can be a result of having no internal frame of reference to perceive the unseen objects, or it can be the result of the mental focus or attention which cause mental distractions. The phenomenon is due to how our minds see and process information.
Mind-body problem	There are three basic views of the mind-body problem: mental and physical events are totally different, and cannot be reduced to each other (dualism); mental events are to be reduced to physical events (materialism); and physical events are to be reduced to mental events (phenomenalism).
Need	A Need is something that is necessary for humans to live a healthy life. Need s are distinguished from wants because a deficiency would cause a clear negative outcome, such as dysfunction or death. Need s can be objective and physical, such as food and water, or they can be subjective and psychological, such as the Need for self-esteem.
Not	This catalog is compiled from a source file. Please do not edit this page manually. This is how to edit it.
Occipital lobe	The occipital lobe is the visual processing center of the mammalian brain, containing most of the anatomical region of the visual cortex. The primary visual cortex is Brodmann area 17, commonly called V_1.
Stimulus	In psychology, a stimulus is part of the stimulus-response relationship of behavioral learning theory.
Binocular rivalry	Binocular rivalry is a phenomenon of visual perception in which perception alternates between different images presented to each eye.When one image is presented to one eye and a very different image is presented to the other, instead of the two images being seen superimposed, one image is seen for a few moments, then the other, then the first, and so on, randomly for as long as one cares to look.

Synchrony	In child development, synchrony is the carefully coordinated interaction between the parent and the child or adolescent in which, often unknowingly, they are attuned to each other's behavior.
Eye	Eye s are organs that detect light, and send signals along the optic nerve to the visual and other areas of the brain. Complex optical systems with resolving power have come in ten fundamentally different forms, and 96% of animal species possess a complex optical system. Image-resolving Eye s are present in cnidaria, molluscs, chordates, annelids and arthropods.
Perception	In psychology. and the cognitive sciences, perception is the process of acquiring, interpreting, selecting, and organizing sensory information. It is a task far more complex than was imagined in the 1950s and 1960s, when it was proclaimed that building perceiving machines would take about a decade, but, needless to say, that is still very far from reality.
Neglect	Neglect means to leave uncared for or to leave undone.
Phi phenomenon	The phi phenomenon is a perceptual illusion described by Max Wertheimer, in which a disembodied perception of motion is produced by a succession of still images.
Hemispatial neglect	Hemispatial neglect is a neurological condition in which, after damage to one hemisphere of the brain, a deficit in attention to the opposite side of space is observed.
Memory	In psychology, memory is an organism"s ability to store, retain, and subsequently retrieve information. In recent decades, it has become one of the principal pillars of a branch of science called cognitive neuroscience, an interdisciplinary link between cognitive psychology and neuroscience.
Working memory	Working memory is a theoretical framework within cognitive psychology that refers to the structures and processes used for temporarily storing and manipulating information. There are numerous theories as to both the theoretical structure of working memory as well as to the specific parts of the brain responsible for working memory.
Storage	The human memory has three processes: encoding (input), Storage and retrieval(output.) Storage is the process of retaining information whether in the sensory memory, the short-term memory or the more permanent long-term memory.

Mood	A mood is a relatively lasting emotional or affective state. They differ from emotions in that they are less specific, often less intense, less likely to be triggered by a particular stimulus or event, however longer lasting.
Mood disorder	A mood disorder is a condition where the prevailing emotional mood is distorted or inappropriate to the circumstances.
Depression	In everyday language depression refers to any downturn in mood, which may be relatively transitory and perhaps due to something trivial.
Major depression	Major depression is a state of intense sadness, melancholia or despair that has advanced to the point of being disruptive to an individual"s social functioning and/or activities of daily living. It is generally acknowledged to be more serious than normal depressed feelings. It often leads to constant negative thinking and sometimes substance abuse or self-harm.
Brain	In animals, the brain, is the control center of the central nervous system, responsible for behavior. The brain is located in the head, protected by the skull and close to the primary sensory apparatus of vision, hearing, equilibrioception, sense of acceleration, taste, and olfaction.
Brain size	When comparing different species, brain size does present a correlation with intelligence. For example, the ratio of brain weight to body weight for fish is 1:5000; for reptiles it is about 1:1500; for birds, 1:220; for most mammals, 1:180, and for humans, 1:50. However within the human species modern studies using MRI have shown that brain size shows substantial and consistent correlation with IQ among adults of the same sex
Energy	The concept of psychic Energy was developed in the field of psychodynamics. In 1874, German scientist Ernst von Brucke proposed that all living organisms are Energy-systems governed by the principle of the conservation of Energy. Brucke was also coincidentally the supervisor at the University of Vienna for first-year medical student Sigmund Freud who adopted this new paradigm.
Feeling	Feeling in psychology is usually reserved for the conscious subjective experience of emotion. As such, it is inherently beyond the reach of scientific method.
Pleasure	Pleasure is commonly conceptualized as somehow opposed to pain or suffering, though it has received much less scientific attention. Pleasure can be brought about in different ways, depending on how every individual senses the feeling of pleasure. Some feel this phenomenon through music, sexuality, drugs, writing, accomplishment, recognition, service, and any other imaginable activity; even pain.
Attribute-value system	An Attribute-value system is a basic knowledge representation framework comprising a table with columns designating "attributes" and rows designating "objects" Each table cell therefore designates the value of a particular attribute of a particular object. Below is a sample Attribute-value system.

Tim	TIM is a series of lesser-known psychedelic drugs similar in structure to mescaline. They were first synthesized by Alexander Shulgin. In his book PiHKAL (Phenethylamines i Have Known And Loved), none of their durations are known.
Audition	An Audition is a sample performance by an actor, singer, musician, dancer or other performer. It involves the performer displaying their talent through a previously-memorized and rehearsed solo piece: for example, a monologue for actors or a song for a singer. Used in the context of performing arts, it is analogous to job interviews in many ways.
Experience	Experience as a general concept comprises knowledge of or skill in or observation of some thing or some event gained through involvement in or exposure to that thing or event. The history of the word experience aligns it closely with the concept of experiment.
Genetics	Genetics is the science of heredity and variation in living organisms.Knowledge of the inheritance of characteristics has been implicitly used since prehistoric times for improving crop plants and animals through selective breeding. However, the modern science of genetics, which seeks to understand the mechanisms of inheritance, only began with the work of Gregor Mendel in the mid-1800s.
Serotonin	Serotonin, is a monoamine neurotransmitter synthesized in serotonergic neurons in the central nervous system and enterochromaffin cells in the gastrointestinal tract of animals including humans. Serotonin is also found in many mushrooms and plants, including fruits and vegetables.
Stress	Stress is the consequence of the failure to adapt to change. Less simply: it is the condition that results when person-environment transactions lead the individual to perceive a discrepancy, whether real or not, between the demands of a situation and the resources of the person"s biological, psychological or social systems.
Vision	Vision is the most important sense for birds, since good eyesight is essential for safe flight, and this group has a number of adaptations which give visual acuity superior to that of other vertebrate groups; a pigeon has been described as "two eyes with wings". The avian eye resembles that of a reptile, but has a better-positioned lens, a feature shared with mammals. Birds have the largest eyes relative to their size within the animal kingdom, and movement is consequently limited within the eye"s bony socket.
Behavior	Behavior refers to the actions or reactions of an object or organism, usually in relation to the environment. Behavior can be conscious or subconscious, overt or covert, and voluntary or involuntary. Human Behavior (and that of other organisms and mechanisms) can be common, unusual, acceptable, or unacceptable. Humans evaluate the acceptability of Behavior using social norms and regulate Behavior by means of social control

Neural development	The study of neural development draws on both neuroscience and developmental biology to describe the cellular and molecular mechanisms by which complex nervous systems emerge during embryonic development and throughout life.
Disease	A Disease or medical problem is an abnormal condition of an organism that impairs bodily functions, associated with specific symptoms and signs. It may be caused by external factors, such as invading organisms, or it may be caused by internal dysfunctions, such as autoimmune Disease s. In human beings, Disease is often used more broadly to refer to any condition that causes extreme pain, dysfunction, distress, social problems, and/or death to the person afflicted, or similar problems for those in contact with the person.
Infection	An infection is the detrimental colonization of a host organism by a foreign species.
Acetic acid	Acetic acid, is an organic chemical compound, giving vinegar its sour taste and pungent smell. Its structural formula is represented as CH_3COOH.
Disulfiram	Disulfiram is a drug used to support the treatment of chronic alcoholism by producing an acute sensitivity to alcohol.
Antidepressant	An antidepressant, is a psychiatric medication or other substance (nutrient or herb) used for alleviating depression or dysthymia ("milder" depression). Drug groups known as MAOIs, tricyclics and SSRIs are particularly associated with the term. These medications are now amongst the drugs most commonly prescribed by psychiatrists and general practitioners, and their effectiveness and adverse effects are the subject of many studies and competing claims.
Bromide	A bromide ion is a bromine atom with charge of −1.
Epilepsy	Epilepsy is a chronic neurological condition characterized by recurrent unprovoked neural discharges. It is commonly controlled with medication, although surgical methods are used as well.
Estradiol	Estradiol is a sex hormone. Labelled the "female" hormone but also present in males, it represents the major estrogen in humans. Estradiol has not only a critical impact on reproductive and sexual functioning, but also affects other organs including bone structure.
Estrogen	Estrogen is a group of steroid compounds that function as the primary female sex hormone. They are produced primarily by developing follicles in the ovaries, the corpus luteum and the placenta.
Gamma-aminobutyric acid	Gamma-aminobutyric acid is an inhibitory neurotransmitter found in the nervous systems of widely-divergent species. It is the chief inhibitory neurotransmitter in the central nervous system and also in the retina.
Hormone	A hormone is a chemical messenger that carries a signal from one cell to another. All multicellular organisms produce hormone s.

Lateralization	Lateralization of brain functions is evident in the phenomena of right- or left-handedness, -earedness and -eyedness. Broad generalizations are often made in popular psychology about certain function being lateralised, that is, located in the right or left side of the brain. These ideas need to be treated carefully because the popular lateralization is ften distributed across both sides. However, there is some division of mental processing.
Postpartum depression	Postpartum depression is a form of clinical depression which can affect women, and less frequently men, after childbirth. Studies report prevalence rates among women from 5% to 25%, but methodological differences among the studies make the actual prevalence rate unclear. PPE is caused by sleep deprivation coupled with hormonal changes in the women"s body shortly after giving birth and may be mild or severe.
Prefrontal cortex	The prefrontal cortex is the anterior part of the frontal lobes of the brain, lying in front of the motor and premotor areas. Cytoarchitectonically, it is defined by the presence of an internal granular layer IV.
Progesterone	Progesterone is a C-21 steroid hormone involved in the female menstrual cycle, pregnancy and embryogenesis of humans and other species. Progesterone belongs to a class of hormones called progestogens, and is the major naturally occurring human progestogen.
Testosterone	Testosterone is a steroid hormone from the androgen group. It is the principal male sex hormone and the "original" anabolic steroid.
Acetaldehyde	Acetaldehyde is a flammable liquid with a fruity smell. Acetaldehyde occurs naturally in ripe fruit, coffee, and fresh bread, and is produced by plants as part of their normal metabolism. It is popularly known as the chemical that causes hangovers. It is toxic, an irritant, and a probable carcinogen.
Activating effect	The arousal-producing effects of sex hormones that increase the likelihood of sexual behavior is called the activating effect.
Androgen	Androgen is the generic term for any natural or synthetic compound, usually a steroid hormone, that stimulates or controls the development and maintenance of masculine characteristics in vertebrates by binding to androgen receptors. This includes the activity of the accessory male sex organs and development of male secondary sex characteristics.
Anterior	Anterior is an anatomical term referring to the front part of the body. The anterior is positioned in front of another body part, or towards the head of an animal. It is the opposite of posterior.
Blood	Blood is a specialized biological fluid consisting of red blood cells.White blood cells also called leukocytes and platelets also called thrombocytes suspended in a complex fluid medium known as blood plasma.

Recess	In education, recess is the daily period, typically ten to thirty minutes, in elementary school where students are allowed to leave the school"s interior to enter its adjacent outdoor playground, where they can play on such recreational equipment or engage in activities.
Chemical	A chemical is a material with a definite chemical composition. All samples of a compound have the same composition; that is, all samples have the same proportions, by mass, of the elements present in the compound.
Discovery	Discovery observations form acts of detecting and learning something. Discovery observations are acts in which something is found and given a productive insight. Serendipity is the effect by which one accidentally discovers something fortunate, especially while looking for something else entirely.
Frontal lobe	The frontal lobe comprises four major folds of cortical tissue: the precentral gyrus, superior gyrus and the middle gyrus of the frontal gyri, the inferior frontal gyrus. It has been found to play a part in impulse control, judgement, language, memory, motor function, problem solving, sexual behavior, socialization and spontaneity.
Gland	A gland is an organ in an animal's body that synthesizes a substance for release such as hormones, often into the bloodstream or into cavities inside the body or its outer surface.
Habit	An habit is an automatic routine of behavior that are repeated regularly, without thinking. They are learned, not instinctive, human behaviors that occur automatically, without the explicit contemporaneous intention of the person. The person may not be paying attention to or be conscious or aware of the behavior.
Need	A Need is something that is necessary for humans to live a healthy life. Need s are distinguished from wants because a deficiency would cause a clear negative outcome, such as dysfunction or death. Need s can be objective and physical, such as food and water, or they can be subjective and psychological, such as the Need for self-esteem.
Other	The Other or constitutive Other is a key concept in continental philosophy, opposed to the Same. It refers, or attempts to refer, to that which is "Other" than the concept being considered. The term often means a person Other than oneself, and is often capitalised.
Ovum	Ovum is a female sex cell or gamete.
Role	A role is a set of connected behaviors, rights and obligations as conceptualized by actors in a social situation. It is mostly defined as an expected behavior in a given individual social status and social position.
Signal	In the fields of communications, signal processing, and in electrical engineering more generally, a signal is any time-varying quantity. Signals are often scalar-valued functions of time, but may be vector valued and may be functions of any other relevant independent variable.

Species	Species refers to a reproductively isolated breeding population.
Steroid	A steroid is a terpenoid lipid characterized by its sterane or steroid nucleus: a carbon skeleton with four fused rings, generally arranged in a 6-6-6-5 fashion. steroid s vary by the functional groups attached to these rings and the oxidation state of the rings. Hundreds of distinct steroid s are found in plants, animals, and fungi.
Stimulus	In psychology, a stimulus is part of the stimulus-response relationship of behavioral learning theory.
Uterus	The uterus or womb is the major female reproductive organ. The main function of the uterus is to accept a fertilized ovum which becomes implanted into the endometrium, and derives nourishment from blood vessels which develop exclusively for this purpose.
Bupropion	Bupropion is an atypical antidepressant that acts as a norepinephrine and dopamine reuptake inhibitor, and nicotinic antagonist.
Chlorpromazine	Chlorpromazine is a phenothiazine antipsychotic. Its principal use is in the treatment of schizophrenia, though it has also been used to treat hiccups and nausea. Its use today has been largely supplanted by the newer atypical antipsychotics such as olanzapine and quetiapine. It works on a variety of receptors in the central nervous system; these include anticholinergic, antidopaminergic and antihistamine effects as well as some antagonism of adrenergic receptors.
Citalopram	Citalopram is an antidepressant drug used to treat depression associated with mood disorders. It is also used on occasion in the treatment of body dysmorphic disorder and anxiety.
Dopamine	Dopamine is a hormone and neurotransmitter occurring in a wide variety of animals, including both vertebrates and invertebrates. In the brain, dopamine functions as a neurotransmitter. Dopamine is also a neurohormone released by the hypothalamus. Its main function as a hormone is to inhibit the release of prolactin from the anterior lobe of the pituitary.
Eating	Eating is the process of consuming nutrition, i.e. food, for the purpose of providing for the nutritional needs of an animal, particularly their energy requirements and to grow.
Fluent aphasia	Receptive aphasia or Fluent aphasia is a type of aphasia often caused by neurological damage to Wernicke"s area in the brain This is not to be confused with Wernicke"s encephalopathy or Wernicke-Korsakoff syndrome. The aphasia was first described by Carl Wernicke and its understanding substantially advanced by Norman Geschwind.
Fluvoxamine	Fluvoxamine is an antidepressant which functions pharmacologically as a selective serotonin reuptake inhibitor. Though it is in the same class as other SSRI drugs, it is most often used to treat obsessive-compulsive disorder.

Imipramine	Imipramine is an antidepressant medication, a tricyclic antidepressant of the dibenzazepine group. Imipramine is mainly used in the treatment of clinical depression and enuresis.
Manic-depressive disorder	Bipolar affective disorder until recently, the current name is of fairly recent origin and refers to the cycling between high and low episodes; it has replaced the older term Manic-depressive disorder. The new term is designed to be neutral, to avoid the stigma in the non-mental health community.
Phenelzine	Phenelzine is a monoamine oxidase inhibitor used as an antidepressant drug.
Norepinephrine	Norepinephrine is a catecholamine and a phenethylamine with chemical formula $C_8H_{11}NO_3$.
Parasympathetic nervous system	The parasympathetic nervous system is a division of the autonomic nervous system, along with the sympathetic nervous system and Enteric nervous system. The ANS is a subdivision of the peripheral nervous system.
Fluoxetine	Fluoxetine is an antidepressant of the selective serotonin reuptake inhibitor class. It is approved for the treatment of clinical depression, obsessive-compulsive disorder, bulimia nervosa, panic disorder and premenstrual dysphoric disorder.
Schizophrenia	Schizophrenia is a psychiatric diagnosis that describes a mental illness characterized by impairments in the perception or expression of reality, most commonly manifesting as auditory hallucinations, paranoid or bizarre delusions or disorganized speech and thinking in the context of significant social or occupational dysfunction.
Paroxetine	Paroxetine is a selective serotonin reuptake inhibitor antidepressant. It was released in 1992 by the pharmaceutical company GlaxoSmithKline. In 2006 it was the fifth-most prescribed antidepressant in the United States retail market, with more than 19.7 million prescriptions.
Sertraline	Sertraline is used medically mainly to treat the symptoms of depression and anxiety. It has also been prescribed for the treatment of obsessive-compulsive disorder, post-traumatic stress disorder, premenstrual dysphoric disorder, panic disorder, and bipolar disorder
Tricyclic	Tricyclic antidepressants are a class of antidepressant drugs first used in the 1950s. They are named after the drugs' molecular structure, which contains three rings of atoms.
Tyramine	In organic chemistry, tyramine is a monoamine compound derived from the amino acid tyrosine.
Alcoholism	Alcoholism is a term with multiple and sometimes conflicting definitions. In common and historic usage, alcoholism refers to any condition that results in the continued consumption of alcoholic beverages despite the health problems and negative social consequences it causes.

Body weight	Body weight is a term that is used in biological and medical science contexts to describe the mass of an organism"s body. Body weight is measured in kilograms throughout the world, although in some countries people more often measure and describe body weight in pounds or stones and pounds and thus may not be well acquainted with measurement in kilograms.
Catecholamine	Catecholamine refers to chemical compounds derived from the amino acid tyrosine containing catechol and amine groups.
Delusion	A false belief, not generally shared by others, and that cannot be changed despite strong evidence to the contrary is a delusion.
Dose	An effective dose in pharmacology is the amount of drug that produces a therapeutic response in 50% of the people taking it, sometimes also called ED-50. In radiation protection it is an estimate of the stochastic effect that a non-uniform radiation dose has on a human.
Emotion	Emotion, in its most general definition, is a complex psychophysical process that arises spontaneously, rather than through conscious effort, and evokes either a positive or negative psychological response and physical expressions, often involuntary, related to feelings, perceptions or beliefs about elements, objects or relations between them, in reality or in the imagination. An emotion is often differentiated from a feeling.
Emotional expression	In psychology, emotional expression is observable verbal and nonverbal behavior that communicates emotion.
Personal life	Personal life is the course of an individual human"s life, especially when viewed as the sum of personal choices contributing to one"s personal identity.
Glutamate	Glutamate is one of the 20 standard amino acids used by all organisms in their proteins. It is critical for proper cell function, but it is not an essential nutrient in humans because it can be manufactured from other compounds.
Hallucination	A hallucination is a sensory perception experienced in the absence of an external stimulus, as distinct from an illusion, which is a misperception of an external stimulus. They may occur in any sensory modality - visual, auditory, olfactory, gustatory, tactile, or mixed.
Intoxication	Intoxication is the state of being affected by one or more psychoactive drugs. It can also refer to the effects caused by the ingestion of poison or by the overconsumption of normally harmless substances.
Negative symptoms	Negative symptoms are indications of deficiency in specific mental functions and of an absence of typical behavior; these can include reduced or inappropriate emotions, lack of eill, loss of verbal expression, and the lack of logic. Negative symptoms are often displayed in the residual phase of schizophrenia.

Nerve	A Nerve is an enclosed, cable-like bundle of peripheral axons (the long, slender projections of neurons.) A Nerve provides a common pathway for the electrochemical Nerve impulses that are transmitted along each of the axons. Nerve s are found only in the peripheral nervous system.
Neurotransmitter	A neurotransmitter is a chemical that is used to relay, amplify and modulate electrical signals between a neurons and another cell.
Control group	A control group augments integrity in experiments by isolating variables as dictated by the scientific method in order to make a conclusion about such variables. In other cases, an experimental control is used to prevent the effects of one variable from being drowned out by the known, greater effects of other variables. this case, the researchers can either use a control group or use statistical techniques to control for the other variables.
Receptor	A sensory receptor is a structure that recognizes a stimulus in the internal or external environment of an organism. In response to stimuli the sensory receptor initiates sensory transduction by creating graded potentials or action potentials in the same cell or in an adjacent one.
Homeostasis	Homeostasis is the property of either an open system or a closed system, especially a living organism, which regulates its internal environment so as to maintain a stable, constant condition.
Adverse effect	In medicine, an adverse effect is a harmful and undesired effect resulting from a medication or other intervention such as surgery. An adverse effect may be termed a "side effect", when judged to be secondary to a main or therapeutic effect, and may result from an unsuitable or incorrect dosage or procedure, which could be due to medical error. adverse effect s are sometimes referred to as "iatrogenic" because they are generated by a physician/treatment.
Speech	Speech refers to the processes associated with the production and perception of sounds used in spoken language. A number of academic disciplines study speech and speech sounds, including acoustics, psychology, speech pathology, linguistics, and computer science.
Thought disorder	Thought disorder describes a persistent underlying disturbance to conscious thought and is classified largely by its effects on speech and writing. Affected persons may show pressure of speech, derailment or flight of ideas, thought blocking, rhyming, punning, or word salad.
Choice Set	A Choice Set is one scenario provided for evaluation by respondents in a Choice Experiment. Responses are collected and used to create a Choice Model. Respondents are usually provided with a series of differing Choice Set s for evaluation.
Blood-brain barrier	The Blood-brain barrier is a membranic structure that acts primarily to protect the brain from chemicals in the blood, while still allowing essential metabolic function. It is composed of endothelial cells, which are packed very tightly in brain capillaries. This higher density restricts passage of substances from the bloodstream much more than endothelial cells in capillaries elsewhere in the body

Monism	Monism is the metaphysical view that there is only one principle, essence, substance or energy.
Psychotherapy	Psychotherapy is an interpersonal, relational intervention used by trained therapists to aid clients in problems of living. This usually includes increasing individual sense of well-being and reducing subjective discomforting experience.
Mechanism	In philosophy, mechanism is a theory that all natural phenomena can be explained by physical causes. It can be contrasted with vitalism, the philosophical theory that vital forces are active in living organisms, so that life cannot be explained solely by mechanism.
5-Hydroxyindoleacetic acid	*5-hydroxyindoleacetic acid* (5-HIAA) is the main metabolite of serotonin in the human body. In chemical analysis of urine samples, 5-HIAA is used to determine the body"s levels of serotonin. 5-HIAA, Quantitative, 24-Hour Urine; Serotonin Metabolite, 24-Hour Urine 24-hour urine volume is measured and recorded on the request form.
Brain-derived neurotrophic factor	Brain-derived neurotrophic factor is exactly as it states; a neurotrophic factor found originally in the brain, but also found in the periphery. More specifically, it is a protein which has activity on certain neurons of the central nervous system and the peripheral nervous system; it helps to support the survival of existing neurons, and encourage the growth and differentiation of new neurons and synapses.
Hippocampus	The hippocampus is a part of the brain located in the medial temporal lobe. It forms a part of the limbic system and plays a part in memory and spatial navigation.
Plasma membrane	A component of every biological cell, the selectively permeable plasma membrane is a thin and structured bilayer of phospholipid and protein molecules that envelopes the cell. It separates a cell's interior from its surroundings and controls what moves in and out.
Tryptophan	Tryptophan is a sleep-promoting amino acid and a precursor for serotonin (a neurotransmitter) and melatonin (a neurohormone). Tryptophan has been implicated as a possible cause of schizophrenia in people who cannot metabolize it properly.
Affect	Affect refers to the experience of feeling or emotion. Affect is a key part of the process of an organism's interaction with stimuli. The word also refers sometimes to affect display, which is "a facial, vocal, or gestural behavior that serves as an indicator of affect."
Prosencephalon	In the anatomy of the brain of vertebrates, the prosencephalon is the rostral-most portion of the brain. The prosencephalon, the mesencephalon, and rhombencephalon are the three primary portions of the brain during early development of the central nervous system.
Generation	Generation, also known as procreation, is the act of producing offspring. A generation can also be a stage or degree in a succession of natural descent as a grandfather, a father, and the father"s son comprise three generations.

529

Impulse	In classical mechanics, an Impulse is defined as the integral of a force with respect to time. When a force is applied to a rigid body it changes the momentum of that body. A small force applied for a long time can produce the same momentum change as a large force applied briefly, because it is the product of the force and the time for which it is applied that is important.
Information	Information as a concept has a diversity of meanings, from everyday usage to technical settings. Generally speaking, the concept of Information is closely related to notions of constraint, communication, control, data, form, instruction, knowledge, meaning, mental stimulus, pattern, perception, and representation. According to the Oxford English Dictionary, the first known historical meaning of the word Information in English was the act of informing, or giving form or shape to the mind, as in education, instruction, or training.
Metabolite	Metabolite is the intermediate and product of metabolism. The term metabolite is usually restricted to small molecules. A primary metabolite is directly involved in the normal growth, development, and reproduction.
Structure	Structure is a fundamental and sometimes intangible notion covering the recognition, observation, nature, and stability of patterns and relationships of entities.
Thalamus	An area near the center of the brain involved in the relay of sensory information to the cortex and in the functions of sleep and attention is the thalamus.
Arachidonic acid	Arachidonic acid is a polyunsaturated fatty acid that is present in the phospholipids of membranes of the body"s cells, and is abundant in the brain. It is also involved in cellular signaling as a second messenger.
Circadian rhythm	The circadian rhythm is a name given to the "internal body clock" that regulates the roughly 24 hour cycle of biological processes in animals and plants.
Electroconvulsive therapy	Electroconvulsive therapy, is a controversial psychiatric treatment in which seizures are induced with electricity for therapeutic effect. It is often used as a treatment for severe major depression which has not responded to other treatment, and is also used in the treatment of mania, catatonia, schizophrenia and other disorders.
Exercise	Exercise is manual activity that develops or maintains physical fitness and overall health. It is often practiced to strengthen muscles and the cardiovascular system, and to hone athletic skills.
Memory	In psychology, memory is an organism"s ability to store, retain, and subsequently retrieve information. In recent decades, it has become one of the principal pillars of a branch of science called cognitive neuroscience, an interdisciplinary link between cognitive psychology and neuroscience.

Rapid eye movement	Rapid eye movement is the stage of sleep during which the most vivid (though not all) dreams occur. During this stage, the eyes move rapidly, and the activity of the brain's neurons is quite similar to that during waking hours. It is the lightest form of sleep in that people awakened during REM usually feel alert and refreshed.
Rapid eye movement sleep	Rapid eye movement sleep is the normal stage of sleep characterized by rapid movements of the eyes. Criteria for Rapid eye movement sleep include not only rapid eye movements, but also low muscle tone and a rapid, low voltage EEG these features are easily discernible in a polysomnogram, the sleep study typically done for patients with suspected sleep disorders.
Sleep	Sleep is the state of natural rest observed throughout the animal kingdom, in all mammals and birds, and in many reptiles, amphibians, and fish.
Transcranial magnetic stimulation	A Transcranial magnetic stimulation is a noninvasive method to excite neurons in the brain.
Animal testing	Animal testing refers to the use of animals in experiments. It is estimated that 50 to 100 million vertebrate animals worldwide — from zebrafish to non-human primates — are used annually and either killed during the experiments or subsequently euthanized.
Arousal	Arousal is a physiological and psychological state involving the activation of the reticular activating system in the brain stem, the autonomic nervous system and the endocrine system, leading to increased heart rate and blood pressure and a condition of alertness and readiness to respond.
Central sulcus	The central sulcus is a prominent landmark of the brain, separating the parietal lobe from the frontal lobe. The central sulcus is the site of the primary motor cortex in mammals, a group of cells that controls voluntary movements of the body.
Cerebral cortex	The cerebral cortex is a structure within the vertebrate brain with distinct structural and functional properties.
Eye	Eye s are organs that detect light, and send signals along the optic nerve to the visual and other areas of the brain. Complex optical systems with resolving power have come in ten fundamentally different forms, and 96% of animal species possess a complex optical system. Image-resolving Eye s are present in cnidaria, molluscs, chordates, annelids and arthropods.
Field	Field is one of the core concepts used by French social scientist Pierre Bourdieu. A field is a setting in which agents and their social positions are located. The position of each particular agent in the field is a result of interaction between the specific rules of the field, agent"s habitus and agent"s capital social, economic and cultural Bourdieu, 1984. Fields interact with each other, and are hierarchical most are subordinate of the larger field of power and class relations.

Social influence	Social influence occurs when an individual"s thoughts or actions are affected by other people. Social influence takes many forms and can be seen in conformity, socialization, peer pressure, obedience, leadership, persuasion, sales, and marketing. Harvard psychologist, Herbert Kelman identified three broad varieties of Social influence. · Compliance is when people appear to agree with others, but actually keep their dissenting opinions private. · Identification is when people are influenced by someone who is liked and respected, such as a famous celebrity or a favorite uncle. · Internalization is when people accept a belief or behavior and agree both publicly and privately.
Motor cortex	Motor cortex is a term that describes regions of the cerebral cortex involved in the planning, control, and execution of voluntary motor functions.
Cytoplasmic streaming	Cytoplasmic streaming is the flowing of cytoplasm in eukaryotic cells. This occurs in both plant and animal cells.
Muscle	Muscle is contractile tissue of the body and is derived from the mesodermal layer of embryonic germ cells. It is classified as skeletal, cardiac, or smooth muscle, and its function is to produce force and cause motion, either locomotion or movement within internal organs.
Primary	In medicine, the reporting of symptoms by a patient may have significant psychological motivators. Psychologists sometimes categorize these motivators into primary or secondary gain. primary gain is internally good; motivationally.
Primary motor cortex	The primary motor cortex works in association with pre-motor areas to plan and execute movements. It contains large neurons known as Betz cells which send long axons down the spinal cord to synapse onto alpha motor neurons which connect to the muscles.
Relaxation	Relaxation is a process or state with the aim of recreation through leisure activities or idling and the opposite of stress or tension
Attention	Attention is the cognitive process of selectively concentrating on one aspect of the environment while ignoring other things. Examples include listening carefully to what someone is saying while ignoring other conversations in the room or listening to a cell phone conversation while driving a car.

Bipolar I disorder	Bipolar I disorder is a sub-diagnosis of bipolar disorder. Diagnosis it requires at least one Manic or Mixed episode, but there may be episodes of Hypomania or Major Depression as well. The essential feature of Bipolar I Disorder is a clinical course that is characterized by the occurrence of one or more manic episodes or mixed episodes. Often individuals have also had one or more major depressive episodes.
Bipolar II disorder	A mood disorder in which a person is mostly depressed but has also had one or more episodes of mild mania is called bipolar II disorder.
Bipolar disorder	Bipolar disorder is a psychiatric condition defined as recurrent episodes of significant disturbance in mood. These disturbances can occur on a spectrum that ranges from debilitating depression to unbridled mania. Individuals suffering from bipolar disorder typically experience fluid states of mania, hypomania or what is referred to as a mixed state in conjunction with depressive episodes.
Hypomania	Hypomania is a state involving combinations of: elevated mood, irritability, racing thoughts, people-seeking, hypersexuality, grandiose thinking, religiosity, and pressured speech.
Mania	Mania is a severe medical condition characterized by extremely elevated mood, energy, and unusual thought patterns. There are several possible causes for mania, but it is most often associated with bipolar disorder, where episodes of mania may cyclically alternate with episodes of clinical depression. These cycles may relate to diurnal rhythms and environmental stressors. Mania varies in intensity, from mild mania to full-blown mania with psychotic features.
Sleep deprivation	Sleep deprivation is a general lack of the necessary amount of sleep. This may occur as a result of sleep disorders, active choice or deliberate inducement such as in interrogation or for torture..
Unipolar	Unipolar depression is a common psychiatric disorder, characterized by a persistent lowering of mood, loss of interest in usual activities and diminished ability to experience pleasure.
Clinical depression	Clinical depression is a common psychiatric disorder, characterized by a persistent lowering of mood, loss of interest in usual activities and diminished ability to experience pleasure.
Anxiety	Anxiety is a physiological state characterized by cognitive, somatic, emotional, and behavioral components.
Laughter	Laughter is an audible expression or appearance of merriment or amusement or an inward feeling of joy and pleasure. It may ensue from jokes, tickling and other stimuli. Inhaling nitrous oxide can also induce laughter; other drugs, such as cannabis, can also induce episodes of strong laughter.
AMPA receptor	The Ampa receptor is a non-NMDA-type ionotropic transmembrane receptor for glutamate that mediates fast synaptic transmission in the central nervous system. Its name is derived from its ability to be activated by the artificial glutamate analog, AMPA. AMPARs are found in many parts of the brain and are the most commonly found receptor in the nervous system.

Amygdala	Amygdala are almond-shaped groups of neurons located deep within the medial temporal lobes of the brain in complex vertebrates, including humans. Shown in research to perform a primary role in the processing and memory of emotional reactions, the amygdala are considered part of the limbic system.
Carbamazepine	Carbamazepine is an anticonvulsant and mood stabilizing drug, used primarily in the treatment of epilepsy and bipolar disorder. It is also used to treat ADD, ADHD, schizophrenia and trigeminal neuralgia.
Depakote	Valproate semisodium (INN) or divalproex sodium (USAN) consists of a compound of sodium valproate and valproic acid in a 1:1 molar relationship in an enteric coated form. It is used in the UK, Canada, and U.S. for the treatment of the manic episodes of bipolar disorder. In rare cases, it is also used as a treatment for major depressive disorder, and increasingly taken long-term for prevention of both manic and depressive phases of bipolar disorder, especially the rapid-cycling variant.
	In the UK semisodium valproate has been sold for a few years as the proprietary drug Depakote and marketed for psychiatric conditions only. It is about five times the price of sodium valproate, which has been marketed for around 30 years as Epilim by the same company for epilepsy and is also available from other manufacturers as a generic product.
	The most severe side effects are ten times higher-than-average incidence rates of serious, irreversible birth defects (teratogenic) such as births of brainless babies (anencephaly.)
Diet	In nutrition, the diet is the sum of food consumed by a person or other organism. Dietary habits are the habitual decisions an individual or culture makes when choosing what foods to eat.
LIP	Lip s are a visible body part at the mouth of humans and many animals. Lip s are soft, movable, and serve as the opening for food intake, as an erogenous organ used in kissing and other acts of intimacy, as a tactile sensory organ, and in the articulation of speech.
	One differentiates between the Upper (Labia superfluos entafada) and lower Lip (Labium inferius.)
Valproic acid	Valproic acid is a chemical compound that has found clinical use as an anticonvulsant and mood-stabilizing drug, primarily in the treatment of epilepsy, bipolar disorder, and clinical depression. It is also used to treat migraine headaches and schizophrenia.
Affective	Affective is the way people react emotionally, their ability to feel another living thing's pain or joy.
Affective spectrum	The affective spectrum is a grouping of related psychiatric and medical disorders which may accompany bipolar, unipolar, and schizoaffective disorders at statistically higher rates than would normally be expected. These disorders are identified by a common positive response to the same types of pharmacologic treatments.

Seasonal affective disorder	Seasonal affective disorder is an affective, or mood, disorder. Most seasonal affective disorder sufferers experience normal mental health throughout most of the year, but experience depressive symptoms in the winter or summer. There are many different treatments for seasonal affective disorder, including light therapies, medication, and ionized-air reception.
Acute	Acute means sudden, sharp, and abrupt. Usually short in duration.
Chronic	In medicine, a chronic disease is a disease that is long-lasting or recurrent. The term chronic describes the course of the disease, or its rate of onset and development
Cognition	In psychology, cognition refers to an information processing view of an individual"s psychological functions. Other interpretations of the meaning of cognition link it to the development of concepts; individual minds, groups, organizations, and even larger coalitions of entities, can be modelled as societies which cooperate to form concepts.
Intelligence	Intelligence is a property of mind that encompasses many related abilities, such as the capacities to reason, plan, solve problems, think abstractly, comprehend ideas and language, and learn. In some cases intelligence may include traits such as creativity, personality, character, knowledge, or wisdom. However other psychologists prefer not to include these traits in the definition of intelligence.
Thorazine	Thorazine is the trade name for chlorpromazine, one of the antipsychotic drugs and a member of the phenothiazine group. It is classified as a low-potency antipsychotic and is used in the treatment of both acute and chronic psychoses, including schizophrenia and the manic phase of manic depression.
Belief	Belief is the psychological state in which an individual is convinced of the truth or validity of a proposition or premise without the ability to adequately prove their main contention for other people who may disagree.
Characteristic	Characteristic has several particular meanings: · in mathematics ● · Euler characteristic ● · method of characteristic s (partial differential equations) · in physics and engineering · any characteristic curve that shows the relationship between certain input- and output parameters, e.g. · an I-V or current-voltage characteristic is the current in a circuit as a function of the applied voltage · Receiver-Operator characteristic · in navigation, the characteristic pattern of a lighted beacon. · in fiction

· in Dungeons ' Dragons, characteristic is another name for ability score .

Duration

A duration is an amount of time or a particular time interval.

Not

This catalog is compiled from a source file. Please do not edit this page manually. This is how to edit it.

Brain damage

Brain damage is the destruction or degeneration of brain cells. It may occur due to a wide range of conditions, illnesses, injuries, and as a result of iatrogenesis. Possible causes of widespread brain damage include prolonged hypoxia, poisoning by teratogens, infection, and neurological illness.

Hearing

Hearing is one of the traditional five senses, and refers to the ability to detect sound. In humans and other vertebrates, hearing is performed primarily by the system: sound is detected by the ear and transduced into nerve impulses that are perceived by the brain.

Hearing impairment

A hearing impairment is a full or partial decrease in the ability to detect or understand sounds.[1] Caused by a wide range of biological and environmental factors, loss of hearing can happen to any organism that perceives sound.

Psychosis

Psychosis is a generic psychiatric term for a mental state often described as involving a "loss of contact with reality".

Substance abuse

Substance abuse refers to the use of substances when said use is causing detriment to the individual"s physical health or causes the user legal, social, financial or other problems including endangering their lives or the lives of others.

Vitamin C

Vitamin C is an essential nutrient for higher primates, and a small number of other species. The presence of ascorbate is required for a range of essential metabolic reactions in all animals and in plants and is made internally by almost all organisms, humans being one notable exception. It is widely known as the vitamin whose deficiency causes scurvy in humans. It is also widely used as a food additive.

Working memory

Working memory is a theoretical framework within cognitive psychology that refers to the structures and processes used for temporarily storing and manipulating information. There are numerous theories as to both the theoretical structure of working memory as well as to the specific parts of the brain responsible for working memory.

Addiction

The term Addiction is used in many contexts to describe an obsession, compulsion such as: drug Addiction (e.g. alcoholism), video game Addiction crime, money, work Addiction compulsive overeating, problem gambling, computer Addiction nicotine Addiction pornography Addiction etc.

In medical terminology, an Addiction is a chronic neurobiologic disorder that has genetic, psychosocial, and environmental dimensions and is characterized by one of the following: the continued use of a substance despite its detrimental effects, impaired control over the use of a drug (compulsive behavior), and preoccupation with a drug"s use for non-therapeutic purposes (i.e. craving the drug.) Addiction is often accompanied the presence of deviant behaviors (for instance stealing money and forging prescriptions) that are used to obtain a drug.

Diagnosis	In general, diagnosis has two distinct dictionary definitions. The first definition is "the recognition of a disease or condition by its outward signs and symptoms", while the second definition is "the analysis of the underlying physiological/biochemical causes of a disease or condition".
Identification	Identification is a term that is used in different meanings in psychoanalysis. The roots of the concept can be found in Freud"s writings. Freud established five concepts of identification of which the three most important concepts will be discussed below. We finalise with the current concept of identification as is mostly seen in psychoanalytic thinking today.
Disability	A disability is a condition or function judged to be significantly impaired relative to the usual standard of an individual or their group. The term is often used to refer to individual functioning, including physical impairments, sensory impairments, cognitive impairments, intellectual impairments or mental health issue.
Storage	The human memory has three processes: encoding (input), Storage and retrieval(output.) Storage is the process of retaining information whether in the sensory memory, the short-term memory or the more permanent long-term memory.
Tremor	Tremor is the rhythmic, oscillating shaking movement of the whole body or just a certain part of it, caused by problems of the neurons responsible from muscle action.
Muscle contraction	A muscle contraction occurs when a muscle fiber generates tension through the action of actin and myosin cross-bridge cycling.
Cerebrovascular accident	Cerebrovascular accident refers to a sudden stoppage of blood flow to a portion of the brain, leading to a loss of brain function.
Concordance	Concordance is an approach at involving the patient in the treatment process to improve compliance and is a current UK NHS initiative
Diabetes	Diabetes is a medical disorder characterized by varying or persistent elevated blood sugar levels, especially after eating. All types of diabetes share similar symptoms and complications at advanced stages: dehydration and ketoacidosis, cardiovascular disease, chronic renal failure, retinal damage which can lead to blindness, nerve damage which can lead to erectile dysfunction, gangrene with risk of amputation of toes, feet, and even legs.

Dopamine hypothesis	The suggestion that schizophrenia may result from excess dopamine activity at certain synaptic sites is referred to as the dopamine hypothesis.
Dopamine hypothesis of schizophrenia	The dopamine hypothesis of schizophrenia is a model attributing symptoms of schizophrenia to a disturbed and hyperactive dopaminergic signal transduction. The model draws evidence from the observation that a large number of antipsychotics have DA-antagonistic effects. The theory, however, does not posit dopamine overabundance as a complete explanation for schizophrenia.
Heritability	Heritability It is that proportion of the observed variation in a particular phenotype within a particular population, that can be attributed to the contribution of genotype. In other words: it measures the extent to which differences between individuals in a population are due their being different genetically.
Rheumatoid arthritis	Rheumatoid arthritis is a chronic, inflammatory autoimmune disorder that causes the immune system to attack the joints. It is a disabling and painful inflammatory condition, which can lead to substantial loss of mobility due to pain and joint destruction.
Heredity	Heredity is the transfer of characteristics from parent to offspring through their genes, or the transfer of a title, style or social status through the social convention known as inheritance.
Hypothesis	A hypothesis consists either of a suggested explanation for a phenomenon or of a reasoned proposal suggesting a possible correlation between multiple phenomena.
Population	In sociology and biology a population is the collection of people or individuals of a particular species. A population shares a particular characteristic of interest most often that of living in a given geographic area.
Sense	Sense are the physiological methods of perception. They and their operation, classification, and theory are overlapping topics studied by a variety of fields, most notably neuroscience, cognitive psychology, and philosophy of perception. The nervous system has a sensory system dedicated to each sense.
Synapse	A synapse is specialized junction through which cells of the nervous system signal to one another and to non-neuronal cells such as muscles or glands. They allow the neurons of the central nervous system to form interconnected neural circuits.
Synapses	Chemical synapses are specialized junctions through which neurons signal to each other and to non-neuronal cells such as those in muscles or glands. Chemical synapses allow neurons to form circuits within the central nervous system. They are crucial to the biological computations that underlie perception and thought.
Trait	An enduring personality characteristic that tends to lead to certain behaviors is called a trait. The term trait also means a genetically inherited feature of an organism.

547

Twin	Twin s are a form of multiple birth in which the mother gives birth to two offspring from the same pregnancy, either of the same or opposite sex.
Twins	Twins are two offspring resulting from the same pregnancy, usually born in close succession. They can be the same or different sex. Twins can either be monozygotic (MZ, colloquially "identical") or dizygotic (DZ, colloquially "fraternal" or "non-identical").
Variance	In probability theory and statistics, the variance of a random variable or somewhat more precisely, of a probability distribution is one measure of statistical dispersion, averaging the squared distance of its possible values from the expected value.
Mutation	In biology, mutation s are changes to the nucleotide sequence of the genetic material of an organism. mutation s can be caused by copying errors in the genetic material during cell division, by exposure to ultraviolet or ionizing radiation, chemical mutagens, or viruses, or can be induced by the organism itself, by cellular processes such as hyper mutation . In multicellular organisms with dedicated reproductive cells, mutation s can be subdivided into germ line mutation s, which can be passed on to descendants through the reproductive cells, and somatic mutation s, which involve cells outside the dedicated reproductive group and which are not usually transmitted to descendants.
Prenatal development	Prenatal development is the process in which an embryo or fetus gestates during pregnancy, from fertilization until birth.
Cytokines	Cytokines are a group of proteins and peptides that are used in organisms as signaling compounds. These chemical signals are similar to hormones and neurotransmitters and are used to allow one cell to communicate with another. The cytokine family consists mainly of smaller water-soluble proteins and glycoproteins with a mass of between 8 and 30 kDa.
Fever	Fever is a frequent medical symptom that describes an increase in internal body temperature to levels that are above normal.
Scolex	The Scolex of the worm attaches to the intestine of the definitive host. In some groups, the scolex is dominated by bothria, which are sometimes called "sucking grooves," and function like suction cups.
Immune system	The most important function of the human immune system occurs at the cellular level of the blood and tissues. The lymphatic and blood circulation systems are highways for specialized white blood cells. These cells include B cells, T cells, natural killer cells, and macrophages. All function with the primary objective of recognizing, attacking and destroying bacteria, viruses, cancer cells, and all substances seen as foreign.
Rubella	Rubella is a disease caused by the rubella virus. It is often mild and an attack can pass unnoticed. However, this can make the virus difficult to diagnose.

Toxoplasma	Toxoplasma gondii is a species of parasitic protozoa in the genus Toxoplasma. Acute stage toxoplasma infections can be asymptomatic, but often gives flu-like symptoms in the early acute stages, and like flu can become, in very rare cases, fatal. Several independent pieces of evidence point towards a possible role of Toxoplasma infection in some cases of schizophrenia and paranoia, but this theory does not seem to account for many cases.
Toxoplasma gondii	Toxoplasma gondii is a species of parasitic protozoa in the genus Toxoplasma. The definitive host of Toxoplasma gondii is the cat, but the parasite can be carried by the vast majority of warm-blooded animals, including humans. Toxoplasma gondii infections have the ability to change the behavior of rats and mice, making them drawn to rather than fearful of the scent of cats. This effect is advantageous to the parasite, which will be able to sexually reproduce if its host is eaten by a cat.
Anatomy	Anatomy is the branch of biology that deals with the structure and organization of living things. It can be divided into animal anatomy zootomy and plant anatomy phytonomy. Major branches of anatomy include comparative anatomy, histology, and human anatomy.
Antipsychotic	The term antipsychotic is applied to a group of drugs used to treat psychosis.
Antipsychotics	*Antipsychotics* are a group of psychoactive drugs commonly but not exclusively used to treat psychosis, which is typified by schizophrenia. Over time a wide range of *Antipsychotics* have been developed. A first generation of *Antipsychotics*, known as typical *Antipsychotics*, was discovered in the 1950s.
Lead	Lead is a poisonous metal that can damage nervous connections and cause blood and brain disorders. Long term exposure to lead or its salts can cause nephropathy, and colic-like abdominal pains. The concern about lead"s role in cognitive deficits in children has brought about widespread reduction in its use. The majority of cases of adult elevate blood lead levels are workplace-related.
Infant	In basic English usage, an Infant is defined as a human child at the youngest stage of life, specifically before they can walk and generally before the age of one.
Probability	Probability is the likelihood that something is the case or will happen. Probability theory is used extensively in areas such as statistics, mathematics, science and philosophy to draw conclusions about the likelihood of potential events and the underlying mechanics of complex systems.
Dorsolateral prefrontal cortex	Brodmann area 46, is part of the frontal cortex in the human brain. Brodmann area 46 roughly corresponds with the dorsolateral prefrontal cortex though the borders of area 46 are based on cytoarchitecture rather than function. It is also encompasses part of granular frontal area 9, directly adjacent on the dorsal surface of the cortex.
Nervous system	The nervous system of an animal coordinates the activity of the muscles, monitors the organs, constructs and also stops input from the senses, and initiates actions.

Temporal lobe	The temporal lobe is part of the cerebrum. It lies at the side of the brain, beneath the lateral or Sylvian fissure. Adjacent areas in the superior, posterior and lateral parts of the temporal lobe are involved in high-level auditory processing.
Ventricle	In the heart, a ventricle is a heart chamber which collects blood from an atrium another heart chamber that is smaller than a ventricle and pumps it out of the heart.
Card Sorting	Card sorting is a simple technique in usability design where a group of subject experts or "users", however inexperienced with design, are guided to generate a category tree or folksonomy. It is a useful approach for designing workflows, menu structure, or web site navigation paths. Card sorting has a characteristically low-tech approach.
Handedness	Handedness is an attribute of human beings defined by their unequal distribution of fine motor skill between the left and right hands. An individual who is more dextrous with the right hand is called right-handed, and one who is more skilled with the left is said to be left-handed.
Planum temporale	The planum temporale is the posterior superior surface of the superior temporal gyrus in the cerebrum. It is a highly lateralized brain structure involved with language.
Wisconsin Card Sorting Test	The Wisconsin Card Sorting Test is a neuropsychological test of "set-shifting", i.e. the ability to display flexibility in the face of changing schedules of reinforcement.
Right hemisphere	The brain is divided into left and right cerebral hemispheres. The right hemisphere of the cortex controls the left side of the body.
AMPT	Alpha-methyl-p-tyrosine (AMPT) is a drug that temporarily reduces brain catecholamine activity by competitively inhibiting tyrosine hydroxylase. It has been used in the treatment of pheochromocytoma. AMPT administration leads to a transient exacerbation of depressive symptoms in patients that have responded to catecholaminergic antidepressants.
Basal ganglia	The basal ganglia are a group of nuclei in the brain associated with motor and learning functions.
Butyrophenone	Butyrophenone is a chemical compound; some of its derivatives are used to treat various psychiatric disorders such as schizophrenia, as well as acting as antiemetics.
Haloperidol	Haloperidol is a conventional butyrophenone antipsychotic drug. It posesses a strong activity against delusions and hallucinations, most likely due to an effective dopaminergic receptor blockage in the mesocortex and the limbic system of the brain.
Lysergic acid diethylamide	Lysergic acid diethylamide, is a semisynthetic psychedelic drug. It is synthesized from lysergic acid derived from ergot, a grain fungus that typically grows on rye. Many clinical trials were conducted on the potential use of it in psychedelic psychotherapy, generally with very positive results.

Caudate nucleus	The caudate nucleus is a nucleus located within the basal ganglia of the brains of many animal species. The caudate nuclei are located near the center of the brain, sitting astride the thalamus. There is a caudate nucleus within each hemisphere of the brain.
Globus pallidus	The globus pallidus is a sub-cortical structure of the brain. It is a major element of the basal ganglia system. In this system, it is a major element of the basal ganglia core, consisting of the striatum and its direct targets: globus pallidus and substantia nigra. The last two are made up of the same neuronal elements, have a similar main afferent, have a similar synaptology, and do not receive cortical afferents.
Hypothalamus	The hypothalamus is a region of the brain located below the thalamus, forming the major portion of the ventral region of the diencephalon and functioning to regulate certain metabolic processes and other autonomic activities.
Putamen	The putamen is a structure in the middle of the brain, which, together with the caudate nucleus forms the dorsal striatum. The putamen is a portion of the basal ganglia that forms the outermost part of the lenticular nucleus.
Glycine	Glycine is the organic compound with the formula $HO_2CCH_2NH_2$. It is one of the 20 amino acids commonly found in proteins, coded by codons GGU, GGC, GGA and GGG. Because of its structural simplicity, this compact amino acid tends to be evolutionarily conserved in, for example, cytochrome c, myoglobin, and hemoglobin. Glycine is the unique amino acid that is not optically active. Most proteins contain only small quantities of glycine. A notable exception is collagen, which contains about 35% glycine.
Mesencephalon	The mesencephalon is archipallian in origin, meaning its general architecture is shared with the most ancient of vertebrates. Dopamine produced in the subtantia nigra plays a role in motivation and habituation of species from humans to the most elementary animals such as insects.
N-methyl d-aspartate receptor	The N-methyl d-aspartate receptor is an ionotropic receptor for glutamate is a name of its selective specific agonist). Activation of NMDA receptors results in the opening of an ion channel that is nonselective to cations. This allows flow of Na^+ and small amounts of Ca^{2+} ions into the cell and K^+ out of the cell.
Tardive dyskinesia	Tardive dyskinesia is a neurological disorder caused by the long-term or high-dose use of dopamine antagonists, usually antipsychotics. Tardive dyskinesia is characterized by repetitive, involuntary, purposeless movements. Features of the disorder may include grimacing, tongue protrusion, lip smacking, puckering and pursing of the lips, and rapid eye blinking.
Amisulpride	Amisulpride is an atypical antipsychotic drug sold by Sanofi-Aventis. Amisulpride is a selective dopamine antagonist. It has a high affinity for D_2 (Ki 2.8 nM) and D_3 (Ki 3.2 nM) dopaminergic receptors.

Aripiprazole	Aripiprazole was approved by the Food and Drug Administration for the treatment of schizophrenia, the sixth atypical antipsychotic medication of its kind.
Clozapine	Clozapine is an antipsychotic medication used in the treatment of schizophrenia. The first of the atypical antipsychotics to be developed, it was first introduced in Europe in 1971, but was voluntarily withdrawn by the manufacturer in 1975 after it was shown to cause agranulocytosis that led to death in some patients. In 1989, after studies demonstrated that it was more effective than any other antipsychotic for treating schizophrenia, the U.S. Food and Drug Administration (FDA) approved Clozapine"s use but only for treatment-resistant schizophrenia.
Olanzapine	Olanzapine is an atypical antipsychotic, approved by the FDA for the treatment of: schizophrenia on 1996-09-30 ; depressive episodes associated with bipolar disorder, as part of the Symbyax formulation, on 2003-12-24; acute manic episodes and maintenance treatment in bipolar disorder on 2004-01-14.
Risperidone	Risperidone is an atypical antipsychotic medication developed by Janssen Pharmaceutica. It was approved by the United States Food and Drug Administration in 1993 for the treatment of schizophrenia.
Compound	Compound when applied to a human habitat refers to a cluster of buildings in an enclosure, having a shared or associated purpose, such as the houses of an extended family. The enclosure may be a wall, a fence, a hedge or some other structure, or it may be formed by the buildings themselves, when they are built around an open area or joined together.
Material	Material refers to physical substances used as inputs to production or manufacturing.
Book	A Book is a set or collection of written, printed, illustrated made of paper, parchment usually fastened together to hinge at one side. A single sheet within a Book is called a leaf, and each side of a leaf is called a page. A Book produced in electronic format is known as an e-Book.
Amino acid	Amino acid is the basic structural building unit of proteins. They form short polymer chains called peptides or polypeptides which in turn form structures called proteins.
Covalent bond	A covalent bond is an intramolecular form of chemical bonding characterized by the sharing of one or more pairs of electrons between two elements, producing a mutual attraction that holds the resultant molecule together.
Ion	An Ion is an atom or molecule which has lost or gained one or more electrons, making it positively or negatively charged.
Nucleus	In neuroanatomy, a cluster of cell bodies of neurons within the central nervous system is a nucleus.

Protein	A protein is a complex, high-molecular-weight organic compound that consists of amino acids joined by peptide bonds. It is essential to the structure and function of all living cells and viruses. Many are enzymes or subunits of enzymes.
Protein channel	A protein channel is a pore-forming protein that help establish the small voltage gradient that exists across the membrane of all living cells, by controlling the flow of ions. They are present in the membranes that surround all biological cells.
Attraction	Attraction refer to a quality to be the cause of the emotion of attraction in a person. An attraction emotion is an interest or desire in something or someone.
Chromosome	A chromosome is a single large macromolecule of DNA, and constitutes a physically organized form of DNA in a cell. It is a very long, continuous piece of DNA, which contains many genes, regulatory elements and other intervening nucleotide sequences.
Egodystonic	Egodystonic is a psychological term referring to thoughts and behaviors, (e.g., dreams, impulses, compulsions, desires, etc.), that are in conflict with the needs and goals of the ego in conflict with a person"s ideal self-image. The concept is studied in detail in abnormal psychology, and is the opposite of egosyntonic. Obsessive compulsive disorder is considered to be an ego-dystonic disorder, as the thoughts and compulsions experienced or expressed are often not consistent with the individual"s self-perception, causing extreme distress.
Pacifier	A pacifier is a rubber, plastic, or silicone nipple given to an infant or other young child to suck upon. In its standard appearance it has a teat, mouth shield, and handle. The mouth shield and/or the handle is large enough to avoid the danger that the child chokes on it or swallows it.
Enzyme	An enzyme is a protein that catalyzes, or speeds up, a chemical reaction. Enzymes are essential to sustain life because most chemical reactions in biological cells would occur too slowly, or would lead to different products, without enzymes.
Neuromodulator	A neuromodulator is a substance other than a neurotransmitter, released by a neuron at a synapse and conveying information to adjacent or distant neurons, either enhancing or damping their activities.
Ethics	Ethics a major branch of philosophy, is the study of values and customs of a person or group. It covers the analysis and employment of concepts such as right and wrong, good and evil, and responsibility
Neuroscience	A field that combines the work of psychologists, biologists, biochemists, medical researchers, and others in the study of the structure and function of the nervous system is neuroscience.
Sex steroid	Sex steroid refers to steroid hormones that interact with vertebrate androgen or estrogen receptors.

Society	A society is a grouping of individuals, which is characterized by common interests and may have distinctive culture and institutions. Society can also refer to an organized group of people associated together for religious, benevolent, cultural, scientific, political, patriotic, or other purposes.
Society for Neuroscience	The Society for Neuroscience is a professional society for basic scientists and physicians around the world whose research is focused on the study of the brain and nervous system.
Issue	In computing, the term Issue is a unit of work to accomplish an improvement in a system. An Issue could be a bug, a requested feature, task, missing documentation, and so forth. The word "Issue" is popularly misused in lieu of "problem." This usage is probably related.

CPSIA information can be obtained at www.ICGtesting.com
Printed in the USA
242086LV00001B/3/P